Religious Routes
to
Gladstonian Liberalism

Religious Routes
to
Gladstonian Liberalism

The Church Rate Conflict in
England and Wales,
1832–1868

J. P. Ellens

The Pennsylvania State University Press

University Park, Pennsylvania

Library of Congress Cataloging-in-Publication Data

Ellens, J. P. (Jacob P.), 1948–
    Religious routes to Gladstonian liberalism : the church rate
conflict in England and Wales, 1832–1868 / J. P. Ellens.
        p.   cm.
    Includes bibliographical references and index.
    ISBN 0-271-01036-3
    1. Church tax—England—History—19th century.   2. Church and
state—England—History—19th century.   3. England—Church
history—19th century.   4. Great Britain—Politics and
government—1837–1901.   5. Liberalism—England—History—19th
century.   I. Title.
BR759.E48   1994
322'.1'094209034—dc20   93-21927
                                                                        CIP

Published by The Pennsylvania State University Press,
University Park, PA 16802-1003

It is the policy of The Pennsylvania State University Press to use acid-free paper for
the first printing of all clothbound books. Publications on uncoated stock satisfy the
minimum requirements of American National Standard for Information Sciences—
Permanence of Paper for Printed Library Materials, ANSI Z39.48–1984.

Contents

Preface

Revolution remade the social fabric of Europe and Britain during the nineteenth century. Those who feared revolutionary violence shuddered as armed mobs took to the barricades in the cities of the continent in 1830, 1848, and again in 1870. Radicals—spanning two generations—assaulted the old order, their hearts quickened by the call to "liberté, égalité, fraternité" that had inspired their spiritual brothers in 1789.

Throughout Europe the politics of prescription fell before the leveling demands of armed democrats. But it was not only the state: the Church too was weighed in the balance by a revolutionary people, and found wanting. For a millennium and a half, since Emperors Constantine and Theodosius had made Christianity the official religion of the Roman Empire, the Christian church had represented the city of God on European soil. In addition, she had developed the power to transform the city of man, as far as possible in a sinful world, into a Christian commonwealth. The Church—authoritative and involuntary—dominated the social landscape like a soaring Gothic cathedral. As in the case of the state, all who were born in the territory under her jurisdiction were subject to her. The Church crowned monarchs and collected ecclesiastical taxes, and her courts settled bequests and matrimonial disputes. The Church founded schools, universities, and hospitals, and under her auspices to the greater glory of God were offered the literature and science, the art and architecture of a millennium.

Revolutionaries violently wrenched from the Church much of her social power. The first French Revolution "nationalized" the vast estates of the Gallican church; nor were these returned when Napoleon recognized that a rapprochement with the Church was expedient. With the abolition of French ecclesiastical taxation, revolutionaries gave notice that the Church was to be a private organization with no financial claim on anyone who did not voluntarily support her. In the European democratic revolutions of the nineteenth century the battle against the Church was waged alongside the political demand for representative institutions made by men who had often replaced God with the god of liberty or the goddess of reason.

In England and Wales too, it seemed for a short time in the 1830s that the established church might be leveled by mobs intent on razing to the ground what they believed to be a den of iniquity and corruption. But there in the long term the most influential critical voices were not those of armed infidels and secularists, but of religious men— Protestant Dissenters. In the 1830s they began to rely on new political weight to insist that the state cease favoring one religious denomination over another, and that the Church of England be disestablished. These political demands were not made in the language of unbelief but in words of faith. The animus behind opposition to established religion was not hatred of religion but genuine belief that the core of the Christian faith was warped when it was propagated at the point of a temporal sword. In England and Wales then, in contrast to much of the continent, the campaign to undo the Constantinian legacy was conducted in the name of Christianity, not against it.

Nevertheless, it would be misleading to claim that Dissenters merely were engaged in a Christian crusade to free the Church from bondage to the state. They moved also toward the ideal of a liberal state freed from the traditional tutelage of the Church and from the directives of the Christian religion, although they did want room for individual Christian conscience in a secular state. Their political teachers were no longer from the Christian tradition of Augustine, Aquinas, Hooker, or Calvin, but in the modern liberal school of Locke and John Stuart Mill. The larger legacy of the political campaign of Dissent in England and Wales to seek the abolition of church rates and the advancement of voluntaryism—the focus of this study—was to create a new liberal state, neutral not only as to contending denominations but to Christianity itself. In light of centuries of Christian history the outcome of the

Dissenters' campaign against the Church of England was scarcely less revolutionary than the conclusion of the antichurch war waged by their violent compatriots on the continent, although it was achieved with infinitely greater subtlety.

Acknowledgments

In writing this book I have become indebted to numerous people. My first debt of thanks is to R. J. Helmstadter, who suggested the church rate topic to me and sagely supervised my work in an earlier version of this study, my 1983 University of Toronto Ph.D. dissertation, "The Church Rate Conflict in England and Wales, 1832–1868." A number of historians in North America have read one of the several drafts of this work, and their queries and critical comments have greatly strengthened this book. I am thankful for the careful reading and other help of R. K. Webb (who suggested the importance of the church rate question to Professor Helmstadter years ago), J. B. Conacher, T. O. Lloyd, J. M. Robson, C. T. McIntire, P. T. Phillips, R. W. Davis, and Denis Paz. A number of historians in the United Kingdom assisted this project either in person or in generous correspondence. I give particular thanks to G.I.T. Machin, the Reverend E. R. Norman, W. R. Ward, Clyde Binfield, D. M. Thompson, D. C. Coleman, J. S. Newton, D. W. Bebbington, and the late Lord Butler. I am thankful to the Marquess of Salisbury and R. H. Harcourt Williams for giving me access to the papers of the third Marquess of Salisbury. I thank Lord Blake for providing access to the papers of Lord Derby when he was provost of The Queen's College, Oxford.

Librarians and archivists in England and Toronto aided this work immeasurably. I am especially thankful to Joan Kenealy of the Greater London Record Office for refusing to believe that the slim packet of notes of minutes of the Church Rate Abolition Society could have been lost. I am thankful too for the assistance given by Malcolm Thomas of Friends' House and the generous hospitality provided by the Reverend Wayne Hankey while I immersed myself in the pamphlets at Pusey House, Oxford.

I am very grateful to Linda Schulte, Roger Grootenboer, and Cynthia Hoekstra for their skill on word processors and for their care and cheerfulness in entering draft after draft of my revisions. Redeemer College in Ancaster, Ontario, is a small undergraduate institution that promotes both scholarship and teaching; I am grateful that it made available both the time and resources to support this project. Peter J. Potter, editor, and Cherene Holland, managing editor, at Penn State Press were always as careful, kind, and obliging in turning my type-script into a book as any author could wish. I thank them kindly.

I am indebted to my parents, Peter and Anne Ellens, for inclining my thoughts to the question of the role of religion in public life. My wife, Kathleen Davis Kennedy, has been more than patient. Her thoughtful questions and well-timed, sensible suggestions retrieved me from more than a few dead ends. I am especially grateful for her invaluable help. To her these pages are warmly dedicated.

Abbreviations

ASCA	British Anti-State-Church Association
LSE	British Library of Economic and Political Science
ERO	Essex Record Office
GRO	Gloucestershire Record Office
GLRO	Greater London Record Office
Hansard	3 Hansard's
HLRO	House of Lords Record Office
PRO	Public Record Office

Introduction

The Confessional State and the Law of Church Rates, 1832

The immediate emphasis of this work is the opposition to, and defense of, the church rate—the property tax levied on ratepayers in England and Wales, regardless of denominational affiliation, for the maintenance of the parish churches of the Church of England. The underlying focus is the role of voluntaryism in building a voluntaryist society, shaping a secular and desacralized liberal state, and drawing Protestant Dissenters into the Liberal party.

Religion was at the core of political conflict in urban constituencies in the generation after the passage of the Parliamentary Reform Act of 1832. Liberals and Tories faced each other as Dissenters and Churchmen. They were divided because of the privileges of Churchmen and the religious grievances of Dissenters more often than because of tensions engendered by inequalities of class and economic interest. Of all the instances of religious discrimination against Dissenters, the obligation to pay church rates became established quickly after 1832 as the greatest Dissenting grievance. In the mid-Victorian period the church rate question served as the symbol of all other Dissenting grievances. It was this question more than any other that galvanized

Dissenters into political action, and ultimately into Gladstone's Liberal party.

The liberalism that evolved in mid-nineteenth-century England and Wales was not of the overly anti-Christian and anticlerical sort often seen on the continent. Instead, the English variety of liberalism was a hybrid species that was given birth through the midwifery of religion (including the participation of High Church and Broad Church Anglicans) and Dissenting voluntaryism.

Voluntaryism was from its inception a disparate mixture. Its oldest element was a deeply held conviction that the core of authentic religion depended on the free submission of the human will to the call of God; true religion, therefore, could not be coerced. Antipathy to coercion in religion accounted as much for the anti-Erastianism of Anglo-Catholics as the fierce ecclesiological independence of Dissenters. This old Christian concern to maintain internal freedom for personal and congregational faith was translated into an ideology of voluntaryism after 1832 when Dissenters turned to politics and the state to force religiously based institutions, including places of worship and schools for instruction, to become free of state interference. Voluntaryists became obsessed with freeing religion from all state influence and control, to separate church and state and to make religion a matter of entirely private concern. By the end of the period voluntaryists, both Dissenting and Anglican, had gone far toward achieving their goal of a society in which religion in public life had become largely vestigial. By 1868 the contours of a secular liberal state were in place; voluntaryism and liberalism had become largely indistinguishable.

No single political issue played as central a role in accounting for the paradoxical development of a desacralized state and society, from principles intended to advance the Christian faith, as the opposition to church rates. On 31 July 1868, when royal assent was given to the bill that abolished compulsory church rates, an end was put to a thirty-six-year conflict that, according to the *Nonconformist*, had "caused more strife and bitterness than any agitation which has ever taken place in England. . . ."[1] In the course of the conflict, church rate opponents

---

1. The *Nonconformist*, 5 Aug. 1868, p. 773; modern historians do not disagree with this assessment, although they use more careful language. Olive Anderson calls the church rate conflict "arguably the longest and hardest of all the politico-ecclesiastical struggles of the mid-nineteenth century . . . ," in "Gladstone's Abolition of Compulsory Church Rates: A Minor Political Myth and Its Historiographical Career," *Journal of Ecclesiastical History*, XXV, no. 2 (April 1974), 191; Owen Chadwick says: "If church and dissent came to blows as never before and never afterwards in the history of

were imprisoned, churches were desecrated by vestry meetings that turned into brawling mob scenes, and the tranquillity of countless towns and villages was shattered. Of all the political-ecclesiastical disputes that figured so strongly in the politics of the period between the first two parliamentary reform bills, none had the steady power of the church rate issue to keep alive the fires of enmity that set Dissenters against Churchmen. That was so in part because only the church rate obligation, of the grievances that remained to remind Dissenters of their continuing second-class citizenship after repeal of the Test and Corporation Acts, was one that Dissenters themselves had the power to begin redressing. The church rate was a local tax that could be levied only with the consent of the majority of the ratepayers gathered in the parish vestry. During the 1830s urban Dissenters began to muster their forces to defeat the church rate. Because Dissenters were at the same time becoming voluntaryists who repudiated the legitimacy of church establishments, vestry church rate contests became an ideal local forum to strike a blow against the church establishment.

The church rate issue went beyond the consideration of money, although the financial aspect was of consequence to many ratepayers and the actual church rate income was crucially important in numerous parishes. The church rate conflict was fought so long and so fiercely because it hinged on allegiance to, or rejection of, the church rate principle — the dictum that all ratepayers, irrespective of their denominational allegiance, owed financial support to the parish churches of the established church. In this respect, the church rate struggle was from the outset quite unlike the antitithe movement of the 1820s and 1830. The opposition to tithes since the eighteenth century reflected primarily on economic grievances, and tithes were debated largely in economic terms. Farmers and agricultural laborers scorned high tithes and high rates indiscriminately as a financial burden. Church rates, on the other hand, were challenged or defended primarily because they illustrated the prerogatives of the established church. Most opponents of tithes could be satisfied with their reduction and later commutation; Dissenting opponents of church rates came to see even the smallest church rate as a symbol of unacceptable ecclesiastical preeminence and began to demand total abolition of the rate.[2]

England, a main cause was the tea-cup parochial squabbles of church rate" (in *The Victorian Church*, I [3d ed.; London, 1971], p. 82).

2. W. R. Ward, "The Tithe Question in England in the Early Nineteenth Century," *Journal of Ecclesiastical History*, XVI (1965), 70, 78, 80–81; J. L. Hammond and Barbara Hammond, *The Village Labourer, 1760–1832* (New York, 1967), p. 248; Eric

The Dissenting opposition to the church rate principle grew out of the frontal attack on the Church made in the 1830s when the Church was widely identified as a part of a corrupt "old order." By 1832 the defenders of the established church had lost several important lines of defense. The repeal of the Test and Corporation Acts in 1828 and Catholic emancipation in 1829 had dislodged the cornerstones of religious discrimination that guaranteed the preeminent status of the Church and gave the state its confessional color.[3] Protestant Dissenters eagerly took advantage of the new political power afforded them by the extended franchise given by the Parliamentary Reform Bill of 1832. But rather than gratefully accepting the new civil privileges extended to them by the constitutional changes between 1828 and 1832, they began a concerted attack against the social and political disabilities under which they continued to live.[4]

The altered constitutional and political status of the Church contributed to the important theoretical debate in the 1830s concerning the ideal relation of church and state. Prominent men such as the rising young Tory W. E. Gladstone, the eminent Scottish Presbyterian Thomas Chalmers, Dr. Ralph Wardlaw, an Independent minister from Glasgow, and the keen young Whig T. B. Macaulay were among those who set forth radically differing church-and-state theories.[5] The

Hobsbawm and George Rudé, *Captain Swing: A Social History of the Great English Agricultural Uprising of 1830* (New York, 1975), pp. 109, 130–131; Eric J. Evans, *The Contentious Tithe: The Tithe Problem in English Agriculture, 1750–1850* (London, 1976), chaps. 2 and 3; Roger J. P. Kain and Hugh C. Prince, *The Tithe Surveys of England and Wales* (Cambridge, 1985), pp. 6, 18, and 32.

3. Owen Chadwick, *The Victorian Church*, I, 7–60; Norman Gash, *Reaction and Reconstruction in English Politics, 1832–1852* (Oxford, 1965), pp. 60–64; G.F.A. Best, "The Constitutional Revolution, 1828–1832, and Its Consequences for the Established Church," *Theology*, LXII, no. 468 (June 1959), 226–234.

4. Owen Chadwick points out that passage of the Municipal Corporations Act had an even more direct effect on the church rate conflict. Before 1835 a considerable number of corporations normally cared for the churches in their patronage. The act divested them of their patronage, making it necessary for church rates to be levied in its stead. Agitation against the church rate tended to develop in towns unaccustomed to church rates. *The Victorian Church*, I, III.

5. W. E. Gladstone, *The State in Its Relations with the Church* (London, 1838); Thomas Chalmers gave a series of lectures in 1838 on "the establishment and extension of national churches as affording the only adequate machinery for the moral and Christian instruction of the people"; Chalmers was answered by Ralph Wardlaw in a series of lectures in 1839 published as *National Church Establishments Examined* (London, 1838); T. B. Macaulay's Whig church and state views are clearly shown in his review

deepest implications of the troublesome church rate question are set in relief against the contested principles that came to the fore in the debates of the 1830s regarding the proper relation of church and state.

It was an indication of the radical focus of the competing theories that the concern was as much about the religious nature of the state as the civil and religious privileges of the Church. In contention was a fundamental issue: should public affairs remain based on a religious footing, in continuity with a millennium of tradition, or be reconstituted on a desacralized basis? Arising out of this dispute were two questions on which much of the division centered. The first was whether the state was divinely instituted, with a transcendent mandate and objectives, or whether it was founded solely in contract and confined to temporal concerns. A related but separate question was whether there ought to be an alliance of church and state, or whether the ecclesiastical and civil communities should be entirely separate. By the late 1830s there were three main political approaches to these questions promoted by spokesmen representing revived Tory, Whig, and voluntaryist Dissenting views. Cutting across and deeply influencing the Whig and Dissenting positions were two powerful intellectual currents— liberalism and utilitarianism.

The Tory position was essentially a medieval Catholic legacy, reformed by Richard Hooker and modified by the exigencies of constitutional change and the spirit of romanticism. It favored an Anglican-Christian nation in which both state and church were divinely instituted and were necessarily allied. The best formulation of this position was given in 1838 by W. E. Gladstone in *The State in Its Relations with the Church*. Gladstone championed a state church to allow an organic state possessing a personality and a national conscience to sanctify "the acts of that personality by the offices of religion. . . ."[6] Although they

"The State in its relations with the Church. by W. E. Gladstone, Esq., . . . ," *Edinburgh Review*, LXIX, 318–380; Gash, *Reaction and Reconstruction*, p. 86, note 1.

6. W. E. Gladstone, *The State in Its Relations with the Church*, p. 39; M. D. Stephen, "Liberty, Church, and State: Gladstone's Relations with Manning and Acton, 1832–1870," *Journal of Religious History*, 1 (1960), 217–232; H.C.G. Matthew, ed., *The Gladstone Diaries*, vol. III, 1840–1847 (Oxford, 1974), pp. xxvi–xxvii; Deryck Schreuder, "Gladstone and the Conscience of the State," in P. Marsh, ed., *The Conscience of the Victorian State* (London, 1979); Perry Butler, *Gladstone: Church, State, and Tractarianism—A Study of His Religious Ideas and Attitudes, 1809–1859* (Oxford, 1982); Boyd Hilton, "Gladstone's Theological Politics," in M. Bentley and J. Stevenson, eds., *High and Low Politics in Modern Britain* (Oxford, 1983), pp. 28–57; Agatha Ramm, "Gladstone's Religion," *Historical Journal*, 28 (1985), 327–340; J. P. Parry, *Democracy*

agreed generally on the nature of the state and society, Tories differed widely in their ideas of the Church. The Tory position included Evangelicals defending the Protestant Reformed church, and Anglo-Catholics proclaiming the prerogatives of a catholic, apostolic church. Because of their high view of the Church, Anglo-Catholics could contemplate separating church and state if the latter's Erastian embrace appeared overbearing enough to threaten the former's integrity.

The nineteenth-century life span of this Tory ideal was short. By the 1840s few Tories persisted in taking seriously the Christian tenet of a state founded by divine sanction.[7] Most Conservatives merely bowed in perfunctory obeisance to their old ideal and satisfied themselves by defending as many vestiges as remained of the alliance of church and state. The forces of religious pluralism and political democracy undermined the traditional Christian view of state and society; the ultras who continued to believe lacked the imagination to rework Christian teaching to fit new social and political conditions.

In contradistinction to the Tory desire for a Christian society, the Whigs tended to aim for a moral society. Under the influence of Locke and liberalism, Whigs exchanged the Tory belief in the divine constitution and aims of the state for a contractual footing and temporal ends. They generally continued to defend an established Erastian church, but on utilitarian grounds. Many were Broad Churchmen whose latitudinarian theology led them to eschew both the Evangelical's "vital religion" and the Tractarian's sacramentalist piety. Instead, they supported the established church as the most efficient means of guaranteeing social and political stability and promoting a moral society.[8]

---

and Religion: Gladstone and the Liberal Party, 1867–1875 (Cambridge, 1986); T. A. Jenkins, *Gladstone, Whiggery, and the Liberal Party, 1874–1886* (Oxford, 1988), chap. 1.

7. Robert Hole, *Pulpits, Politics, and Public Order in England, 1760–1832* (Cambridge, 1989), chaps. 1, 12, 13, 16. Robert Hole has shown convincingly that little remained of serious Christian political theory by 1832. What did remain was social theory in which the Christian faith and the established church continued to play a central role. During the nineteenth century even when Christian theory, whether political or social, was weak or incoherent, Anglicans and many Dissenters continued to feel by ingrained faith, tradition, or habit that public recognition and support of the Christian faith were necessary foundations of a good society. Thus the voluntaryist campaign to relegate Christian faith to the private sphere was fought tenaciously albeit ultimately unsuccessfully, due in part to the absence of a systematic Christian theory of politics and society that could go beyond nostalgia for an idealized past to incorporate the fact of growing political participation of non-Anglicans — Protestant Dissenters and Roman Catholics.

8. For studies arguing that Whig social policy was influenced by a liberal theology

Voluntaryist Dissenters sought to establish a moral and voluntaryist society. Like the Whigs, they saw the state as an entirely conventional institution, established for the protection of life and property. Like Whig political theory, voluntaryist political philosophy was not identifiably Christian. It was tied more closely to political liberalism and class interests than to religious confession. Unlike the Whigs, however, voluntaryist Dissenters (especially the militants among them) were eager to separate church and state, believing that the integrity of each was compromised by alliance with the other. Proponents of this view did not wish to withdraw all Christian influence from the state; but they rejected any corporate Christian activity by the state, trusting that the influence of individual Christians would provide the Christian conscience of the state.[9]

The voluntaryist rejection of the establishment principle was probably confined to a very small minority of Protestant Dissenters in 1832. But between 1834 and 1838 the voluntary principle came to dominate the outlook of Baptists and Congregationalists. English Presbyterians, who by the early nineteenth century had mainly become Unitarians, were not uniformly opposed to the establishment principle, but they were being pushed out of the leadership of Dissent by 1836. The development of voluntaryism in the 1840s was encouraged by the disruption in Scotland; the precedent of Free Scottish Presbyterianism became a model for voluntaryist organization in England and Wales. Quakers were opposed to an established church but on spiritual

---

that sought to promote a moral society led by an inclusive and latitudinarian national church, see Ellis Archer Wasson, *Whig Renaissance: Lord Althorp and the Whig Party, 1782–1845* (New York, 1987); J. P. Ellens, "Lord John Russell and the Church Rate Conflict: The Struggle for a Broad Church, 1834–1868," *Journal of British Studies*, 26 (April 1987), 232–257; Richard Brent, "The Whigs and Protestant Dissent in the Decade of Reform: The Case of Church Rates, 1833–1841," *English Historical Review*, 102, no. 405 (Oct. 1987), 887–910; Brent, *Liberal Anglican Politics: Whiggery, Religion, and Reform* (Oxford, 1987); T. A. Jenkins, *Gladstone, Whiggery, and the Liberal Party, 1874–1886* (Oxford, 1988). A criticism of the revisionist view of Brent and others and sympathy for Dissenting aspirations was shown especially by "liberal Anglican Whigs" is given by R. W. Davis, who has given the apt reminder that the Whig party as a whole was the party of constitutional and religious liberty. See R. W. Davis, "The Whigs and Religious Issues, 1830–1835," in R. W. Davis and R. J. Helmstadter, eds., *Religion and Irreligion in Victorian Society* (London, 1992).

9. See Richard J. Helmstadter, "The Nonconformist Conscience," in Peter Marsh, ed., *The Conscience of the Victorian State* (Syracuse, 1979), pp. 135–172; Gerald Parson, "From Dissenters to Free Churchmen: The Transitions of Victorian Nonconformity," in *Religion in Victorian Britain*, vol. I, *Traditions* (Manchester, 1988), chap. 2.

grounds. They did not generally join voluntaryist Dissenters in political assaults on the establishment.

The numerous and respectable Wesleyan Methodists, who distanced themselves from Dissent, were in the 1830s generally loyal to the establishment principle, although the Primitive Methodists, the New Connection, and the various groups that seceded from the Wesleyans during the 1850s were drawn to voluntaryism. But the Wesleyans generally supported the church rate as an arm of the establishment principle, and defended both as essential to maintain a Christian nation. Only in the mid-1860s, as the development of ritualism alienated them from the Church, did Wesleyans become more openly critical of church rates. Then they began to support moderate Churchmen in seeking church rate reform. The growing Wesleyan antipathy to church rates by 1865 would actually be one of the factors that encouraged Gladstone to take an active role in seeking to repeal compulsory church rates, lest Wesleyans begin to repudiate their traditional support for, or at least tolerance of, the establishment principle.[10]

Some conservative Congregationalists and Baptists who believed that churches ought to be voluntary institutions nevertheless opposed disestablishment. They retained a traditional corporate view of the religious responsibilities of the state and feared, as did Tories, that separation of church and state would lead to an irreligious or atheistic state and society. This fear points to a theme central to the church-state debate, and implicit in the church rate controversy—secularization. This process occurred on two related but distinct levels. The first involved the institutional separation of church and state and will be called secularization. The second entailed the religious redirection of the state from its traditional Christian orientation and will be described as desacralization.[11]

10. Gash, *Reaction and Reconstruction*, pp. 64–65; Chadwick, *The Victorian Church* I, 374–386.

11. A century-old paradigm associates secularization and the putative decline of religion in modern Western societies with the process of modernization seen in the growth of capitalism and urbanization. With varying emphases, such a view is often assumed in Owen Chadwick, *The Secularization of the European Mind in the Nineteenth Century* (Cambridge, 1975); David Martin, *A General Theory of Secularization* (New York, 1979); and Bryan Wilson, *Religion in Sociological Perspective* (Oxford, 1982). Some sociologists and historians have questioned whether it is fruitful to talk of the decline of religion and suggest rather that religion in modernized societies has retained its potency although having taken on new forms. See Jacques Ellul, *The New Demons* (Oxford, 1976); Jeffrey Cox, "Is Secularization a Useful Concept? No, Not Even in

The voluntaryist Dissenting aim of separating church and state, and abolishing church rates, can be seen on this first level simply as deriving from the Protestant conviction that religion could prosper only when free. Secularization thus merely meant freeing ecclesiastical institutions and religion from state control. Desacralization connotes a more radical process. Whigs as well as Dissenters contributed to it by looking increasingly and uncritically to liberalism and utilitarianism to provide the theoretical rationale for the state's foundation and purpose. In this, voluntaryist Dissenters, and particularly the militants, greatly outstripped the Whigs. The voluntaryists insisted that the state and other social institutions should relinquish their traditional transcendent orientation in exchange for a this-worldly replacement. This desacralization was truly revolutionary, although it was only gradually accomplished. For most moderate Dissenters the approach to a desacralized state was unconscious. Because of their antipathy to church establishments they paid little attention to the religious orientation of social institutions and adopted immanent social values by default.

The organized opposition to church rates, which came to the fore in the 1830s as part of the overt challenge to the established church, continued after the imminent threat to the Church died down by the late 1830s. Church rate opposition became the favored means of transforming the frontal attack of the 1830s into practical politics. Voluntaryists sought to erode the nationality of the Church by a process of gradual disestablishment. At the same time the growth of the anti–church rate movement came to play a pivotal role in drawing mid-nineteenth century Dissenters into the political process.

Before the late 1860s, when Gladstone took in hand the cause of abolishing compulsory church rates, Dissenters had coalesced into a political community. The decades long opposition to church rates had bridged differences among moderate and militant voluntaryist Dissenters. Gladstone's willingness to seek the repeal of compulsory church rates won him the allegiance of mid-Victorian Dissent. Without this support, the formation of Gladstonian liberalism would not have occurred. The resolution of the church rate question was a key to unlock the possibilities of post-1867 politics.

Twentieth-Century Britain," paper read at the Southern Conference on British Studies, 1984; David Lyon, "Rethinking Secularization: Retrospect and Prospect," *Review of Religious Research*, vol. XXVI, no. 3 (March 1985), 228–243; Rodney Stark and William Sims Bainbridge, *The Future of Religion* (Berkeley, 1985).

II

Church rates were an ancient legal obligation in England and Wales. The parson was bound by common law to repair the chancel of the parish church, and the parishioners were to maintain its nave, although custom frequently decreed that parishioners were liable for the upkeep of the chancel as well. But the origins and legal basis of the obligations of parishioners toward the parish church were clouded in obscurity. Dissenters who came to dispute their obligation to maintain the church happily appropriated the laconic observation by Richard Burn, in his authoritative *The Justice of the Peace and Parish Officer*, that "formerly" bishops had the obligation to maintain parish churches because they impropriated the tithe. When the right to the tithe (a quarter of which was meant for church repair) was conferred on rectors, they also assumed the obligation for the church.[12] Maintenance of the parish church had long since passed from rectors to parishioners. This was usually fulfilled through the levying and paying of a church rate, known also as a levy, cess, lay, or ley in different parts of the country. But everywhere, the church rate, like all other rates, was a property tax paid by occupiers of lands and buildings, levied as a percentage in the pound of the annual assessed value of the property occupied.[13]

Church rates, which were levied at least as early as 1370, supplied the funds to maintain the fabric of church and churchyard and provided the things "necessary for the decent performance of Divine Service."[14] Besides being used for repairs, church rates also supplied the bread and wine for Holy Communion, paid the sexton and bell ringers, and often cared for the village clock as well as the washing of surplices and the lighting of the church.

Church rates were paid by the ratepayers of the parish, the basic political and ecclesiastical unit of administration. The parish was that area served by one church, and politically it could be practically defined as "a place making a separate poor rate."[15] Church rates were levied by the authority of what was commonly referred to as "the parishioners in vestry assembled." The vestry meeting had been, at

12. Richard Burn, *The Justice of the Peace and Parish Officer*, vol. I (28th ed. rev. by J. Chitty and Thomas Chitty; London, 1837), p. 667.
13. Bryan Keith-Lucas, *The Unreformed Local Government System* (London, 1980), p. 137.
14. W. E. Tate, *The Parish Chest* (Cambridge, 1946), p. 281, notes 12–15.
15. Keith-Lucas, *The Unreformed Local Government System*, p. 76.

least since the fourteenth century, "the assembly of the whole parish, met together in some convenient place for the despatch of the affairs and business of the parish. . . ."[16]

To vote in the vestry one had to have lived in the parish for one year and a day and paid the latest poor rate, to which all inhabitants of the parish, whether owning or occupying lands and houses, were assessed. The local franchise thus belonged to women who paid poor rates independently as well as to men, and to the small as well as the great. But in fact it was the practice to omit the cottages of the laboring classes from the rate book. By 1832 few properties of less than £10 in annual value were assessed, which meant that in industrial towns like Manchester and Birmingham only about one-quarter of the householders paid the poor rate.[17]

As a further complication, poor rates were sometimes compounded. In such a case cottages of the poor were put on the rate books, but the rate was paid by the owner rather than the occupier. This practice became more common following the enactment of the 1818 Parish Vestry Act, and the right to vote of the "compound tenant" came to be disputed in church rate contests, as it did in parliamentary and municipal elections, following the reforms of 1832 and 1835. Bryan Keith-Lucas observed that "the working classes in general made no contribution to the poor rate."[18] As they were therefore also exempt from church rates, it is understandable that working men and secular radicals expressed little interest in the church rate controversy after the 1830s, when it became a particularly middle-class Nonconformist grievance.

The vestry meeting was presided over by the minister if he were present. Generally two churchwardens were chosen in the annual Easter vestry by consent of the minister and parishioners. When agreement was lacking the minister was entitled to choose one and the parishioners the other. Aliens, Papists, Jews, and the underaged were prohibited from being elected, but neither poverty nor Dissent could be cited by the archdeacon as cause to disqualify the parish's choice.[19]

16. Burn, *Justice of the Peace*, VI, 131; Tate, *Parish Chest*, p. 14; see also Keith-Lucas, *The Unreformed Local Government System*, p. 75.

17. Burn, *Justice of the Peace*, I, 671, 672; VI, 133; Keith-Lucas, *The Unreformed Local Government System*, pp. 77, 139.

18. Keith-Lucas, *The Unreformed Local Government System*, pp. 139, 140. (Sturges Bourne's Parish Vestry Act, 58 Geo. III, c. 69.)

19. Burn, *Justice of the Peace*, I, 685, 686; VI, 132. According to 58 Geo. III, c. 69,

Churchwardens joined surveyors of highways, parish constables, and overseers of the poor as the principal unpaid parish officers. Churchwardens served primarily in an ecclesiastical capacity as guardians or keepers of the church and its contents, although in some places such as the Manchester they also had sole responsibility for the poor.[20] The churchwardens provided the vestry meeting with an estimate of funds needed for the coming year and requested that the parishioners levy a particular rate to supply that need. To obtain a legal rate a motion had to be seconded by a parishioner and supported by a majority of those present, indicated by a show of hands or in case of doubt by dividing ayes and noes on opposite sides of the room. Finally the record of the proceedings in the vestry minutes and the assessment form needed to be signed by both churchwardens and by several parishioners.[21]

On the face of it, the parishioners assembled in vestry had the final word on the making of rates. Burn seemed to state that point, declaring: "The churchwardens have no power to make any rate themselves exclusive of the parishioners, who are to meet for that purpose, and when they are assembled, a rate made by the majority present shall bind the whole parish, although the churchwardens voted against it."[22] The freedom of parishioners to make or not to make a rate was not so straightforward, however. Tempering the freedom of the parishioners was the old common law obligation to maintain the parish church. That duty was supervised by the ecclesiastical courts. Burn asserted that if a church fell into disrepair, "the parishioners may be compelled by that court to repair the body of the church, and they might be excommunicated until it is repaired, except those who are willing to contribute."[23] Furthermore, churchwardens could be sued for neglecting or refusing to call a meeting to make a necessary rate.

Excommunication by the Church of those not conforming to her discipline was clearly an inadequate punishment by 1832. But the dictum concerning parochial obligations remained. One body of legal

---

s. 2, if the rector or vicar were absent the parishioners meeting in vestry were entitled to elect their own chairman, who had a casting vote.

20. Burn, *Justice of the Peace*, I, 691 (43 Eliz. c. 2, s. 1); Keith-Lucas, *The Unreformed Local Government System*, pp. 86, 87.

21. Burn, *Justice of the Peace*, I, 670–675.

22. Ibid., p. 670.

23. Ibid., p. 668.

opinion held that in case parishioners should refuse to levy a church rate, the churchwardens might make one without their concurrence, as they could be punished in the ecclesiastical courts for neglecting to maintain the church and it would be unfair to punish them for the obstinacy of others. Burn believed this view to be questionable law, but it convinced many Churchmen, aggravated feelings in numerous parishes, tempered the militancy of others, and was only finally declared in error in the Braintree decision of 1853—the legal ruling that will be discussed in Chapter 2.[24]

The view that churchwardens could unilaterally levy church rates in case of a refusal by the vestry was given qualified support at a critical time by a report issued in 1832 by the commissioners appointed to investigate the ecclesiastical courts. They acknowledged that in theory churchwardens might indeed have that power but could not practicably exercise it in the present state of the law. They therefore recommended that churchwardens be given the power to appeal to the quarter sessions, which should have the authority to make a church rate if the vestry refused or levied an inadequate one. The commissioners further recommended that payment of church rates should be enforced just like payment of poor rates, as there was in their view no material difference between them.[25] Thus in 1832, as church rate contests were heating up and Dissenters were beginning to deny the legitimacy of ecclesiastical taxation, defenders of the establishment were given ammunition to strengthen the church rate system by making it less ecclesiastical and more political.

The commissioners' recommendations were in tune with legislation passed in 1813 to facilitate more efficient recovery of legally levied church rates. The statute 53 Geo. III, c. 126 enabled churchwardens to bypass the ecclesiastical courts, whose powers of enforcement had proved cumbersome and expensive. This act empowered two justices of the peace, upon the request of one churchwarden, to recover delinquent church rates by distraining the recusant's goods and selling them to recover the rate plus costs. This procedure could be used to enforce payment of any church rate not exceeding £10 whose validity was not challenged in an ecclesiastical court.[26]

24. Ibid., p. 670.

25. Great Britain, *Parliamentary Papers*, "Report of Commissioners Appointed to Inquire into the Practice and Jurisdiction of Ecclesiastical Courts in England and Wales," 1831–1832 (199) XXIV. 1, pp. 47, 48.

26. Burn, *Justice of the Peace*, I, 675–677. (53 Geo. III, c. 127, s. 7, "for the more

By 1832, when church rates became a divisive issue, statute law had significantly bolstered the conventions governing them. Furthermore, legislation in 1818 and 1819 reorganized vestries, making them less open and popular. In response to the explosive need for increased poor relief Parliament introduced legislation drafted by William Sturges Bourne to "take control of poor relief out of the hands of the poor themselves."[27] The Parish Vestries Act of 1818 provided that henceforth all vestry elections should give more weight to the votes of larger ratepayers. Parishioners with up to £50 of assessed value were given one vote. Each additional £25 valuation earned them an additional vote, up to a limit of six votes. In addition, those not paying rates were not only prevented from voting as before, but were actually excluded from attending vestry meetings. In the following year the vestry was weighted even more heavily in favor of property by an amendment that enfranchised joint stock companies and nonresident ratepayers.[28]

This system of plural voting was often ignored because of its unwieldiness. But it was used when a parishioner demanded a poll. It was here that Sturges Bourne's acts had a sharp impact on the church rate question. As church rates became ever more hotly contested, parishioners increasingly demanded polls in their attempts to reverse undesirable decisions. In a poll each ratepaying parishioner could vote, whether or not he had attended the disputed vestry. The time allotted to polling gave both sides additional opportunities to agitate, and the careful attribution of plural votes to larger ratepayers enormously exacerbated the ill feelings of Dissenters toward Churchmen, who tended to benefit from plural voting.

In 1818 and 1819 the church building acts created new ecclesiastical districts with statutory authority to levy church rates. Under the authority of these acts, church rates could be levied to repay monies expended by church commissioners to purchase new sites for churches; money could be borrowed on the rates; and in extraparochial places, where church rates had not previously been levied, a justice of the peace could appoint two or more churchwardens with the power to levy church rates subject to the ordinary constraints of church rate law. The statute 58 Geo. III, c. 45 provided that new "district

---

easily and speedily recovering church rates or chapel rates of limited amounts . . . ," p. 675.)

27. Keith-Lucas, *The Unreformed Local Government System*, p. 98.
28. Ibid., pp. 98, 99; Burn, *Justice of the Peace*, VI, 131–134.

churches" built or acquired in a parish should raise their own church rates, functioning essentially as a new parish. At the same time, ratepayers in such districts remained liable for church rates to the original parish church as well for a period of twenty years.[29] This stipulation greatly enlarged the number of church rate opponents and accounted for a considerable number of the Churchmen who joined Dissent in opposing the rate. The "new church rates" were especially distasteful to many Dissenters because the levying of a church rate to repay a loan obtained for building a new church could be enforced by common law. Churchwardens actually could be compelled to levy a church rate by a mandamus obtained from the Court of King's Bench.[30] Finally, the management of the new churches was actually taken out of the hands of those obliged to maintain them. The 1819 act provided that the commissioners could appoint a "select vestry" of twenty-six persons from among "the substantial inhabitants" to maintain the new church, elect a churchwarden, and levy rates.[31] Thus in two decades prior to 1832 legislation concerning parishes and rates had both increased the aggravation of church rates, making them seem a pressing grievance, and reinforced their defenses, encouraging Churchmen to rely on them.

A final word should be said about the actual financial importance of church rates. An important parliamentary paper published in 1839 revealed that the total amount of church rates received in England and Wales in 1832 was £446,247. This sum serves as the most accurate account of the economic weight of church rates at the outset of the conflict. In addition, churchwardens in 1832 received the sum of £41,489, which had been collected as poor rates. It was common practice in small parishes, in which the collection of a small church rate would have been uneconomical, for churchwardens to get a share of the poor rate. To the Church's loss, this practice was disallowed by the Poor Law Amendment Act of 1834.[32] The return further showed the amounts received in 1832 from other local rates: county rates

---

29. Burn, *Justice of the Peace*, I, 679–682. (58 Geo. III, c. 45 and 59 Geo. III, c. 134.)

30. Ibid. (58 Geo. III, c. 45, s. 14 and 60, and 59 Geo. III, c. 134, s. 24.)

31. Ibid., p. 682. (Geo. III, c. 134, s. 30.)

32. Great Britain, *Parliamentary Papers*, "Amount of Church Rates in the year ending Easter 1827; of Church Rates and other Monies Received and Expended by the Churchwardens in the year ending Easter 1832; and of Church Rates and other Monies Received and Expended in the year ending Easter 1839," 1839 (in 562), XLIV. 47, p. 48.

amounted to £761,901, and poor rates to £8,622,920.[33] In comparison, particularly to the annual poor rate income, the amount derived from church rates does not seem overly large. Nevertheless, it was important to the Church in financial as well as in symbolic terms. Church rate income may have accounted for as much as 12 percent of the total revenues of the Church, calculated by the church commissioners to have amounted in 1832 to £3,738,951 exclusive of voluntary payments and church rates.[34] The Church would therefore not part lightly with the church rate, particularly as Churchmen were becoming increasingly aware of the need for extra funds to finance church expansion to meet the spiritual needs of the unchurched in industrial England. But the church rate was a local tax, and its financial importance was felt first on the parish level. In many parish churches the annual church rate was financially all-important. A defeat—and particularly repeated defeats—of the church rate could make it difficult to meet the costs of maintaining a church. That was so because churches that were denied a rate could not fall back on a tradition of voluntary contributions. Church rate refusals therefore could hurt churches especially in poor parishes, which lacked wealthy benefactors to fill the deficiency of a rate.

Although the church rate was not the most financially onerous of the local rates, its financial bite was sharp enough to make most Dissenting ratepayers receptive to the voices of those voluntaryists in the 1830s who began to question the legitimacy of an ecclesiastical tax. The hypothetical case of a small Dissenting shopkeeper may illustrate that point. A five-penny rate levied on the property he occupied, valued at £20 per annum, would make his share of the parish church rate amount to 8s.4d. That sum would equal approximately one-half percent of an annual income of £80. Translated into a current income of, let us say, £20,000, this would amount to a bill of £100 owed to the parish church. In years when extraordinary repairs were needed the church might very well demand an eight-penny or even a one- or two-shilling rate, considerably increasing the amount owed to the church. If our shopkeeper was becoming more antagonistic to the established church and was being swayed by the appeal of voluntaryism, his annual church

33. Ibid., p. 50. See also Great Britain, *Parliamentary Papers*, "Poor Rates, County Rates, Highway Rates, and Church Rates," 1830–1831 (52), XI. 205, p. 211.

34. Great Britain, *Parliamentary Papers*, "First Report of Commissioners on the State of the Established Church, with reference to Duties and Revenues," 1835 (54), XXII. 1, pp. 23–25.

rate could easily begin to seem intolerably unfair and burdensome. In the coming chapter we shall show how between 1832 and 1841 the church rate came to be seen as an unjust tax—"that impious impost"—the opposition to and defense of which developed into a political and ecclesiastical conflict that was not to be resolved for thirty-six years.

I

Origins of the Church Rate Conflict and the Birth of Voluntaryism, 1832–1838

The church rate was a local tax like the poor rate, county rate, lighting rate, or highway rate. During the 1820s and early 1830s all rates were increasingly complained of as excessive and financially burdensome. But it would be difficult to document any claim before 1832, in the approximately fifteen thousand parishes of England and Wales, that the church rate was inherently unjust or unlike other rates. In 1832, however, ratepayers in a number of parishes crossed a historic divide. They denied the legitimacy of an ecclesiastical tax. By the spring of 1834 large and influential sections of Protestant Dissent singled out the church rate as "that unjust impost," and many parish vestries in towns and cities throughout the land refused to levy the rate upon which depended the maintenance of the parish church.

The church rate question became such a thorny problem to resolve partly because of the nature of Dissenting opposition to the rate. Had Congregationalists and Baptists begun to balk at paying the church rate simply on the grounds of individual conscientious objections to supporting a faith at variance with their own, governments might more easily have found the means to extricate them from their dilemma. But between 1832 and 1838 the ethos of Dissent was being transformed. The principle of voluntaryism—the repudiation of religious establishments and compulsion in religion—increasingly became the animus of political Dissent and began to provide its raison d'être. Voluntaryism provided the ideological framework that allowed Dissenters to weave particular grievances into a unified political movement. The voluntaryist context of the anti–church rate cause made it difficult for Churchmen to redress the grievance for fear of undermining the establishment principle.

The conflict was further complicated because the voluntaryist principle also became the line of division among Dissenters. Between 1832 and 1838 most vocal political Dissenters became either moderate or militant voluntaryists. Both opposed church rates as products of compulsory religion, but they disagreed bitterly on tactics and on how consistently to apply their voluntaryist beliefs. Moderates generally saw the church rate primarily as a "practical grievance" and trusted in their alliance with the Whigs for redress. Militants often wished to use their opposition as a means to overthrow the church establishment and were eager to take an independent political stance. By 1838 disappointment with the Whigs, focused on their failure to satisfy Dissenting church rate demands, allowed militants to gain the upper hand in Dissenting politics.

II

In 1831 and 1832, while the Church was being savagely attacked for the corruption of its finances and organization, first individuals and then entire urban vestries took the step—unprecedented since the late seventeenth century—of refusing to levy church rates. Previously, of course, individuals had failed to pay, and the statute 53 Geo. III, c. 127 had been enacted to facilitate more efficient enforcement of church rates. In Sheffield the parish had actually refused to make a church rate since 1819.[1] But Sheffield's case was a local one and did not materially challenge the principle of ecclesiastical taxation. Except for

---

1. E. R. Wickham, *Church and People in an Industrial City* (London, 1957), p. 71. The majority of the parishioners refused to make a church rate in protest against the claim of pew owners in the parish church to exclusive ownership of the pews.

the Quakers, whose case was unique, Dissenters had until 1832 generally accepted their obligation to pay church rates. That pattern of acquiescence began to break down in the reform crisis of the 1830s.

The growth of vestry church rate refusals emerged from and gave focus to the widely perceived need for church reform. Prominent Churchmen such as Lord Henley proposed reforms dealing with nonresidence, pluralism, and blatantly unequal clerical incomes, giving the Churchmen hope that if these evils were remedied the establishment might yet set Dissent at defiance.[2] But the *Patriot*, established in 1832 as a national voice for evangelical Dissent on public issues, argued that even wide-ranging reforms could not reconcile Dissenters to the Church. Articulating the rationale of voluntaryism that was beginning to shape the outlook of numerous Dissenters, the *Patriot* asserted that the very existence of an establishment was a stumbling block:

> that which is daily becoming the chief reason for Dissent— namely, a conviction that religious establishments of all kinds are unfavorable to the progress of religion—would operate with undiminished force. . . . our ancestors quarreled with the church, because it was not reformed up to the point at which they could conscientiously join her; whereas we cannot enter her, let her be ever so reformed in other respects, while she remains the ally—or mistress—or rather the slave of the state.[3]

Critics of the unreformed Church received a focal point for their anger in October 1831, when bishops sitting in the House of Lords divided with the majority against the Parliamentary Reform Bill. In response, a number of persons in Manchester refused to pay their church rate.[4]

Opponents of the Church were fortunate that the burden of church rates was actually being increased due to the church building acts of 1818 and 1819, which gave newly created parishes a statutory right to

2. Concrete measures to effect proposals made by Lord Henley included the formation of the Church Reformation Society, whose provisional committee reported a meeting under Lord Henley's chairmanship on 8 October 1832. Lord Henley urged members to save the Church by working for ecclesiastical reforms including the termination of pluralities and nonresidence of clergy, better pay and training for clergy, and the commutation of tithes. No mention was made of church rates. *Patriot*, 31 Oct. 1832, p. 329.

3. Ibid., 27 June 1832, p. 185.

4. *Manchester Times*, 29 Oct. 1831, p. 764.

levy church rates. Vestry meetings in Manchester were agitated during 1831, even before the reform bill crisis, about additional church rates required to outfit and maintain the four "new government churches" that had been built in Manchester. It was revealed that the building of each of the four new churches in Manchester had cost the parishioners £2,500 in addition to the £50,000 expended by the government. A leader in the militant *Manchester Times* predicted that the additional burden of rates for "unneeded" government churches, in the midst of excitement about "ancient wrongs," could be made into such an issue that the fight could be enlarged against church rates in general.[5]

The *Manchester Times* had presciently identified the catalytic role that the "new rates" might play in mobilizing Dissenting opinion against the principle of church rates. This was so particularly because this new grievance was felt at a time when, as the *Patriot* was to say in June 1832, the raison d'être of Dissent was being transformed daily.[6] Numerous contemporaries agreed that the church rate conflict originated with the introduction of the new church rates. Writing to Disraeli in 1862, William Hale, archdeacon of London and redoubtable defender of church rates, dated the beginning of opposition from the church building movement.[7] It was paradoxical that these statutory rates remained compulsory after the ancient common law rates were made voluntary in 1868.

In the decade before 1830 the Protestant Dissenting Deputies, established in 1732 to seek the repeal of the Test and Corporation Acts and to represent the interests of Congregationalists, Baptists, and Presbyterians in and around London, handled several church rate grievances, all relating to the church building acts. On 30 November 1827, Thomas Pewtress attended a committee meeting of the deputies to describe legal proceedings being taken against him for recovery of church rates under the church building acts. The committee, preoccupied at that time with the Test and Corporation Acts, exhibited little interest in the issue but did resolve to monitor any new legislation that might extend or alter the powers of the church building commissioners.[8] The committee of the deputies had taken a tentative step toward

5. Ibid.; W. R. Ward, *Religion and Society in England, 1790–1850* (London, 1972), pp. 178–179.

6. See note 3.

7. Hale to Disraeli, 16 July 1862, Hughenden Papers, B/XXI/H/19, LSE microfilm 131.

8. Minutes of the Protestant Dissenting Deputies, 30 Nov. 1827, Guildhall MSS. 3083, VI, 246, 247.

church rate opposition by deciding to attempt to prevent the extension of church rates: By December 1829 a full meeting of the deputies, after having received in the preceding year several appeals for aid to contest liability to new rates, resolved to adopt a policy of assisting those who appealed against the new church rates.[9]

Soon after the first personal objections to new rates by individuals, entire parishes refused to levy a rate for new churches in their jurisdiction. The first of such cases to be reported concerned the refusal of the parishioners of Lambeth to maintain the new church of St. John the Evangelist in the Waterloo Road, although they continued to levy and pay rates for St. Mary's, their parish church, through 1836. With an unfortunate dearth of detail the *Patriot* reported on 23 May 1832: "In consequence of the refusal of the parishioners of Lambeth to grant a rate for the expenses of the new church in the Waterloo-road, the Rector declined preaching on Sunday evenings, urging as a reason that he could not afford to be at the expense of lighting the church from his yearly income. The church has consequently been closed on Sunday evenings for a long time."[10]

It did not take long for Dissenters to expand their opposition from new church rates to those of greater antiquity. In a rowdy vestry meeting in the parish of Manchester, held on 1 June 1832 in the Collegiate Church, the crowd hooted down not only accounts relating to new churches but also numerous accounts of dubious legality that had been accepted in quieter times, including two charges for dinners for the swearing-in of churchwardens and sidesmen.[11] Such incidents reflected the larger protest against privilege and corruption that was convulsing civil and national politics. Another sign of trouble was the admission by the churchwardens that last year's three-penny rate had netted only £3,872 out of a total of £5,000 to £6,000 that should have been collected. This fact reflected the widespread popular refusal of

9. Ibid., 27 Nov. 1829 and 18 Dec. 1829, VII, 165–169.

10. *Patriot*, 23 May 1832, p. 143; Lambeth Churchwardens' Accounts, 1829–1839, Minet Library, London. Unfortunately the Lambeth Vestry minutes prior to October 1834 have been lost. However, churchwardens' accounts show that church rates were paid from 1829 to 1836. It can be surmised that the Lambeth parishioners agreed to levy their traditional church rate for St. Mary's, Lambeth, but declined to levy a rate for the new district church of St. John the Evangelist. St. Mary's rector, George D'Oyly, apparently used the collected monies to maintain both churches as well as he could, compensating for his lack of funds by declining to preach in St. Mary's on Sunday evenings.

11. *Manchester Guardian*, 2 June 1832; Ward, *Religion and Society*, pp. 178, 179.

individuals to pay following the bishops' vote on the reform bill. In addition, churchwardens had long exempted Quakers and cottages of the poor from church rate obligations. Such discreet enforcement of the law had long made the church rate levy a tolerable and humane tax. Now, however, as the battle lines between Church and Dissent hardened, militant Dissenters often challenged the validity of the rate on the grounds that it had been inconsistently enforced. In forcing churchwardens to be less discriminating in their collection of church rates, Dissenters succeeded in raising social tensions within parishes and in enlarging the number of those having an interest in abolishing the rate.[12]

At the conclusion of the vestry meeting a half-penny rate was granted as an amendment to the motion for a one-penny rate asked by the churchwardens.[13] It was a tenuous compromise. In one year's time the Manchester vestry had moved well beyond objections to new church rates. In 1832, although not yet refusing to recognize church rates altogether, it had so narrowly defined their legitimacy as to make them a questionable asset for the Manchester churches.

The evolution in England and Wales toward a forthright rejection of the church rate principle was given a boost by the example of Ireland. In April 1832 the *Spectator* observed that the revolt against tithes now occurring in Ireland could not fail to extend to England. But the commutation of tithes would not suffice; it was but a change in the form of payment. The writer predicted, with reference to church rates, that "the next question to be agitated will be, the propriety of payment in any shape."[14] The Irish church cess, the equivalent of the church rate, was as vexatious as the tithe. On 12 July 1832 Edward Stanley, the future fourteenth earl of Derby and chief secretary for Ireland, promised in a speech on the Irish tithe that he would soon relieve Irish Catholics from church cess. The *Patriot* called on Stanley to extend his promise to cover English church rates. Furthermore, the *Patriot* challenged English Dissenters to appropriate Stanley's argument to suit English requirements.[15] Three days after the introduction in the Commons of the Irish Church Temporalities Bill, which included abolition of church cess, E. B. Pusey wrote despondently that "The

12. Ward, *Religion and Society*, pp. 178, 179; Burn, *Justice of the Peace*, I, 678.
13. *Manchester Guardian*, 2 June 1832.
14. *Spectator*, 7 April 1832, p. 325.
15. *Patriot*, 18 July 1832, p. 208; G.I.T. Machin, *Politics and the Churches in Great Britain, 1832–1868* (Oxford, 1977), pp. 31–32.

question of Church Rates I suppose we shall soon have in England, for Ministers will scarcely refuse to the Dissenters, what they grant to the R.C.s."[16]

The pressure on the government to relieve English Dissenters from compulsory church rates developed as suddenly and dramatically in Birmingham as in Manchester. In a vestry meeting held in St. Martin's on 5 April 1831 to elect a parish churchwarden for the seven churches in Birmingham, there were signs of political tension related to the parliamentary reform bill and some dissatisfaction with the previous year's wardens. But there was no indication that church rates were in any jeopardy. The parishioners elected as parish churchwarden W. Weston, a merchant committed to economy in local government. Weston, a Churchman, made it clear that his commitment to economy would not undermine his faithfulness to the Church or cause him to neglect his duty as churchwarden.[17]

A year later on Easter Tuesday the ratepayers met again in St. Martin's to choose new churchwardens. The rector wisely attempted to tap the spirit of economy that last year had motivated Churchmen as well as secular radicals and Dissenters. He nominated Weston as rector's warden for having so efficiently fulfilled his duties in the previous year. Thomas Chilton Salt, a Churchman and one of two nominees belonging to the Birmingham Political Union, was elected as parish warden. Salt endeared himself to the boisterous crowd by making a pledge that went a step beyond the one made by Weston the year before, committing himself to collect as few rates as legally possible and pledging to appeal to the legislature to abolish church rates.[18]

When the vestry met again on 7 August 1832 to levy new states, the mood of the crowd in St. Martin's was more hostile. Weston, who had tried valiantly to balance his pledge to maintain the church with a zeal for economy, was thoroughly grilled about legally unexceptionable expenditures. Salt's request for a four-penny rate was set aside for a month pending a committee's investigation of the estimates. The vestry meeting was ultimately turned into an anti–church rate forum when a Mr. Pare introduced a series of resolutions condemning church rates as unjust. Pare's resolutions, made after the rector angrily vacated the

16. Pusey to Gladstone, 15 Feb. 1833, Pusey Papers, Liddon, vol. I.
17. *Birmingham Journal*, 9 April 1831.
18. Ibid., 28 April 1832.

chair to loud cheers, received the support of all but four or five of those present and were forwarded to Joseph Hume for presentation to the Commons. The *Patriot* congratulated itself that this meeting and several others were a response to its challenge, issued several weeks earlier, to Dissenters to mobilize against church rates.[19]

The adjourned vestry meeting met again on 4 and 18 September 1832. In both meetings Weston and Salt complained that the parishioners had shown a lack of trust in them. Both conscientiously had attempted to reduce church rates while striving to keep their oaths to raise the necessary funds to maintain the churches for which they were liable. But the parishioners were moving rapidly beyond a demand for reduction to the abolition of church rates. The meeting of 18 September, which was frequently in uproar, was again adjourned for a fortnight without refusing a rate altogether out of the widespread (if legally questionable) opinion that the churchwardens could compel the making of a rate by appealing to the archdeacon or the Court of King's Bench.[20]

The Birmingham vestry met again on 2 October after the auditors had succeeded in checking the old accounts. Despite the rector's plea that the meeting "not be disgraced by the noise and tumult which had characterized former meetings," the proceedings were frequently drowned out by groaning, hooting, hissing, and scenes of great confusion. Numerous impassioned speeches and more fervent exclamations from the audience made it clear that the majority of the gathered parishioners opposed making any church rate at all. Joseph Parkes, the leader of Birmingham radicalism, regretting that the popular mood seemed to demand an outright refusal of a church rate, argued that the proper approach was an appeal to the reformed Parliament to abolish church rates as part of a full body of ecclesiastical reform. Despite his arguments the meeting closed with an overwhelming vote for a three-month adjournment — a virtual rejection of the church rate.[21] The *Morning Chronicle* warned that the government must pay immediate attention to the popular opposition to compulsory religion. Several months earlier the *True Sun* had issued a similar warning. Reforms must be made soon because influential places like Birmingham, Wakefield, Huddersfield, Bristol, and Lambeth had begun to resist the Church's

19. Ibid., 11 Aug. 1832; *Patriot*, 15 Aug. 1832, p. 241.
20. *Birmingham Journal*, 8 Sept. 1832; 22 Sept. 1832.
21. Ibid.

claims, "and the spirit which animates them is spreading itself through-out the length and breadth of the land."[22]

In Manchester a more militant faction of Dissenters and radicals readied itself to battle the Church. Led as in 1831 by Archibald Prentice, proprietor of the *Manchester Times*, the militants resumed the church rate contest at the Easter vestry of 1833 called to elect churchwardens and sidesmen. Prentice nominated an alternate slate to the one proposed by the senior churchwarden, and he won the backing of a large majority of those present. Victory was thwarted, however, by a demand for a poll of the parish, to be conducted under the plural voting provisions of Sturges Bourne's vestry acts. After a heated protest against plural voting, Prentice and a substantial number of followers resolved to refrain from voting. The resulting poll was lopsided. The establishment list won by 770 to 26 persons—and by 2,059 to 25 votes.[23]

When the Manchester vestry met again on 20 May 1833 to consider the churchwardens' request for a half-penny church rate, George Hadfield, the fiery Congregationalist solicitor, led the attack by moving an amendment for a six-month adjournment of the meeting that carried overwhelmingly.[24] As noteworthy as this massive support for the effective refusal of the church rate was the amount of support the rate received from non-Anglicans in Manchester. The Wesleyan churchwar-den James Wood enthusiastically defended the church rate principle.

22. *True Sun*, 29 Aug. 1832.

23. *Manchester Guardian*, 13 April 1833; 20 April 1833. The passions evoked by the plural voting provisions of Sturges Bourne's Vestry Acts, in Manchester and other parishes, were accurately predicted by *The Times* on the occasion of the easy passage of the first bill through Parliament. *The Times* warned that if the bill were not altered "it will effect a great deal towards the subversion of the existing order of society in this kingdom." *The Times*, 7 May 1818; see also *Courier*, 21 April 1818.

24. *Manchester Times*, 25 May 1833; *Manchester Guardian*, 25 May 1833; Ward, *Religion and Society*, p. 179. The argument in Manchester on 20 May 1833 against an adjournment illustrated how tenuously church rates were intertwined with the entire system of local rates. The viability of church rates was threatened by alterations to the fragile organism of local rating as surely as by direct attacks against church rates. Following enactment of the Poor Law Amendment Act, the church rate system was more deeply exposed to the assaults of Dissenters, not only because small uneconomic church rates were now lost, but in numerous parishes church rates now were needed for the first time. Prior to 1834 it had been the practice in many parishes to take money for ecclesiastical purposes out of the poor rate; that avenue was legally closed in 1834. Such was the case in Minchinhampton, Lord John Russell's borough, where a church rate was first asked, and refused, on 20 October 1836. *Patriot*, 27 October 1836.

Samuel Fletcher, unlike Wood, did oppose the church rate principle but rejected Hadfield's proposed means of extinguishing it. Fletcher counseled the parishioners to "submit to the rate while it was law, but petition the legislature to alter the law."[25]

Manchester's Dissenting newspapers reflected the same division. Archibald Prentice's *Manchester Times* echoed Hadfield's appeal to reject the rate at all costs and likewise fulminated against the ruling of the vestry's chairman that the amendment should be decided by a poll of the parish, subject to Sturges Bourne's law. Like Fletcher, the *Manchester Guardian*, which objected to the church rate principle, urged Dissenters to levy and pay church rates until the law freed them from that obligation. The *Guardian* cautioned its readers against Hadfield's amendment on religious, social, and political grounds. It feared that the militants were resisting the rate "far more in the spirit of political agitation than of religious Dissent." It warned that the agitation was giving influence to those whose stations and characters did not merit it, while the political ferment endangered the reforms Dissenters could expect from their Whig friends in government.[26] The dispute between Fletcher and Hadfield and between the *Manchester Guardian* and the *Manchester Times* was a microcosm of a divided Dissent combating the claims of the Church.

In the poll of 25 May 1833 the militant Dissenters feverishly drummed up votes for the amendment to adjourn for six months. They won narrowly by a vote of 3,514 to 3,512, although the number of persons for the amendment was a comfortable if irrelevant 2,668 to 1,446. The jubilation of the militants was short-lived, however, as James Wood—that staunch Wesleyan establishment man—demanded a scrutiny of the poll book. It took two months to sort through the unpleasant complexities of Manchester voting. After a great number of votes for the six-month adjournment amendment were disqualified on the grounds that they had been given by voters who had not paid the most recent poor rate, the rate was declared carried by a vote of 3,269 to 3,113.[27]

25. *Manchester Times*, 25 May 1833; Ward, *Religion and Society*, p. 179. Although Ward is correct to say that both James Wood and Samuel Fletcher supported the rate, he does not adequately distinguish their respective positions. Wood supported the establishment doctrine and the principle ascribing legitimacy to church rates. Fletcher denied both but insisted on making and paying particular church rates until the law prescribing them could be changed.

26. *Manchester Guardian*, 25 May 1833; *Manchester Times*, 25 May 1833.

27. *Manchester Times*, 10 Aug. 1833; 1 June 1833; Ward, *Religion and Society*, p. 180.

The churchwardens waited until late August 1834 before asking for another rate, hoping that the church rate legislation introduced by Lord Althorp in April 1834 (to be discussed later) might relieve them of that task. When that proposed legislation was withdrawn, they requested a small rate of a half-penny. But the request met a hostile reception in a meeting of approximately two thousand parishioners on 27 August. The United Dissenters' Committee had effectively appealed to parishioners in Manchester's out-townships to form subcommittees and to pay their poor rates to qualify as church rate voters. In a clamorous meeting in which he spoke violently against the Church, Hadfield introduced an amendment to adjourn for six months. When the vote was called, "an immense forest of hands were held up" favoring the amendment, while only "a solitary few at the back part of the wardens' pew" supported the rate. The radical *Manchester Times* claimed that the vestry meeting's rejection of the rate was an event "of *national* importance." It claimed that the example of Manchester had spread such resistance to church rates through the land that the government had been induced to introduce the Althorp Bill.[28]

The six-day poll that ensued immediately upon the vestry's rejection was a tumultuous affair marked by minor violence and voting irregularities. During the first four days the Church Protection Society effectively brought in rate supporters from outlying townships. There were numerous charges that the outlying townships allowed the unqualified to vote and that the "rabble," according to the Tory *Manchester Courier*, had been tempted by drink to join Dissent—many voting twice. These efforts prevailed, and the rate was defeated amid scenes of exuberance by a vote of 7,019 to 5,897.[29]

The *Courier* was confident that the defeat was but a temporary one, since scrutiny would show the majority of legal votes to be for the rate. On the face of it, that prediction was accurate enough. After a recount lasting until late November in which 1,665 votes—almost half from Salford—were stricken from the poll books, the rate was declared to have carried by a majority of 358 votes.[30] It was a shallow victory for the Church. In the following year a church rate was again requested, and again the vestry massively rejected it. But this time the wardens

28. *Manchester Times*, 23 and 30 Aug. 1834.
29. *Manchester Courier*, 6 Sept. 1834; Ward, *Religion and Society*, p. 181.
30. *Manchester Courier*, 6 Sept. 1834; *Manchester Times*, 29 Nov. 1834; Ward, *Religion and Society*, pp. 181, 182.

conceded defeat and did not demand a poll. In following years church rates in Manchester became voluntary, and Dissenters tended to pay their share. But this was a mark of Dissenting strength, not of weakness. In particular it marked the victory in Manchester of the voluntaryist ideal proclaimed by the militant Dissenters. Their voluntary contribution to the church's maintenance underlined their local victory against compulsory ecclesiastical taxes.[31]

The drama of the proceedings in Manchester against the church rate may have been surpassed by the events in Birmingham. In that city's town hall on 5 December 1834 a great crowd of perhaps eight thousand people hooted down a proposed four-penny rate in a meeting designated by the Whig *Morning Chronicle* as "one of the most remarkable meetings ever held in this country on a religious subject."[32] For three years no church rate payment had been enforced in Birmingham, and in recent vestry meetings many Dissenters had voted for a rate believing that the legislature would soon repeal such rates. In Birmingham as in the entire Dissenting world, there was division between moderates, who were committed to constitutionalism and the Whig alliance, and militants, who proclaimed "salvation" by disestablishment and were distrustful of the Whigs. It was widely believed that Birmingham High Churchmen and Tories had attempted to take advantage of Dissenting disunity to reimpose a rate at the instigation of W. Spooner, archdeacon of Coventry, following the king's dismissal of Melbourne's government in November.[33]

If Birmingham Churchmen were motivated by such political considerations, they were disappointed. The high-handed behavior of William IV had the effect of reuniting militant and moderate Dissenters throughout the country. In Birmingham Dissenters "rose as it were *en masse*" to oppose the church rate.[34] According to the *Patriot* the methods of the Church party led many liberal Churchmen and even Quakers, who were traditionally passive, to play a part in opposing the rate.[35]

31. Ward, *Religion and Society*, p. 182. Ward correctly observes that beginning about 1837 some of the steam went out of the church rate conflict. However, he may be mistaken when he interprets the payment of voluntary church rates by Manchester Dissenters as a sign of complacency.

32. *Morning Chronicle*, 8 Dec. 1834; *Birmingham Journal*, 6 Dec. 1834.

33. *Morning Chronicle*, 8 Dec. 1834; *Birmingham Journal*, 6 Dec. 1834; *Patriot*, 10 Dec. 1834, p. 420.

34. *Birmingham Journal*, 6 Dec. 1834; H. R. Martin, "The Politics of the Congregationalists" (unpublished Ph.D. dissertation, Durham University, 1971), p. 125.

35. *Patriot*, 17 Dec. 1834.

Both sides organized, formed committees, and placarded the city in the week before the vestry meeting, giving Birmingham the appearance "of a strongly contested election." The vestry opposition to the rate was headed by the Reverend T. McDonnell, a fiery and witty Irish Catholic priest; G. F. Muntz of the Political Union; Joseph Sturge, who was to lead the Complete Suffrage Union; and Joshua Scholefield, Birmingham's radical M.P. But the greatest impact was made by the Reverend Timothy East, the Congregationalist minister at Steel-house Lane, Birmingham, when he declared, "I have never yet gone for separation of Church and State: —I go for it today." Upon that declaration the meeting erupted in "Thunders of applause," the like of which the *Birmingham Journal* professed never before to have heard in any popular assembly.[36] The editor of the *Birmingham Advertiser* delivered a scathing attack against Dissenters for allying themselves with freethinkers and infidels against the Protestant establishment. He reminded them that Dissenters often spoke of propagating "their common Christianity" on occasions such as meetings of the Bible Society, in which Churchmen and Dissenters worked together. He asked Timothy East to consider whether the course of "genuine religion" would be promoted best by joining with infidels or by aiding the Church to instruct their countrymen. But the political tensions surrounding the 5 December 1834 vestry meeting were sufficiently powerful to keep moderate Dissenters from being swayed by appeals to an ecumenical evangelical conscience. The ranks of moderate and militant Dissenters remained unbroken, and the requested rate was rejected by all but perhaps 150 of 7,000 to 8,000 votes.[37]

In the vituperative poll of the parish that followed, church rate opponents were able to solidify their victory. Despite handbills appealing to Methodists (and to female householders who were assessed the poor rate) to save the Church, the rate was defeated by a vote of 6,699 to 1,723.[38] In Birmingham as in Manchester, many moderate Dissenters had been swayed by the allure of militant voluntaryism. Most of those not yet convinced by its claims could agree to join militants in opposing a rate that both disdained. The defiant refusal to levy church rates by largely Dissenting vestries in Birmingham,

36. *Birmingham Journal*, 6 Dec. 1834; Judith F. Champ, "Priesthood and Politics in the Nineteenth Century: The Turbulent Career of Thomas McDonnell," *Recusant History*, 18 (May 1987), 289–303.

37. *Birmingham Advertiser*, 11 Dec. 1834; *Birmingham Journal*, 6 Dec. 1834.

38. *Birmingham Journal*, 6 Dec. 1834; *Aris's Birmingham Gazette*, 15 Dec. 1834.

Manchester, Rochdale,[39] and at least thirty-four other places in England by August 1833 reflected the new sense of worth and national importance felt by Protestant Dissenters. The Whig *Morning Chronicle* was so impressed with the growth in numbers and power of Dissenters that, following the Birmingham church rate refusal in October 1832, it declared that the "Protestant Dissenters of England and Wales are no longer to be trifled with. . . ."[40]

III

In the early 1830s Dissenters developed rudimentary national institutions to give direction to vigorous local anti–church rate agitation and to address the national government with demands for legislation to grant them full equality with Churchmen. On 19 December 1831, with the prospect of a reformed Parliament that would need to consider extensive ecclesiastical reforms, leading Dissenters met in the Congregational Library and resolved to found a journal that, as the *Patriot* said of itself in its first issue on 22 February 1832, should be "the accredited organ of communication between the Dissenters and the public."[41] The weekly *Patriot* was directed by twelve trustees and edited by the Congregationalist Josiah Conder, who was already promoting the cause of religious equality in the *Eclectic Review.*[42]

By the spring of 1833 a central organization to speak for Dissent

39. For a thorough account of the important church rate questions in Rochdale from 1826 to 1849, see Ward, *Religion and Society*, pp. 183–189; G. M. Trevelyan, *The Life of John Bright* (London, 1913), pp. 35–41; K. Robbins, *John Bright* (London, 1979), pp. 25–27.

40. *The Kent Herald* claimed to have seen a list of thirty-seven places in England where payment of church rates had been refused. Cited in *Birmingham Journal*, 24 Aug. 1833; *Morning Chronicle*, 8 Oct. 1832. For the changing demography of Dissent, see the contemporary discussion in *Congregational Magazine*, "Supplement," 1829, p. 689; ibid., new series, vol. II, 1834, pp. 59, 60; for recent discussion, see R. Currie, A. Gilbert, and L. Horsley, *Churches and Churchgoers: Patterns of Church Growth in the British Isles Since 1700* (Oxford, 1977); Richard Brent, "The Whigs and Protestant Dissent in the Decade of Reform: The Case of Church Rates, 1833–1841," *English Historical Review*, vol. 102, no. 405 (Oct. 1987), 889.

41. *Patriot*, 2 Jan. 1833; 22 Feb. 1833.

42. Raymond G. Cowherd, *The Politics of English Dissent* (New York, 1956), p. 70; Eustace R. Conder, *Josiah Conder: A Memoir* (London, 1857), p. 273; *Patriot*, 1 May 1833, p. 144.

seemed as essential as a national journal. On 5 March 1833 a deputation from the general body of the Dissenting ministers of the three denominations—Presbyterian, Congregationalist, and Baptist—took the initiative to request the Dissenting Deputies to provide centralized leadership to obtain redress from the grievances currently felt by Dissenters.[43] There was considerable agreement concerning the immediate grievances from which Dissenters wished relief: the exclusive validity for all but Quakers of the Anglican marriage ceremony; the liability of Dissenters' chapels to poor rates; the universal obligation to pay church rates and other ecclesiastical dues; the denial to Dissenting ministers of the right to officiate at burial services in parochial churchyards; the lack of an acceptable national registration of births; and the effective exclusion of Dissenters from the universities. As early as November 1832 the *Congregational Magazine* had published a list of grievances that was identical to the deputies' list, with the exception of the reference to the liability of chapels to the poor rate.[44]

The Dissenting Deputies were ready to provide the requested leadership and resolved to form "The United Committee appointed to consider the Grievances under which Dissenters now labour, with a view to their Redress." The United Committee was to consist of the Committee of the Dissenting Deputies, the elected executive of twenty-one members who did most of the work of the deputies; twelve delegates from the Dissenting ministers; and three each from the Scottish secessionist United Associate Presbytery, the Protestant Society for the Protection of Religious Liberty, the Wesleyan Methodist Conference, and the Society of Friends.[45] The Protestant Society, which was formed by John Wilks in 1811 to oppose Lord Sidmouth's aborted attempt to register Dissenting preachers, agreed to send delegates but objected that it merited more than three.[46] The Society of Friends and the Wesleyans both declined to send delegates without

43. Minutes of Dissenting Deputies, 5 March 1833, Guildhall MSS. 3083, VIII, 151–153.

44. Ibid.; *Congregational Magazine*, Nov. 1832, p. 703.

45. Minutes of Dissenting Deputies, 5 March 1833, Guildhall MSS. 3083, VIII, 152, 153; 15 March 1833, fol. 156; Bernard Lord Manning, *The Protestant Dissenting Deputies*, ed. Omerod Greenwood (Cambridge, 1952), pp. 2, 36.

46. Machin, *Politics and the Churches*, p. 16; Minutes of Protestant Society for the Protection of Religious Liberty, 18 March 1833, Dr. Williams's Library, MS. 38.194; Minutes of the United Committee Appointed to Consider the Grievances under which Dissenters now labour with a view to their redress, 19 March 1833, Guildhall MS. 30886.1, fols. 4–6.

stating a cause—although the reluctance of the Quakers to engage in politics as a body was well known, as was the Wesleyan unwillingness to associate with Dissent against the Church.[47]

The United Committee's first action was to appoint a subcommittee of grievances to enumerate and attribute priorities to Dissenting complaints. The subcommittee stated at the outset that it believed its mandate to be restricted to dealing with the "specific and practical grievances" that plagued Dissenters. Showing their moderate colors, the members of the subcommittee refused to comment on whether the very existence of a religious establishment actually constituted the major Dissenting grievance, but they did assert that the national mood was certainly not ready to seek disestablishment.[48]

The subcommittee identified the primary grievances as the compulsory Anglican marriage ceremony and the liability of Dissenters to church rates, Easter offerings, and other ecclesiastical dues. As an indication of the traditionally moderate approach of the deputies, the subcommittee characterized the four remaining wrongs complained of by Dissenters as "inconvenience," not grievances. The subcommittee cautioned the United Committee against confusing genuine religious grievances with mere diminutions of their respectability—a distinction not frequently made by Dissenters in coming decades—because Parliament might refuse to concede its legitimate demands on the basis of allegedly unreasonable expectations.[49]

On 25 April 1833 the United Committee set out to influence the Grey government. The committee's memorial addresses to Earl Grey pressed him to include relief from church rates and the marriage law as part of the ecclesiastical reform promised in the king's speech at the opening of Parliament. The memorial reminded Grey that the United Committee had hitherto refrained from encouraging its constituents to petition the government. The committee did not expect immediate liberation from all their grievances, "nor would they think of prescrib-

47. Minutes of United Committee, 25 April 1833, Guildhall MS. 3086.1, fols. 35, 36; 19 March 1833, fol. 4; For discussion of the general social and political postures of the Wesleyans and Quakers, see respectively David Hempton, *Methodism and Politics in British Society, 1750–1850* (Stanford, 1984); and E. Isichei, *Victorian Quakers* (Oxford, 1970).

48. Ibid., fols. 7–14. The subcommittee of seven consisted of Henry Waymouth, the chairman of the Dissenting Deputies; William Smith, the former chairman; the eminent Congregationalist Joshua Wilson; the Unitarian Reverend Robert Aspland; the Baptist Reverend Dr. Cox; the Reverend Dr. Bennett; and Sheriff Peek.

49. Ibid., fols. 15–28; Manning, *Dissenting Deputies*, pp. 16, 17.

ing either the time or the mode of such Redress." They did, however, importune Grey to grant Dissenters justice concerning their ecclesiastical grievances, on the basis of "the greatly increased and increasing numbers and intelligence, the social responsibility and moral worth, the political influence, in a word the national importance of the Protestant Dissenters of England and Wales."[50]

Not all Dissenters were happy with the conciliatory approach of the United Committee. On November 1833 George Hadfield, the militant Manchester Congregationalist and later M.P. for Sheffield, wrote a blistering letter to the *Leeds Mercury* charging that Dissenters were foolish to trust the government, whose planned measure of church reform would undoubtedly strengthen the establishment rather than favor Dissenters. Hadfield implicitly censured the leadership of the United Committee, asserting that English Dissent had actually "misled the Government itself by asking trifles, when we ought to have been contending for great principles. What signifies a small church-rate, when we should be contending against a corrupt State Church?"[51] The letter was a dramatic one, producing "a great sensation in the north of England" and leading some Churchmen to plead for the formation of church defense associations.[52] Hadfield's letter illustrated the growing friction in the country between moderate Dissenters who sought relief from practical grievances resulting from the privileged position of the established church, and more militant Dissenters eager to launch a frontal attack against the very principle of established religion.

George Hadfield was not alone in criticizing the United Committee for its cautious spirit. On 6 November 1833 a deputation of three ministers representing the Congregational Union informed the members of the United Committee that Dissenters in the country were urging the union to take "decisive measures." The deputation urged the United Committee to adopt a more militant posture. It should issue a statement setting forth the grievances of Dissenters "and putting forward the question of a National Establishment as the main point." The ministers warned that if the United Committee refused to take such a stand, "the Congregational Union must."[53]

50. Minutes of United Committee, 2 May 1833, Guildhall MS. 3086.1, fols. 50–62.

51. *Leeds Mercury*, 16 Nov. 1833, p. 8.

52. *Manchester Times*, 30 Nov. 1833; *Standard*, 4 Dec. 1833; *Manchester Guardian*, 30 Nov. 1833.

53. Minutes of United Committee, 6 Nov. 1833, Guildhall MS. 3086.1, fols. 89–91. The Congregationalist deputation consisted of the Reverend John Blackburn, the Reverend Andrew Reed, and the Reverend John Hunt.

The United Committee accepted the challenge and formed a subcommittee charged with preparing a declaration setting forth the grievances from which it would seek redress in the coming session of Parliament, together with a prominent statement "of the great principle" that the union of church and state in any form was unscriptural.[54] The final version of the "Brief Statement of the Case of Protestant Dissenters" that was adopted by the United Committee on 30 December stated five "practical grievances" from which Dissenters required immediate redress. Preceding that statement was the single declaration that Dissenters asked for the removal of the listed grievances in the belief that any mixture of law with religion corrupted the latter, a principle said to be the "primary ground of Religious Nonconformity." The declaration reassured Churchmen, however, that Dissenters did not intend to begin a disestablishment campaign but would leave that "great question" to the providential "progress of events."[55]

In the conclusion of the "Brief Statement," the committee called on Dissenters throughout the country to form associations and to adopt resolutions and petitions to support their claims. As a reminder of the moderate aims of the committee, the statement ended with this provision: "They also suggest, that while, in their applications to Parliament, they firmly, but temperately, avow their principles, they limit the *prayer* of the Petitions to the Redress of practical grievances."[56] Copies were sent to editors of the leading London journals. The Congregational Union adopted the "Brief Statement,"[57] and Dissenters readied them-

54. Ibid., 26 Nov. 1833, fol. 102. The name of the subcommittee was the "subcommittee appointed to prepare a declaration of Dissenters' Grievances."

55. *Patriot*, 8 Jan. 1834, p. 13. The five practical grievances complained of were: "1. the lack of a legal registration of births, marriages and deaths unencumbered by the need to conform to Anglican rites. 2. compulsory conformity to Anglican rites in the marriage ceremony. 3. the denial to Dissenters of the right of burial in parochial cemeteries by Dissenting ministers using their own forms. 4. the exclusion of Dissenters from the full privileges of Oxford and Cambridge without conforming to the Established Church. 5. the liability of Dissenters to the payment of church rates and other ecclesiastical demands." The minutes of the United Committee do not give the rationale for listing the grievances in this order. The priority given to the first two reflects the fact that Parliament was already dealing with them. The "Brief Statement" was also published in an expanded and widely circulated pamphlet in 1833: *The Case of the Dissenters, in a Letter Addressed to the Lord Chancellor* (5 editions; London, 1833).

56. *Patriot*, 8 Jan. 1834, p. 13.

57. See Minutes of United Committee, 4 and 20 Jan. 1834, Guildhall MS. 3086.1, fols. 123, 138–139.

selves to follow its guidelines for their assault on Parliament in the coming session.

In the half-year following the publication of the United Committee's "Brief Statement," Dissenters throughout the country held meetings and signed petitions, many of which were modeled on its pattern of stating the anti–state church principle and going on to pray for relief from practical grievances. By mid-August 1834 the House of Commons had received 1,134 petitions with 352,910 signatures asking for relief from Dissenting grievances.[58] But it was indicative of the extent to which the United Committee was pushed into action by Dissenters in the country that a significant number of petitions predated the publication of the "Brief Statement."[59]

A deputation from the United Committee met with Earl Grey on 15 January 1834 and with Lord John Russell, the home secretary, on 20 January. Both officials agreed that Dissenters had real grievances. Both also indicated that it might be difficult to satisfy Dissenters on the church rate question. Russell observed "that the abolition of church rates could hardly be advocated without involving the question of the connection between Church and State."[60] Grey gave a forceful warning that it was his strong opinion that an established church was necessary and that if Dissenters should attempt to effect the disunification of church and state they would find it "the surest way . . . to make their Friends their Foes."[61]

Despite such warnings, militant Dissenters did publish petitions and memorials demanding disestablishment of the Church. Scores of

58. Great Britain, House of Lords Record Office, *Reports of the Select Committee of the House of Commons on Public Petitions. Session 1834,* "Forty-seventh Report of the Select Committee on Public Petitions. 11–15 August 1834," p. 609.

59. Great Britain, House of Lords Record Office, *Public Petitions and Appendix. 1833 vol. 2,* "Fortieth Report of the Select Committee on Public Petitions. 16 August 1833," p. 1560.

60. Minutes of United Committee, 22 Jan. 1834, Guildhall MS. 3086.1, fols. 144, 142; Younger Whigs, including Russell, were motivated to grant greater religious freedom, moved in part by an active broad churchmanship and liberal theology. Because they aspired to build a broad inclusive church, however, they were often as averse as older Whigs to demands for disestablishment. See Brent, "The Whigs and Protestant Dissent," *English Historical Review*; *Liberal Anglican Politics*; and Ellens, "Lord John Russell," *Journal of British Studies*.

61. Minutes of United Committee, 22 Jan. 1834, Guildhall MS. 3086.1, fols. 141, 142.

pamphlets were published in 1834 advocating the same.[62] By 15 August 1834 sixty-three petitions with 72,274 signatures urging the separation of church and state had been received by the House of Commons.[63] The *Patriot* and progovernment newspapers warned that if militant Dissenters insisted on fighting a battle on abstract principles, they courted defeat. The *Patriot* counseled that Dissenters should address Parliament for redress from practical grievances; each concession was a gradual abandonment of the state church principle.[64]

For precisely that reason many Tories refused to grant any of the practical demands of Dissenters. The Tory *Standard* called on Churchmen to defend the Church by signing "A Declaration of the Laity of the Church of England." In that declaration Anglican laymen pledged to maintain the church establishment "unimpaired," declaring their conviction (which was the heart of the Tory view of a Christian society) "that the consecration of the State by the public maintenance of the Christian Religion is the just and paramount duty of a Christian people. . . ."[65] Such appeals were successful in eliciting as many as 1,520 petitions with 204,834 signatures in defense of the church establishment during the 1834 parliamentary session.[66]

Moderate Dissenters counseled the pursuit of redress from practical grievances rather than the abstract question of disestablishment not only out of fear of antagonizing Churchmen, but also because of a realistic appreciation of differences among Dissenters. The *Patriot* bluntly acknowledged: "in the former almost all Dissenters agree; in the latter they do not."[67]

The *Congregational Magazine* agreed with this assessment. It believed

---

62. Many pamphlets advocating the separation of church and state, along with (but usually independent of) other pamphlets urging redress from "particular grievances," were published in 1834. A good selection can be consulted in the Congregational Library, London (boxes D.9.e to D.14.c.). The argument "By Mathetes" was typical. The author urged that ecclesiastical reform that did not disestablish the Church would be unsatisfactory in that it would retain the Church's chief defect. "By Mathetes," *Religious Reform Impracticable, Without Separation from the State* (London, 1834).

63. Great Britain, HLRO, *Reports on Public Petitions. Session 1834*, "Forty-Seventh Report of the Select Committee on Public Petitions. 11–15 August 1834," p. 607.

64. *Patriot*, 29 Jan. 1834, pp. 36, 37; *Morning Chronicle*, 13 Jan. 1834; *Globe and Traveller*, 27 Feb. 1834.

65. *Standard*, 13 Jan. 1834.

66. Great Britain, HLRO, *Reports on Public Petitions. Session 1834*, "Forty-Seventh Report of the Select Committee on Public Petitions. 11–15 August 1834," pp. 607–608.

67. *Patriot*, 29 Jan. 1834, p. 37.

that there were four distinct groups of Dissenters in 1834 holding different views about what course to follow on the question of disestablishment and practical grievances: the first group cared only about obtaining redress from practical grievances; the second, believed to be fairly small in number, probably preferred to retain the established church so long as Dissenters were freed from practical annoyances; the third wished to petition immediately for separation of church and state under the mistaken opinion that this view was more prevalent than it was in fact; the fourth, which included the *Congregational Magazine* and which the editor believed to be the largest group, held that church and state ought to be separated but that it was inexpedient to demand that from Parliament now. This group believed that Dissenters should concentrate first on freeing themselves from their most immediate grievances.[68]

The initiative on introducing a motion to abolish compulsory church rates was taken on 18 March in the Commons by Edward Divett, a backbench Liberal member for Exeter. Divett, who had received the support of the United Committee since giving notice of his intention in early February, moved for abolition on the grounds that the bitterness felt by Dissenters toward the Church in most parishes, particularly in large towns, might yet be assuaged.[69] After defending his motion, Divett acceded to a request by Lord Althorp, chancellor of the exchequer, to withdraw it because the government intended to introduce a measure dealing with church rates.[70]

On 21 April Althorp presented the government's plan to abolish church rates and substitute a fixed annual sum of £250,000 from the land tax for the support of parish churches and chapels. Althorp called on the legislature to adopt his measure because church rates were indeed unfair to Dissenters and because they were also unsatisfactory to the Church in light of the refusals to levy them in different parishes. His plan would "place the maintenance of parochial churches and chapels on a better footing" and affirm the establishment principle that the legislature was obliged to maintain the nation's church.[71]

68. *Congregational Magazine*, new series, vol. II, Jan. 1834, pp. 62, 63.
69. Great Britain, *Hansard's Parliamentary Debates*, XXII (18 March 1834), 385, 386; Minutes of United Committee, 7 Feb. 1834, Guildhall MS. 3086.1, fol. 163.
70. *Hansard*, XXII (18 March 1834), 389.
71. Ibid. (21 March 1834), 1013, 1012–1063; Althorp was one of the new morally earnest Whigs devoted to enlarging religious freedom within a revitalized and inclusive national church; Ellis Archer Wasson, *Whig Renaissance: Lord Althorp and the Whig Party, 1782–1845* (New York, 1987).

Dissenters and radicals in the House denounced Althorp's plan. Outside Parliament, Dissenting organizations encouraged the sending of petitions and the holding of meetings with members of Parliament to thwart the plan. The United Committee, the Protestant Society, and a special meeting of the deputies essentially agreed that the plan was particularly objectionable because it deprived vestries of the power they now had to refuse rates altogether. The plan imposed new burdens on Scotland and Ireland and actually strengthened the alliance of church and state,[72] which of course was what Grey and Althorp intended.

Tories were ambivalent about the plan. The evangelical *Record* believed that it was a wise measure, and the ultra-Tory Sir Robert Inglis, who represented Oxford, said he could not oppose the measure vigorously since it did recognize the duty of government to make public provision for Christian worship. But he castigated the Dissenters, moderates as well as militants, for seeking the demise of the establishment.[73]

Faced with the displeasure of the Dissenters, the government quietly dropped Althorp's proposal.[74] After the earlier introduction of what they considered to be an unsatisfactory marriage bill and Althorp's failed church rate plan, Dissenters became disillusioned with the Whigs. The Manchester committee of the "United Dissenters" characteristically called on Dissenting electors to adopt an independent political course on the voluntary principle, and to support only candidates willing to seek a speedy separation of church and state. But even the Whiggish *Patriot* adopted a less conciliatory tone. On 7 May Josiah Conder's leader still advised a "purely disinterested" support for the Whigs to prevent the Tories from coming to power, but it reluctantly agreed to join the militants in making the voluntary principle the rallying point for all Dissenters.[75]

72. Cowherd, *English Dissent*, p. 89; Minutes of Protestant Society, 28 April 1834, Dr. Williams's Library, MS. 38.194; Minutes of United Committee, 25 April 1834, Guildhall MS. 3086.1, fols. 202, 203; Minutes of Dissenting Deputies, 29 April 1834, Guildhall MS. 3083, VIII, 213–218.

73. *Record*, 24 April 1834; *Hansard*, XXII (21 April 1834), 1024–1029; *Standard*, 22 April 1834.

74. The government felt it to be inexpedient to push a church rate bill through the Commons although a majority of 256 to 140 divided in favor of Althorp's motion. *Hansard*, XXII (21 April 1834), 1059.

75. *Patriot*, 7 May 1834, pp. 149–152; Machin, *Politics and the Churches*, p. 45.

IV

The voluntaryist principle had by 1834 become the dogma in whose name Dissenters demanded the abolition of church rates. But although that principle was invaluable in giving a philosophic basis to a burgeoning political movement, it also divided Dissenters. Probably a minority of Congregationalists and Baptists continued to accept the validity of an established church. But they neglected politics, and their public impact was consequently small. The most important conflict with Dissent was therefore between moderate and militant voluntaryists. The voluntaryism of the former was mainly latent; the moderates concentrated on seeking redress from practical grievances. But the voluntaryism of the militants was active and aggressive. They were eager to make separation of church and state a concrete political demand.

The London Dissenting leadership avoided giving public exposure to the militants' views for fear of alienating the Whigs, and also out of concern that the militants might usurp their leading role in Dissent. Therefore the United Committee shied away from calling large public gatherings that might give militants a respectable forum. But on 28 April 1834, in light of popular dissatisfaction with Earl Grey's attempt to redress Dissenting grievances and particularly because of anger about Althorp's church rate scheme, the United Committee concluded that an emergency had arrived that necessitated inviting Dissenting delegates from throughout England and Wales to a meeting about the civil and religious rights of Dissenters.

In an attempt to ensure a moderate meeting, the United Committee restricted participants to those invited by Robert Winter, the committee's secretary. In addition, a subcommittee was delegated to formulate resolutions to be endorsed by the proposed meeting.[76] Nevertheless, the United Committee found that it could not easily compel Dissenters of Nottingham and Manchester, where the claims of voluntaryism had taken deepest root, to accept its narrow terms of reference.

Militant Dissenters in Manchester were already incensed with the United Committee for having turned down a request on 22 April to call a public meeting to petition the legislature "for the dissolution of the alliance of church and state and leaving religion entirely to volun-

76. Minutes of United Committee, 28 April and 5 May 1834, Guildhall MS. 3086.1, fols. 206–209.

tary support."[77] A meeting of the Manchester "Committee of United Dissenters" on 5 May resolved not to send delegates for the purpose given in the invitation, as it disapproved of the United Committee's course of allegedly concealing from Parliament and the government that nothing short of the complete separation of church and state would satisfy Dissenters. Because of the current crisis, the "United Dissenters" did agree to send six delegates, including Thomas Harbottle and George Hadfield. The delegates were pledged to seek a public declaration demanding disestablishment, and any petition or memorial regarding "practical grievances" they signed had to indicate clearly that redress was looked for merely as a means to the end of "an entire separation for Church and State."[78]

The well-attended London meeting was held on 8 May 1834 and chaired by the moderate and respected Congregationalist Edward Baines. Robert Winter had asked John Angell James, the Evangelical Congregationalist pastor of the Carr's Lane Chapel in Birmingham, to move the official declarations on practical grievances, as the United Committee wanted a moderate man from outside London for that task. Angell James represented his own congregation since the Birmingham delegation considered him too moderate. The meeting passed the United Committee's resolutions, foremost of which was the declaration that Dissenters ought to be freed from church rates on the same principles that led to repeal of church cess in Ireland.[79]

But the meeting was marred by clashes between militant and moderate voluntaryists. The spirit of agreement was broken as soon as Angell James moved the first United Committee resolution. Thomas Harbottle moved an amendment that called on the meeting to recognize "the great principle of separation between Church and State." He stated also that he was bound by an agreement with Manchester Dissenters not to participate in the meeting if this point were rejected. The Reverend J. Gilbert of Nottingham, who seconded his amendment, said he was similarly bound.[80]

---

77. *Manchester Times*, 3 May 1834; Minutes of United Committee, 22 April 1834, Guildhall MS. 3086.1, fols. 195–200; Minutes of Dissenting Deputies, 16 April 1834, Guildhall MS. 3083, VIII, 208–212; Minutes of Protestant Society, 14 April 1834, Dr. Williams's Library, MS. 38.194.

78. *Patriot*, 7 May 1834, p. 156.

79. Martin, "Politics of the Congregationalists," p. 118; Minutes of United Committee, 8 May 1834, Guildhall MS. 3086.1, fols. 232–235.

80. *Patriot*, 10 May 1834, p. 163.

The amendment brought to the fore the differences that had been simmering for months between the moderate voluntaryist Dissenting leadership centered in London and the more militant voluntaryist Dissenters with strength in Manchester and Nottingham. In the three-hour discussion that followed, the moderate leaders all asserted that none of them disagreed with the principle formulated by Harbottle. The only question, said Edward Baines, was "whether under present circumstances it was desirable it should be placed in the foreground."[81] It was precisely the affirmative answer to that question that distinguished militant voluntaryists from the moderates. But finally a compromise was reached, and all but three votes were given to a new first resolution, introduced by Angell James and supported by Harbottle and Gilbert, that recognized "the great and leading principle of full and complete separation of Church and State, as the true basis on which equal rights and justice can be secured to all classes of his Majesty's subjects."[82]

Although the militant voluntaryists had failed to win the support of the meeting for a policy of making the separation of church and state the first goal of Dissent, they had gained support for the assertion that the voluntaryist principle was the true basis for achieving a just settlement of all the practical grievances besetting Dissenters. That was saying more than moderate Dissenters wished to say and was more radical than the "Brief Statement" of December 1833. What was more, this argument had taken place in public, and Churchmen—Whigs as well as Tories—were alarmed.[83]

The spirit of voluntaryism, which was committed equally to voluntarily maintained religion and the separation of church and state, was gaining visibility in 1834, as it was being transformed from an ecclesiastical tenet to a political principle.[84] It was this introduction of the voluntary principle into political debate through petitions and public

81. Ibid., 14 May 1834, p. 167; Brent mistakenly portrays Angell James as one of the militant provincial delegates who "won control" to pass "a violent pro-disestablishment motion" rather than, more accurately, as the moderate chairman who acquiesced to the will of the militants only reluctantly. Brent, "The Whigs and Protestant Dissent," p. 891.

82. *Patriot*, 10 May 1834, p. 157; *Leeds Mercury*, 17 May 1834.

83. *Morning Chronicle*, 9 May 1834; *Standard*, 9 May 1834.

84. Machin, *Politics and the Churches*, p. 46. The ecclesiastical position had been clearly formulated in Article 1 of the Congregational Union of England and Wales, which was adopted in 1833 at its third general meeting: "the power of a Christian Church should in no way be corrupted by union with temporal or civil power. . . ."

meetings that disturbed moderate Dissenters. The formation of the British Voluntary Church Society, in response to a resolution passed at the Dissenting conference in London of 8 May 1834, also served to popularize the idea of "voluntary" religion. The society was aligned with the Voluntary Church Association of Scotland. But it did not frighten moderate Dissenters because it explicitly rejected antagonizing Churchmen or using a political tone, and it restricted its membership to evangelical Dissenters.[85] Partly for those reasons it was soon scorned by militant Dissenters eager to make voluntaryism a political question.

The tactics and agenda of the militant voluntaryists sufficiently alienated Robert Winter that he resigned on 24 December 1834 as secretary of the United Committee. He alleged that the "impudence of some Dissenters" had greatly delayed the cause of Dissent and injured the Whig government. He charged that the United Committee had been unwilling to check a course that would "bring down Protestant Dissenters from the high ground of Christian Independence . . . to the much lower grade of a mere political party."[86]

It might have been more accurate to say that the United Committee was unable to stem a tide. In April 1834 the *Eclectic Review* detected a revolutionary movement, of very recent origin, toward voluntaryism.[87] That change from the traditional Dissenting acceptance of religious establishments represented the beginning of a fundamental transformation in the ethos of Dissent. In the early eighteenth century Dissenters hardly questioned the union of church and state. In 1832 the *Eclectic Review* said that most Dissenters probably did not oppose the existence of an established church. Leading London and provincial Evangelical Congregationalists cautioned against a hasty opposition to the established church, since the public identified religion with the establishment.[88]

The militant voluntaryist Dissenters who provoked Robert Winter were quite unlike the cautious and respectable leaders whose dominance was unquestioned until 1832. Eminent ministers like Robert

85. *Patriot*, 10 May 1834, pp. 156, 157; 4 June 1834, pp. 201–206.

86. Minutes of Dissenting Deputies, 31 Dec. 1834, Guildhall MS. 3083, VIII, 251, 252.

87. *Eclectic Review*, 3d series, XI (April 1834), 320; Machin, *Politics and the Churches*, p. 46.

88. R. K. Webb, *Modern England: From the Eighteenth Century to the Present* (New York, 1970), p. 39; Norman Gash, *Reaction and Reconstruction in English Politics* (Oxford, 1965), p. 64; Martin, "Politics of the Congregationalists," p. 62.

Hall, Rowland Hill, and John Clayton eschewed politics after sympathy shown by Dissenters to the American and French revolutions
engendered political tensions. Even deeper than the social and political
motives that were grounds for political restraint was the power of the
Evangelical Revival that had shaped the Dissenting leadership as
deeply as the evangelical party in the established church, making
cooperation natural. What was to become the mainly Congregationalist
London Missionary Society was organized in 1795 as an ecumenical
venture intended to contain all Evangelicals—Churchmen no less than
Wesleyans, Congregationalists, and Baptists. According to Herbert
Skeats, nearly all the most eminent Congregationalist ministers early
in the century had close personal associations with the evangelical
party, and there was a "tacit compact that the Church should not
be attacked."[89]

The pre-1830 evangelical Dissenting leaders had no desire to attack
a church with many of whose clergy they shared an evangelical
commitment to oppose the forces of irreligion. If an ecclesiastical
establishment could help stop the spread of atheism they would not
weaken it. They could be content if the Dissenting interest were given
a respected place in the old order.

The exponents of militant voluntaryism who began demanding a
hearing in the 1830s were brash, middle-class representatives of the
new industrial towns. Unlike the older evangelical Dissenting worthies,
they were not content to defend the prerogatives of the Dissenting
interest. The militant voluntaryists were the nineteenth-century shock
troops of liberation. They were guided in part by a developing "politi-
cized"[90] theology that freely synthesized the liberal creed with the
Protestant Christian one. For those motivated by the logic of militant

89. Skeats and Miall, *The Free Churches*, pp. 443, 444; Roger H. Martin, "The Place
of the London Missionary Society in the Ecumenical Movement," *Journal of Ecclesiastical History*, XXXI, no. 3 (July 1980), 283–300.

90. E. R. Norman popularized the term "politicization of religion" in his 1978
Reith Lectures. His discussion of the twentieth-century transformation of Christianity
through the adoption of the political values and language of advanced liberalism and
Marxism is suggestive for considering analogous development in the theology of
nineteenth-century Dissent. E. R. Norman, *Christianity and the World Order* (Oxford,
1979). For a detailed academic discussion of the social and political ideas of Churchmen
seen as reflections of the secular ideas, both radical and conservative, current in each
generation, see E. R. Norman, *Church and Society in England 1770–1970* (Oxford, 1976);
Brian Stanley, "Nineteenth-Century Liberation Theology: Nonconformist Missionaries
and Imperialism," *Baptist Quarterly*, vol. XXXII (Jan. 1987), pp. 5–18.

voluntaryism, seeking disestablishment of the Church of England became the first priority; and pursuing relief from "practical grievances," unless expressly done as a means of achieving the separation of church and state, was to deal with trifles. Cooperation with secular radicals was quite in order if that would hasten the birth of a voluntary society; cooperation with Anglican Evangelicals was precluded by higher political goals. Churchmen, and those Dissenters who feared desacralization, therefore accused voluntaryist Dissenters of hating the Church more than they hated infidelity.

The militant Dissenters who were becoming spellbound by the message of voluntaryism gradually replaced the passionate commitment to the transforming power of the Gospel that had earlier drawn them together with Evangelical Anglicans with an equally passionate devotion to the idea of liberty and the commitment to separate church and state. Although their concern for a purified church was genuine enough, there are indications that their deepest concerns were shifting from the evangelical faith of their forebears to the postulates of ecclesiastical and political liberty. Along that route lay one of the paths that led to the desacralization of modern society.

Within the Dissenting world, voices ranging from those of moderate voluntaryists to conservative pro-establishment Dissenters attempted to temper the demands of the militant voluntaryists. Some moderates like Edward Baines feared that imprudent demands might alienate the Whigs. Others were apprehensive that Dissenters might lose their spiritual integrity through political organization. Discounting the Wesleyans, all moderate Dissenters after 1832 agreed (although conservative Dissenters did not) that the separation of church and state was a goal to be desired. It was the mark of moderates that they believed it either expedient or wrong to force the issue of disestablishment through direct political pressure.

One prominent moderate Dissenter, John Angell James, disapproved of the course taken by the militant voluntaryists. In a letter to the *Patriot* in January 1835 he formally dissociated his views and those of his congregation from recent militant resolutions approved by the Birmingham Dissenting Deputies.[91] Earlier, in a Christmas address to his congregation, he had outlined the principles and duties of Dissent-

---

91. *Patriot*, 21 Jan. 1835, p. 20; For divisions among Dissenters, centered on the issue of voluntaryism, see J. P. Ellens, "Protestant Dissent in Mid-Nineteenth Century England: A House Divided," *Fides et Historia*, vol. XVIII, no. 1 (Jan. 1986), 15–24.

ers. Angell James affirmed at the outset the Congregationalist view
that "a church of Christ is a spiritual, voluntary, and independent
community. . . ." He further outlined reasons to oppose an established
religion, but he rejected making the dissolution of the union of church
and state the main subject of appeals to the government. He agreed
with the Dissenting committees and journals that believed such an
attack to be inopportune since it would delay the granting of redress
from practical evils and since it would hurt the Whigs and help the
Tories. Angell James further distanced himself from the militant
voluntaryists by arguing that disestablishment should be sought not by
political agitation but only by diffusing "sound scriptural sentiments."
He insisted that Dissenters act as ecclesiastical bodies, and not "in
league with infidels and Radicals."[92]

Numerous moderate Dissenters had views on the establishment that
were in practice not dissimilar from the position of conservative
Dissenters. The eminent moderate Congregationalist theologian, the
Reverend Dr. J. Pye Smith, reassured Lord Holland on 6 March
1834: "The theory of a separation of the State & the Church need
alarm no one. . . . Wild unreflecting & comparatively few (I trust) are
the men of any intelligence who wish Government to effect such a
result. Some time probably it will take place in a spontaneous way,
easily and happily, the issue of a long course of cautious meliora-
tions. . . ."[93]

Unlike the moderates, conservative Dissenters defended the existence of an established church on principle. "A Nonconformist of the
Old School" challenged Dissenters who declared ecclesiastical taxes
illegitimate to read the words of the two hundred ejected ministers, the
original Nonconformists—to be reminded that they thought otherwise.
He quoted from Dr. John Owen, Dr. Philip Doddridge, Dr. Isaac
Watts, and Matthew Henry, all of whom supported compulsory payments to the national church. The author implored Dissenters not to
join infidels in their attacks on the Church.[94] Conservative Dissenters
favored spiritual over temporal activity, and thus they did not seriously

92. The address was given on 25 December 1833 and printed as a tract in the year
following: John Angell James, *A Pastor's Address to His People: On the Principles of
Dissent, and the Duties of Dissenters* (London, 1834), pp. 9, 10–15, 55–57.

93. Pye Smith to Holland, 6 March 1834, Holland House Papers, Add. MS. 51838,
fol. 237.

94. A Nonconformist of the Old School, *Primitive Nonconformity Opposed to Modern
Dissent* (London, 1837), pp. 3–12.

add their weight to that of moderate voluntaryists in attempting to tame the demands that militant voluntaryists began to make in the 1830s.

V

Between 1834 and 1836 Lord Melbourne's government worked to pass legislation that might satisfy a turbulent Dissenting world. The sticking point was to find a church rate solution that would placate Dissenters while also satisfying the establishment principle. Hints from the Whigs in 1836 to the effect that Dissenters should not expect total church rate abolition temporarily drew militant and moderate Dissenters together. The moderates began to rely on "pressure from without," and not for the last time militants demoted their radical demands for disestablishment of the Church to a secondary place in the hope that exerting unified pressure on the government might yield a church rate victory.

The Whigs were eager for political reasons to keep the militant voluntaryists at bay. To that end, Lord Melbourne, who replaced Grey as prime minister in July 1834, authorized Lord John Russell to cooperate with Lord Holland and Henry Waymouth, chairman of the Dissenting Deputies, to prepare reforms for the coming parliamentary session in 1835 that might "conciliate the Dissenters" while "strenuously" resisting the "separation of Church and State."[95] Although he expressed hope that satisfactory bills might be introduced to satisfy most of the Dissenters' grievances, Russell was pessimistic about setting the church rate question to rest. He noted that William Howley, the archbishop of Canterbury, was "very anxious" that the question should be settled. Russell added, "So am I, if it can be—but I know of no other plan than our scheme of last year." Russell suggested that they faced a dilemma, as the state had to ensure that provision was made for repair of the national churches but the Commons was not prepared to fix a charge of £250,000 per year on the consolidated fund without strong proof that church revenues could not defray the expense. The best course Russell could suggest, and he realized it was

95. Russell to Holland, 17, 24 Aug. 1834, Holland House Papers, Add. MS. 51677, fols. 150, 154; Machin, *Politics and the Churches*, p. 47; Brent, "The Whigs and Protestant Dissent," 899–901.

not a happy one, was to retain church rates for some years until reform of the Church's finances might disclose a surplus that could replace the rate. Only at that point could they be abolished.[96]

In October the deputies sent Russell thanks for the government's intentions, particularly concerning their marriage bill. Russell wryly wrote to Holland that he might deserve thanks, "but that we shall obtain them, with that ugly Church-rate question hanging over our heads, I very much doubt." Although Dissenters were disappointed with the Whigs' slowness to act on their grievances they rallied behind them in force after Melbourne's dismissal from office. On 25 November 1834 Dissenters formed a central committee to organize opposition to Peel and give selective support to Whigs who had aided Dissenters.[97]

Sir Robert Peel, who formed a government in December, was entirely preoccupied during his brief administration in 1835 with urging church reform and the redress of Dissenters' grievances, both of which were aimed at purifying and safeguarding the Church. Peel told the bishop of Exeter that if Dissenters were to be placated, the marriage ceremony and church rates required immediate attention. Peel said he assumed that the Church could not object if the government were to replace church rates with funds from another source, so long as the state maintained the principle of public recognition of the establishment. But Peel also hinted that conservative church rate legislation would likely provide a substitute of considerably smaller value than that raised by the rate.[98]

Peel was perhaps fortunate in that he was saved from having to disappoint the Church on the question of church rates. That prospect was left to the Whigs, who, in alliance with radicals and Irish repealers, defeated the government's Irish Tithe Bill on an amendment giving the state the right to appropriate surplus funds of the Irish church.[99] Peel left office on 8 April 1835, having succeeded in convincing the hierar-

96. Russell to Holland, 26 Oct. and 24 Aug. 1834, Holland House Papers, Add. MS. 51677, fols. 170 and 156.
97. Ibid., 13 Oct. 1834, fol. 164; Minutes of United Committee, 18 Nov. 1834, Guildhall MS. 3086.1, fols. 285, 286; *Patriot*, 26 Nov. 1834, p. 404; Machin, *Politics and the Churches*, p. 49.
98. Peel to Bishop of Exeter, 22 Dec. 1834, "Copy. Most Private," Peel Papers, Add. MS. 40407, fols. 107, 108; G. Kitson Clark, *The Making of Victorian England* (New York, 1969), pp. 156, 157; Machin, *Politics and the Churches*, pp. 48–50; Gash, *Reaction and Reconstruction*, p. 70.
99. Machin, *Politics and the Churches*, pp. 51, 52.

chy to join an ecclesiastical commission to reform the Church. It was then left to the Whigs to deal with Peel's commission.

Soon after resuming office, Melbourne appealed to the archbishop of Canterbury as well as the bishops to continue on as ecclesiastical commissioners. They agreed but, newly emboldened, attached the condition that the government had to accept the recommendations already made by the commissioners and agree to resist any motions made in the Commons hostile to the Church. After protracted negotiations, Melbourne was able to give the required assurances, subject to the provision that the pledge to resist hostile ecclesiastical motions should be understood to apply neither to the resolutions already made on the Irish Tithe Bill "nor relating to Church Rates."[100] The archbishop replied that they could probably be satisfied with the provision concerning church rates if some qualification were added, such as "that no part of the Church Property is to be applied to make good any deficiency, which may be occasioned by the abolition of these rates."[101] Melbourne replied after a delay of several days and explained that he had isolated the question of church rates because he believed it possible that the issue might be pressed so strongly in the Commons "as to render the introduction of some measure impossible to be avoided. . . ."[102] He then promised: "it is not our intention to depart from the principle of Lord Althorp's measure of last year, which we understand to be that it is the duty of the State to provide that the Churches of the Establishment are to be kept in decent and sufficient repair."[103] This reassurance sufficed to win the commitment of Howley and the other bishops to stay on as commissioners. Melbourne had used the words suggested by Russell, but he had omitted Russell's telling aside, "how this is to be done is another matter."[104] In two years' time the bishops were to charge that the government's church rate plan of 1837 was a betrayal of Melbourne's pledge.

The Whigs needed to appease Dissenters as well as Churchmen. After Russell had announced to the Commons on 20 May 1835 that

100. Melbourne to Howley, 25 April and 18 May 1835, "Copy," Russell Papers, PRO 30/22 1 E, fols. 59, 60, 115; correspondence between Melbourne and Howley, 5–18 May, "Copies," ibid., fols. 76, 95, 97–100, 102, 114, 115.
101. Howley to Melbourne, 19 May 1835, "Copy. Confidential," ibid., fol. 143.
102. Melbourne to Howley, 23 May 1835, "Copy. Confidential," ibid., fol. 147.
103. Ibid., fols. 147, 148.
104. Howley to Melbourne, 30 May 1835, "Copy," ibid., fol. 154; Lord John Russell, Memorandum, 1835, "Copy," ibid.

the government would deal only with English municipal and Irish church reform that session, the United Committee issued a veiled threat of harm to the government in case of a general election unless the government promised now to introduce further reforms concerning Dissenters early in the next session. The government agreed, telling a United Committee deputation that it would announce to Parliament its intention of introducing early in the next session a bill for the registration of births, marriages, and deaths, a marriage bill, and a measure to discontinue the present mode of payment of church rates if the United Committee would publish a resolution supporting the government's position. This was agreed to. Dissenters were benefiting from the Whig's weak position in the Commons as well as the sympathy of liberal Anglicans such as Russell in the cabinet, and the official leadership of Dissent at least was prepared to be patient with the government.[105]

But this conciliatory spirit had already been jeopardized by the actions of John Childs of Bungay, Suffolk. On 12 May 1835 this prosperous Congregationalist printer was interned in Ipswich county gaol for having refused to acknowledge the authority of the consistorial court at Norwich, which prosecuted him for declining to pay his 1834 church rate of seventeen shillings six pence.

The Bungay churchwardens had chosen to enforce Childs's church rate through the ecclesiastical court rather than the magistrates, using the statute 53 Geo. III, c. 127 in hope of preventing a recurrence of the unrest of the previous year. In that year the goods of one of the two defaulters of Bungay's 1833 church rate—a rate which had until then always been paid quietly—were distrained for sale, obtained by townspeople, and returned to the original owners after having been paraded through the town in a boisterous demonstration against the churchwardens.[106]

Lord John Russell agreed with Joseph Hume that it was regrettable that the churchwardens had gone to the ecclesiastical court instead of relying on the magistrates to distrain Childs's goods for the recovery of the church rate, as was routinely done to Quakers who refused to pay their church rates. Russell was embarrassed to be so painfully reminded

105. Machin, *Politics and the Churches*, p. 53; Minutes of United Committee, 28 May 1835, Guildhall MS. 3086.1, fols. 321, 322; Minutes of United Committee, 6 July 1835, Guildhall MS. 3086.1, fols. 325, 327; Brent, "The Whigs and Protestant Dissent," p. 900.

106. *Ipswich Journal*, 16, 23 May 1835; *Hansard*, XXVIII (25 May 1835), 56-60.

that the church rate question demanded a resolution. He stated that the government wished to abolish church rates but intimated that the question was stalled because Dissenters disagreed with the government's principle, outlined by Althorp (now Earl Spencer), that any abolition scheme must recognize Parliament's obligation to maintain the nation's churches.[107]

Outside Parliament, Childs was beatified as a prisoner of conscience. His plight was the main theme at the twenty-fourth anniversary meeting of the Protestant Society. The Dissenting Deputies did no more than petition both houses of Parliament; they took no step to rouse Dissenters in the country. On 23 September 1835 Childs's imprisonment ended after some Ipswich Dissenters to whom Childs had committed his affairs paid his rate with costs, on the grounds that the principle of resistance had been maintained. Childs was escorted into Bungay "by some thousands of persons, with flags, banners, and music, and the liveliest expression of triumph. . . ."[108] The demonstration favoring Childs had been localized, as can be seen in the scarcity of petitions sent to Parliament, but the gentlemen directing Dissenters' affairs in London had been given notice that there were Dissenters in the country ready to take steps considerably beyond those advocated by London. In 1836 in Bungay itself the number of defaulters on a legally enacted rate rose to forty-one, and Churchmen voluntarily paid their arrears for the sake of peace.[109]

At the beginning of 1836 the moderate London leaders of Dissent brimmed with confidence that their faith in the Whigs was about to be rewarded. The United Committee was informed by a government spokesman on 18 January that the government was preparing a bill for the registration of births, deaths, and marriages as well as an amended marriage bill, and the committee was invited to appoint a "professional individual" to work with the government's draftsman.[110] Josiah Conder, the editor of the *Patriot*, proclaimed euphorically that

107. *Hansard*, XXVIII (25 May 1835), 53, 54, 61, 62.

108. *Patriot*, 13 May 1835, p. 156; 20 May 1835, p. 173; 27 May 1835; *Standard*, 26 May 1835; Minutes of Dissenting Deputies, 22 May 1835, Guildhall MS. 3083, VII, 265–269; *Bury and Norwich Post*, 27 March 1835; *Ipswich Journal*, 30 May 1835.

109. There were twenty-one petitions with 5,504 signatures complaining about John Child's imprisonment sent to Parliament by 12 Aug. 1835. Great Britain, HLRO, *Reports on Public Petitions*. Session 1835, "Thirty-seventh Report . . . 10–12 Aug. 1835," p. 275; *Sun*, 11 April 1836.

110. Minutes of United Committee, 18 Jan. 1836, Guildhall MS. 3086.2, fols. 3; Minutes of Dissenting Deputies, 23 Dec. 1835, Guildhall MS. 3083, VIII, 287.

"universal religious freedom so long claimed by the suffering Dissenters of this country . . . is on the eve of being granted by a liberal
Government. . . ."[111]

The cabinet discussions during March, on a church rate position
paper formulated by Russell, might have inclined Conder to greater
restraint had he known of them. Russell had apparently broken the
church rate into two parts. The first, meant for the maintenance
of church services, could be left to the voluntary contributions of
churchgoers. The second, for the upkeep of the church fabric, should
be paid from public revenues in order to retain the establishment
principle.[112] Russell's distinction won general approval. Charles Poulett
Thompson articulated the primary assumption upon which Russell and
most of his colleagues were ready to act. If a Dissenter were relieved,
said Thompson, "from the so-called grievance of conscience which
consists in the direct payment of Church Rates, he has no right, *as a
Dissenter*, to object to the (apportioning) of any part of the Public
Revenues to the support of the Church, unless he is prepared to
contend for the abolition of Establishment and the substitution of the
voluntary principle. . . ." He believed that only a few "violent Dissenters" took that view.[113] Only Sir John Cam Hobhouse, who had
frequent contacts with Dissenters, objected that from what he knew of
Dissenters "nothing will satisfy them except leaving the Churchmen to
take care of the Church and the chalice too."[114]

Thompson disagreed with Russell about the timing of a church rate
bill. Russell had apparently argued that they had a duty to introduce
one as soon as they had the chance of passing one. All the cabinet
ministers who responded, with the exception of Viscount Howick,
agreed strongly with Thompson that they should refuse to bring in a
bill until Parliament had studied the report of the Ecclesiastical Commission and had passed a bill reforming the Church's finances. Thompson's view was that Parliament would undoubtedly find, as the ecclesiastical report seemed to indicate, that the Church would have no

111. *Patriot*, 29 Feb. 1836, p. 69.
112. Cabinet discussion on Lord John Russell's paper on church rates, March
1836, Russell Papers PRO 30/22 2A, fols. 323–335. Russell's own paper is not included
in this collection, but his views may be surmised from the reactions of his colleagues
and particularly from an extensive summary compiled by Poulett Thompson (fols.
334, 335).
113. Poulett Thompson, ibid., fol. 334.
114. Sir John Cam Hobhouse, ibid., fol. 323.

surplus funds after caring for its parochial clergy. He felt, and the cabinet agreed, that it would then not be difficult to show the need to devote other public revenues to maintain the fabric of the churches.[115] Spring Rice, the chancellor of the exchequer, agreed that a church rate bill should be delayed lest its introduction jeopardize a church reform bill and other bills dealing with Dissenters' grievances. He argued that if those other bills did succeed, "the *momentum* of that success may drive a Church rate bill satisfactorily through."[116]

Dissenters only learned of the government's plan to delay the introduction of a church rate bill from Russell's reply to Lord Stanley's query in the Commons concerning the government's intentions. Russell hinted on 2 May 1836, and confirmed on 20 June, that a church rate bill would not be introduced before Parliament had passed the Dissenters' marriage and registration bills and had dealt with the appropriation of church revenues on the basis of the Ecclesiastical Commissioners' report, which had not yet been presented. Russell stated therefore that he could not bring in a church rate bill that session, although one would be essential before the end of the next. Dissenters' sense of betrayal at this information was deepened by Russell's cold reply in the Commons to Joseph Hume on 20 June that Dissenters had no cause to feel great anxiety concerning the government's intentions, since he had consistently made it clear that any bill that was introduced would follow Althorp's principle: that church rates would not be abolished unless the state provided a substitute. Russell also denied promising that the equivalent was to come from the Church's own revenues. He concluded by saying that in meetings with Dissenters he had made it clear "that he did not mean to bring forward any Bill that would accomplish their wishes."[117]

Dissenters were stung into action. The London leadership's alter-ation in attitude toward the Whigs was remarkable. The *Patriot*, which less than three months before had expected a new era of religious liberty to be ushered in by the Whigs, now declared: "Upon the question of Church-rates they are to be trusted no longer. Relief from this grievous impost, this unjust exaction upon the Dissenters, is not to be expected—even from a Whig administration—unless we take the business into our own hands, and deal with the Whigs as we would

115. Poulett Thompson, ibid., fols. 334, 335.
116. T. Spring Rice, ibid., fol. 324.
117. *Hansard*, XXXIII (2 May 1836), 499–501; (20 June 1836), 611, 612.

have done, long ago, with the Tories. . . ."[118] On 19 May a deputation of the United Committee met with Melbourne and Russell and requested that if they did not plan to abolish the church rate they not attempt to legislate upon the question at all, but allow it to be settled in the vestries. In other ways, too, moderate Dissenters appeared ready to adopt more militant actions than had hitherto been the case as they began to pursue the still controversial politics of electoral pressure. The *Patriot* advocated choosing candidates on the basis of their church rate views, although it admitted that in the past it had insisted that a man's general policy be judged. But a pledge to abolish church rates was now deemed a valid criterion because the question involved "great principles of such fundamental interest. . . ."[119]

Of perhaps even greater import was the *Patriot*'s decision to challenge Dissenters to begin emulating members of the Society of Friends by practicing "passive resistance" to the church rate. That practice entailed refusing to pay a legally levied rate and allowing one's goods to be seized under the statute 53 Geo. III, c. 127. Josiah Conder wrote that Dissenters were beginning to rethink the view that the law ought to be obeyed so long as it remained.[120] The undertaking of passive resistance meant that church rates could be challenged even in parishes where Dissenters were numerically too weak to prevent the legal making of a rate.

By the end of the parliamentary session of 1836 the Whigs had fulfilled their pledge to pass bills giving Dissenters a fairly satisfactory marriage ceremony and civil registration of births, deaths, and marriages. But as Lord Holland ruefully observed, the failure to deal with church rates "somewhat diminished the satisfaction" with which the "suspicious Dissenters" accepted that gift.[121] The Dissenting Deputies did pass a resolution thanking the government. But the emphasis of the meeting was on the grievances that remained.[122] From this point, one grievance stood out above the rest. For the next three decades,

118. *Patriot*, 11 May 1836, p. 165.

119. Minutes of United Committee, 23 May 1836, Guildhall MS. 3086.2, fol. 22; *Patriot*, 18 May 1836, p. 180; D. A. Hamer, *The Politics of Electoral Pressure* (London, 1977), pp. 60–61.

120. *Patriot*, 27 April 1836, p. 143; 25 May 1836, p. 197; 8 June 1836, pp. 214, 215; 20 June 1836, p. 228.

121. Lord Holland's Journal, 1836, Holland House Papers, Add. MS. 51871, pp. 949, 950.

122. Minutes of Dissenting Deputies, 31 Aug. 1836, Guildhall MS. 3083, VIII, fol. 383.

only the church rate question consistently commanded the passions of
Dissent. It drew militants and moderates together in apparent
harmony.

In mid-August 1836, as Parliament was about to be prorogued, the
Patriot made it clear that it no longer relied solely on the good graces
of the Whigs. It called on Dissenters to mobilize and to use the
politics of pressure to ensure that they received satisfaction. The editor
declared emphatically: "The Church-rate question *must be settled out of
Parliament.*" On 6 and 13 September 1836 a group of men, most of
whom were prominent members of the Committee of Dissenting
Deputies, met in the *Patriot* office to discuss forming an association to
secure the complete abolition of church rates.[123] A circular letter
published by the provisional committee of what was to become the
Church Rate Abolition Society reviewed steps taken by Dissenters and
the government to deal with the church rate grievance. It pointed out
that until now Dissenters had depended on Parliament to abolish the
tax. It was clear now that satisfactory relief would be granted only if
Dissenters organized. They were asked therefore to attend a meeting
in London on 19 October to establish a society that would effect
their goal.[124]

At the inaugural meeting of the Church Rate Abolition Society there
were no extreme calls for making disestablishment a central tenet of
the society. The overriding concern was to found an association that
would make it clear to the government that only the entire abolition of
church rates, without any form of commutation, was acceptable.
The tone of the day was firm and moderate. Charles Lushington, a
Churchman and M.P. for Ashburton, presided over the meeting. He
had been chosen to ensure a moderate tone and as a reminder that
numerous Churchmen were embarrassed that Dissenters were obliged
to maintain the Church contrary to their consciences. The new society
was chaired by Richard Peek, soon to become sheriff of London, and
led by a committee of twenty. It was closely linked in outlook to the

123. *Patriot*, 17 Aug. 1836, p. 309; Notes of Minutes of the Church Rate Abolition
Society, 1836 to 1839, 6 and 13 Sept. 1836, GLRO, Ac. 72, 62 (pt.). The Minutes of
the Church Rate Abolition Society are no longer extant. The only MS. records that
remain are brief notes of the original Minutes, made by T. H. Boykett.

124. Circular Letter of the Provisional Committee of the Church Rate Abolition
Society," *Patriot*, 22 Sept. 1836, p. 357.

Dissenting Deputies and to the *Patriot*. Its sense of affinity was facilitated by meeting in 5 Bolt Court, the *Patriot*'s address.[125]

Dissenters and reformers hailed the meeting of 19 October and the formation of the Church Rate Abolition Society. The *Morning Chronicle* believed that the events of the nineteenth had "sealed the doom of Church-rates." The *Patriot* exulted that metropolitan Dissenters could no longer be reproached for apathy; they could now be expected to lead. Even the militant *Leicestershire Mercury* gave its commendation.[126] In a popular address made on 1 November, the Church Rate Abolition Society urged people to form local associations in correspondence with the London society. These local societies should send delegates to a projected meeting in London at the commencement of the next parliamentary session. Parliament should be petitioned and, above all, M.P.s pressured to back abolition.[127]

Dissenters began to follow the example of Quakers, who traditionally allowed their goods to be distrained rather than paying ecclesiastical taxes of any kind. The *True Sun* wrote that a public sale in Aston of goods distrained in lieu of church rates had been canceled because the auctioneer complained of "such a throng of customers, some of them ugly ones, amounting to many thousands." The editor also pointed to a seizure of goods in Dover from eight ratepayers, five of whom were Quakers. He emphasized that for rates amounting to approximately £12, goods valued at nearly £90 had been seized. He believed that Dissenters and liberal Churchmen would not allow such injustices to continue.[128]

125. *Patriot*, 20 Oct. 1836, pp. 417–419, 422–423. Probably the majority of the committee governing the Church Rate Abolition Society (CRAS) were members of the Dissenting Deputies. Included in the committee were such prominent deputies as Richard Peek, Josiah Conder, J. Remington Mills, Thomas Pewtress, Apsley Pellatt, Joshua Wilson, and Thomas Wilson. B. L. Manning wrongly asserts that there was friction between the deputies and CRAS. It is true that the deputies were never willing to give CRAS a monopoly on the church rate question, but that was because the deputies believed they had responsibility for the full range of Dissenters' grievances; Manning, *Dissenting Deputies*, p. 187. Machin follows Manning's incorrect lead in pointing to dissension between CRAS and the deputies, and in seeing CRAS as representing a "new and harder tone in English Dissenting organization"; Machin, *Politics and the Churches*, p. 56.

126. *Morning Chronicle*, 20 Oct. 1836; *Patriot*, 20 Oct. 1836, p. 420; *Leicestershire Mercury*, 17 Dec. 1836.

127. *Patriot*, 3 Nov. 1836, p. 452.

128. *True Sun*, 20 Sept. 1836.

Wider publicity was now given to the annual reports that the Society of Friends had meticulously made since 1681 of the total value of goods distrained from members in place of defaulted ecclesiastical taxes. The "Epistle" from the society's yearly meeting of 1836 indicated that members had suffered the loss of upwards of £11,000 in that year.[129] Until 1852 the Friends did not differentiate sums relating to tithes, church rates, and other ecclesiastical taxes. Although tithes would have accounted for the largest share of the total, church rate abolitionists happily used the entire figure to illustrate the evil of the compulsory principle.

During the closing months of 1836 the Dissenting world seemed to be undergoing a transformation. In anticipation of Parliament's projected opening on 31 January 1837, militant and moderate Dissenters alike demanded that compulsory church rates be entirely abolished. The *Leicestershire Mercury* claimed there was "scarcely a village in the kingdom to which the excitement has not spread." The town of Leicester was, as A. T. Patterson has shown, an example of those urban areas in which the chasm between Church and Dissent became the key to politics in the early and mid-Victorian period, and church rates were the point of conflict. In city after city massive public meetings formed local church rate abolition societies and petitioned both houses of Parliament. Invariably they stated clearly that compulsory support of religion was alien to Christianity and demanded complete abolition of compulsory church rates. From Manchester a petition bearing 36,000 signatures was sent to the Commons. The Leicester town council responded favorably to a request by the Church Rate Abolition Society that civic corporations join the petitioning drive. The Dissenters' new strength in local government, resulting from the municipal reform of 1835, was quickly turned to the advantage of the anti–church rate fight.[130]

Occasionally, however, Dissenters still spoke in favor of the church rate. In one such case, in a vestry meeting in Chelmsford, Essex, which levied a rate of seven pence over the noisy objections of a Dissenting minority, a man named King defended the church rate. He gave a

129. *Epistles from the Yearly Meetings of Friends*, vol. I, 1681–1769 (London, 1858), p. 2; vol. XXV, 1836–1846, "The Epistle from the Yearly Meeting Held in London, 18–28 May 1836."

130. *Leicestershire Mercury*, 17 Dec. 1836; 28 Jan. 1837; *Patriot*, 23 Jan. 1837, p. 47; 2 Jan. 1837, p. 1; A. T. Patterson, *Radical Leicester, 1780–1850* (Leicester, 1954), pp. 247–259; Machin, *Politics and the Churches*, pp. 54, 55.

classic conservative Dissenter's speech, denying that ecclesiastical taxes were unscriptural and arguing that "great good arises in this country from the existence of a Church Establishment. . . ." He saw it as self-evident that a country professing to be Christian should have a Christian government which ensured that religious instruction was provided for the nation.[131] But his was now clearly a minority voice in the Dissenting world, and few of the Dissenters who shared his view spoke up.

Churchmen became alarmed by the growing anti–church rate agitation couched in voluntaryist language. The evangelical *Record* warned that Dissenters "rightly perceive, that it is by the road of *Church-rates* they are most likely to attain the final accomplishment of their entire desires."[132] Archbishop Howley had arrived at a similar position. Howley reminded Peel that he had been willing to sacrifice church rates in 1834 only as an attempt to stop religious animosities. But he charged that the language of Dissenters in the past year showed, "beyond doubt, that they seek the abolition of this charge as the first step in the subversion of the Church as an Establishment; and the introduction of what is called the voluntary system."[133] Because the existence of the establishment was at stake, he believed the time had come for them to defend the church rate.

By the end of 1836 Howley stood in opposition not only to Dissenters but to Russell as well, who had been able to convince Melbourne and the cabinet to adopt a church rate plan that Russell believed would be satisfactory to the Dissenters."[134] Despite Howley's determined opposition to the plan, which had been discussed with him, Russell was determined to persevere with it as their "only escape from the support of Church Rates on the one hand, or the adoption of the voluntary principle."[135]

The Church Rate Abolition Society staged an impressive meeting in London on 1 February 1837 to coincide with the opening of Parliament. There were four hundred delegates, representing church rate abolition societies and Congregationalist and Baptist congregations from England, Wales, and Scotland as well as the Dissenting Deputies and the

131. *Essex Standard*, 20 Jan. 1837.

132. *Record*, 9 Jan. 1837.

133. William Howley to Peel, 30 Jan. 1837, "Private," Peel Papers, Add. MS. 40423, fol. 21.

134. Minutes of United Committee, 27 Jan. 1837, Guildhall MS. 3086.2, fol. 52.

135. Russell to Melbourne, 31 Dec. 1836, Broadlands MS. MEL/RU/24.

Protestant Society, gathered with the single focus of demanding the entire abolition of church rates. The delegates, cheered on by the presence of approximately fourteen hundred onlookers, firmly declared their opposition to any form of commutation. Resolutions were passed to petition both houses of Parliament and to arrange meetings with M.P.s—although a resolution to exact pledges from M.P.s was voted down, reflecting the meeting's moderate tone.[136]

Josiah Conder regarded it as "the most effective public meeting he ever attended," and he believed it would give a death blow to church rates. He further exulted that it had been "unalloyed by a single *faux paus*." Unlike the large public meeting of 8 May 1834 following the demise of the Althorp church rate plan, no mention had been made of separation of church and state. But Churchmen charged that the delegates had deliberately concealed their "ulterior objects." The *Patriot* denied this. It acknowledged that Dissenters did ultimately seek civic equality but asserted that they had no designs on church property.[137]

It was clear in early 1837 that Churchmen were deeply divided on whether church rates should be abolished. A considerable number of prominent Churchmen who attended the anti–church rate conference of 1 February had argued that the rate should be repealed as a means of strengthening the Church. Partly because of the backing of Churchmen, the *Morning Chronicle* was hopeful that church rates would soon fall. But support of the repeal movement, which was particularly popular among liberal Broad Churchmen,[138] was vigorously opposed by Evangelicals and High Churchmen. The Reverend E. Tottenham's view was typical of those who believed liberal Churchmen to be shortsighted: "I am really astonished at these assertions, when I know that the general levying of a Church rate is the only existing way whereby at present the government really recognizes its obligation to provide for the religious instruction of the people."[139]

Conservative Churchmen perceived, as Archbishop Howley had,

136. Minutes of Dissenting Deputies, 25 Jan. 1837, Guildhall MS. 3083, VIII, fol. 432; Minutes of Protestant Society, 30 Jan. 1837, Dr. Williams's Library, MS. 38.194; *Morning Chronicle*, 3 Feb. 1837; *Patriot*, 2 Feb. 1837, pp. 73, 77–79.

137. Josiah Conder to "My Dear Friend," 13 Feb. 1837, quoted in E. R. Conder, *Josiah Conder: A Memoir* (London, 1857), p. 280; *Patriot*, 9 March 1837, p. 156.

138. *Morning Chronicle*, 3 Feb. 1837; Brent, "The Whigs and Protestant Dissent," pp. 902–904.

139. E. Tottenham, *A Speech on the Subject of the Established Church and Church Rates* (London, 14 Feb. 1837), p. 2.

that the mere demand for the entire abolition of church rates, as made by even moderate Dissenters, fundamentally challenged the basis of an established church. Instead of simply arguing practically that it was unfair to tax Dissenters for the churches of the establishment, Dissenters were openly stating the presupposition out of which they opposed the compulsory church rate—namely, their belief that religious acts were illegitimate unless freely performed. This was the heart of the voluntaryism that had been adopted by Dissenters in the preceding few years. Conservative Churchmen understood that it threatened the establishment even though most moderate Dissenters were as yet disinclined to seek disestablishment of the Church.

The fear of voluntaryism motivated Churchmen throughout the land to defend church rates and the establishment principle, and they proved that they too could send petitions. Defenders of the Church were particularly heartened by a great public meeting held on 18 February 1837 to counter the antirate meeting of 1 February and to react against the report by the *Morning Chronicle* that the government planned to force the Church on its own resources. The gathering, chaired by the Evangelical Lord Ashley and attended by some two thousand people, pledged support for the church rate as an immemorial property of the Church. The meeting called on the government to acknowledge that the Church's resources were inadequate to meet the needs of a greatly expanding population, and it requested that Parliament grant it additional funds to meet the needs of the country. This strong defense of the church rate was based on the traditional Christian view of the state, to be elaborated by Gladstone in 1838 and offered here as the first resolution: "it is the bounden duty of a nation to establish and preserve the public worship of Almighty God. . . ."[140]

VI

In March 1837, after weeks of intensive lobbying and petitioning by all sides, T. Spring Rice, the liberal Anglican chancellor of the exchequer, placed the government's long-anticipated church rate proposal before the House in committee. The core of the plan, which closely resembled a cabinet proposal of August 1836, was that church rates

140. *Standard*, 2 Feb. 1837; 15 Feb. 1837; *John Bull*, 19 Feb. 1837, p. 92.

would be abolished and churches maintained instead from a fund of at least £250,000, which was to come from the surplus income that the government said could be created by the better management of church lands. To realize that aim, it was suggested that management of ecclesiastical property be transferred from bishops, deans, and chapters and vested in a commission.[141]

Spring Rice explained that his proposal attempted to halt a "progressive evil" that threatened the Church. He compared church rate resistance to a plague spot that could not be localized but would "spread its contagion generally." He argued as a liberal Anglican that his proposal strengthened the Church by appeasing Dissenters' attacks against it. He denied that it was accurate to charge, as defenders of the existing law did, that the government wanted the Church to relinquish a fixed mode of maintaining itself. He argued that practice and law already allowed the majority in any vestry to refuse to repair a church[142]—a "right" that was soon to be tested in the courts in the Braintree case.

The government plan was debated with considerable passion for several days until the House divided 273 to 250 in favor of the resolution on 16 March, allowing a bill to be introduced. The bill had its second reading on 23 May, but with a drastically reduced majority. The radical M.P. Joseph Hume approved fully the principle of Spring Rice's proposal, because "it placed the burden of maintaining the fabric of the Church on its own property."[143] Precisely for that reason Sir Robert Inglis disdained it. His opposition expressed not only the old Tory view, but also the conservatism of Peel when he said that even if a fund could be found to fill the Church's needs, "yet the nationality of the Church of England would be destroyed, and it would be considered as a Church not supported by the nation, but by itself."[144] This was denied by Spring Rice and the cabinet, who alleged that, contrary to the voluntary principle, their plan recognized the state's obligation to maintain the Church by providing for the reorganization of its finances.[145] They also worked from the Erastian assumption that the

141. Cabinet church rate proposal, Aug. 1836, Russell Papers, PRO 30/22 2B, fol. 341; *Hansard*, XXXVI (3 March 1837), 1225–1229.
142. *Hansard*, XXXVI (3 March 1837), 1211, 1210; Brent, "The Whigs and Protestant Dissent," pp. 903, 904.
143. *Hansard*, XXXVI (3 March 1837), 1267.
144. Ibid., 1255.
145. Ibid., 1218.

Church's surplus funds were public: when the Church maintained itself, it was publicly provided for. That seemed an unacceptable argument to many Churchmen.

In the debate on 22 May 1837 Andrew Johnstone, the Evangelical M.P. for St. Andrew's, moved an amendment to the new church rate bill providing that surplus funds be used to extend religious instruction to unchurched areas. Johnstone denied that a concession such as Spring Rice proposed could lead to peace since Dissenters "had told them" that they would be satisfied only when they obtained their goal of separating church and state. Edward Baines, the member for Leeds, called that an unfounded charge and declared that so far as he knew Dissenters had no such intention. But it was clear that the voice of militant Dissent had been heard. John Hardy, Liberal M.P. for Bradford, quoted from a report of the 8 May 1834 London meeting — chaired by Baines himself — at which the first resolution adopted had stated that "full and complete separation of Church and State" was the true basis on which equal rights could be assured. Baines acknowledged that he had presided over the meeting in question, but he countered by asserting that "upon that occasion the chairman and his friends were outvoted. In fact it was not the petition of Dissenters, but of Radicals." Baines might better have explained that he and the moderate majority present had accepted the resolution only as an expression of their views of ecclesiastical polity, which they did not intend to translate into political demands. His rationalization fell flat. The *Record* disdained it as "paltry Jesuitry."[146]

Perhaps the strongest objection to the government plan was a practical one. The second report of the Ecclesiastical Commission had just been published; it had drawn the chilling picture of a church unable to provide sufficient clergy and places of worship for a rapidly growing urban population. It delivered the pessimistic judgment that "the Resources, which the Established Church possesses, and which can properly be made available to that Purpose, in whatever way they may be husbanded, or distributed, are evidently quite inadequate. . . ."[147] Gladstone expressed the view of Tories and not a few Whigs when he asked how a "Christian Legislature" could pass a

146. Ibid., XXXVIII (22 May 1837), 930–940; *Record*, 25 May 1837.
147. Great Britain, *Parliamentary Papers*, "Second Report of Commissioners on the State of the Established Church, with reference to Duties and Revenues," 1836 (86), XXXVI, 1.

measure that appropriated the only resources the Church might use in the attempt to "enlighten the religious darkness."[148]

The sharpest attacks in the Commons were leveled at Russell for having reversed his consistent statements in the Commons, until as late as 20 June 1836, that the government was committed to the principle enunciated by Althorp—that the Church should be maintained by public funds. Peel, who had been fully briefed by Archbishop Howley on the latter's correspondence with Russell, denounced the Spring Rice plan as having been repudiated by the authority of Russell himself.[149]

Most serious for the government was a letter on 10 March 1837 signed by the majority of the ecclesiastical commissioners informing Melbourne that they would cease acting on the commission so long as the church rate bill was pending.[150] In an exchange of letters in which Melbourne attempted to mollify Archbishop Howley, the archbishop reminded the prime minister that Melbourne had assured him in a letter of 26 May 1835 that the government would not depart from the principle of Lord Althorp's bill. In reply a week later, Melbourne acknowledged that the passage Howley had quoted from Melbourne's letter of 26 May "was not present to my memory, when I determined upon proposing the measure for the Abolition of Church Rates in the year 1836." He went on to say, however, that had he recalled it he would have acted differently only in feeling bound to inform Howley "of the change, which had taken place in my opinion."[151] The government had made a political decision to give in to the Dissenters in the hope of buying religious peace. It did so on the pretext, as expressed by Russell, that it now seemed that the Church had sufficient resources to make up for the loss of church rates.[152]

Dissenting committees hailed the Spring Rice plan with delight. The Committee of the Dissenting Deputies formed a subcommittee, with representation from the Church Rate Abolition Committee, to organize a petition drive in favor of the bill.[153] The combined efforts of Dissent-

148. *Hansard*, XXXVII (15 March 1837), 496.
149. Ibid. (13 March 1837), 315; William Howley to Peel, 4 March 1837, "Private," Peel Papers, Add. MS. 40423, fols. 83, 84.
150. The Ecclesiastical Commissioners to Melbourne, 10 March 1837, "Copy," Russell Papers, PRO 30/22 2E, fols. 124–127.
151. Howley to Melbourne, 9 Jan. 1838, "Copy," Melbourne to Howley, 15 Jan. 1838, "Copy," Russell Papers, PRO 30/22 3A, fols. 47–49, 57.
152. *Hansard*, XXXVII (14 March 1837), 445.
153. Minutes of Protestant Society, 27 March 1837, Dr. Williams's Library, MS. 38. 194; Minutes of United Committee, 8 March 1837; 27 March 1837, Guildhall MS.

ers showed impressive results. By 17 July 1837 a total of 2,325 petitions bearing 674,719 signatures, calling for abolition of church rates, and favoring the government bill had been received by the Commons.[154]

After the Spring Rice plan was given initial approval on 16 March by a majority of twenty-three in the Commons, the *Patriot* applauded a victory over the formidable alliance of the Church and the Tories. But church rate defenders could claim the smallness of the majority as a victory for the Church.

The church defense movement had been slower off the mark than had the abolitionist forces. The archdeacons belatedly called on the clergy seriously to begin encouraging petitions in defense of the rate.[155] Clergy and people responded, inspired by fear of disestablishment, sending in 3,194 petitions with 330,123 signatures.[156] Lord Holland felt they had been all too successful. He believed that the Conservative party had seized the church rate question as a convenient way to rouse the Church against the Whigs. He observed cynically on 2 April 1837: "With this view innumerable petitions from the most remote rural parishes were procured by Archbishops, Rural Deans and other clerical vermin that infest the country. . . ."[157]

The mustering of Churchmen in the cause of church defense had considerable effect. In the second vote on the Spring Rice bill on 23 May, 287 members were in favor and 282 against. The plan's majority had been reduced from twenty-three to five. The reason, said the *Morning Chronicle*, was the absence of Whigs on whom Dissenters had the right to count and the presence of an effective whip on the conservative side.[158] The *Patriot* was sober too, although still hopeful, but it blamed the government for not persisting with Althorp's plan.

3086.2, fols. 69–83; Minutes of Dissenting Deputies, 29 March 1837, Guildhall MS. 3083, IX, fol. 4; 3 April 1837, fols. 14–16.

154. Great Britain, HLRO, *Reports on Public Petitions*. Session 1837, "Twenty-third Report . . . 7–17 July 1837," p. 470.

155. *Patriot*, 16 March 1837, p. 172; *Record*, 16 March 1837; *John Bull*, 19 March 1837, p. 138; *Standard*, 13 March 1837.

156. Great Britain, HLRO, *Reports on Public Petitions*. Session 1837, "Twenty-first Report . . . 24–30 June 1837," p. 442.

157. Lord Holland's Journal, 2 April 1837, Holland House Papers, Add. MS. 51871, p. 10003.

158. *Hansard*, XXXVIII (23 May 1837), 1073; *Morning Chronicle*, 25 May 1837; Gash, *Reaction and Reconstruction*, p. 73.

But the *Morning Chronicle* as well as the Tory press assumed that the Spring Rice bill was dead.[159]

The government proposed that the measure be postponed until a select committee could report on the administration of church property. The United Committee accepted that plan in good faith, confident that the committee's findings would show the church rate bill to be practicable. The government was eager to postpone consideration of church rates, as it had become clear that the Whig gentry was not willing to abolish them if it would appear that such a reform undermined the established church. In the general election of 1837, held on the death of William IV, the Whig majority was reduced, making the government entirely dependent on the Irish members. The church rate question had been the biggest issue of the election. Melbourne blamed it for the Whigs' poor showing, saying that he had been told "of many clergymen who were formerly with us but who now have gone against us."[160] The election had shown the government how far it could go in placating Dissenters. As H. R. Martin said: "Politically, church rate abolition had become too dangerous, and the election was, in effect, a defeat for Dissenting aspirations."[161]

In the wake of the general election, the government reviewed its obligations to the Spring Rice bill. Russell was convinced that it was impossible to carry a bill in the Lords that was opposed in the Commons by all the Tories. He told Melbourne on 11 August: "It remains to be considered what course will be most useful to the country, and creditable to us. I think we may give up the Church rate bill without any difficulty."[162] Ten days later Russell reiterated to Melbourne that they could not hope to carry the church rate bill, and he went further to say that they "must limit any advantage to be gained from the Church lands to the increase of small livings."[163] So Russell had capitulated to the Church. Even before the Select Committee on Church Leases was established, he had conceded that any surplus

159. Gash, *Reaction and Reconstruction*, p. 73; *Standard*, 24 May 1837; *Record*, 25 and 29 May 1837; *Patriot*, 25 May 1837.

160. *Hansard*, XXXVIII (12 June 1837), 1383–1386, 1405–1408; Minutes of United Committee, 31 May 1837, Guildhall MS. 3086.2, fols. 88, 89; Machin, *Politics and the Churches*, pp. 61, 62; Melbourne to Holland, 22 Sept. 1837, Holland House Papers, Add. MS. 51558, fol. 149.

161. Martin, "Politics of the Congregationalists," p. 160.

162. Russell to Melbourne, 11 Aug. 1837, Broadlands Papers, MEL/RU/38/2.

163. Ibid., 21 Aug. 1837.

funds should go to church extension rather than to replace church rates. Melbourne agreed but cautioned against hastily relinquishing their bill or the select committee. Russell concurred "that it would not be wise formally to abandon our Church rate plan." So the plot was laid to stall the Dissenters with the cynical charade of a select committee and the promise of renewed government backing of the bill after an investigation of the legal and financial state of church lands.[164]

Russell rationalized that they had done what they could. They had "proposed two bills—one objected to by the Dissenters—the other by the Church. I do not think we are bound to revive those Bills, or propose another, till a better temper prevails. In the mean time, we may propose our Committee, but not till February. Reasons enough for this delay."[165] In the meantime Russell counseled that they attempt to close their ranks. He believed they should concentrate on getting the goodwill of the radicals, most of whom he believed to be "reasonable enough," and particularly radically inclined Whigs. He suggested that this group would especially appreciate making the ballot an open question and removing the Tories from the political command of the army.[166]

The moderate Dissenting leadership was quite innocent of the understanding between Melbourne and Russell. On 6 November 1837, near the opening of a new parliamentary session, the United Committee considered what steps to take. It decided with utter simplicity to confer first with the government, since "they possess such grateful confidence and cordial regard for the present Administration" and did not wish to "interfere with their plan"! Russell suggested at a 16 November meeting with a United Committee delegation that they should not exert themselves "until the question was again brought under the consideration of Parliament."[167]

164. Ibid., 28 Aug. 1837; Brent's thesis that younger Whigs such as Russell acted on liberal Anglican principle when they refused to give in to voluntaryism is sound if one remembers the reminder of Davis that the younger Whigs were not so unlike their older leaders. Dissenters therefore could not charge that they had been betrayed when such Whigs were unyielding in insisting that church rate legislation must not undercut the establishment principle. Brent does not point out, however, that Russell could be as cynical as older Whigs in the course of his political dealings with Dissenters. Brent, "The Whigs and Protestant Dissent," pp. 906–910; Davis, "The Whigs and Religious Issues."

165. Russell to Melbourne, 13 Sept. 1837, Russell Papers, PRO 30/22 2F, fol. 113.

166. Ibid., fols. 113, 114.

167. Minutes of United Committee, 6 Nov. and 23 Nov. 1837, Guildhall MS. 3086.2, fols. 104, 106.

After the general election of July 1837 the church rate question seemed to lose steam. As the administration moved ever so slowly toward appointing a church leases committee, moderate Dissenting leaders sat in embarrassed inactivity. The Church Rate Abolition Society held a public meeting on 8 May 1838, after Russell had finally moved for the appointment of the Select Committee on Church Leases on 3 July. It was a somewhat dispirited gathering except for a rousing speech by Daniel O'Connell, who admonished his hearers to "agitate, agitate, agitate." But because they were committed to waiting on the government they found agitation senseless, and only five petitions seeking the abolition of church rates were signed in 1838.[168]

An effort was made to develop a more comprehensive organization to represent the civic interests of Dissent. On 26 March 1838 Josiah Conder moved that the United Committee become a national representative body. But the plan collapsed for lack of interest, and the United Committee itself was allowed to dissolve after 9 July. When the Select Committee on Church Leases requested reappointment in the autumn of 1838 the *Patriot* was suspicious, but it went along when parliamentary approval was given to the request on 10 February 1839. The *Patriot* argued that the ministers had "so far redeemed their pledge. . . ." For the rest, it recommended that Dissenters should continue to follow the advice of the Church Rate Abolition Society.[169]

In the six years from 1832 to 1838 Protestant Dissenters, led by the moderate leadership centered in London, had won redress from three important disabilities. Dissenters' chapels had been freed from liability to poor rates, and Dissenters had won the right to use their own marriage service as well as a fairly acceptable mode of registering births, deaths, and marriages. But the course of reform seemed to be foundering by 1838 on the church rate question. Conservative Churchmen had identified the fate of church rates with that of the establishment, and the Whig gentry had rallied round the Church in its time of danger and voted to retain the bulwark of church rates. Melbourne and Russell were politically astute enough to see that it was

168. *Patriot*, 9 May 1838, p. 302; Great Britain, HLRO, *General Index to Public Petitions, 1833–1852*, p. 133.
169. Minutes of United Committee, 26 March 1838, Guildhall MS. 3086.2, fol. 130; 23 April 1838, fols. 136–139; 9 July 1838, fols. 142–147; *Patriot*, 1 Nov. 1838, p. 708; 14 Feb. 1839, p. 100.

now more expedient to bow to the Church, and safer to disappoint the Dissenters.

The failure to attain abolition of compulsory church rates by 1838 was due to the Church's success in arguing that abolition was a step toward disestablishment. But the Church's ammunition was provided by militant Dissenters, who had expanded the church rate question by insisting that it be approached only through the gospel of militant voluntaryism. These militants thoroughly lost faith in the Whigs after 1837. They lost faith also in the moderate men of the Church Rate Abolition Society, and moderates came to be discredited because of their ineffectiveness and their ties to unresponsive Whigs. With no prospect of an imminent resolution to the church rate question, the militants took the initiative to pursue their voluntaryist agenda.

II

The Impact of Voluntaryism,
1838–1853

The period from 1838 to 1853 opened under the pall of disappointed hopes that Melbourne's administration would pass legislation to repeal church rates. The institutions representing especially London-based moderate Dissenters—the *Patriot*, the Dissenting Deputies, the Church Rate Abolition Society (CRAS), and the new Religious Freedom Society—were vilified for their alleged indolence, their subservience to the Whigs, and their ineffectual championing of the cause of church rate martyrs. The moderate Dissenting leadership was discredited, although it was in fact adopting an active voluntaryism, including an insistence that only total abolition of church rates and not exemption from them would satisfy Dissenters. The moderates were overtaken by militant provincial voluntaryists and some aggressive metropolitan groups such as the Baptist ministry, who appropriated the leadership of Dissent.

In the early 1840s militant voluntaryists succeeded in bringing to the fore the issue of disestablishment. In 1844 the Anti-State-Church Association (ASCA) was formed with the primary aim of separating church and state. For a time the particular grievances of Dissent including church rate obligations were overshadowed by the ASCA disestablishment campaign, until in 1848 the moderate Dissenting Deputies again took up the church rate question. By now the deputies sought church rate repeal explicitly within a voluntaryist framework. By 1853 Dissenters' hopes to achieve abolition of rates appeared more realistic in light of the Braintree legal decision that confirmed the right of a vestry majority to refuse to make a rate, and in light of a new willingness of Churchmen, especially Anglo-Catholics, to revise their view of the national Church and to consider exempting Dissenters from church rate obligations. In this climate the ASCA decided that the time was ripe to begin to cooperate with the Dissenting Deputies. The ASCA soon became the leading political organization among Dissent and used the campaign against church rates as a means of seeking its larger goal of a disestablished Church and a voluntary society.

From November 1838 to November 1840 Dissenting politics were inextricably tied to the fate of church rate martyrs. On 23 November 1838 John James, a Congregationalist farmer from Llanelly, Carmarthenshire, was jailed by the consistory court of St. David's for refusing to pay costs arising from a suit brought against him by the Reverend Ebenezer Morris. James was punished for failing to attend the parish church, which was his duty as churchwarden. He was freed within weeks when friends paid his costs,[1] but not before another Dissenting churchwarden—David Jones, a poor Unitarian—was incarcerated for contempt of the same court. His troubles began when he declined to supply the Communion elements for the Llanon parish church, the second of the livings held by Morris, after the overwhelmingly Dissenting vestry refused to lay a church rate. After spending seven months in gaol, Jones was released by Lord Denman of the Court of Queen's Bench because the writ under which he had been imprisoned was technically irregular. But in 1840 Morris obtained another writ to imprison Jones for nonpayment of court costs. On 8 February Jones fled on foot in a greatly agitated state ahead of a bailiff said to be in pursuit of him. He was stricken in flight "with a dangerous disorder" and died two days later.[2]

1. *Leeds Mercury*, 1 Dec. 1838; *Patriot*, 29 Nov. 1838, pp. 772, 773; Machin, *Politics and the Churches*, pp. 104–105. See also W. T. Morgan, "Disciplinary Cases against Churchwardens in the Consistory Courts of St. David's," *Journal of the Historical Society of the Church in Wales*, X (1960), 17; *Patriot*, 20 Dec. 1838, p. 820.

2. *Morning Advertiser*, 11 Dec. 1838; Machin, *Politics and the Churches*, pp. 104–105;

The "martyrdom" of James and Jones played a role in pushing moderate Dissenters toward a more militant voluntaryism. The Board of "Baptist Ministers in London and Westminster," chaired by the eminent F. A. Cox, declared on 11 December 1838 that it was now clearly the duty of Dissenters to seek "the speedy severance of the Established Church from the present degrading and unholy alliance with the State." But the London leaders of Dissent did not move so quickly—nor did they distinguish themselves. The Dissenting Deputies supported John James with misgivings. They decided not to take Jones's case because it was legally weak, and they satisfied themselves with contributing £20 to a subscription in his aid.[3] The deputies' decision not to fight for Jones was legally sound but politically unwise. They had neglected an opportunity to impress Church and government with their commitment to religious liberty, and to consolidate their leadership of Dissent. Instead, they had acted anemically and had given militant Dissenters grounds for challenging their power.

The credibility of the London Dissenting leadership was destined to be undermined more grievously during the eighteen-month imprisonment of John Thorogood. This obstreperous liberal shoemaker from Chelmsford, Essex, was imprisoned on 16 January 1839 after disregarding the ruling of London's consistory court, to which he had himself appealed, after being summoned by the magistrates for failing to pay a church rate bill amounting to 5s.6d. The rate in question was a six-penny rate levied on 30 December 1837 by the Chelmsford vestry with but five hands raised in opposition. Chelmsford was a solid Church and Tory parish that took little notice of Dissenters. The vestry book on this occasion did not even deign to note the existence of dissentient voices.[4]

Because they constituted a minority, Chelmsford's church rate opponents had begun appealing to the law to fight the rate. They had succeeded in having a rate levied on 1 August 1836 declared invalid on technical grounds. Thorogood had been one of fourteen men called before the magistrates for declining to pay the rate made in its place on

Welshman, 14 Feb. 1840; *Patriot*, 23 May 1839, p. 349; 24 June 1839, p. 423; 27 June 1839, p. 432.

3. *Patriot*, 13 Dec. 1838, p. 801; Minutes of Dissenting Deputies, 7 and 14 Dec. 1838, 23 Jan. 1839, Guildhall MS. 3083, IX, fols. 246–299.

4. *Morning Chronicle*, 22 Jan. 1839; *Essex Herald*, 25 Sept. 1838; 2 Oct. 1838; *Essex Standard*, 18 Jan. 1839; *Patriot*, 4 March 1839, p. 142; *Chelmsford Chronicle*, 5 Jan. 1838; Chelmsford Vestry Book, 30 Dec. 1837, ERO, MS. D/P 94/8/16.

18 January 1837. Their cases were dismissed when they stated their intention of disputing the rate's validity. But the churchwardens had chosen not to pursue them in the ecclesiastical courts.[5] That victory had perhaps emboldened Thorogood to face those courts alone in 1838.

The Dissenting Deputies reacted to Thorogood's imprisonment by sending a deputation to Lord Melbourne requesting immediate attention to church rates and proceedings in the ecclesiastical courts. Melbourne replied at their meeting of 24 May 1839 that the government was willing to reform the courts but lacked the parliamentary support to repeal church rates. Melbourne further unsettled them by saying "that he supposed every man must continue to pay his Church Rates," as the church leases committee "was not expected to report any surplus such as had been hoped for."[6] The basis of the moderation of the Dissenting Deputies and the Church Rate Abolition Society had now been undermined because their counsel since 1837 to wait patiently for the government to keep its promise to repeal church rates depended on a favorable report on church leases.

By the autumn the archbishop had rejected that part of the government's plan concerning church lands that might have provided a fund to replace church rates. Russell meanwhile was reconciled to seeing the Church happy, to which, as he wrote Melbourne, he was "more inclined" than to Dissenters. Russell was relieved in any event to have "one of the two parties with us."[7] As the government's attitude became clearer, even moderate Dissenting leaders became willing to adopt a more independent and militant stance.

Under the impetus of Josiah Conder, the genteel Congregationalist editor of the *Patriot*, Dissenters organized the Religious Freedom Society (RFS) in April 1839 to advance the cause of voluntaryism. As Conder wrote when advocating the society's formation, the question was bigger than simply a tithe or church rate question; "it is all of these combined. . . ." The RFS complemented the work of the Evangelical Voluntary Church Association, which relied on religious persuasion to pursue religious equality. The new society was openly

    5. Chelmsford Vestry Book, ERO, MS. D/P 94/8/16; *Chelmsford Chronicle*, 31 March 1837.
    6. Minutes of Dissenting Deputies, 31 May 1839, Guildhall MS. 3083, IX, fols. 364, 365.
    7. William Howley to Lord John Russell, 16 Nov. 1839, Russell Papers, PRO 30/ 22 3D, fols. 121, 122; Russell to Melbourne, 30 Oct. 1839, Broadlands Papers, MEL/ RU/107/1.

political and depended on its parliamentary business committee to monitor legislation and to influence Parliament. The society's moderation was revealed in its address, 5 Bow Court, which it shared with the *Patriot* and CRAS; the names of its directors indicated the same. Charles Lushington, a liberal Anglican M.P., served as the first chairman. J. Remington Mills, Robert Peek, and Josiah Conder, who served respectively as deputy chairman, treasurer, and secretary, were leading figures in the Dissenting Deputies and CRAS. The London-based moderate Dissenting leaders were beginning to put the voluntary principle at the head of their political program.[8]

The formation of the RFS failed to satisfy more militant and especially provincial Dissenters. The mistrust of the militants reflected growing exasperation with the CRAS and Dissenting Deputies for giving little apparent support to the jailed Thorogood and stalling on church rate opposition during the tenure of the church leases committee. Such militant criticism of the metropolitan Dissenting societies received an enthusiastic hearing in the town of Leicester. Leicester's Voluntary Church Society and the *Leicestershire Mercury*, which reflected the views of J. P. Mursell, the minister of the Harvey Lane Baptist Chapel, and the Reverend Edward Miall, Congregationalist pastor of the Bond Street Independent Chapel, challenged Leicester's Dissenters to undertake a more radical opposition to church rates and the established church. After 1836 only St. Margaret's and St. Martin's among Leicester's five parishes still levied church rates. St. Margaret's was run by a select vestry elected annually by the ratepayers. Spurred on by the *Leicestershire Mercury*, the parishioners elected a slate of antirate vestrymen in 1837. They refused to levy a church rate despite protracted attempts by the courts to compel them to do so.[9]

In St. Martin's Dissenters seemed unable to outvote the church rate. Since 1836 growing numbers of Dissenters had followed the radical advice of the *Leicestershire Mercury* neither to pay nor to allow distraint of their goods. William Baines, a member of Edward Miall's congregation, refused to pay his assessment for the six-penny rate set on 17 May 1838 and with other recusants, as they were frequently named in Dissenting newspapers, declared a bona fide objection to the rate's

8. Conder, *Josiah Conder*, pp. 284–286; *Patriot*, 15 April 1839, p. 237; 16 May 1839, pp. 334, 335; 15 Nov. 1838, p. 740; 20 May 1839, p. 339.

9. Machin, *Politics and the Churches*, p. 105; *Leicestershire Mercury*, 26 May 1838; 24 Nov. 1838; 26 Jan. 1839; 2 Feb. 1839; 12 Oct. 1839; 20 April 1839; 29 June 1839.

validity, which only an ecclesiastical court could hear. Baines then repeatedly disregarded citations to appear before the Court of Arches (the court of the archbishop of Canterbury) and was pronounced "'contumacious and in contempt.'" He was ultimately jailed on 13 November 1840.[10] We shall return to his case later.

During the months preceding Baines's imprisonment the militant *Leicestershire Mercury* campaigned to ensure that future "church rate martyrs" would not be consigned to endure incarceration unaided.[11] The implied general criticism of the leadership of the existing metropolitan Dissenting bodies was particularized in a series of letters written to the *Sun* in February 1839. The edition of 2 February carried a letter from the former church rate martyr John Childs, of Bungay, Suffolk, charging that the CRAS had betrayed the cause of Dissenters by its inaction since the establishment of the Select Committee on Church Leases. Even more seriously, Childs hinted darkly that the CRAS had received large sums of money but had never published an account of its finances. The auditors of the CRAS accounts replied, expressing their full satisfaction with the records, but the following week Robert Besley, a former CRAS committee member, charged that the audit of October 1838 had been a delusion and maintained that there had indeed been "gross MISMANAGEMENT and MISAPPLICATION" of the society's funds. As an example he pointed to the disbursement of "a considerable sum" to the *Patriot* for reporting public meetings on church rate subjects.[12]

Besley had resigned from the committee of the CRAS three months earlier, believing he stood alone in objecting to the "do-nothing policy of [the] last 2 years." The damage of Besley's letter was reinforced by one from Leicester's prospective church rate martyr, William Baines, who thanked the paper for exposing the "uselessness" of the CRAS.[13] The organization did not outlive the year. Its remaining records indicate, as its critics had made so painfully public, that the CRAS had

10. *Leicestershire Mercury*, 8 Sept. 1838; 19 May 1838; 8 Sept. 1838; 5 Jan. 1839; David Cornick, "William Baines in Leicester Gaol—A Note," *Journal of United Reformed Church History Society*, 3 (Oct. 1986), 388–391.

11. *Leicestershire Mercury*, 26 Jan. 1839.

12. *Sun*, 2 Feb. 1839; 7 Feb. 1839; 16 Feb. 1839.

13. Notes of Minutes of the Church Rate Abolition Society, 3 Nov. 1839, GLRO, Ac. 72.62 (pt.); letter dated 5 Feb. 1839 in the *Sun*, reprinted in the *Leicestershire Mercury*, 16 Feb. 1839.

functioned only torpidly since the government had promised to establish a select committee on church leases in 1837.[14]

The *Leicestershire Mercury* was not content to trace the problems
of the CRAS to 1837. The paper representing Leicester's militant
voluntaryists regarded "the very origin of this Society as illegitimate. . . ."
The editor wrote that to be acceptable Dissenting societies must be
"dependent for their authority, and directed in their movements by,
the great body of Dissenters, and not constitute the hobby of the purse-
proud bashaws of the metropolitan suburbs."[15] Class and politics now
separated militant from moderate Dissenters more than their stance on
voluntaryism, which moderates were adopting as well. The *Leicestershire
Mercury* believed that antipathy toward radical democracy prevented
Dissenters from achieving their aims. To succeed they must control the
legislature, which they could do only if Dissenters would lose their
middle-class fear of extending the franchise to the class below them.
They should leave the Whigs and join "the Radicals heart and hand, in
their attempts to bring about the absolute ascendancy of the democratic
principle and insure the interest of the many."[16]

This advice had already been taken to heart in Leicester. The
Reverend J. P. Mursell, leader of the voluntaryist Baptists (who
seemed to be replacing Unitarians as the point men for local radicalism), and the militant Congregationalist minister Edward Miall had
been in the forefront of those seeking parliamentary and municipal
democracy as well as reforms that specifically affected Dissenters. The
Leicestershire Mercury began counseling provincial Dissenters to cease
waiting for a lead from the CRAS and to "look to their own energies
for their deliverance."[17]

On 30 July 1839 Thomas Slingsby Duncombe, the radical M.P. for
Finsbury, called the attention of the House of Commons to the case of
John Thorogood, who had by then spent six months in gaol. A small

14. Notes of Minutes of the Church Rate Abolition Society, GLRO, Ac. 72.62
(pt.). The notes indicate a gap in the minutes between 18 March 1837 and 3 April
1838; on 11 Dec. 1839 T. H. Boykett requested remuneration for his services. The
matter was postponed because of small attendance. This was the last recorded meeting.

15. *Leicestershire Mercury*, 23 Feb. 1839.

16. Ibid., 27 Oct. 1838.

17. Arthur Mursell, *James Philippo Mursell: His Life and Work* (London, 1886),
pp. 23–31, 38–41, 44–46; Patterson, *Radical Leicester*, chaps. 10–12; *Leicestershire
Mercury*, 9 March 1839.

House voted forty-two to twenty-two in favor of altering the church rate law early in the next session to prevent the recurrence of such an imprisonment.[18]

By late 1839 Thorogood was complaining loudly that he was being treated as a felon in the Chelmsford gaol, a charge denied by the gaol's governor. Thorogood also reproached the leaders of metropolitan Dissent for deserting him. Going further, he inculpated T. H. Boykett, on the CRAS executive, for giving him the advice that led to his imprisonment. In a letter to the *Sun* Thorogood alleged that Boykett had dissuaded him from heeding the summons of the consistory court and contesting the validity of his church rate, as had been his intention, on the grounds that his refusal would further the cause of religious liberty. Boykett was said to have assured Thorogood "that they would move heaven and earth in the cause if I should be committed." Boykett replied that he had warned Thorogood of the "enormous expenses" contesting the rate might involve, and that he had advised Thorogood not to heed his citation only after Thorogood had "expressed perfect willingness to go to prison . . . alleging that he could work at his trade as well in prison as out of it."[19] Both men had clearly been very naive; neither understood the workings of the judicial or penal system. The liberal *Morning Advertiser* mocked Boykett's feeble defense, denigrated the "miserable mess" made of Thorogood's case in Parliament, and declared it had lost all confidence in the Religious Freedom Society. The account of recriminations among the Dissenters was carried with savage glee by conservative newspapers.[20] Thorogood's martyrdom had become a greater embarrassment to Dissent than to the Church.

In December 1839 the Leicester Voluntary Church Society published a declaration signed by J. P. Mursell, Edward Miall, J. M. Davis, and William Baines, calling for the organization in every town in England and Wales of associations with the sole object of extinguishing church rates. Each association should be an independent local body. In open criticism of existing Dissenting political bodies, they pledged to avoid their deleterious centralization of power. The

18. *Hansard*, XXXXIX (30 July 1839), 998–1007.

19. Great Britain, *Parliamentary Papers*, "Memorandum of the Visiting Justice and Governor of the Gaol of Chelmsford, Transmitted to the Secretary of State for the Home Department, with reference to the Treatment of John Thorogood, a Prisoner in that Gaol," 1839 (444), XXXVIII. 397, pp. 397, 398; *Sun*, 26 Nov. 1839; 28 Nov. 1839.

20. *Morning Advertiser*, 29 Nov. 1839; see *Standard*, 28 Nov. 1839; *Essex Herald*, 3 Dec. 1839.

Patriot objected that such a network of associations already existed in the Church Rate Abolition Society,[21] although it was in fact on the verge of expiring. But whatever its fate, Leicester's voluntaryists had taken the initiative to bypass London by urging the building of a national confederation of Dissenting pressure groups outside the control of metropolitan Dissent.

On 11 February 1840 Duncombe asked leave to introduce a bill in the Commons that would immediately discharge John Thorogood and amend the church rate law. His reform was based on a scheme first suggested by the *Edinburgh Review* in October 1839. According to Duncombe's plan Dissenters who declared that they conscientiously dissented from the Church and agreed not to participate in vestries dealing with church affairs should be exempted from church rate obligations. Duncombe's motion lost by the substantial margin of 117 to 62 votes. Russell opposed Duncombe's motion and objected strongly to Duncombe's characterization of Thorogood as a prisoner of conscience. Thorogood was in gaol for contempt of court, asserted Russell, not for refusing to pay a church rate. His case therefore did not permit Parliament's interference.[22]

Dissenters and liberal newspapers were angered by what they interpreted as aristocratic contempt for Thorogood and Dissenters. Russell's speech had the important effect of further radicalizing moderate Dissenters. The *Cheltenham Examiner* actually asserted that the "breach between Leicester and London is healed. . . ." That prognostication was premature, but the *Patriot* did move toward a more militant position. It believed Russell clearly had indicated that Dissenters need no longer look to the Whigs for redress of their grievances. Concurring with the *Eclectic Review*, the *Patriot* advised Dissenters to depend on their own resources.[23] Despite remaining social and political differences with militant provincial Dissenters, Josiah Conder's moderate *Patriot* had moved closer to their view of the Whigs and the need for an independent political stance.

Russell rejected exempting Dissenters as brusquely as he had treated Thorogood's claim to clemency. Russell repudiated exemption on the Broad Church grounds upon which he had consistently defended

21. *Leicestershire Mercury*, 21 Dec. 1839; *Patriot*, 23 Dec. 1839, p. 837; 6 Jan. 1840, p. 12.

22. *Hansard*, LII (11 Feb. 1840), 87–94, 116, 117.

23. *Examiner*, 16 Feb. 1840; *Morning Chronicle*, 12 Feb. 1840; *Globe*, 17 Feb. 1840; *Patriot*, 20 Feb. 1840; 2 March 1840, p. 140; *Cheltenham Examiner*, 26 Feb. 1840.

church rates and the establishment: "it was for the common good, and that was a principle which entitled them to ask for that burden to be laid upon all."[24] The *Patriot* indicated that it could be satisfied with either exemption from, or total repeal of church rates. Duncombe had said that leading Dissenters whom he had consulted found his exemption plan equitable, and Edward Baines, the leading Dissenter in Parliament, supported it. However, three months later the Committee of the Dissenting Deputies declared its opposition to a similar exemption plan. The deputies insisted on full abolition of church rates.[25] The refusal to be satisfied with exemption indicated the growing impact of voluntaryism among moderate Dissenters. Even in London they were coming to believe that exemption of Dissenters implied mere toleration; they demanded equality.

The acceptance of voluntaryism as a practical principle among moderate Dissenters was given a boost in the spring of 1840 by the campaign led by Oxford University's tireless Protestant High Church M.P. Sir Robert Inglis for government-financed Church extension. Inglis called on Parliament to follow the precedents of 1818 and 1824 to give parliamentary grants to build churches for an unchurched urban population. The RFS mobilized to mount determined opposition to any further extension of the political privileges enjoyed by the Church. At a large public meeting in London's Freemasons' Hall on 19 March 1840, organized by the RFS and chaired by the Duke of Sussex, resolutions were passed opposing the Inglis church extension scheme. The meeting rejected allocating tax money for church extension not only because that violated the rights of Dissenters but even more because it contravened the rights and consciences of unbelievers. As the *Patriot* said, this sensibility marked a new stage in the development of the religious freedom principle—from toleration of Dissenters to equal rights for all, including the enemies of Christianity.[26]

Following an intensive petition campaign by both sides, the Inglis motion was debated in the Commons on 30 June 1840. Russell opposed it, arguing that no additional ecclesiastical burden should be asked of those not of the Church because to do so would create great dissatisfaction harmful to the Church. The motion was then defeated by a vote of

24. *Hansard*, LIII (11 Feb. 1840), 97; Ellens, "Lord John Russell," pp. 244, 245.

25. *Patriot*, 13 Feb. 1840, p. 100; *Hansard*, LII (11 Feb. 1840), 103–107; Minutes of Dissenting Deputies, 29 May 1840, Guildhall MS. 3083, IX, 449, 450.

26. *Hansard*, LV (30 June 1840), 271–326; *Patriot*, 12 March 1840, p. 164; 23 March 1840, pp. 185, 188.

168 to 149. The expansion of the Church's political power had been thwarted. Peel, who had supported Inglis, refused to use parliamentary funds to build churches once he came to power, fearing as Russell had in 1840 that the opposition would harm the Church. The Religious Freedom Society, which had become more committed to voluntaryism, proposed a concrete plan to monitor legislation affecting religious freedom and to work to return members of Parliament dedicated to advancing religious liberty.[27]

Moderate Dissenting leaders in the Dissenting Deputies, Religious Freedom Society, *Patriot*, and *Eclectic Review*[28] were adopting an active voluntaryist posture such as militant Dissenters had long recommended. Yet it was less clear that ordinary Dissenters were as committed. The *Patriot* believed that if Dissenters had been truly committed to religious liberty the number of petitions against church extension should have been doubled. It is noteworthy that although only 202,586 signatures could be found to counter the 216,176 in favor of church extension in 1840, 1,255,730 petitioned in the first session of the following year for repeal of the Corn Laws.[29] Dissenting leaders regretted not being able to match anti–corn law petitions, as they had hoped to be able to emulate the Anti–Corn-Law League.

By the summer of 1840 Thorogood had been in gaol for sixteen months. There was a general consensus in the House of Commons that the imprisonment had been long enough and that a way should be found to extricate Thorogood. That proved difficult. On 24 July Duncombe moved that the crown show clemency and release the prisoner. But the motion was withdrawn after the attorney general stated that such a motion entailed advising the crown to break the law. Dr. John Nicholl, judge of London's consistory court, argued that ecclesiastical courts lacked the discretion to free a contumacious prisoner who persisted in refusing to submit. New legislation was needed to free Thorogood. Nicholl and the government submitted separate

27. *Hansard*, LV (30 June 1840), 354–358; Machin, *Politics and the Churches*, p. 150; Gash, *Reaction and Reconstruction*, pp. 89–91; *Sir Robert Peel* (London, 1972), pp. 382, 383; *Patriot*, 9 April 1840, p. 228.

28. *Eclectic Review* had taken on a more militant tone and openly called for disestablishment since 1837, when the Baptist minister Dr. Thomas Price became editor. Machin, *Politics and the Churches*, p. 73.

29. *Patriot*, 2 July 1830, p. 468; Great Britain, HLRO, *Reports on Public Petitions*. Session 1840, "Forty-sixth Report . . . 3–11 Aug. 1840," p. 1023; ibid., Session 1841, "Thirty-fifth Report . . . 16–22 June 1841," pp. 894, 895.

ecclesiastical courts bills. Nicholl's was more severe, insisting that the original church rate and all legal costs be paid before a prisoner might be released. The government bill simply allowed the court to free the offender after he had served a twelve-month sentence. After Nicholl withdrew his bill the government bill went to the Lords, where one amendment generously reduced the mandatory prison term for contempt of an ecclesiastical court to six months and another reintroduced Nicholl's principle that payment of the rate and legal costs was a prerequisite for releasing a prisoner.[30]

On 13 November Thorogood was released under the provisions of the statute 3 and 4 Vict. c. 93 after an unknown party paid his rate and costs, saying that he counted his "life as nothing compared to the idolatry of paying to what I believe a most un-christian Church."[31] Thorogood's imprisonment had hardly weakened the Church. The payment of his rate and costs by an anonymous benefactor had maintained the principle of obligatory church rates and the honor of ecclesiastical courts. But discredit had come to the leadership of the metropolitan Dissenting societies, giving provincial militants an opportunity to fill the breach.

II

On 13 November 1840, the day Thorogood was released from gaol, William Baines of Leicester was imprisoned. Three days later Leicester's Voluntary Church Society convened a public meeting to support Baines. The enthusiastic gathering, presided over by the newly liberated Thorogood, resolved to rely on its own strength rather than government favor and to conduct Baines's case more energetically than Thorogood's had been. The *Leicestershire Mercury* gloated about the "almost innumerable visitors" Baines received, and the largest ward in the borough of Leicester actually elected him as town councillor.[32]

On 23 January 1841 at a second public meeting attended by Leicester's mayor and parliamentary representatives, the Reverend

30. *Hansard*, LV (24 July 1840), 939–954; (25 July 1840), 980; (30 July 1840), 1161, 1162; (1 Aug. 1840), 1189–1193; (5 Aug. 1840), 1281–1287; (7 Aug. 1840), 1386–1389; (8 Aug. 1840), 1395, 1396.

31. *Sun*, 14 Nov. 1840.

32. *Leicestershire Mercury*, 21 Nov. 1840; 23 Jan. 1841; 27 Feb. 1841.

J. P. Mursell exhorted his audience not to trust the Dissenting leaders of the "London Committees" or to rely on the government but to "get up the 'pressure from without.' "[33] The Leicester voluntaryists' campaign for religious liberty coincided with their attempt to wrest the control of Dissenting affairs out of the hands of the moderates in London. The *Leicestershire Mercury* stated its view clearly: "The great battle of Voluntarism, *versus* Coercion, must be fought in the provinces. The London Dissenters, with most honourable exceptions, seem half indifferent to it. . . . Going to jail for conscience sake, is quite an unfashionable way of serving the good cause. It is not gentlemanly."[34]

As the *Leicestershire Mercury* issued its condemnation, moderate Dissenting bodies, including the Congregational and Baptist unions, were attempting to organize a coordinated anti–church rate petition drive. However, the plan foundered in January 1841 for lack of funds. Within a month of the failure of the London bodies Edward Miall and J. P. Mursell, Leicester's leading voluntaryist ministers, had taken the initiative to contact M.P.s sympathetic to church rate repeal. John Easthope, liberal M.P. for Leicester, agreed to attempt to introduce a bill in the Commons seeking unconditional repeal.[35]

Despite the organizational lassitude of the moderate Dissenters, they did continue to gravitate toward a more thorough voluntaryism. On 25 January 1841 the *Patriot* announced that it now agreed with the position earlier arrived at by the Dissenting Deputies: that only the entire abolition of church rates, and not exemption from them, could satisfy the demands of voluntary religion. The Religious Freedom Society humbly sent a representative to Leicester's Voluntary Church Society on 11 March to ask that the introduction of Easthope's church rate bill be postponed to give London time to initiate petitions. But the cooperation of London with Leicester was to no avail. Easthope's bill was challenged on procedural grounds by Russell and others and was withdrawn after the first reading on 8 June.[36]

33. Ibid., 30 Jan. 1841.
34. Ibid., 23 Jan. 1841.
35. Minutes of Dissenting Deputies, 27 Nov. 1840, Guildhall MS. 3083, X, 11–14; Minutes of Protestant Society, 24 Nov. 1840, Dr. Williams's Library, MS. 38.194; Minutes of Dissenting Deputies, 20 Jan. 1841, Guildhall MS. 3083, X, 40, 41; *Patriot*, 22 Feb. 1841, p. 127.
36. *Patriot*, 25 Jan. 1841, p. 52; 15 March 1841, p. 169. Easthope had proposed that the bill be brought in, but not be debated until the motion for the second reading, because of the pressure of business before the House of Commons. Dr. Nicholl and

On 23 June 1841 William Baines was freed after (as the Tory *Leicester Journal* snidely reported) "having paid, or procured to be paid, or allowed to be paid" a total of about £385 in court costs—a sore point denied by the *Leicestershire Mercury*. Both sides honored their heroes. Leicester Churchmen raised a subscription to reward their churchwarden, who had prosecuted Baines, for having vindicated the law. On 23 July Baines was honored at a testimonial meeting. Some speakers caustically criticized the RFS. The meeting resolved that the alliance of church and state was the master grievance and agreed that dissolution of that alliance should become the first priority of Leicester's Voluntary Church Society.[37]

Militant provincial Dissenters did not believe that the existing Dissenting parapolitical bodies or the Dissenting press would contend for the disestablishment of the Church in a way satisfactory to them. They finally responded by establishing their own weekly newspaper in London. The *Nonconformist*, first published on 14 April 1841, was edited by Edward Miall, who gave up his Leicester pastorate to make separation of church and state his life's mission.[38] The need for a militant voluntaryist paper with a national circulation was agreed upon in one of the regular gatherings of militant Dissenters hosted by Cyrus R. Edmonds, headmaster of the Leicestershire Proprietary School for the sons of ambitious middle-class men of the midland counties. J. P. Mursell and Edward Miall represented the impatient provincial militants. Also present were two eminent metropolitan Baptists with advanced views: Dr. Thomas Price, since 1837 editor of the *Eclectic Review*, and Dr. F. A. Cox, an influential figure in the Baptist Union.[39]

The *Nonconformist* demanded that Dissenters should recognize the alliance of church and state as the fundamental evil and make disestablishment their primary objective. Miall castigated moderate Dissenters for having fought their war on the periphery and stated that he

---

Sir Robert Inglis objected that this approach was improper procedure. Russell, who would not otherwise have opposed the first reading, indicated that he would not support Easthope in the face of this opposition. *Hansard*, LVIII (11 May 1841), 185–187; (8 June 1841), 1314.

37. *Leicester Journal*, 25 June 1841; *Leicestershire Mercury*, 26 June 1841. It was disclosed in the House of Commons in 1858 that Baines's benefactor had been a Mr. Biggs, a Leicester magistrate. *Hansard*, CL (13 May 1858), 569; *Leicester Journal*, 22 Jan. 1841; *Leicestershire Mercury*, 24 July 1841.

38. Arthur Miall, *Life of Edward Miall* (London, 1884), pp. 28–33; C. Binfield, *So Down to Prayers: Studies in English Nonconformity, 1780–1920* (London, 1977), chap. 5.

39. Mursell, *James Philippo Mursell*, pp. 52–55.

disdained the phrase "the PRACTICAL grievances" of Dissenters.[40] In fact, few leading moderate Dissenters continued to speak of practical grievances after 1837; although the *Nonconformist* was loath to acknowledge it, moderate Dissenters had, since 1837, moved steadily to voluntaryism.

Some of Miall's most eloquent writing was that which pleaded for a purified Church cleansed from the interference of the state. His ardent entreaties for religious freedom and a spiritual Church stood squarely within the religious tradition of the Protestant reformation and the Evangelical Revival. Nevertheless, it was an open question whether Dissent could retain its spiritual integrity while devoting its energies to a sustained political campaign for religious equality. Even so committed a political activist as J. P. Mursell expressed misgivings. He warned at the Baines testimonial: "Let us take care that we do not mar our piety; we shall make a tremendous sacrifice, too great to be made, if we lose our devotedness to Christ, and suffer it to dissipate into the mean spirit of a political contest, especially as religion constitutes our strength."[41]

The *Nonconformist* argued that political Dissent could retain its spiritual identity by keeping its political principles consonant with New Testament directives. It believed that one such principle—liberty—was presently being transgressed by a legislature that did not respect its bounds: "At present we have government in excess. . . . Restriction meets us everywhere—regulates our markets, impedes our commerce, cripples our industry, paralyses our religion. . . . The utmost liberty, compatible with social order, we take to be the inalienable right of all men."[42] With a simple guilelessness the *Nonconformist* intermingled the economic, political, and ecclesiastical liberty of liberalism with the liberty promised by the Gospel. The liberalism inherent in voluntaryism

40. *Nonconformist*, 14 April 1841, p. 1; 21 April 1841, p. 15. Miall helped to create the myth that older Dissenting leaders had been apolitical and had shied away from taking responsible political action. This point is made by Mark D. Johnson, *The Dissolution of Dissent, 1850–1918* (New York and London, 1987), chap. 1. Miall's view, and that of his confederates, was partly devious—an attempt to underline his own importance and to win support from Dissenters. It was in part genuine, if erroneous, based on the belief that only militant voluntaryism was true to the ethos of historical Dissent. In fact, it could be argued that voluntaryism was an innovation and deviation from evangelical Dissent. However, Miall was able to denigrate the consistency of older Dissenters with growing ease because evangelical Dissent itself was rapidly being won over to voluntaryism.

41. *Nonconformist*, 28 July 1841, p. 277.

42. Ibid., 14 April 1841, p. 1.

offered a type of salvation. The passions of mid-nineteenth-century Dissent were redirected to yearn for the establishment of an earthly kingdom of peace and justice to be inaugurated with the lifting of government restrictions from commerce and religion. A danger for Dissent was that its new fascination with temporal liberation might eclipse its experience of the transcendent liberation from sin and damnation that was the animus of evangelical Dissent. The politicization of Dissent provided a subtle vehicle for its desacralization.

In the general election of 1841 Dissenters showed that they were more disillusioned with the Whigs than they had been in 1837. The *Patriot* had challenged Dissenters to return their own members. But in general, Dissenters' hopes for a politically independent posture were disappointed. When Peel formed his administration in September 1841 Dissenters could hope for little from either party; nor did they have much strength in themselves. Norman Gash has concluded that "the retreat into voluntaryism in fact was a retreat from politics."[43] On 11 June 1842 Russell replied to the second request (having disregarded the first) of Henry Waymouth, chairman of the Dissenting Deputies, for Russell's aid and advice in seeking church rate abolition from Peel. Russell firmly declined, saying it would be useless for the weakened Liberal party to make any such attempt in light of its recent failure when in power. Another indication of the malaise besetting moderate Dissenters was the Religious Freedom Society's appeal to the Protestant Society late in 1842 for a contribution to enable it to pay its bills. The Protestant Society's meager £20[44] could not prevent the expiration of the Religious Freedom Society in 1843.

On 16 June 1842 Sir John Easthope asked leave to introduce a bill in the Commons to abolish church rates and to substitute other provisions to maintain the churches of England and Wales. The motion was defeated by a vote of 162 to 80. Peel opposed Easthope's substitute because it included pew rents, which Peel believed to be harmful to the poor. Russell favored the proposal so long as it was certain that the substitute would suffice. The sharpest criticism came from the radical

43. Machin, *Politics and the Churches*, pp. 73, 74; *Nonconformist*, 23 June 1841, p. 194; 14 July 1841, p. 249; Gash, *Reaction and Reconstruction*, p. 76. It is perhaps more accurate to say that in the short term voluntaryism represented a "retreat from politics." In the long term Dissenters followed the route of voluntaryism to find their identification as liberals.

44. Minutes of Dissenting Deputies, 11 June 1842, Guildhall MS. 3083, X, 141, 142; Minutes of Protestant Society, 25 Nov. 1842, Dr. Williams's Library, MS. 38.194.

M.P. for Rochdale, Sharman Crawford. He reproached Easthope for failing to attack the alliance of church and state—the root of the church rate evil. The *Patriot* objected that it was quite legitimate to distinguish the related evils, seeking the immediate abolition of rates while postponing the disestablishment question until Parliament was prepared for it. The *Patriot* further scorned the militant Crawford as "the representative, not so much of Rochdale, as of a scattered band of young, zealous, ardent, but inexperienced, not to say ill-informed Voluntaries. . . ."[45]

III

Militant voluntaryists were increasingly unwilling to be hobbled by the cautions of moderates. In the summer of 1842 Miall wrote a series of articles in the *Nonconformist* on the evils of the church-state alliance and proposed a convention to discuss organizing a disestablishment campaign. That invitation fell on deaf ears, but in the following year the introduction of Sir James Graham's Factory Bill gave militants an unprecedented opportunity. Graham's bill, which provided for government-inspected factory schools, favored the Church and galvanized into opposition not only Baptists and Congregationalists but Wesleyans and Catholics too. The force of that temporary alliance caused the government to withdraw the measure. As a consequence of the controversy, considerable numbers of moderate Dissenters became receptive to the militant belief that religious liberty was held only precariously, and that only disestablishment of the Church could prevent the establishment from enlarging its powers.[46]

By the autumn of 1843, two new militant societies believed superfluous by the *Patriot*—the East London Religious Liberty Society and the Metropolitan Anti-State-Church Association—competed in attempting to convince London Dissenters to mobilize to dismember the alliance of church and state. On 2 October 1843 a group of seventy-six Dissenting ministers from the midland counties gave Edward Miall

45. *Hansard*, LXIII (16 June 1842), 1613–1639; *Patriot*, 20 June 1842, p. 420.

46. Machin, *Politics and the Churches*, pp. 151–160; Anti-State-Church Association, Proceedings of the First Anti-State-Church Conference, Held in London, April 30, May 1 and 2, 1844 (London, n.d.).

the support he lacked in London. The group challenged London ministers to summon a convention to consider how best to seek the separation of church and state. That approach was supported by the *Eclectic Review* but opposed by the *Patriot*, which feared that "wild schemes are afloat. . . ." It suggested that Dissenters' civil interests would be most safely protected if the Congregational and Baptist unions would emulate the Wesleyans and establish political committees or affiliate with an existing London society.[47]

When the appeal by the midlands ministers failed, Edward Miall convened a meeting in Leicester on 7 December 1843 to form a provisional committee with the objective of organizing a convention. Representing London were the men who had also played an active role in the founding of the *Nonconformist*—Baptist militants Drs. Thomas Price and F. A. Cox. The widely respected Cox was asked to chair the meeting. As hoped, his presence and conciliatory manner disarmed some of the mistrust of moderate London Dissenters.[48]

By 1 January 1844 the *Patriot* had been won over to the idea of an anti–state church conference, in part because of the confidence it felt in the provisional committee. The *Patriot* was particularly pleased because the committee agreed that a new society initially should concentrate on diffusing voluntaryist principles among Dissenters themselves, before initiating a disestablishment campaign. Josiah Conder attempted to convince his fellow Dissenting Deputies to adopt his own cautious endorsement of the conference. But on 14 February 1844 the subcommittee of the deputies that had been delegated to formulate a position on the separation of church and state was deadlocked between moderate and militant factions. Conder's moderate position conflicted with a militant set of resolutions proposed by James Cook Evans that called for repealing all laws favoring certain sects and applying the property now devoted to particular religious bodies to national purposes. After a month's adjournment, a special meeting of the deputies attended by Edward Miall chose the Evans list of militant

47. *Nonconformist*, 6 Sept. 1843, p. 611; *Patriot*, 2 Nov. 1843, p. 756; 16 Nov. 1843, pp. 790–791; 7 Sept. 1843, p. 631; A. H. Welch, "John Carvell Williams, the Nonconformist Watchdog (1821–1907)" (unpublished Ph.D. dissertation, University of Kansas, 1968), pp. 9–13; *Patriot*, 2 Oct. 1843, p. 685; 6 Nov. 1843, p. 764.

48. ASCA, Proceedings of First Anti-State-Church Conference, pp. 5, 6; *Nonconformist*, 13 Dec. 1843, p. 833; 27 Dec. 1843, p. 865; Welch, "John Carvell Williams," pp. 13–15.

resolutions and endorsed the holding of a conference.[49] Militant voluntaryists were no longer confined to the provinces. They had won a
majority even among the respectable deputies.

From 30 April to 2 May 1844 upwards of seven hundred delegates
met at the Crown and Anchor Hotel in the Strand. They agreed to
form the British Anti-State-Church Association (ASCA). The association was to be governed by a council of five hundred and an executive
committee of fifty. The council met annually and the executive met
fortnightly—both were elected at triennial conferences. The object of
the society was "the liberation of religion from all governmental or
legislative interference."[50]

Because of a fear of radicalism and secularism, many leading Dis-
senters, laymen, and ministers abstained from supporting the ASCA.
Of the religious denominations, only the Baptist Union sent official
representatives to the founding conference. Only three prominent
London Congregational ministers attended—the Reverend John Bur-
net of Camberwell; Dr. John Pye Smith, president of Homerton
College; and the Reverend Dr. John Campbell, editor of the *British
Banner*. But both Pye Smith and Campbell had misgivings.[51] The *Leeds
Mercury* gave no editorial comment on the ASCA for at least a month.

Prominent Congregationalists like the Reverend John Angell James,
Dr. Robert Vaughan (who founded the *British Quarterly Review* in 1845
to counter the voluntaryist *Eclectic Review*) and the Reverend John
Blackburn actively opposed the ASCA. All feared that the spirituality
of evangelical Dissent was threatened by the militant voluntaryism of
the ASCA. Blackburn objected in his *Congregational Magazine* that the
ASCA illegitimately intended to use political means to achieve religious
ends, and that the religious influence of Dissent would necessarily
diminish because the ASCA was "to consist of Christians, Socinians,
and men of no religion. . . ."[52] That misgiving was shared by other
evangelical Dissenters. The religious heterogeneity of the ASCA mem-

49. J. Guinness Rogers, *The Story of the Struggle for Religious Equality* (London,
1882), pp. 46, 47; *Patriot*, 1 Jan. 1844, pp. 4, 5; Minutes of Dissenting Deputies, 23
Jan. 1844–13 March 1844, Guildhall MS. 3083, X, 286–323.

50. *Nonconformist*, 1 May 1844, p. 285; William H. Mackintosh, *Disestablishment and
Liberation* (London, 1972), pp. 27, 28; Martin, "Politics of the Congregationalists,"
p. 301; ASCA, Proceedings of First Anti-State-Church Conference, p. 149.

51. Welch, "John Carvell Williams," p. 15; Mackintosh, *Disestablishment*, pp. 27, 28.

52. *Congregational Magazine*, 1844, p. 383, quoted in David M. Thompson, *Nonconformity in the Nineteenth Century* (London, 1972), p. 127.

bership also diverged sharply from the first principle of the older Evangelical Voluntary Church Association, that members should be "Evangelical Christians holding the Voluntary Principle."[53] The voluntaryism of the ASCA frightened evangelical Dissenters like Blackburn, Vaughan, and Angell James because it was based on a theology that was increasingly concerned with temporal matters, and a view of the state that was frankly secular.

All Dissenters but a conservative minority assented to the preeminent aim of the ASCA—to free the Church from the constrictions of the state. Older evangelical Dissenters agreed with the ASCA that the Church's pollution stemmed from the state-church legacy of Christendom inaugurated by Constantine: "Prior to his interference, the church had wooden cups, and golden ministers; but after it, she had golden cups, and wooden ministers."[54] Older evangelical Dissenters differed from voluntaryists about what characterized a spiritual church. The voluntaryist definition was shaped increasingly by the development of a "new evangelism" in the mid-nineteenth century. A new generation of ministers not directly influenced by the Evangelical Revival began to deemphasize the doctrine of justification that was central to the revival's call for spiritual conversion in favor of sanctification. The realization of sanctification was sought in the active participation of Dissenters in the life of the nation.[55] In that spirit Edward Miall urged in an important and sophisticated book that churches could increase their spirituality by devoting their energies to improving the physical conditions of the poor. He maintained that "the Churches would lose nothing of their spirituality in such increased attention to temporal affairs, so long as their own motive and end were spiritual. . . ."[56]

In fact, the spirituality of Dissent was ultimately compromised. This did not occur because of the temporal activism of the voluntaryists—the participation of older evangelical Dissenters in political and social questions had been much more widespread than Miall usually acknowl-

53. John Burnet, *The Church of England and the Church of Christ* (London, n.d.), inside cover.

54. David Young, *The Law of Christ for Maintaining and Extending His Church* (London, 1846), pp. 58–61.

55. Johnson, *The Dissolution of Dissent*, chap. 1; Boyd Hilton, *The Age of Atonement: The Influence of Evangelicalism on Social and Economic Thought, 1785–1865* (Oxford, 1988), pp. 281–297.

56. Edward Miall, *The British Churches in Relation to the British People* (2d ed.; London, 1850), p. 295.

edged. But it had much to do with the failure of voluntaryists to maintain an integrated Christian vision of the society they wished to build. It was particularly in their view of the state that voluntaryists came under the thrall of desacralized ideals. In its influential *Anti-State-Church Catechism* the ASCA inculcated the lesson that a state church was objectionable because its existence involved the misconception of the proper ends of civil government. The catechetical definition of the proper ends of government was given with the certainty of inerrancy: "Civil government is the means by which the members of a community combine to seek certain ends. Those ends are temporal, and only temporal. They are such as the members of the community naturally appreciate and desire, viz., the preservation of life, liberty, and property. Religion is not one of them."[57]

The *Catechism*'s blueprint for a state owed more to Locke than to Scripture, reflecting the pervasive influence of the Enlightenment on evangelicalism from its birth in the eighteenth century.[58] The ASCA championed the creation of both a secular state and an independent spiritual church, quite unconscious of the divergent authorities for each. This view of a state unconcerned with the transcendent was Gladstone's greatest fear. It would have seemed incomprehensible to medieval Europe as it does now to the Moslem world. But this concept of a desacralized state had also been shunned by Dissenters in the recent past. In 1834 the *Congregational Magazine* explained that in seeking the separation of church and state Dissenters wished only to prevent the state from favoring one *sect or denomination* over another. They most certainly did not mean to divorce *religion* from the concern of the state. The *Congregational Magazine* explained that if the word *church* were understood as the universal Christian church, "the Dissenters were anxious that the union between the Church and the State should be still more intimate; that the obligations of the Christian religion should be recognized by all in authority and enforced by public homage and example; that the civil observance of the Christian Sabbath

57. A. J. Morris, *The Anti-State-Church Catechism Adapted for Popular Use* (London, 1845), p. 191.

58. Bebbington has made a strong case that the influence of the Enlightenment was as decisive for the orthodox as the heterodox in the eighteenth century. Those transformed in the evangelical revivals of that age nevertheless eagerly appropriated the spirit of optimism, reliance on experience, and love of John Locke that captivated many who were turning against the Christian tradition. D. W. Bebbington, *Evangelicalism in Modern Britain: A History from the 1730s to the 1980s* (London, 1989), chap. 2.

should be secured by protective enactments. . . . "[59] This older evangelical ideal of a nondenominational Christian state and society was
repudiated by the ASCA and voluntaryist Dissenters. It was spurned
because it clashed with the secular liberal vision of the state that
Dissenters had incorporated into their voluntaryism. This synthesis
of political liberalism with Dissenting Protestantism constituted the
politicization of Dissent. The voluntaryism that resulted provided the
coach (with the ASCA the enthusiastic coachman) that was to carry
men and women from Dissent to liberalism.

In the four years following its formation the ASCA worked to win
the minds of Dissenters and to make the existence of a religious
establishment a matter of public debate. Church rates were temporarily
displaced as a parliamentary concern, although they remained contentious in the vestries and the courts. Several parliamentary questions
allowed the ASCA to champion voluntaryism and to gain respectability,
although not without underlining continuing divisions between moderate and militant voluntaryists. At the same time Churchmen became
more disunited in their positions on the establishment principle.

One of the first issues addressed by the ASCA was the annual
parliamentary grant of *Regium Donum* to poor Dissenting ministers in
Ireland. The Dissenting Deputies and a rather somnolent Protestant
Society helped bring the question, which had long embarrassed voluntaryists, before Parliament in 1845. After six years of pressure the
government agreed to terminate the grant.[60] The ASCA and the
Nonconformist, which faithfully published its views, urged Dissenters
not to lose sight of the primary evil—the existence of an established
church. The ASCA organized one hundred meetings throughout the
country during the year preceding its annual meeting on 2 May 1848.
Equally important, leading moderate Dissenters like Edward Baines,
Jr., and the Independent ministers of Leeds, who had kept aloof from
the ASCA, joined its ranks in 1847. The *Patriot* felt justified in claiming
in 1847 that the ASCA now spoke for the voluntaries of Great Britain.[61]

In 1845 Peel proposed extending an enlarged grant to the Roman
Catholic college at Maynooth as part of a plan to conciliate Ireland.

59. *Congregational Magazine*, new series, II (1834), 358.
60. Minutes of Protestant Society, 28 April 1845; 26 May 1845, Dr. Williams's
Library, MS. 38.194; Minutes of Dissenting Deputies, Guildhall MS. 3083, XI,
172–200; Skeats and Miall, *The Free Churches*, pp. 502, 503.
61. Martin, "Politics of the Congregationalists," pp. 321, 322. Martin refers to the
Patriot, 7 May 1847, p. 312.

The bill deeply divided Churchmen and the Conservative party. It was objected that the bill subverted the Protestant nature of the established church and was a step toward concurrent endowment of the Irish Catholic church. Many Dissenters also rallied against Maynooth. Initially they looked to the Anti-Maynooth Committee, which was composed of Evangelical Anglicans, Congregationalists, Presbyterians, and Wesleyans and chaired by a conservative Dissenter, Sir Culling Eardley Smith. But this cooperation foundered on the voluntary question. Militant voluntaryists seceded from the committee, insisting that the establishment of Catholicism could be averted consistently only by rejecting establishments altogether. But conservative and moderate Dissenters remained in the Anti-Maynooth Committee. The Reverend John Blackburn praised the Church of Ireland and called for a united Protestantism to prevent the establishment of Catholicism. The split among Dissenters continued after the Maynooth bill passed with the formation of the anti-Catholic Evangelical Alliance, chaired by Eardley Smith and including the Reverend John Angell James.[62]

Russell and the Whigs had incurred the wrath of militant voluntaryists by supporting Peel's Maynooth bill. They further alienated the voluntaryists in 1846, after they had replaced Peel's Conservative government, with their decision to enlarge government grants to teacher training colleges. The voluntaryists' unsuccessful battle to oppose the extension of government and church involvement in elementary education gave moderates as well as militants the determination to adopt an independent political stance and thoroughly break with the Whigs in the general election of the summer of 1847. The *Patriot* echoed the *Nonconformist's* declaration that "the allegiance we have given to the Whigs, must be henceforth given to truth."[63] A Dissenters parliamentary committee chaired by the Congregationalist textile manufacturer Samuel Morley drew up a list of fifty-three voluntaryist candidates. The Dissenting Deputies named sixteen candidates for the

62. Martin, "Politics of the Congregationalists," p. 325; Machin, *Politics and the Churches*, pp. 169–177; cf. also J. Blackburn, *The Three Conferences Held by the Opponents of the Maynooth Endowment Bill* (London, 1845); A. S. Thelwall, *Proceedings of the Anti-Maynooth Committee* (London, 1845); E. R. Norman, *Anti-Catholicism in Victorian England* (London, 1968); J. Wolffe, "The Evangelical Alliance in the 1840s: An Attempt to Institutionalise Christian Unity," in W. J. Sheils and D. Wood, eds., *Voluntary Religion* (Oxford, 1986), pp. 333–346.

63. *Patriot*, 19 April 1847, p. 252; 17 May 1847, p. 340; Machin, *Politics and the Churches*, pp. 183–185; *Nonconformist*, 31 March 1847, p. 189.

London boroughs and insisted that candidates on the hustings should pledge to oppose giving religious bodies and schools government funds to vote for abolition of church rates and ecclesiastical courts. The voluntaryists had considerable success, electing perhaps twenty-six members pledged to disestablish the Church and another sixty committed to resisting new state endowments of religion. The Dissenting Deputies were elated to have elected all of the candidates they sponsored, and the *Nonconformist* exulted that Dissenters had had "a taste of independence, and they will never again forget it."[64]

No less significant than the growing voluntaryist opposition to the establishment principle was the modification of that principle by leading Churchmen. Gladstone had frightened his Oxford constituents by voting for the Maynooth bill, although he had resigned from Peel's administration out of an anguished sense of duty to act consistently with the principle (which he had publicized only several years earlier in *The State in Its Relation with the Church*) that government should endow only truth.[65] As he wrote to his friend R. J. Phillimore, the Anglo-Catholic Peelite M.P. for Tavistock, Gladstone had become convinced that because of recent political changes, "it is now impossible to regulate the connection between Church and State in this country by reference to an abstract principle."[66] Gladstone did believe Churchmen should strive to maintain the Church's national status in substance, but to do so Gladstone believed that the Church needed to part "earlier, and more freely and cordially, than heretofore with such of her privileges here and there, as may be more obnoxious than really valuable."[67] This new viewpoint would come to have an important bearing on Gladstone's stand on the church rate question.

---

64. *Nonconformist*, 4 Aug. 1847, p. 557; Minutes of Dissenting Deputies, 4 June 1847, Guildhall MS. 3083, XI, 394–396; 13 July 1847, fols. 400–403; 20 Dec. 1847, fols. 432–442; Machin, *Politics and the Churches*, pp. 185–192; J. B. Conacher, *The Peelites and the Party System* (Newton Abbot, 1972), pp. 220–232; Miall, *Edward Miall*, p. 128.

65. John Morley, *The Life of William Ewart Gladstone*, vol. I (London, 1905), pp. 270–281; M.R.D. Foot and H.C.G. Matthew, eds., *The Gladstone Diaries*, vol. III, 1840–1847 (Oxford, 1974), Feb. 1844–Jan. 1845, especially 9 Jan. 1845, pp. 424, 425; R. J. Helmstadter, "Conscience and Politics: Gladstone's First Book," in *The Gladstonian Turn of Mind: Essays Presented to J. B. Conacher*, ed. by Bruce Kinzer (Toronto, 1985), pp. 3–42.

66. Gladstone to R. J. Phillimore, 15 Feb. 1847, Gladstone Papers, Add. MS. 44276, fol. 84.

67. Ibid., 24 June 1847, fol. 111.

Before he gave any public indication of an altered approach to church rates, Gladstone's liberalized stance on the establishment principle was revealed when he voted early in the first session of Parliament in 1847 for Russell's bill to allow Jews to sit in Parliament. Pusey, who had earlier acclaimed Gladstone's concern for a Christian state, felt stricken by what he believed to be his friend's "irreligious act, which one looks upon as a renunciation of Christianity on the part of the state and a preparation for its final apostasy."[68] Gladstone did not deny Pusey's diagnosis but retorted that the battle for a Christian state had been lost since 1813 when Parliament had allowed the admission of Unitarians. Gladstone observed that the state was in fact becoming secular in England as surely as elsewhere. He would therefore fight as well as he could to defend and adjust the holy interests of the Church within a secular state.[69]

IV

Early in 1848 the Dissenting Deputies began to reemphasize the church rate question. Moderate Dissenters had been stung into action by a controversial decision on 8 February 1847 by the Court of Queen's Bench that the churchwardens and a minority of the parishioners of Braintree, Essex, had made a valid church rate despite the opposition of the majority of the parish. Lord Denman ruled for the minority rate on the grounds that common law prescribed that parishioners had the duty to maintain the fabric of their parish church; repairs were a duty, " 'not a mere voluntary act.' "[70]

The ruling of Queen's Bench confirmed the contention of conservatives in the Church and the law that the common-law obligation of parishioners to maintain their parish church implied that parishioners could not legally refuse to make a church rate, the time-honored means of maintaining parish churches. Protestant Dissenters and some liberal legal experts agreed that the law did enjoin the maintenance of parish churches but argued that no common-law sanctions existed to compel

68. Pusey to Gladstone, 13 Dec. 1847, Pusey Papers, Liddon Volumes, p. 274.
69. Gladstone to Pusey, 14 Dec. 1847, "Private," ibid., pp. 282–285.
70. Gosling v. Veley and Another, judgment by Lord Denman in the Court of Queen's Bench, 8 Feb. 1847, *English Reports*, CXV, 558.

an unwilling vestry majority to make a church rate; a rate was valid only if made with the consent of the majority.

Legal proceedings initiated in Braintree, Essex, in 1837 were to define what constituted a valid church rate. The mastermind behind the parochial organization to defeat the rate in Braintree was Samuel Courtauld, a Unitarian, radical, and prosperous proprietor of a firm with power-driven silk crape factories in Braintree, Bocking, and Halstead, Essex.[71] The Braintree case followed a tortuous course through eight courts for sixteen years from 1837 to 1853. It actually consisted of two cases. In the first, Veley v. Burder (1837–41), a rate made by churchwardens alone was declared to be illegal. In the second case, Gosling v. Veley (1841–53), ultimately decided by the House of Lords, a rate made by the wardens together with a minority of voting ratepayers was also found to be invalid.

In 1848, before the final House of Lords' ruling, Dissenters were faced with the judgment made by the Court of Queen's Bench that churchwardens had the power to make a binding rate without the assent of the majority in vestry. The Dissenting Deputies determined that church rates should again be brought to the foreground of political debate.

Josiah Conder, a perpetual member of the Committee of Dissenting Deputies, explained that the deputies' decision entailed a deliberate rejection of the militant voluntaryist policy, which had dominated the Dissenting political agenda since 1837, of concentrating on the abstract question of disestablishment. Conder declared that the militants' policy had failed. He did not deny the validity of the voluntaryist principle; all but a minority of conservative Dissenters had by then adopted that view. But he stated the position that moderate voluntaryists were beginning boldly to reassert: "it was unwise to cease from agitating practical grievances, and especially that of Church-rates. The one ought to have been done, without having the other undone."[72]

The committee of the deputies embarked swiftly in the spring of 1848 on its plan of bringing the church rate question before Parliament. Bernal Osborne, the radical member for Middlesex, agreed to sponsor an abolition bill after Charles Lushington, the liberal Anglican M.P. for Westminster, politely declined. A legal subcommittee drafted a

71. D. C. Coleman, *Courtauld's: An Economic and Social History*, vol. I (Oxford, 1969), pp. 70–74.

72. *Patriot*, 17 Sept. 1849, p. 596.

church rate bill. It also wrote an extensive statement for Osborne's use, outlining the objections to church rates and the deficiencies in existing church rate law. The planned assault on Parliament did not lack for enthusiasm, but it did reflect parliamentary inexperience. At the end of June Osborne convinced the deputies that they should not proceed that session because of the constraints of time.[73]

The renewed parliamentary attention to church rates was facilitated by the fact that parochial church rate opposition had not ceased when Parliament became indifferent after the impasse of 1837. A parliamentary report issued in 1845 indicated that over a recent two-year period the rate had amounted to an average annual income of £285,276. That was a decrease of £77,827 from the £363,103 collected in 1839. Of the 10,070 separate returns, 1,100 recorded not requiring a church rate. In this category were endowed churches and those maintained by the lord of the manor in cases where a large landowner occupied all or most of a parish. Other such returns referred to churches depending for maintenance on pew rents, or to district churches or chapels of ease, which lacked authority to levy rates. Over the two-year period there were 281 church rate refusals. Approximately 73 of these were single refusals and 208 were repeated refusals.[74]

Church rate defenders could take heart that the percentage of church rate refusals was relatively low. However, the small number of recorded church rate refusals imperfectly indicated the level of opposition to rates. Several Welsh parishes reported the routine making of rates but the inability to enforce their collection. The parish Llanystyndwy explained that the danger was too great. In the parish of Henry's Moat, Dissenters (who formed the majority) declined to attend vestry meetings, and "many refuse or put off payment of the rate. . . ."[75] Another mode of opposition common throughout England and Wales

73. Minutes of Dissenting Deputies, 4 Feb. 1848, Guildhall MS. 3083, XI, 446; 13 March 1848, fols. 456–457; 20 March 1848, fol. 457; 14 April 1848, fols. 459–463; 30 June 1848, fol. 467.

74. Great Britain, *Parliamentary Papers*, "Abstract of Returns Relating to Church Rates," 1845 (428), XLI.51. All the figures I have given represent my own calculations. The report is a detailed and important one but was of limited use to M.P.s because all the figures were left in raw form; they were neither compiled nor summarized. Not all the parochial returns refer to the same two-year period. Some were for 1840–1841, while others referred to 1841–1842. In Norfolk, which had a great number of single-owner parishes, 100 of 485 parishes reported not requiring church rates.

75. *Parliamentary Papers*, 1845 (428), LXI.51, pp. 369, 378.

was the levying of a rate of perhaps a half-penny; such a nominal rate could not be collected economically. The report gave hope to church rate defenders, too. Several parishes reported that although rates had been refused in the late 1830s, they were granted again in the early 1840s.[76] That phenomenon probably reflected the temporary decline of the abolitionist cause after 1837 and a feeling of uncertainty, exacerbated by the Braintree case, as to whether the law could compel the making of a rate.

In numerous parishes throughout England and Wales, Dissenters — and in some parishes disaffected Churchmen — waged a war of attrition against church rates. In the parish of St. Martin's, Leicester, a minority persistently battled the levying and enforcement of the rate until triumphing in 1849, when enough Churchmen decided that the cost to the reputation of the Church and of religion outweighed the value of the establishment principle that they had so tenaciously defended.

During the imprisonment of William Baines from November 1840 to June 1841, controversy centered on the absence of the parish vestry book. Dissenters demanded the right of reading the records to ensure that current church rate income would not be used illegally to cover deficits caused by growing defaults of church rates. In the "very numerous and animated" vestry meeting of 4 July 1839, the previous year's accounts passed by the narrow margin of eighty-nine to eighty-five votes. A four-penny rate was levied with a majority of seven votes, although the majority in a subsequent poll was ninety-seven.[77]

In the following July a five-penny rate seemed to pass quietly. But at a vestry meeting on 27 August 1841 a hardening of attitudes accompanied the absence of the conciliatory vicar, the Reverend H. D. Erskine, who had left the parish. The chairman, elected from the parishioners in the vicar's absence, refused to hear an amendment for a six-month adjournment. In protest the Dissenters left the meeting "in a body,"[78] and the requested three-penny rate passed unanimously. The *Leicestershire Mercury* encouraged Dissenters to refuse payment and to suffer distraint of their goods, as that course of action unfailingly struck "a heavy blow . . . at the system which oppresses them."[79]

76. Ibid., pp. 79, 171, 175.

77. *St. Martin's, Leicester Vestry Book*, no. 22, 4 and 5 July 1839; *Leicestershire Chronicle*, 4 July 1839.

78. *St. Martin's, Leicester Vestry Book*, no. 22, 10 July 1840; *Leicestershire Chronicle*, 28 Aug. 1841.

79. *Leicestershire Chronicle*, 28 Aug. 1841; *Leicestershire Mercury*, 28 Aug. 1841; *St. Martin's, Leicester Vestry Book*, no. 22, 27 Aug. 1841.

At the vestry meeting of 14 July 1842, presided over by St. Martin's new vicar, the Reverend Charles John Vaughan, both a proposed rate and the previous year's accounts were unsuccessfully opposed; Churchmen outnumbered Dissenters three to one. The legality of numerous items in the accounts was challenged, including the payment of ten shillings to a lawyer to draw up the notice summoning the vestry meeting. The meeting was told that the great amount of litigation and disputation surrounding the enforcement of the annual church rate had necessitated the use of a legal person to preclude legal challenges to the notice's validity.[80]

During the next four years Dissenters were unable to prevent the levying of church rates. At the vestry meeting of 23 July 1846 they were bested by a vote of seventy to sixty-six in the making of a galling one-shilling rate requested for extraordinary repairs. The antirate faction could gloat that the churchwardens were able to collect but half of the budgeted £1,436. That was an unusual case; passive resistance never became extensive enough at St. Martin's to prevent the collection of the greater part of the annual church rate.[81]

Finally on 20 May 1847 church rate opponents won a measure of revenge for the defeats they had suffered year after year. They pressed their attack against the accounts of the previous year, including the legality of items such as the cost of ringing the church bells on the anniversary of the restoration of Charles II and after the election of churchwardens. More compelling was the legal argument that the accounts could not pass so long as a portion of the previous year's rate remained uncollected. Dissenters gleefully pointed out that the delinquent parishioners were Churchmen who could afford to pay. An amendment passed seventy-four to fifty-four for a month's adjournment in which wardens should collect the arrears and correct the accounts. William Baines observed that although he objected conscientiously to the church rate principle, he did not mind using technical means of subverting the rate.[82]

A month later the accounts were again rejected. But a small majority of 117 to 107 did pass a proposed ten-penny rate to pay for a new roof

80. *St. Martin's, Leicester Vestry Book*, no. 22, 14 July 1842; *Leicestershire Chronicle*, 16 July 1842.

81. *St. Martin's, Leicester Vestry Book*, no. 22, Churchwardens' Accounts, 23 July 1846; ibid., 1839–1849.

82. *St. Martin's, Leicester Vestry Book*, no. 22, 20 May 1847; *Leicestershire Mercury*, 22 May 1847.

for the chancel. The objection that common law allotted repairs of the chancel to the parson was rejected with the explanation that no glebe or tithe existed at St. Martin's to maintain the chancel.[83] At the vestry meeting of 10 August 1848 the accounts were again rejected, but a seven-penny rate was passed by a vote of seventy-eight to fifty and confirmed in a poll by 176 to 106 votes.[84]

The victory for which Dissenters in St. Martin's had fought so long finally came in the vestry meeting of 23 August 1849. The requested church rate was defeated by a vote of eighty to fifty-six. A two-day poll confirmed that rejection by a majority of twelve in a poll of 394. The *Leicestershire Mercury* said later that the Dissenters had never despaired of ultimate victory, because "as each successive occasion for asking for a rate came on, they found their position was strengthened." The paper went on to say that the courts that had once been hostile to church rate opponents had become steadily more empathic. In cases in which they distrained money from those who refused to pay rates, the courts had begun to insist that churchwardens provide a bill of particulars to ensure that distrained funds were used only to repair the church building. Some courts had even insisted that no rate could be laid unless it could be proved that no alternative resources existed. Liberal magistrates, said the *Leicestershire Mercury*, had become increasingly disgusted with needing to sign distress warrants and sometimes substituted their own funds rather than doing so.[85] The cumulation of years of disputes and unrest ultimately had convinced enough Churchmen by 1849 that the Church might be better served by their abstensions or votes against the annual church rate.

One last awkward attempt was made to retain church rates in St. Martin's at the vestry meeting of 20 June 1850. The chairman refused to hear several amendments that replaced the proposed three-penny rate with voluntary contributions. A large meeting of Dissenters and "not a few liberal Churchmen" gathered that evening to oppose church rate by fiat.[86] The *Leicestershire Chronicle* regretted that the question had

    83. *Leicestershire Mercury*, 19 June 1847; *St. Martin's, Leicester Vestry Book*, no. 22, 17 June 1847; an authority stating that repairs of the chancel fell to the parson, while parishioners had responsibility only for the nave, was Burn, *Justice of the Peace*, I, 667.
    84. *St. Martin's, Leicester Vestry Book*, no. 22, 10 Aug. 1848; *Leicestershire Mercury*, 12 Aug. 1848.
    85. *Leicestershire Mercury*, 25 Aug. 1849; *St. Martin's, Leicester Vestry Book*, no. 22, 23 Aug. 1849.
    86. *Leicestershire Mercury*, 22 June 1850.

been reopened after the decision of the previous year. It accurately observed that it was "tolerably certain that it has only been reopened to be for ever set at rest. The system cannot now be maintained. . . ."[87] The church did not again demand a rate. The abolition of the church rate had been won gradually in yet another parish.

The next attempt to achieve national abolition of compulsory church rates was made by J. S. Trelawny on 13 March 1849. The Liberal and Anglican member for Tavistock moved a simple resolution in the House of Commons that immediate steps be taken to abolish church rates. The militant *Nonconformist* responded grumpily: "It is but a minor branch of a great subject — but since others are willing to work for its excision, we would not show ourselves insensible to the value of their efforts."[88] Six months later the *Nonconformist* was more pointed in its criticism of the *Patriot* and *Morning Chronicle* for exhorting Dissenters to give more systematic attention to their practical grievances, and to church rates in particular. The *Nonconformist* responded disdainfully that Parliament was unlikely to take them seriously so long as Dissenting ministers and officers attended vestry meetings to propose amendments seeking mere reductions of proposed rates. It asserted the militant view that they should offer passive resistance, refusing payment altogether. It was ironic, in light of the *Nonconformist*'s bravado, that the militant ASCA readily paid the church rate assessed on its own headquarters. In 1852 the ASCA executive committee authorized payment of a £4 5*s*. church rate bill. Despite some discussion about the decision, the executive did not seriously consider passive resistance.[89]

The Dissenting Deputies worked feverishly, and at short notice, to support Trelawny's parliamentary attempt. The church rate subcommittee issued a "Statement on Church Rates" that was sent to a number of M.P.s.[90] In the House of Commons Trelawny defended his resolution, arguing that although the law might require parishioners to maintain their church it provided no adequate strictures to enforce the making of a rate. He recounted also that in 1847 and 1848 two

87. *St. Martin's, Leicester Vestry Book*, no. 22, 20 June 1850; *Leicestershire Chronicle*, 22 June 1850; *Leicester Journal*, 21 June 1850.

88. *Nonconformist*, 14 March 1849, p. 206.

89. Ibid., 19 Sept. 1849, p. 746; Minutes of the British Anti-State-Church Association (ASCA), 23 Sept. 1852 and 21 Oct. 1852, Greater London Record Office (GLRO), A/LIB/1, II, 407, 418, 419.

90. Minutes of Dissenting Deputies, 2 March 1849, Guildhall MS. 3083, XII, 40; 5 March 1849, fols. 41, 42; 11 March 1849, fol. 45.

additional church rate martyrs had been briefly interned—James Bidwell of St. Botolph's, Cambridge, and J. Simmonds of Munsley, Buckinghamshire. W. P. Wood, the Liberal M.P. for Oxford and a "strong high-Churchman," introduced an amendment that Dissenters be exempted "from contributing to Church Rates, and from taking any part in levying, assessing, or administering the same."[91] But Russell's administration, despite its weakness, made no attempt to curry favor with Dissent. The home secretary, Sir George Grey, dismissed exemption as "a premium on Dissent."[92] Russell resolutely rejected both options and reiterated the old Erastian Whig praise of an established church "as a great tribute and national homage to religion."[93] It was noteworthy, however, that no one wished to retain the law as it stood. Gladstone articulated a common view that "the evils attending the present system were enormous," but, like members on both sides of the House, he objected to voting for an abstract resolution, insisting that an actual bill was needed to offer a good substitute. The majority found both alternatives unsatisfactory, defeating Wood's exemption amendment by a vote of 183 to 20 and Trelawny's resolution by a vote of 119 to 84.[94]

Although they had not succeeded in securing a vote for abolition, the Dissenting Deputies had elicited considerable parliamentary support for reform of the church rate system. Outside of Parliament there were also stirrings from unexpected quarters. The Society of Friends began to show a political interest in the church rate issue. The Dissenting Deputies had requested the aid of the Friends on behalf of Trelawny's motion. But the Quakers, as they were commonly called, consistently eschewed politics as a body, and members were periodically admonished to be wary of political agitation as a threat to spirituality.[95]

Friends were further set apart from Dissent because special laws regulated their church rate obligations. These had been enacted to

91. *Hansard*, CIII (13 March 1849), 639–651; *Dictionary of National Biography*, XXI, 852.

92. *Hansard*, CIII (13 March 1849), 655.

93. Ibid., *674, 675.*

94. Ibid., *672, 684.*

95. Minutes of Dissenting Deputies, 9 March 1849, Guildhall MS. 3083, XII, 43; Society of Friends, London Yearly Meeting. Meeting for Sufferings Minutes, 3 Dec. 1841, Friends' House MS., XLV, 134; Society of Friends, London Yearly Meetings Minutes, 24 May–2 June 1843, Friends' House MS., XXV, 3.

protect Quakers from the exactions of ecclesiastical courts and imprisonment—two dangers to a group that consistently refused to pay
ecclesiastical taxes. The statute 5 and 6 Wm. IV, c. 74 raised from £12
to £50 the value of church rate obligations below which ecclesiastical
courts were denied jurisdiction in cases involving Friends. In effect, the
act meant that magistrates routinely distrained the goods of Quakers in
lieu of church rates.

In 1849 when the Society of Friends first distinguished the kinds of
ecclesiastical taxes for which their goods were distrained, church rates
appeared particularly objectionable. This was so because the excess
value of distrained goods was markedly higher for church rates than
for other ecclesiastical taxes. The actual value of goods distrained for
church rates in 1849 was only £1,262 compared to the sum of £6,638
that satisfied the rent charge—the substitution since 1839 of the
commuted tithe.[96] But whereas the value of property distrained for
rent charges exceeded the original demand by only 8 percent, the
excess value of distraints for church rates was 56 percent. The Friends'
committee appointed to examine the accounts of "sufferings" for 1849
therefore asked the Meeting for Sufferings whether the time had not
come to apply to the legislature for relief "from the impost itself
or from the oppressive exactions to which Friends in the country
are exposed."[97]

In 1850 Trelawny attempted to have Parliament reconsider abolishing church rates. As was the case with Osborne in 1848, the motion
was withdrawn because of timing difficulties,[98] reflecting the still
rudimentary organization of parliamentary church rate opponents.
Trelawny had initiated his appeal to the Commons independently, but
the deputies who had decided to make church rate abolition their
priority for that parliamentary session enthusiastically supported him.
They supplied Trelawny with the statistical information he requested
as well as the statement of facts prepared earlier for Bernal Osborne.[99]

The deputies succeeded in influencing the government in 1851. They
negotiated with Russell and the earl of Carlisle to amend the Church

96. Society of Friends, Sufferings Minutes, 5 Dec. 1849, Friends' House MS.,
XLVI, 64; Eric J. Evans, *The Contentious Tithe* (London, 1976), chap. 6.

97. Society of Friends, Sufferings Minutes, 4 Jan. 1850, Friends' House MS.,
XLVI, 65.

98. Minutes of Dissenting Deputies, 26 July 1850, Guildhall MS. 3083, XII, 137.

99. Ibid., 30 Nov. 1849, fol. 71; report for 1849 given to the annual meeting of
Dissenting Deputies, 18 Jan. 1850, fol. 80.

Building Acts Amendment Bill. The clauses that both houses agreed to withdraw would have allowed commissioners to levy church rates for new churches built under the act.[100] This victory by the deputies indicated the limits to the political influence enjoyed by Dissent in 1851. Russell and Carlisle would fight to retain the Church's existing privileges; they would not persist in seeking to extend them in the face of determined opposition.

Early in 1851 the Dissenting Deputies were given the opportunity subtly to shape Parliament's consideration of the church rate question. J. S. Trelawny requested their assistance in conducting a House of Commons select committee that he had been authorized to chair. His mandate was to analyze how the law of church rates operated through-out the land. Because of the intimate involvement of Dissent in the committee, it was able to contribute significantly to defining the problem for which Parliament would be asked to legislate.

The committee of the deputies eagerly accepted. It immediately formed a subcommittee to supply Trelawny with evidence, and it suggested a list of names of M.P.s who should serve on the select committee. A "legal gentleman"—Robert Hull Terrell, who served for many years as secretary of the Dissenting Deputies and who was well acquainted with the law and practice of church rates—was retained for a fee not to exceed one hundred guineas, to collect and digest evidence to be laid before the select committee.[101] A list of people was compiled who should give evidence before the Trelawny committee. Trelawny summoned as witnesses those whom the deputies had invited to attend, and he even relied on a list of questions prepared at his request by the deputies.[102] The deputies received the cooperation of the ASCA in procuring evidence for the select committee.[103]

Militant and moderate voluntaryists had not forgotten their differ-ences, however. Sharp discord was aroused by the question of "Papal Aggression" when it was proposed to restore territorial titles to the

100. Minutes of Dissenting Deputies, 1 Feb. 1851, Guildhall MS. 3083, XII, 157, 158; 30 June 1851, fols. 203–204; report for 1851 given at the annual meeting of the Dissenting Deputies, 16 Jan. 1852, fols. 233–239.
101. Ibid., 14 April 1851, fol. 176; 25 April 1851, fol. 183; Minutes of the subcommittee on church rates, 21 April 1851, fol. 177; 28 April 1851, fols. 191–193.
102. Minutes of Dissenting Deputies, 25 April 1851, Guildhall MS. 3083, XII, 183, 184; 5 May 1851, fols. 194–196; 2 May 1851, fols. 192, 193.
103. Ibid., 26 May 1851, fol. 199; *Nonconformist*, 21 May 1851, pp. 397, 398; Minutes of ASCA, 15 May 1851, GLRO A/LIB/I, II, 220, 221 and insert.

Catholic hierarchy. For moderate Dissenters allegiance to Protestantism generally overwhelmed their voluntaryism. Angell James in the
Evangelical Alliance eagerly supported Russell's Ecclesiastical Titles
Bill, as did the *Patriot*.[104] At the end of March a majority of the deputies
objected to the amended Titles Bill as inadequate to defend the
"independence of the Crown and the honour of the country." The
Nonconformist caustically asked how the deputies could possibly push
for a more stringent measure without encroaching on religious liberty.[105] But the ASCA, which generally spoke for militant voluntaryism, was itself probably too divided to adopt a position on the
question.[106]

The Dissenting enthusiasm for anti-Catholic legislation indicated
that the ASCA had not by 1850 won mass support for militant
voluntaryism. The *British Quarterly Review* still criticized the militants,
as did the Reverend John Campbell's large-circulation newspapers.
Campbell attacked both the radical politics and the alleged theological
liberalism of the militants. He also resigned from the ASCA after
having served as a member of its executive committee. Campbell
judged the ASCA's six years of work a failure and blamed it for
the decay of piety in the churches. He charged that revival, not
disestablishment, was needed to restore vigor to the churches.[107]

V

Feuding Dissenters closed ranks in opposition to Lord Derby, who
formed a government on 22 February 1852 after Palmerston, aided by
Irish Liberals and Peelites, brought down the Russell government.
Derby alarmed Dissenters by declaring at the outset that his adminis-

104. *Patriot*, 17 March 1851, p. 172; 20 March 1851, p. 180.

105. Minutes of Dissenting Deputies, 31 March 1851, Guildhall MS. 3083, XII,
171; 15 Nov. 1850, fols. 140, 141; 3 Jan. 1851, fol. 148; 10 Jan. 1851, fol. 151;
Nonconformist, 2 April 1851, p. 257.

106. Machin, *Politics and the Churches*, p. 222.

107. *Christian Witness*, published in 1844; *Christian's Penny Magazine*, published in
1846; *British Banner*, published in 1848; Martin, "Politics of the Congregationalists,"
p. 439.

tration "would uphold the Church Establishment in all its integrity . . . and seek to extend its influence. . . ."[108]

In the general election campaign that followed Derby's accession to power militant voluntaryists were drawn by circumstances to move from their preoccupation with disestablishment to join moderate Dissenters in seeking the repeal of church rates and other Dissenting grievances. The ASCA was in an unstable financial position and, with the *Nonconformist*, counseled voluntaryists to reject their policy of abstention and independence (followed in the election of 1847) and to support candidates who would pledge to work to abolish church rates or ecclesiastical courts, even if they would not espouse disestablishment. Derby was now the enemy, and the Whigs were weaker than in 1847 and would need an alliance with Dissenters and radicals.[109] The *Nonconformist* was pleased with the election results. It claimed that thirty-eight Dissenters had been returned and that there were now twenty-four voluntaryist M.P.s, fifteen new members who were potential voluntaryists, and twenty-five sympathizers.[110]

The Dissenting Deputies had only one object in 1852: to obtain the immediate abolition of church rates. They worked with J. S. Trelawny and J. A. Hardcastle, both Liberal and Anglican M.P.s, to introduce an abolition bill, but both attempts failed in the press of parliamentary business prior to the July election.[111]

Of greater political weight than Dissenting pressure to abolish church rates was the impact within the Church of changing views about the value of rates and the establishment itself. Anglo-Catholic clergy and M.P.s were beginning to believe that relinquishing the Church's right to support from all ratepayers might be an acceptable sacrifice in return for the spiritual independence of the apostolic Church. Five years of Russell's Erastian hand in church affairs—most notably the ruling in 1850 by the judicial committee of the Privy Council in the Gorham case, which implied that the Church must comprehend both the evangelical and Anglo-Catholic doctrines of baptism—convinced many Anglo-Catholics that it was unsafe to persist

---

108. Machin, *Politics and the Churches*, p. 228; *Nonconformist*, 3 March 1852, p. 166; *Guardian*, 3 March 1852, p. 144; *Record*, 1 March 1852.

109. Minutes of ASCA, 26 June 1852, GLRO A/LIB/1, II, 380; *Nonconformist*, 17 March 1852, p. 197; Martin, "Politics of the Congregationalists," p. 463.

110. *Nonconformist*, 4 Aug. 1852, p. 697; Machin, *Politics and the Churches*, p. 248.

111. Minutes of Dissenting Deputies, 16 Jan. 1852, Guildhall MS. 3083, XII, 223; 13 Feb. 1852, fol. 251; 6 April 1852, fol. 258; 28 May 1852, fol. 275.

in their old Tory theory of the union of church and state.[112] Only a few Anglo-Catholics went so far as to recommend disestablishment to escape Erastianism, but many became more receptive to the concept of granting church rate concessions.

On 19 July 1852, immediately following the general election, Lord Stanley, the progressive conservative heir to the fourteenth earl of Derby, wrote Disraeli, who was chancellor of the exchequer, that Churchmen might concede church rate reform in return for a restoration of convocation, which especially Anglo-Catholics believed essential to safeguard the independence of the Church.[113] On the same day C. J. Blomfield, the Protestant High Church bishop of London, informed Derby that Churchmen as well as Dissenters now generally felt the "urgent necessity of making some speedy settlement of the question of Church Rates."[114] Blomfield later sent Derby a detailed outline of how the rate question might be resolved. The basic point was that those who did not consider themselves members of the Church should register their names to that effect. They would be exempt from paying church rates. Concomitantly, they would forfeit all rights to rent church pews and to receive the sacraments and could no longer be elected as churchwardens or vote in vestry on church matters.[115]

Spencer Walpole wrote Derby that Samuel Wilberforce, the moderate Anglo-Catholic bishop of Oxford, strongly favored Blomfield's plan, as did Gladstone, "both in point of principle and also of expediency."[116] In fact as early as 1843 Gladstone had written privately that in the future "public rating with exemptions" for declared Dissenters

112. J.P.B. Kenyon, "High Churchmen and Politics, 1845–1865" (unpublished Ph.D. dissertation, University of Toronto, 1967), pp. 159–167. Anglo-Catholics were appalled that a state institution, the Judicial Committee of the Privy Council, forced the Church to accept both doctrines of baptism. The Reverend T. M. Neale asked in a tract, "A few Words of Hope," "Is it possible that, after all, she is a mere State Establishment, set up by men, and by men to be thrown down?" (quoted in the *Nonconformist*, 20 March 1850, p. 221). Other Anglo-Catholics began seriously to question the supremacy of the Crown in ecclesiastical affairs and insisted on the need for synods to declare church doctrine. William Dodsworth, *A House Divided Against Itself* (London, 1850); William J. Irons, *The Present Crisis in the Church of England. Illustrated by a Brief Inquiry as to the Royal Supremacy* (London, 1850).
113. Lord Stanley to Disraeli, 19 July 1852, Hughenden Papers B/XX/5/554, LSE microfilm, film 131; Kenyon, "High Churchmen," pp. 225–241.
114. Blomfield to Derby, 19 July 1852, "Private," Derby Papers 127/6.
115. Blomfield to Derby, "Church Rates" (printed), Derby Papers 127/6, put down by 12 Aug. 1852.
116. Spencer Walpole to Derby, 20 Sept. 1852, Derby Papers 153/1; Gladstone to

might be the "least undesirable alternative" available. He continued that the withdrawal of interference in church affairs by Dissenters would actually "be a very great relief to the Church. . . ."[117] Within a few years of publication of *The State in Its Relations with the Church*, Gladstone was willing to modify the establishment principle to gain social peace and to attain greater spiritual independence for the Church.

Wilberforce avidly backed Blomfield's plan, arguing that the expected House of Lords Braintree decision on the legality of rates made by minorities would not favor the Church. They should act now if they wished to retain the rating principle. But he went on to show that his primary concern was not the church rate. He hoped to use exemption from church rates as a means of cleansing the English church of those who were not one with it. He confided to Henry Phillpotts, the Protestant High Church bishop of Exeter:

> I should be ready to surrender the power of taxing Dissenters for Church Rates even if we had clear legal means of enforcing our claim, if in exchange we could get the inestimable privilege of declaring who are and who are not members of the church. The exercise of this power seems to me to be that which is above all other things we need for maintaining what you as well as I value far more than Church Rates, our *spiritual* existence. Now I am confident we can never have so fair a chance of obtaining the means of having any declared *not* to be members of the church as by the process of self-excommunication. . . .[118]

The tendency of Anglo-Catholics to see exemption of Dissenters as a boon to the Church was rejected by Broad Church Whigs and by Protestant High Churchmen as a danger to the Christian character of

---

Samuel Wilberforce, 15 Aug. 1852, Bishop Samuel Wilberforce Papers d. 35, fols. 120, 121; 12 Sept. 1852, fol. 122. On 12 September Gladstone said that his concern was "to obtain spiritual relief for the Church at the minimal expense of a very valueless fiscal right. . . ."

117. Gladstone to Dr. W. F. Hook, 30 March 1843, "Private," Gladstone Papers, Add. MS. 44213.

118. Samuel Wilberforce to Phillpotts, 21 Oct. 1852, "confidential letter," Spencer MSS. quoted in G.C.B. Davies, *Henry Phillpotts, Bishop of Exeter, 1778–1869* (London, 1954), p. 353.

state and society. Phillpotts declared that the central assumption on which the exemption argument was based, that those not receiving benefits from the Church should be relieved of its upkeep, was "glaringly false." He contended that all benefited from the "religious character of their neighbours" and therefore that all should maintain the parish churches that were necessary to form that character.[119]

Phillpotts argued also on practical grounds that it was untimely to legislate on church rates. He contended that they should wait until the House of Lords ruled on the Braintree case, a decision believed to be imminent. But numerous Churchmen such as Spencer Walpole argued that the possibility of a ruling unfavorable to the Church actually strengthened the case for legislation. He presciently argued that after a decision that might declare illegal all but rates made by a majority in vestry, Dissenters might not accept the need for legislation. In a similar vein, Wilberforce argued that Blomfield's exemption scheme should be introduced now so Churchmen might gain something " 'by their qualified surrender.' "[120] Derby was perhaps less impressed with such arguments for church rate reform than by the case made by retentionist Protestant High Churchmen. No serious effort to alter the rate was made until the formation of Aberdeen's coalition government.

On 26 May 1853 R. J. Phillimore, the Anglo-Catholic Peelite M.P. for Tavistock, moved to introduce a bill to exempt declared Dissenters from paying church rates. Those declaring themselves would lose their rights to the ministrations of the Church, as well as their vestry vote on church rates and the management of church property. Sir William Clay, an Anglican voluntaryist M.P. for Tower Hamlets, introduced an amendment similar to the Spring Rice resolution of 1837: that church rates be abolished and replaced by pew rents and the surplus from the better organization of church lands.[121]

The Dissenting Deputies and the ASCA actively supported Clay. Their backing was marked by a deemphasis of petitioning and a move toward more direct pressure on M.P.s, who were reminded that they had been elected because of their pledge to vote to repeal church rates. The deputies had been the first to negotiate with Clay to bring in an abolition plan as early as December 1852. They had objected to Clay's

119. Phillpotts to Derby, 26 Aug. 1852, Derby Papers 142/3.
120. Bishop of Oxford to Phillpotts, 9 Sept. 1852, "confidential letter," Spencer MSS., quoted in Davies, *Henry Phillpotts*, p. 352; Spencer Walpole to Derby, 15 Sept. 1852, Derby Papers 153/1.
121. *Hansard*, CXXVII (26 May 1853), 567–588, 588–604.

wish to offer a substitute, and Clay had agreed to make it clear to the House that part of the proposal was his own and not that of Dissenters. Both the deputies and the ASCA disdained Phillimore's exemption plan because it conflicted with the voluntaryist principle of universal religious liberty, and because it would have reinstituted church rates in numerous parishes—eight thousand out of fifteen thousand, according to the *Nonconformist*—where rates were no longer levied.[122]

Phillimore relied very strongly on the evidence that had been provided by the 1851 select committee chaired by J. S. Trelawny, with the close cooperation of Dissenters. Phillimore argued for reform on the grounds of the ineffectiveness of the present system. He pointed out, as the 1851 parliamentary paper had, that church rates were virtually extinct in the large manufacturing towns in the north of England. Furthermore, when rates could not be refused, they were easily evaded by granting nominal rates and electing Dissenting churchwardens. In other cases church rates were invalidated in courts on the grounds that they were retrospective, based on unequal assessments, or devoted to illegal ends. Phillimore ascribed considerable weight to the view that church rates were socially divisive. He quoted testimony from Dr. Stephen Lushington, judge of London's consistory court, that the existing mode of maintaining churches had led to "great social evils," and that in his career he had seen church rates cause "greater feuds than any other subject that I know."[123]

Phillimore's proposal was attacked by Dissenting M.P.s, who argued for Clay's amendment. One conservative Dissenter, however, Edward Ball, the protectionist member for Cambridgeshire, opposed both Phillimore and Clay. He declared his belief in the value of an established church—to the intense chagrin of Miall, the member for Rochdale.[124] Oxford's formidable Sir Robert Inglis opposed both Phillimore and Clay, but true to his old Protestant High Church view he objected

122. Minutes of Dissenting Deputies, 7 Dec. 1852, Guildhall MS. 3083, XII, 290; 9 March 1853, fols. 329, 330; 14 April 1853, fol. 339; 18 April 1853, fols. 341, 342; *Nonconformist*, 11 May 1853, p. 369; 27 April 1853, p. 329; Minutes of ASCA, 13 April 1853, GLRO A/LIB/1, II, 489.

123. *Hansard*, CXXVII (26 May 1853), 567–578; Great Britain, *Parliamentary Papers*, "Report from the Select Committee of the House of Commons on Church Rates," House of Lords Sessional Papers. 1851, XXXII.1, pp. 307–309, 314; the career of Stephen Lushington, including his role in the church rate question, is covered by S. M. Waddams, *Law, Politics, and the Church of England: The Career of Stephen Lushington, 1782–1873* (Cambridge, 1992).

124. *Hansard*, CXXVII (26 May 1853), 607–623.

in particular to Phillimore's plan to exempt Dissenters. He declared (as Phillpotts had the year before) that if the Church relinquished the compulsory support of the nation it would "cease to be a national church. . . ."[125] Among the Whigs, Sir George Grey, who voted for Clay's amendment, took great exception to Phillimore's proposal to exclude Dissenters from parish churches. Voicing the inclusive latitudinarianism that was so offensive to Anglo-Catholics, Grey asserted that he would not wish to see the demise of occasional communion of Dissenters in the established church, or their sharing in its marriage and funeral rites. Russell antagonized Dissenters by arguing against both proposals, although he did vote to allow Phillimore to bring in a bill. He argued that it was unwise to remove rates because Dissenters would merely attack other parts of the establishment. Furthermore, he believed Parliament should wait for a judicial decision in the Braintree case. He argued also that, unlike the situation in 1837, there was little pressure on Parliament to legislate. Rates were paid in rural areas. He believed that from 1840 to 1853 there had not been "many great practical evils" as a result of "the present state of the law."[126]

Phillimore's resolution lost by a vote of 207 to 185, and Clay's amendment was defeated by the larger margin of 220 to 172 votes. The vote was an important one and indicated that Parliament was once again giving serious attention to church rates. There had been considerable movement of opinion on both sides of the House. The Anglo-Catholic *Guardian* was delighted that included in the minority favoring Phillimore was the "whole staple of the Conservative party."[127] It was indeed noteworthy that of the twenty-eight Peelites in the Commons who voted on Phillimore's motion, twenty-two supported exempting Dissenters and only six were opposed. Among Anglo-Catholics fourteen, of whom five were Peelites, voted for Phillimore and three against. More important than numbers was the fact that supporters of Phillimore included the leading members of Aberdeen's cabinet. Each member with a seat in the Commons had voted in favor.[128] Notable supporters in the Conservative party included Lord Stanley, Disraeli,

125. Ibid., 613, 612–627.
126. Ibid., 636, 627–637; *Patriot*, 2 June 1853, p. 368.
127. *Hansard*, CXXVII (26 May 1853), 643–647; *Guardian*, 1 June 1853, p. 349.
128. *Nonconformist*, 1 June 1853, p. 430; *Hansard*, CXXVII (26 May 1853), 643–646; J. B. Conacher, *The Aberdeen Coalition, 1852–1855* (Cambridge, 1968), app. A; Kenyon, "High Churchmen," app. III, p. 468; *Hansard*, CXXVII (26 May 1853), 643–646.

Walpole, Sir John Pakington, and Lord John Manners. In opposition to Phillimore had been, said the *Guardian*, several conservatives, the bulk of the Whigs, almost all the radicals, and all the Dissenters. The *Nonconformist* was happy that a good number of the Whigs had supported Clay and particularly that eminent Whigs such as Lord Robert Grosvenor and Sir George Grey had broken with their leaders (both Palmerston and Russell had voted for Phillimore).[129]

The movement among conservatives to favor exempting Dissenters was attributable partly to support of religious liberty among Peelites, and partly to concern for the catholicity rather than the nationality of the Church by Anglo-Catholics. But the greatest impact on the conservatives was probably made by the pamphlet "The Church Rate Question Considered," which was published the day before the debate by Lord Stanley, the future fifteenth earl of Derby. Even the *Nonconformist* credited its publication, rather than the presence of Dissenters in the Commons, with the high quality of the debate.[130] It was a sign that, as important as was the pressure of Dissenters against the rate out of doors, within Parliament in 1853 church rate debate would be shaped largely by Churchmen with differing views on the Church and its relations with the state.

Stanley's pamphlet incorporated elements of Peelite concern for religious liberty and Anglo-Catholic consideration for the Church's spiritual welfare. Its effectiveness resulted from its practical message—a refusal to pursue the implications of abstract establishment theories. Stanley relied heavily on the influential parliamentary report of 1851 to show that the church rate had caused great dissension. He argued that conservatives should remove from the legal and social system whatever threatened to divide the community, so long as important national interests were safeguarded. He urged that the exemption of Dissenters from church rates best achieved that goal. Stanley said that based on grounds of right and of expedience the claim of Dissenters "to be exempted from ecclesiastical taxation appears unanswerable."[131] In a manner most congenial to Anglo-Catholics, he concluded that the Church would benefit: "the freedom of internal action of which the Church of England is now deprived, would be in a great measure restored to her by a legal definition of Church-member-

129. *Guardian*, 1 June 1853, p. 349; *Nonconformist*, 1 June 1853, p. 430.
130. *Nonconformist*, 1 June 1853, p. 438.
131. Lord Stanley, *The Church Rate Question Considered* (London, 1853), p. 40.

ship, which might supersede the highly constitutional, exceedingly ancient, but practically quite obsolete assumption that every individual composing the nation, is in connection with the National Church."[132]

Even the evangelical *Record*, which was unyielding in its attachment to a Protestant constitution in church and state, had been convinced by Stanley's tract that the present state of church rates had to be remedied. But it insisted that any legislation must begin with the awareness that it dealt with "a National Church . . . entitled to national privileges. . . ." The *Record* condemned as based on a fallacy any supposition that the church was "a *sectarian* body. . . ." It anathematized Phillimore's motion; it was "substantially a Puseyite measure, and aims at the separation of Church and State."[133] This conflict between establishmentarians and Anglo-Catholics, between the *Record* and the *Guardian*, gave an indication of the difficulty the Church was to have, despite its potential parliamentary power, in resolving the church rate question on terms favorable to itself.

In August 1853 the House of Lords, in its judicial capacity, handed down that final ruling in the Braintree case that defenders of the church rate had dreaded. The Lords ruled that although parishioners were under a common-law obligation to maintain their parish church, churchwardens were powerless to levy rates in the absence of majority consent.[134] Because the levying of a rate was the sole legally prescribed means of maintaining the church, that obligation in effect had been declared voluntary wherever the majority was disinclined to fulfill it.

The House of Lords Braintree ruling became the landmark in the church rate conflict. For Dissenters the decision meant one thing: the majority in vestry might legally refuse to make a rate. The Braintree decision was a signal to abolitionists to concentrate their attentions on abolishing the church rate in their own parishes.[135] Churchmen realized that the real parochial assault on the church rate was about to begin. They recognized too that the church rate law, as it stood after the Braintree ruling, was a broken reed. Churchmen therefore turned to Parliament. New legislation to enforce the common-law obligation to maintain the parish church now appeared indispensable.

132. Ibid.
133. *Record*, 30 May 1853.
134. Gosling v. Veley, judgment in the House of Lords, 12 Aug. 1853, in *English Reports*, X, 627–681.
135. *Nonconformist*, 3 Oct. 1855, p. 725; *Leicestershire Mercury*, 20 Aug. 1853; *Leeds Mercury*, 27 Aug. 1853.

The *Nonconformist* believed that the new parliamentary session of 1852–53 marked the beginning of a new period—an ebbing of the fortunes of the Church, which had for the past fifteen years been regaining vitality. It was encouraged by votes on church rates, a burials bill, and especially the passing of the Clergy Reserves (Canada) Bill. It was certain that there was a new respect for voluntaryism in Parliament and that voluntaryists in the Commons were now able to influence the shape of legislation. The *Nonconformist* concluded that "prudence dictated the priority of giving increased attention to Parliamentary business."[136] The implication for the church rate question was that in the period to follow a more political ASCA would adopt opposition to church rates, which since 1848 had been the domain of the Dissenting Deputies, as a key issue in its battle for a voluntary church and society.

From 1853 the ASCA and the Dissenting Deputies could cooperate in seeking the abolition of church rates. Both now agreed, with varying degrees of emphasis and conviction, in the voluntaryist cause. It was a paradox that weighty voices in the Church and Parliament began to conclude that exempting Dissenters from church rate obligations might resolve the church rate conflict only after most influential Dissenting leaders had determined that their voluntaryist ideal could be satisfied by nothing short of total abolition.

136. Minutes of ASCA, "Report Read at Public Meeting, 4 May 1853," GLRO A/ LIB/1, II, 501.

III

The Liberation Society and the Assault on Church Rates, 1853–1859

The Braintree decision hung as a two-edged sword over the church rate conflict after 1853. Church rate abolitionists eagerly trumpeted the rights of majorities in vestry to defeat a rate and rallied in parishes throughout the country to oppose the tax. The rate's defenders replied that the legal ruling had confirmed the ancient common-law obligation of the parish to maintain its church. They now looked to Parliament to put church rate law on a stronger footing.

Leadership of the church rate abolition cause passed from the Dissenting Deputies to the Anti-State-Church Association after 1853. The ASCA was reorganized in that year to become an influential political pressure group and renamed the Society for the Liberation of Religion from State Patronage and Control—usually called the Liberation Society. For a decade after 1853 church rate abolition served as the premier issue of the Liberation Society. The society's leaders, including Edward Miall, became increasingly pragmatic. They saw in the church rate question a means of winning a degree of political influence, and an opportunity to achieve a following among the mass of Dissenters unlikely to be motivated to fight a sustained campaign for church disestablishment.

A total of thirteen church rate bills and measures were introduced in Parliament between 1853 and 1859. It was a tribute to the growing effectiveness of the Liberation Society's electoral and parliamentary machinery that increasing numbers of M.P.s pledged, and could be held to their pledges, to vote to abolish church rates. By 1854 most Churchmen in Parliament favored some sort of church rate reform. But deep divisions among Churchmen between 1853 and 1859 would prevent both the Liberal and Conservative parties from agreeing on a suitable compromise measure.

II

The Braintree ruling in August 1853 set off an explosion of parochial church rate contests not seen since the period from 1834 to 1837. Scores of parishes had hitherto levied at least a nominal rate to prevent a minority from laying a larger one. Following the decision that a binding church rate could be made only by a majority in vestry, abolitionists rallied enthusiastically in parish after parish to defeat the rate. That trend was so pronounced that in 1859, disregarding two and a half decades of agitation, London's Archdeacon William Hale actually attributed to the Braintree ruling the blame for "the commencement of the church rate agitation."[1]

The increase in parochial church rate agitation followed on the heels of the decision in the spring of 1853 by the ASCA to concentrate on intervening in parliamentary affairs. "It was," said a publication on the fifteenth anniversary of the founding of the ASCA, "a great opportunity for the Society and was fully turned to account."[2]

While preparations were still being made for the Triennial Conference of 3 November at which the ASCA became the Liberation Society,[3] Miall had suggested to his readers that the name of the *Nonconformist* also be changed to reach a wider audience. He pleaded

1. *Morning Post*, 27 May 1859.
2. Liberation Society, *The "Liberation Society": A Jubilee Retrospect* (London, 1894), p. 29.
3. *Nonconformist*, 13 April 1853, pp. 292, 293; 9 Nov. 1853, pp. 897, 898; Minutes of ASCA, 3 March 1853, GLRO A/LIB/1, II, 468; 10 March 1853, fol. 474; Welch, "John Carvell Williams," pp. 32–34.

that the paper's name was misleading, making its aim seem narrowly sectarian. Miall argued that its name alienated liberal Churchmen and kept its circulation down among the working classes. He asserted: "The *Nonconformist*, we are told, needs no change but in name, to become representative of the Radical cause in this Country."[4] A preponderantly unfavorable response from his readers prevented Miall from having his way. Miall keenly regretted being unable to merge the Dissenting "distinctiveness" of his paper's religious liberty cause, which he believed was "on the eve of becoming a truly national undertaking,"[5] into a large political movement. Delegates at the ASCA Triennial Conference were readier to alter their society's name. Edward Baines explained in the *Leeds Mercury* that the old title had often been seriously misunderstood to imply opposition to the Anglican church itself, or even to religion. He remonstrated that "a more serious mistake could scarcely be committed. . . . their motive was a Christian motive, and their object a Christian object."[6]

But other changes were initiated at the Triennial Conference that caused some to question whether the Liberation Society would continue as an avowedly Christian organization. The delegates were swayed by the Baptist Dr. C. J. Foster, professor of jurisprudence at London University, to expunge from the society's constitution the second clause, which stated:

> Inasmuch as the province of law is to regulate overt acts, and of religion, to affect the conscience and the heart—law by compulsion, religion by persuasion—and where compulsion begins, persuasion ends; the authority of law can only be consistently employed in aid of religion to protect its free exercise; and the objects of both are obstructed, as well as the teaching of Christianity disregarded, when law is applied to direct the affairs, prescribe the instruction, or maintain the worship of any religious body.[7]

Foster objected that the phrase "the teaching of Christianity" implied at least a degree of religious exclusivism. He declared that he wished

4. *Nonconformist*, 7 Sept. 1853, p. 718.
5. Ibid., 2 Nov. 1853, p. 878.
6. *Leeds Mercury*, 12 Nov. 1853.
7. *Patriot*, 7 Nov. 1853, p. 732.

to belong to a nonsectarian society that could appeal alike to Catholics, Jews, and others in the community. He challenged the delegates to settle the question whether theirs "was a religious or a non-religious institution." The Evangelical Congregationalist the Reverend John Blackburn believed "they were contending for the Christian religion."[8] Miall disputed Foster's claim that they must choose to be religious or political: "The Society was a religious one, inasmuch as it endeavoured to sway the thoughts and feelings of a large portion of the community by religious considerations, believing that was the strongest agency that could be employed. It was a political Society as every step it took, must be political in its character. . . ."[9] But Foster held his ground, Miall conceded, and the majority agreed to reconstitute the society as a political institution with no reference to Christianity. The *Patriot* expressed misgivings, and the Wesleyan *Watchman* asked ironically whether it was not surprising that after having changed their name to avoid offending fellow Christians, "the liberators of religion have given up Christianity itself as in any way distinctively belonging to their Society?"[10]

Some of the implications of this constitutional change were not apparent for several years. The literature of the Liberation Society continued to use scriptural arguments for separating church and state (especially when it was believed that its audience was receptive to that idiom). But whereas only a few decades earlier evangelical Dissenters and Anglicans had converged in Bible and missionary societies in the unity of the Christian gospel, voluntaryist Dissenters in 1854 called on men of all ecclesiastical creeds and none to make their home in the Liberation Society, united in their allegiance to the holy grail of liberty. The language of Mill and Locke would reign in public affairs; the language of the Gospel was relegated to the chapel's private domain. The constitutional amendment adopted by the Liberation Society marked a definite step in its desacralization.

8. Ibid.

9. Ibid., p. 733; tensions between religion and politics, short- and long-term goals, and rivalries between London and the provinces were a familiar pattern in the history of the Liberation Society. David M. Thompson, "The Liberation Society, 1844–1868," in Patricia Hollis, ed., *Pressure from Without in Early Victorian England* (London, 1974), p. 230.

10. *Watchman*, 9 Nov. 1853, p. 365; *Patriot*, 7 Nov. 1853, p. 732. Although contemporaries realized that the religious change in the constitution of the Liberation Society was a matter of some moment, A. H. Welch barely mentions it; Welch, "John Carvell Williams," p. 32. It was not noticed at all by William H. Mackintosh; Mackintosh, *Disestablishment*.

The most important structural innovation initiated at the 3 November conference was the agreement to follow the example of the Anti-Corn-Law League by forming two standing committees. An electoral subcommittee was to work in the constituencies to increase the number of M.P.s committed to religious liberty. A parliamentary subcommittee, chaired by the talented Dr. Foster and including Miall, was to lobby and monitor legislation, acting in effect as a whip for the society. With these committees the Liberation Society was to integrate electoral and parliamentary influence to make it a power to be reckoned with and to become, along with the Anti-Corn-Law League, the United Kingdom Alliance, and the National Education League, one of the effective electoral pressure groups of the Victorian period.[11]

The Dissenting Deputies were not yet ready to acknowledge the new standing of the Liberation Society. On 20 February 1854 the latter sent a collegial letter to the deputies inviting them to unite or cooperate with the parliamentary subcommittee. After a lengthy delay and protracted discussion, the deputies replied coolly that the parliamentary work envisioned by the Liberation Society had long been done by the deputies. They could see no advantage in union, although they would happily cooperate on "particular questions" with "the Deputies as representing the Metropolis, and the Liberation Society the Provinces. . . ."[12] The committee of the Liberation Society was provoked to reply that the society "has a numerous constituency in London, where, as the centre of its operations, it exerts no inconsiderable influence, and more especially in respect to Parliamentary business."[13]

III

In the spring of 1854 many church rates were defeated or opposed for the first time, and even staunch church rate defenders believed it

11. *Patriot*, supplement, 7 Nov. 1853, p. 740; *Nonconformist*, 9 Nov. 1853, p. 908; Minutes of Liberation Society, 30 Jan. 1854, GLRO A/LIB/2, fol. 36; Welch, "John Carvell Williams," pp. 31, 32; Martin, "Politics of the Congregationalists," pp. 521, 522; Hamer, *Electoral Pressure*, pp. vii, 94.

12. Minutes of Liberation Society, 4 Feb. 1854, GLRO A/LIB/2, fols. 39, 40; Minutes of Dissenting Deputies, 29 April 1854, Guildhall MS. 3083, XIII, 5; 9 May 1854, fol. 6; 12 May 1854, fol. 7; 18 May 1854, fol. 10; 2 June 1854, fol. 20.

13. Ibid., 14 July 1854, fol. 24.

essential that a government bill be introduced to terminate the controversy. The *Record* fervently hoped Palmerston might succeed in finding a compromise that would satisfy the Church and Dissent. That hope was Miall's greatest fear: "The only thing we dread is a compromise— and this we have the greatest reason to apprehend from a Coalition Government."[14]

Miall's dread was groundless. The Aberdeen government could agree on no bill and apparently hoped a private member's bill might accomplish what it could not. Of the two private members' bills introduced, the one presented by C. W. Packe, the Conservative member for South Leicestershire, on 9 May 1854 failed even to attract the Conservatives. Packe's bill entailed breaking the rate into two parts: one for maintenance of the church services, from which Dissenters might be exempted, and the other for the building, which could be enforced against all ratepayers. His bill was dismissed with disdain by the liberal press, and Packe withdrew it on 14 June, expressing disappointment that the government had not introduced a bill.[15]

Church rate abolitionists placed their hopes in an outright abolition bill introduced in the Commons on 23 May by Sir William Clay, the Liberal and Anglican M.P. for Tower Hamlets. The bill had been drafted by the parliamentary committee, which represented the deputies and the Liberation Society, and adopted by Clay. The various Dissenting committees then devoted themselves to securing petitions favoring its passage. Dr. Foster's parliamentary subcommittee facilitated the parliamentary presentation of the petitions.[16]

When Clay introduced his bill on 23 May he explained that unlike the previous year's, his abolition bill did not include a legal substitute for the rate. He was confident, in light of the unprecedented church building program of the past fifty years, that the Church need not fear abolition of the church rate. Clay stated at the outset of his speech that since he had last spoken two important changes had occurred: the

14. *Nonconformist*, 24 May 1854, p. 425; *Record*, 13 Feb. 1854; Minutes of Dissenting Deputies, 3 March 1854, Guildhall MS. 3083, XII, 116.

15. *Hansard*, CXXXIII (9 May 1854), 88; CXXXIV (14 June 1854). The *Patriot* pointed out that Packe's bill would have created "for the first time, a statutory obligation in the matter of an ecclesiastical tax . . ." (*Patriot*, 18 May 1854, p. 332); *Nonconformist*, 24 May 1854, p. 426.

16. Minutes of Dissenting Deputies, 12 May 1854, Guildhall MS. 3083, XIII, 7; 18 May 1854, fol. 9; 2 June 1854, fols. 18, 19; *Nonconformist*, 14 June 1854, p. 486; Minutes of Liberation Society, 16 May 1854, GLRO A/LIB/2, fol. 83.

Braintree decision and the publication of the religious census of 1851. Clay asserted that the latter had made "the most extraordinary disclosures" that Dissenters made up half the religious portion of the population.[17] The new official evidence of the numerical strength of Dissent was raised time and again during the debate as an indication of the absurdity of universal church rate obligations.

Clay reminded members that the church rate issue must be dealt with in light of the Braintree decision. That decisive ruling had settled two further questions besides determining that a legal rate depended on the majority in vestry. First, it affirmed that the rate was a personal tax, not "a perpetual obligation upon property." Second, legal authorities had established "that there was a common law liability to maintain the fabric, yet it was obvious that there was no means of enforcing it."[18] It was this practical dilemma facing legislators in the post-Braintree era that inspired the *Morning Chronicle* to label the church rate question "a perfect political hedgehog. Turn it which way you will, it presents its spines."[19] Robert J. Phillimore, the Peelite member for Tavistock, acknowledged the spines: "He did not pretend to offer a positive opinion as to how the law was to be carried into effect, but certainly no legal obligation could exist without a legal remedy."[20] His position, like that of all defenders of the rate, was to underline that the House of Lords had reinforced the ancient obligation of parishioners to maintain their parish church. His, and their, difficulty was to recommend a politically acceptable manner of enforcing that obligation.

In the debate on the motion for the first reading of Clay's bill, Lord Stanley came out in favor of abolition. He continued to prefer exempting Dissenters, but he felt that option had been lost with the failure of Phillimore's bill in 1853. Over Russell's objections the House agreed, by a margin of 129 to 62 votes, to bring in Clay's bill.[21]

During the lengthy debate of 21 June 1854 on the motion for the second reading, Russell spoke most forcefully against Clay's bill. He responded to John Bright's eulogy of the efficient working of the voluntary principle in America, retorting that it suited the social and

17. *Hansard*, CXXXIII (23 May 1854), 807, 809, 810; Patterson, *Radical Leicester*, pp. 230–231.
18. Ibid., 806.
19. *Morning Chronicle*, 22 June 1854.
20. *Hansard*, CXXXIV (21 June 1854), 441.
21. Ibid., CXXXIII (23 May 1854), 818–820, 824, 825, 829–836.

political system of that country but was inappropriate for Britain. Britain had, said Russell, a national church, a hereditary aristocracy, and a monarchy, "and all these things stand together." He would oppose the church rate abolition bill as "tending to subvert one of the great institutions of the State."[22] Russell also indicated that the government intended to settle the question in the next session. But it would hold to one great principle — that the land must maintain the nation's parochial churches. They were, asserted the consistently Broad Church Russell, in one stroke antagonizing both Dissenters and Anglo-Catholics, "national property" — not the possession of one sect.[23]

The day's most important speech was by Gladstone, to whom as chancellor of the exchequer fell the task of sketching the direction the government would follow in legislation projected for the following year. Gladstone conceded, as most members of both sides now did, that there was "an irresistible case" for changing the church rate law. But he wished to find an alternative to the extreme positions of retention and abolition. He admitted to a strong belief that the rate should not be entirely abolished because it functioned well in most of the country's rural parishes. He guessed that in no more than five hundred of the nation's eleven thousand parishes had a church rate ever been refused or contested. He suggested tentatively that prospective legislation might merely give legal recognition to the fact that some parishes had ceased levying rates, while leaving the situation in other, mostly rural parishes unchanged. In fact, the legislative principles suggested by Gladstone were compatible with the draft of the bill that he had framed and sent to Aberdeen the previous November. No action had been taken on it, probably because of disagreement within the cabinet.[24]

22. Ibid., CXXXIV (21 June 1854), 475.

23. Hansard, CXXXIV (21 June 1854), 474; Patriot, 25 May 1854, p. 348. The editor bitterly branded Russell as a "plagiarist" who had borrowed his arguments from the most bigoted Conservatives, to whom he had been ostensibly opposed all his life. Guardian, 31 May 1854, p. 435; Ellens, "Lord John Russell," pp. 247, 248.

24. Hansard, CXXXIV (21 June 1854), 449–455. Gladstone had suggested a church rate plan in two parts. In the first, any parish in a town, or a parish with more than two thousand inhabitants, could place itself under this act by majority vote. In such parishes the law of church rates would be suspended. In these parishes the communicant member could choose a vestry that could elect churchwardens and collect voluntary contributions. It seems likely that Russell would have taken exception to this first part of Gladstone's draft of November 1853. In part two of his draft, Gladstone provided that in all parishes not choosing to adopt this act, the church rate law should continue as before, subject to several conditions. The most important of

A letter by "Earnest" to the *Nonconformist* a week after the debate of 21 June commended Gladstone's speech because nothing in it precluded him from supporting Clay in the next session. Earnest went on to predict: "Gladstone, be it remembered, is probably destined to influence the legislation of the country long after Lord John Russell has ceased to be the marplot of the party who were once proud of his leadership."[25] Reflecting on the church rate and university tests debate, the *Nonconformist* noted the significance of "the disposition to place the State-Church question on the ground of expediency, and to abandon all Divine-right arguments. . . ."[26] It was that tendency in Gladstone's argument that the reformist *Morning Chronicle* found particularly compelling. Gladstone's suggestion of distinguishing between urban and rural parishes was "obviously not so much an assertion of principle as an attempt to meet a difficulty by walking around it. It is practical. . . . It says nothing about Church and state theories, but it offers a method of scrambling on."[27]

The defeat of Clay's bill by a margin of 209 to 182 votes was a pyrrhic victory for church rate defenders. The liberal *Daily News* exulted, "Another Such Victory, and Church Rates Are Lost."[28] The *Leeds Mercury* gloated that almost all Liberals in the House had voted for abolition against a majority consisting of cabinet ministers and Tories. Conservative papers, sobered by their slim majority, hoped the government would use the time gained to pass a compromise bill such as Gladstone had suggested.[29]

Dissenters recognized that work awaited them. As many as 143

---

these was the provision allowing Dissenters to declare themselves as such in order to be exempt from church rate obligations. Both parts of his bill resembled Phillimore's bill of 1853. Part one prefigured the bill that was actually passed in 1868. Memorandum: "Church Rates," 27 Nov. 1853, Gladstone Papers, Add. MS. 44742, fols. 193–196.

25. *Nonconformist*, 28 June 1854, p. 526.

26. Ibid., p. 527. Another sign of the practical bent to church rate discussion in this period can be seen in the tone of *The Times*, 24 May 1854, which came out for abolition. The church rate question was one of "fact," not of "theory." It felt that philosophers could readjust church-state questions after abolition.

27. *Morning Chronicle*, 22 June 1854.

28. *Hansard*, CXXXIV (21 June 1854), 475–478; *Daily News*, 22 June 1854.

29. *Leeds Mercury*, 24 June 1854; *Patriot*, 22 June 1854, p. 412; *Church and State Gazette*, 23 June 1854, p. 38; *Morning Herald*, 22 June 1854. The editor of the *Herald* acknowledged doubts that the Aberdeen ministry would still exist in the coming year, but hoped that whoever was then in power would redeem the pledge made by Russell and alluded to by Gladstone.

Liberals had been absent from the division. *The Times* explained that "the Treasury screw was put upon all the dependents of Government." The *Nonconformist* included a list of the delinquent Liberals, and "Earnest" urged that constituents begin "squeezing the squeezable and getting rid of the stubborn."[30]

The *Nonconformist* triumphantly predicted that the Clay division would hasten the decisive struggle in Parliament as the Braintree decision had liberated Dissenters in the vestry. It also believed that Gladstone's view of the contrast between urban and rural parishes would color that struggle. The *Nonconformist* urged therefore that in this new phase of the conflict the fight should be carried to every quiet village and hamlet; church rate opposition would then be seen as a national, not an urban problem.[31] Within three months Gladstone confided to Sidney Herbert that he feared "that I have myself damaged the Church Rate question by a clumsy and imperfect allusion to a particular *form* of proceeding. . . ."[32]

In October and November 1854 Gladstone privately circulated several church rate proposals, attempting to influence fellow cabinet ministers to accept a compromise plan that would quash the present "mixed" vestry in favor of a voluntary vestry of communicants or regular churchgoers who would rate themselves. In parishes not adopting such an act, Dissenters could be exempted from the obligation to pay the traditional rate. In each case the possibility of agreement foundered on the clash between Gladstone's Anglo-Catholic and Russell's inclusive Broad Church views of the Church. Russell objected about one proposal that Gladstone's plan "avowedly abolishes the church as a National Church, and makes it a sect of Church People falsely calling itself Church of England."[33] Sidney Herbert's reaction to Gladstone's efforts was the most ominous of all. After seeing yet another of the several plans circulated by Gladstone, Herbert agreed

30. *The Times* claimed that government pressure had led twenty-two government members to abstain from voting. *The Times*, 23 June 1854; *Nonconformist*, 28 June 1854, p. 526.

31. *Nonconformist*, 2 Aug. 1854, p. 633.

32. Gladstone to Sidney Herbert, 31 Oct. 1854, Gladstone Papers, Add. MS. 44210, fol. 156.

33. Russell Memorandum, 19 Jan. 1855, Gladstone Papers, Add. MS. 44291, fol. 228; "Proposal for a new Act of Parliament to be called the Church-dues Act," n.d., follows 16 Nov. 1854, ibid., fols. 216, 217; Sidney Herbert–Gladstone correspondence, 30 Oct. to 3 Nov. 1854, ibid., Add. MS. 44210, fols. 149–158; George Grey to Gladstone, 11 November 1854, ibid., fol. 151.

that it was the best of the plans proposing to limit compulsory rates to Churchmen he had seen. Nevertheless he predicted: "but Sir W. Clay will win the race ultimately."[34]

IV

On 20 January 1855, just ten days before the fall of his coalition government, Aberdeen advised the queen that the cabinet intended to introduce a church rate bill in the House of Commons to counter Clay's expected abolition bill.[35] No government bill was forthcoming that session, but Dissenters used their new parliamentary committee to cajole reluctant backbench Liberals to support Clay's bill. The year marked the first occasion that a majority in the Commons voted in principle to abolish church rates.

As first Derby and then Russell attempted unsuccessfully to form governments, the *Nonconformist* exuded confidence that the present was a "peculiarly propitious" time to attain church rate repeal. No administration, Liberal or Conservative, observed the *Nonconformist*, could afford "to risk being put in a minority on a matter of such public importance as Church Rates" while conducting an increasingly unpopular war.[36] The Liberation Society seized the opportunity. On 5 February it decided to demote in status its other ecclesiastical concerns: Irish *Regium Donum*, the Maynooth grant, and Dissenters' burials. It

34. Sidney Herbert to Gladstone, 10 April 1854, "private," Gladstone Papers, Add. MS. 44210.

35. Aberdeen to Queen, 20 Jan. 1855, in Arthur H. Gordon, ed., *Selections from the Correspondence of the Earl of Aberdeen*, vol. XI. It is not known which bill the cabinet had adopted. It does seem likely, however, that it would have been one of those circulated by Gladstone. Only nine days earlier Gladstone had responded to a church rate proposal by a W. Butler of Wantage, forwarded by Bishop Samuel Wilberforce. At that time Gladstone was still firmly committed to creating a dual system, with a voluntary rate and an exclusive church vestry in places where a rate had been defeated, and the continuation of church rates, with exemptions for Dissenters, in the majority of parishes. In the same letter, however, Gladstone also acknowledged that party difficulties were great. Gladstone to Wilberforce, 11 Jan. 1855, Bishop Samuel Wilberforce Papers, d. 36, fol. 44; Wilberforce to Gladstone, 10 Jan. 1855, Gladstone Papers, Add. MS. 44343; "Heads of a Bill for the Support of Churches and Chapels, Services, etc. without having recourse *to Church Rate*," n.d., "copy," Gladstone Papers, Add. MS. 44343, fols. 276, 277.

36. *Nonconformist*, 7 Feb. 1855, p. 97.

resolved "that the entire force of the Society should be directed upon the Anti-Church-rate movement. . . ."[37]

On 20 March the *Nonconformist* called for the formation in every town and parish of local committees under the central direction of the Liberation Society. It added that members of these committees *"need not be members of the Liberation Society*. Their sole object will be the abolition of Church-rates. . . ."[38] It is difficult to imagine the *Nonconformist* making such a concession much before 1853. For the first nine years of the ASCA's life, collaboration with nonvoluntaryists was disdained. The ASCA had adopted each particular case involving state entanglement with religion primarily as a podium from which to preach the voluntaryist gospel. Now the *Nonconformist* advocated that in the quest to influence individual votes they should eschew public meetings and rely on "quiet, noiseless exertion. . . ."[39] Miall and the Liberation Society were moving increasingly in the direction of downgrading their long-term goal of disestablishing and disendowing the Church whenever opposition to those objectives threatened more immediate prospects of political power that the church rate question afforded.

Sir William Clay's bill to abolish church rates, which was introduced in the Commons on 29 March 1855, again provided no substitute for a repealed rate. Several Conservatives opposed the introduction of the bill, but there was widespread feeling that it ought to be given a hearing. Several M.P.s expressed hope that the government would introduce a compromise bill, as had been promised by the Aberdeen administration. Palmerston, the new prime minister, who had experienced the difficulty of fashioning a solution while in Aberdeen's cabinet, demurred that "it is exceedingly difficult to maintain the law, and it is exceedingly difficult to alter it in a satisfactory mode. . . ."[40] Palmerston then suggested that they ought to allow the abolition bill to be introduced. The majority agreed by a margin of 155 to 76 — a gain of twelve votes over the majority on the first reading the previous year.[41]

---

37. Minutes of Liberation Society, 5 Feb. 1855, GLRO A/LIB/ 13, fol. 24.
38. *Nonconformist*, 20 March 1855, p. 217.
39. Ibid.
40. *Hansard*, CXXXVII (29 March 1855), 1355–1367.
41. Ibid., 1369. The strength of their showing did not surprise Dissenters. They had won a crucial majority of ninety-one, in 1854, on James Heywood's amendment to admit Dissenters to Oxford (Oxford University Reform Bill). The *Liberator* pointed out that the size of that majority "had awakened our friends to a knowledge of a strength which, up to that time, they had not expected, and they put forth all that strength this year (1855) on the church-rate issue." *Liberator*, 1 March 1857, p. 45.

During April supporters of Clay's bill maintained their momentum, and Palmerston became sufficiently alarmed at the prospect that the bill might succeed that he privately told the bishops that they should act lest the church rate be entirely lost. The archbishops and bishops met in early May and "agreed unanimously!" wrote a relieved Samuel Wilberforce, to report to the ministers that if the church rate was to be altered it must be along the principles contained in Phillimore's 1853 bill, which offered Dissenters an exemption from church rates.[42] On 14 May 1855, two days before the Commons' second-reading debate on Clay's abolition bill, the Evangelical Archbishop J. B. Sumner introduced a bill in the Lords to reform the church rate law. The bill, which was indebted to both Phillimore and Gladstone, aimed to abolish the rate in parishes where is was no longer levied and to exempt Dissenters in parishes where the majority supported the rate. The bill was disallowed after the speaker ruled it to be a money bill, which could not originate in the Lords.[43] In retrospect a few years later, the Liberation Society congratulated itself that "the Primate of the Anglican Church himself had reached the position occupied in 1840 by the Radical member for Finsbury [T. S. Duncombe]."[44]

On 16 May 1855 Clay's abolition bill was brought on again. The Liberal M.P. Charles Lushington declared that it was hopeless to expect the matter to be settled as a private member's bill. He chided the government for not yet having brought in its own bill. Palmerston retorted that M.P.s were themselves unable to devise a plan capable of satisfying Parliament. But he did acknowledge that the government was presently unable to draft a suitable bill, an admission that the *Morning Chronicle* labeled "a pitiable confession of incompetency.[45]

Dissenters acknowledged, however, that they were indebted to Palmerston for leaving the question open. The cabinet ministers Sir

42. Wilberforce to Gladstone, 5(?) May 1855(?), "Most Private," Gladstone Papers, Add. MS. 44343; *Parliament and the Church-Rate Question: An Historical Sketch* (London, 1861), p. 15.

43. *Hansard*, CXXXVII (14 May 1855), 464; CXL (5 Feb. 1856), 255; Gladstone to Wilberforce, 28 May 1855, Bishop Samuel Wilberforce Papers d. 36, fol. 56. Some Churchmen were dismayed that an archbishop might propose a bill which effectively abolished an immemorial right belonging to the Church. See George Martin, *Observations on a Bill on Church Rates, Presented to the House of Lords, by the Archbishop of Canterbury* (Exeter, 1855).

44. *Parliament and the Church-Rate Question: An Historical Sketch* (London, 1861), p. 15.

45. *Hansard*, CXXXVII (16 May 1855), 684–690; *Morning Chronicle*, 18 May 1855.

William Molesworth and R. Vernon Smith voted for Clay, as did a number of lesser administration figures. The abolition measure passed by 217 votes to 189. The previous year's minority of twenty-seven had been converted to a majority of twenty-eight.[46] The achievement of that majority can be credited largely to a lack of direction in the Liberal party—a deficiency cleverly exploited by the Liberation Society's parliamentary subcommittee and its chairman, Dr. C. J. Foster. The *Liberator* recalled later: "on the morning of the expected division, every member who could not be relied on to vote against us, received from the chairman of our Parliamentary committee the distinct promise of a majority in favor of the bill. The prophecy no doubt contributed to its own fulfillment, and the promised majority came."[47] Churchmen were angered by Palmerston's handling of Clay's bill: the *Record* insisted that the government should have introduced its own bill, and the *Guardian* asked why the primate's measure had not been accepted. On 25 July Clay withdrew his bill in the face of Palmerston's continuing objections to it.[48]

One of the most important contributions to the abolitionist cause was the commencement in July of the monthly *Liberator*. It performed an invaluable service as the house organ of the Liberation Society, stimulating and guiding the many bodies now "engaged in local struggles." The paper was meant to replace some of the thousands of circulars and letters that the executive committee had sent to the localities during the past two years.[49] Parochial church rate opponents were further aided by the publication in 1855 of what was usually referred to as "The Vestryman's Guide." The treatise was commissioned by the Liberation Society and written by a barrister, Alfred Wills. It clarified in lay language the complexities of church rate law. Equipped with Wills's handbook, amateur parochial lawyers learned

46. *Patriot*, 21 May 1855, p. 340; *Wesleyan Times*, 21 May 1855, p. 329. The editor agreed with Lord Seymour that the principle of Clay's bill had been made an open question "because no member could be returned for a large town who was not opposed to Church-rates"; *Hansard*, CXXXVIII (16 May 1855), 692–694.

47. *Liberator*, 1 March 1857, p. 45. It seems unlikely the weight of petitions would have convinced many M.P.s to go over to Clay. A mere 1,603 petitions with 150,052 signatures demanded abolition, compared to nearly 675,000 signatures for the Spring Rice measure in 1837. Great Britain, HLRO, *Reports on Public Petitions*. Session 1854–1855, "61st Report . . . 6–14 Aug. 1855," p. 1144.

48. *Record*, 21 May 1855; *Guardian*, 23 May 1855, p. 393; *Hansard*, CXXXIX (25 July 1855), 1374, 1375.

49. *Liberator*, July 1855; *Nonconformist*, 18 July 1855, p. 550.

to prevent both the laying and the enforcement of rates. Before the year was out the *Liberator* boasted, "that rates are now being opposed and defeated by the superior knowledge of minorities, with as much facility, and with nearly as much frequency, as they have been by the mere voting power of majorities."[50] This was a sophisticated assault on the church rate, far removed from the symbolic protest of the lonely church rate martyr.

V

The pressure now brought to bear on the church rate by skilled parishioners, and by committees becoming adept at manipulating parliamentary opinion, bore fruit in 1856. In that year Palmerston's government tentatively accepted Clay's abolition bill, subject to amendments that were reluctantly agreed to by Dissenters. Had Palmerston persevered, the question might have been resolved rather differently from the way it ultimately was.

In February *The Times* called the government's attention to the fact that a civil war was actually raging throughout the country on the church rate question. Churchmen were chided for not yet having proposed a scheme to satisfy reasonable people.[51] The *Nonconformist* exhorted voluntaryists to renew the pressure in what was believed to be "a final struggle." This time readers were told that "petitions and vestry contests have already done their work, and need not be repeated. . . ." Their one object should be to increase Clay's majority, and that, counseled the *Nonconformist*, should be accomplished "by *prompt personal correspondence* with *members of* Parliament."[52]

In the beginning of 1856 the Palmerston cabinet considered several church rate proposals. Grey suggested that they name a small committee to consider the various schemes afloat, choose a plan that might preempt Clay from bringing in another abolition bill, and demonstrate (according to E. D. Steele) Palmerston's commitment to liberal princi-

---

50. Alfred Wills, *A Treatise on the Powers and Duties of Parish Vestries* (London, 1855); Minutes of Liberation Society, 12 July 1854, GLRO A/LIB/2, fol. 97; 8 Feb. 1855, fol. 145; 2 March 1855, fols. 150–152; *Liberator*, Nov. 1855, p. 72.

51. *The Times*, 19 Feb. 1856; *Nonconformist*, 20 Feb. 1856, p. 114.

52. *Nonconformist*, 13 Feb. 1856, p. 97.

ples and the sincerity of his professions of goodwill to Dissent.[53] Early in the parliamentary session M.P.s had several church rate bills to consider. C. W. Packe, the Conservative member for South Leicestershire, introduced a bill on 5 February 1856 that, like his bill of two years before, distinguished between the fabric and the church service. His view had evolved, however; he now wished to abolish entirely the rate for the service. The fabric rate should be paid by owners of property rather than occupiers, a provision that Packe believed would relieve nineteen out of twenty Dissenters.[54]

The one bill of importance whose anticipated reintroduction had cajoled Palmerston's cabinet to attempt to devise an alternative was Sir William Clay's Church Rates Abolition Bill. When it came up for its second reading on 5 March, Clay could remind each member of the pressure he had felt from the electorate—a tribute to the Liberation Society's effectiveness. He stated that the reduced number of petitions requesting abolition—26, with 3,088 signatures, compared to the 1,599 petitions of the previous year—indicated that the people trusted Parliament to legislate. He also drew their attention to the language of petitions defending the rate. Only 8 petitions with 370 signatures spoke against abolition; the rest, 756 petitions with 28,938 signatures, merely opposed abolition "without provision of an equivalent."[55] It appeared that the country was prepared for reform of the church rate system.

Lord John Manners, the Conservative member for Colchester, repudiated Clay's proposed substitute of voluntary donations as a chimera because they could not be relied on. With fellow Anglo-Catholic Stafford Northcote, Manners had begun to champion the church rate as vigorously as Sir Robert Inglis had until his retirement from the Commons in January 1854. Unlike the Protestant High Church Inglis, however, Manners favored exempting Dissenters on the condition that they relinquish all rights of interference in church affairs.

In reply to Manners and Northcote, Sir George Grey declared that

---

53. Sir G. Grey to Palmerston, 8 Jan. 1856, "Private," Broadlands Papers, GC/GR/2455/1,2; E. D. Steel, *Palmerston and Liberalism, 1855–1865* (Cambridge, 1991), p. 70.

54. *Hansard*, CXL (5 Feb. 1856), 253–258. Notice of intention to introduce another church rate reform bill had been given by John Lloyd Davies, M.P. for Cardigan. Davies's bill proposed to exempt from the rate Dissenters who declared that they were not members of the Church of England and that they had contributed to the congregation of which they were members. Davies withdrew his notice because of the other bills in the field.

55. *Hansard*, CXL (5 March 1856), 1862, 1860–1862; Great Britain, HLRO, *Reports on Public Petitions*. Session 1856, "57th Report . . . 25–29 July 1856," pp. 1301, 1302.

especially in populous towns where rates were all but forgotten, such bills as Packe's were unworkable; the clock could not be turned back. He announced that the government had formulated a church rate proposal that it would introduce in the form of amendments to Clay's bill. Grey's proposals recognized "immediate abolition" of rates in parishes where they had not existed for a certain length of time. "Prospective abolition" was possible in the future for any parish where the majority of ratepayers might desire it. In what the government hoped would be most cases, especially in rural parishes, the rate would continue as before, subject to the right of Dissenters to exempt themselves upon the simple declaration that they were not members of the established church.[56]

This position on rural parishes resembled the one Gladstone had held since 1854. Grey could not win the support of Gladstone and the other Anglo-Catholics, however, because he refused to limit the parochial rights of exempted Dissenters. He declared that the Church should continue to comprehend as many men as possible. It was just that latitudinarian tenet that men like Gladstone and Sir William Heathcote were striving most urgently to correct.[57] It was clear that important disagreement continued within the Whig cabinet as well. Lord John Russell, the colonial secretary, declared his opposition to the government amendments. He emphasized that the ancient obligation to maintain parish churches remained in force after the Braintree decision. Now that that obligation could be evaded the Church had a legitimate grievance, and Parliament ought to provide a substitute for lost revenues. Unlike his Whig colleagues, Russell was unwilling to modify that Erastian doctrine. Following the decision, he continued to search for reforms that would allow the continuation of the national provision for parochial churches, such as the Scottish practice of demanding that the heritors—holders of real property—maintain the churches.[58] It is clear that Russell was isolated in the cabinet. Palmer-

56. *Hansard*, CXL (5 March 1856), 1896-1903.

57. Ibid., 1903, 1904; "Memorandum," 1856, Gladstone Papers, Add. MS. 44746, fols. 53-60; Sir William Heathcote to Gladstone, 28 March 1856, Gladstone Papers, Add. MS. 44208, fol. 130.

58. *Hansard*, CXL (5 March 1856), 1912-1919; Sir David Dundas to Russell, 30 March 1856, Russell Papers, PRO 30/22 13 A, fols. 305, 306; ibid., 2 April 1856, PRO 30/22 13 B, fol. 4; enclosed letter on Scottish Church Rate Law, Professor G. Ross to Sir David Dundas, 30-31 March 1856, ibid., fols. 5-13; Dean of Ely, G. Peacock, to Russell, 14 May 1856, ibid., fol. 47.

ston dismissed his views, stating that Russell had been unable to propose a good alternative. In the division that followed, Clay's bill, subject to the promise of Grey's amendments, passed by a majority of 221 to 178 votes.[59]

The previous year's majority of twenty-eight had grown to forty-three. Only Russell among cabinet ministers had voted in opposition. Conservatives had generally voted against the measure, although considerable numbers were absent. It was noteworthy, too, that ten Peelites and three independent Conservatives, including Lord Stanley, had voted with the government. Equally important were the "no" votes of Anglo-Catholic Peelites: W. E. Gladstone, Sidney Herbert, R. J. Phillimore, and Roundell Palmer, as well as the Erastian Peelite Sir James Graham. As their 1853 votes in favor of Phillimore's exemption bill had shown, they favored reform.[60] But they could not accept freeing Dissenters from church rates without freeing the Church of Dissenters.

The government's amendments created consternation among Dissenters, who had long agreed that only complete abolition of the rate would satisfy their voluntaryist agenda. The *Nonconformist* was initially very reluctant to agree to the amendments, but it conceded later that Grey's proposals did allow Dissenters to retain their parochial rights and claims to church property. It advocated, with the Dissenting Deputies, that the amendments should be adopted under protest because they did secure practical abolition, and because acceptance was necessary to prevent the breakup of the anti–church rate coalition.[61]

Several weeks later, at the Liberation Society's fourth Triennial Conference, a militant minority protested that their leaders had betrayed the society's voluntaryist ideal. Edward Baines expressed the view of the leaders: they "feared that Sir William Clay would be separated from them if they rejected the amendments."[62] The Liberation Society faced an awkward predicament. Since committing itself to

59. *Hansard*, CXL (5 March 1856), 1919–1927.

60. Ibid., 1924–1927; *Nonconformist*, 12 March 1856, pp. 161, 162; Conacher, *Aberdeen Coalition*, app. A and B.

61. *Leeds Mercury*, 6 March 1856; 17 April 1856; *Patriot*, 24 March 1856, p. 146; *Nonconformist*, 19 March 1856, p. 177; Minutes of Dissenting Deputies, 7 March 1856, Guildhall MS. 3083, XIII, 94, 95; 21 April 1856, fol. 102; 28 April 1856, fols. 103, 104; Minutes of Liberation Society, 19 March 1856, GLRO A/LIB/2, fols. 252, 253; ibid., 29 March 1856, GLRO A/LIB/13, fols. 27, 28.

62. *Patriot*, 9 May 1856, p. 230; *Nonconformist*, 8 May 1856, pp. 310, 311.

the church rate conflict in 1853, it had in fact needed to relegate its premier goal of disestablishment to a lower position. When it decided to lead the opposition to church rates it had become leagued with groups for whom the church rate conflict was not meant as a means of disestablishment. Among these groups were moderate Dissenters and liberal Churchmen who viewed the rate as a practical evil. Those not committed to radical voluntaryism, for whom Clay had been a spokesman, now felt that Grey's amendments promised all they had fought for, and all Dissenters deserved.

Militant voluntaryists like the Reverend H. Toller of Market Harborough asserted that the executive's position "appeared to him inconsistent with the great principle of the Society, which was, that Government should not interfere in any way with the religious opinions of its subjects; whereas the Amendments it was proposed to accept recognised that right of interference by offering exemption from church-rate on profession of Dissent from the Establishment."[63] Toller's militant resolution actually said no more than what had been for years the standard fare in the Liberation Society and the ASCA. For more than a decade Dissenters had agreed that exemption would not suffice. They insisted on universal voluntaryism in religion. But now, although it was clear that under Grey's scheme the rate would remain in numerous rural parishes where Dissenters were few, the Liberation Society leadership argued that it was politically expedient to accept the government offer.

The chairman of the parliamentary subcommittee, Dr. C. J. Foster, admitted that he had actually been consulted by the government on the wording of the amendments. The strongest speech in favor of the executive was by Edward Miall. He admonished members of the Liberation Society not to flatter themselves to think that the majority for Clay's bill indicated acceptance of voluntaryism. He stated that Dissenters had so developed their strength in the constituencies "as to make it necessary for gentlemen to do what they don't like." But if the amendments were rejected by Dissenters the government would table the bill, and "every one of these half-hearted gentlemen" would blame unreasonable voluntaryists. Miall then called on the conference to make concessions so they would not be emasculated as a political force. Miall, one of the original militant voluntaryist founders of the Liberation Society, disclosed that he was urging that society to follow

63. *Patriot*, 9 May 1856, p. 230; *Nonconformist*, 16 April 1856, p. 249.

what David Thompson has called its "steady move from the extreme to the middle ground." It was not enough to adhere to their principles; they must also "maintain the character of practical men; men who can not only spout to the country, but sit down and settle things in the house."[64] Nearly one-third of the members were unconvinced and insisted that the amendments be rejected. But a two-thirds majority backed the Liberation Society's decision to acquiesce. It was a choice that the *Nonconformist* declared retrospectively in 1868 to have been the society's one misstep in its conduct of the church rate question: "an unprecedented and an unrepeated weakness."[65]

There were signs of continuing division within the Liberation Society following the Triennial Conference. On 10 May Herbert Skeats wrote a letter highly critical of the *Nonconformist* and of Miall, its editor. He said that some readers felt the paper had changed its tone, and that five years ago "the Editor would have unhesitatingly ranged himself with the minority" at the Triennial Conference.[66] Miall's reply was unusually bitter. If the *Nonconformist* had changed in tone, he said, a great deal of the blame rested on the paper's constituency. Miall bewailed the paltry financial support Dissenters had given—the number of readers greatly exceeded that of subscribers. Steps such as changing the paper's name, which might have brought commercial success, had been rejected at the request of readers. Miall's anger was compounded by the disappointment and weariness that he admitted to have found in his battle for voluntaryism: "Hope is a great element of strength. But hope snatched from before your eyes again and again just as you are stretching forth your hand to realise it, draws with it no inconsiderable amount of spontaneous energy."[67] Here was a rare glimpse into the psyche of an ambitious man. Miall long had tried to hold in tandem allegiance to the voluntary principle and the desire for political success. He had grown weary clutching both poles at once, in the face of the establishment's hostility and the imperfect support of his own Dissenting constituency. Miall was ready to accept a slight postponement of the full realization of the voluntaryist ideal now that it seemed that a small concession might resolve the church rate question

64. *Patriot*, 9 May 1856, p. 230; Thompson, "The Liberation Society," p. 214.

65. *Patriot*, 9 May 1856, p. 230; *Nonconformist*, 5 Aug. 1868, p. 775.

66. *Nonconformist*, 14 May 1856, p. 335; 2 Jan. 1856. Skeats also complained that from 1853 to 1856 Miall had been too busy as M.P. for Rochdale to devote himself to the *Nonconformist*.

67. Ibid., 14 May 1856, p. 333.

in terms constituting a considerable political achievement, and a degree of respectability.

Clay withdrew his bill on 27 June after the government had stalled for more than three months on going into committee, and after the chancellor of the exchequer denied that the government actually had adopted the bill's principle. The Liberation Society's executive committee adopted a statement releasing itself from its commitment to Grey's amendments. The *Liberator* claimed a victory over the government: "whether so intending or not, they have really given up the principle of church-rates, and have furnished us with a reason for rejecting in future a halting measure."[68] The government's failure to push an amended abolition bill through the Commons marked a turning point in the church rate question. The government had lost a golden opportunity to settle the question, in the Commons at least, in a way most favorable to the establishment principle. Acceptance of the bill, although relinquishing universal rates, might have retained church rates in large parts of country. Now, because the government had hesitated to retain a partial victory, abolitionists—their coalition intact—resolved to win a total one.

As was the usual pattern after a skirmish in Parliament, church rate abolitionists looked to the vestries. But this time, urged the *Liberator*, rather than using their strength in the parishes as an inducement to Parliament to settle the question, they should exterminate the church rate system themselves. Recent prorate petitions had demanded that rates not be abolished without the granting of an equivalent. The *Liberator* urged parish vestries to work so effectively that soon there would be "nothing left for which a substitute can be demanded."[69] As a sign of its determination to conduct a serious parochial church rate campaign, the Liberation Society agreed to publish new tracts and bills and to reprint old ones, in order to build a stock of ninety thousand bills and tracts at a cost of £95.

The Liberation Society also resolved to emulate another of the electoral tactics of the Anti-Corn-Law League. It intended to register potential electors favoring religious liberty in the counties and to purchase £50 rent charges in order to create more. The society was

68. *Hansard*, CXLII (27 June 1856), 2087–2090; *Nonconformist*, 2 July 1856, p. 473; Minutes of Dissenting Deputies, 6 June 1856, Guildhall MS. 3083, XIII, 106; 11 July 1856, fols. 107–108; Minutes of Liberation Society, 3 July 1856, GLRO A/LIB/2, fol. 290; *Liberator*, 1 Aug. 1856, p. 160.
69. *Liberator*, 1 Sept. 1856, p. 179.

guided by an elaborate analysis done by Dr. Foster, based on figures provided by the 1851 religious census, estimating the size, class, and location in each county of potential voluntaryist voters.[70] Foster's statistics suggested that there were twenty-five counties in which they might hope eventually to return religious liberty candidates. At present, however, these constituencies returned approximately fifty members, of whom thirty-two consistently voted against Dissenters. Foster's plan was simple: "As soon as all their friends were placed on the register, they would be able to overpower their opponents at the elections."[71]

On 30 June the Liberation Society took action on this recommendation and commissioned agents in eleven selected counties to register Dissenting voters. Agents were promised one shilling for each Dissenter placed on the register.[72] The parliamentary setback on the church rate question had induced the Liberation Society to develop political machinery that could increase voluntaryism as a political force and contribute to the formation of a reformed Liberal party.

The parliamentary fortunes of Clay's abolition bill and Grey's amendments also galvanized church rate defenders to act. In May 1856 the Committee of Laymen was formed, reflecting frustration with Palmerston's failure to introduce a compromise bill. Conservative Churchmen were beginning to believe that they must cease entrusting the Church's welfare to a friendly government. Anglican laymen had decided that the Liberation Society must be countered with their own pressure group. The Committee of Laymen was chronically underfunded. Its chief spokesman was the honorary secretary, John M. Knott. The committee consisted of Conservative M.P.s, including both High Churchmen and Evangelicals. Among the former were Spencer Walpole, Lord John Manners, and Lord Robert Cecil, the future marquess of Salisbury. Evangelical members included Sir John

70. Minutes of Liberation Society, 22 Sept. 1856, GLRO A/LIB/2, fols. 296–297; 20 Oct. 1856, fols. 303–305.

71. *Liberator*, January 1856, pp. 9–13, 19–20. The county constituencies targeted by Dr. Foster were: °Bedfordshire, Buckinghamshire, °Cambridgeshire, North Durham, °North Essex, South Essex, °West Gloucestershire, South Hampshire, Hertfordshire, Huntingdonshire, North Leicestershire, South Leicestershire, Middlesex, °East Norfolk, South Northhampton, °North and °South Northumberland, °East Somerset, °East and °West Suffolk, East Surrey, East Sussex, North Warwickshire, Isle of Wight, and °North Wiltshire. The counties chosen by the Liberation Society were those above marked with an asterisk. Minutes of Liberation Society, 30 June 1856, GLRO A/LIB/2, fols. 288, 289.

72. Minutes of Liberation Society, 30 June 1856, GLRO A/LIB/2, fols. 288, 289.

Pakington and Richard Spooner. The committee tended to defend a Protestant constitution in church and state, thus ensuring consistent coverage and support by the evangelical *Record*.[73]

The Committee of Laymen was appalled by Grey's amendments. It believed that church rate opponents had already been offered far too many concessions. The committee argued that in fact church rates were paid consistently in the vast majority of parishes and could be retained by some judicious reforms. It urged that redress be given to disgruntled Churchmen belonging to district churches. These members were obliged to support the parish mother church from which they derived no benefit. The committee hoped to isolate militant voluntaryists and to shift the discussion from church rates to the continued existence of the established church.[74]

VI

In 1857 the general election—which temporarily returned Palmerston to power—precluded what had become since the Braintree decision an annual parliamentary debate on Clay's Church Rate Abolition Bill. The government remained in a quandary over what seemed an insoluble church rate dilemma. On 9 February 1857 the home secretary, Sir George Grey, stated in reply to a query by Sir John Pakington that the government did not intend to introduce a church rate bill that session. He added that with sufficient time the government would have brought in a bill based on its 1856 amendments. Three days later Sir William Clay again brought in his abolition bill, this time entirely devoid of any provisions for a substitute.[75]

Church rate opponents were disillusioned with Palmerston. They were anxious for Clay's bill to continue its advance lest the cause of church rate abolition appear to regress. In a reversal of the previous year's policy the Liberation Society decided to promote petitioning

73. *Record*, 19 May 1856.
74. Ibid., Statement of the Past Proceedings in Parliament, with a View to the Abolition of Church Rates, and Reasons for an Immediate Settlement of the Question (London: Tyler and Reed Printers), in Gladstone Papers, Add. MS. 44796, 12 March 1849, fol. 72.
75. *Hansard*, CXLIV (9 Feb. 1857), 343, 344; 12 Feb. 1857, 576, 577.

again. The *Liberator* acknowledged that some of "our friends" believed that "we rested too much on our oars in 1856."[76]

Mobilization behind Clay's bill was only beginning when Palmerston's ministry fell on 3 March, on Richard Cobden's motion censuring Palmerston's support of the Canton bombardment. The Liberation Society's electoral and parliamentary subcommittees were temporarily amalgamated in the effort to return voluntaryist candidates in the impending general election. Miall's "Information for Electors" was widely circulated, and constituents were sent abstracts of the voting records of their M.P.s. The liberal *Daily News* urged that electors pledge to support church rate abolition as one of the tests of Liberal candidates—"a vague profession of Palmerstonianism (we must have the word for we have the thing) will not suffice."[77]

The Society of Friends also involved itself in the election. Quakers were urged to duplicate their efforts in the antislavery campaign by declining to vote for anyone supporting "that which they believe to be morally and religiously wrong." The Committee for Sufferings, which had initiated the appeal to the Friends on 6 February, had acted out of concern for the critical point that it believed Clay's bill had reached. The committee restated the principle that Quakers ought always to eschew political excitement and to pursue political objects such as church rate repeal "on Christian grounds, and in a Christian spirit. . . ."[78] It said also, however, that it feared that "in many districts, the danger has been rather of a want of zeal than of an excess of it, more particularly when the demand is small, and the mode of enforcing it has not been particularly oppressive."[79]

---

76. *Liberator*, 1 March 1857, p. 44; *Nonconformist*, 25 Feb. 1857, p. 141; letter to the editor by "An Ecclesiastical Reformer" in *Daily News*, 2 March 1857; Minutes of Liberation Society, 2 March 1857, GLRO A/LIB/2, fol. 332.

77. Machin, *Politics and the Churches*, pp. 280–282; *Daily News*, 10 March 1857; *Nonconformist*, 11 March 1857; Minutes of Liberation Society, 9 March 1857, GLRO A/LIB/2, fols. 333–335; 23 March 1857, fols. 338, 339; 6 April 1857, fol. 347. On the basis of Steele's analysis it appears that some in the Liberal party may have been more "Palmerstonian" than Palmerston himself. He appears to have favored a larger degree of parliamentary and ecclesiastical reform than some of his more cautious cabinet colleagues were prepared for; Steele, *Palmerston*, pp. 73–79.

78. Yearly Meeting, London (20–29 May 1857), in *Extracts from the Minutes and Proceedings of the Yearly Meeting of Friends, Held in London, 1857–1866* (London, n.d.), pp. 52, 53.

79. Ibid., p. 50. The Society of Friends had in fact begun to seek church rate repeal more actively since the Braintree decision. Petitions to that effect from the Meeting for

The *Record* was discomfited that a few active men in what it persisted in calling the Anti-State-Church Committee were able to force almost any candidate to pledge for abolition. It lamented that the Committee of Laymen was "much at a loss, for want of the proper support which Churchmen, if they were alive to the danger, could so easily render it."[80] On 27 March the Committee of Laymen advertised in the *Record* that funds were desperately needed during the present election campaign to counter the misinformation of the Liberation Society, which could count on £2,000 to £3,000 per annum. At that point the Committee of Laymen had garnered a mere £162.[81]

On the face of it, the *Record*'s foreboding was not fulfilled. Palmerston was returned to power, and the most prominent of the forty-eight Liberals who had helped to bring him down just weeks before, including Cobden, Bright, Miall, and Sir William Clay, lost their seats. The *Record* gloated that in the new House Dissenters "as a distinct *clique*, will scarcely be known."[82] The *Nonconformist* mourned: "we have suffered defeat—a mortifying and disastrous defeat."[83] In fact, as the sober calculations of Dr. Foster's electoral committee showed several days later, the Commons religious liberty party had actually grown in size by perhaps thirty-six M.P.s. The Liberation Society attributed the expansion to the unremitting work of the electoral committee. It was indeed striking that in the counties, where the committee had worked since July 1856, sixteen new religious liberty members were returned and only three lost.[84]

In the new Parliament the anti–church rate mantle of the fallen Clay

---

Sufferings, or the Yearly Meeting, had been sent to the Commons or to both Houses in 1836, 1838, 1841, 1850, 1853, 1854, and 1855. In 1854 the Meeting for Sufferings had also made a personal application to the government to seek abolition. Individual Quakers had often found ways to fulfil their church rate obligations while technically refusing to do so. See E. Isichei, *Victorian Quakers* (Oxford, 1970), pp. 135, 136, 148.

80. *Record*, 18 March 1857.

81. Ibid., 27 March 1857. Contributions were to be sent to one of several conservative publishers: F. and J. Rivington, Hatchard and Son, Selley, Jackson and Halliday, or to the Hoare family bank, one of whose proprietors, Henry Hoare, was beginning to take an important role in church defense.

82. Ibid., 1 April 1857; Machin, *Politics and the Churches*, p. 284.

83. *Nonconformist*, 1 April 1857, p. 250.

84. Minutes of Liberation Society, 6 April 1857, GLRO A/LIB/2, fols. 342–346. The electoral committee's schedule of "religious liberty" M.P.s gained, lost, and exchanged was: "I—re-elected, 40; II—comparative gains in new members: (1) English and Welsh boroughs—47, (2) English and Welsh counties—16, (3) Scotland—3; III—comparative losses: (1) English and Welsh boroughs—24, (2) English and

was assumed by J. S. Trelawny, like Clay an Anglican and a Liberal. Trelawny was far from being a voluntaryist. He simply believed the Church would prosper better without compulsory rates. He approached the Dissenting Deputies, rather than the more militant Liberation Society, about introducing an abolition bill. But after Palmerston stated in the Commons that the government planned to offer a bill that session, Trelawny withdrew his notice of a motion. Palmerston had been less than forthright about his government's readiness to legislate. Only ten days earlier the home secretary, Sir George Grey, had confided to Gladstone that he "almost despaired of a satisfactory solution."[85]

The cooperation of Trelawny and the Dissenting Deputies masked the deputies' declining power in relation to the Liberation Society. In the attempt to redress that situation the secretary, Hull Terrell, wrote to London Dissenting congregations to describe the work of the deputies, "showing the distinction between the objects and labours of the Deputies and the Liberation Society with a request for special contributions to the Deputies towards their extraordinary expenses."[86] Later in the year, 128 congregations in the metropolitan area not represented by a deputy were invited to send a representative. Only eight did so; only one congregation heeded the plea for a special subscription, sending £5. Faced with a dwindling income, the deputies could rely on little but their remaining respectability. Their subscription income declined from a meager £75 in 1856 to a mere £47 two years later. In comparison, contributions to the Liberation Society amounted to approximately £2,552 from May 1855 to May 1856.[87] The deputies' greatest efforts in 1857 were expended in negotiating for the remaining funds of another redundant Dissenting society, the Protestant Society for the Protection of Religious Liberty. Negotiations had begun in 1854 with its two remaining members following the death of John

---

Welsh counties—3, (3) Scotland—3; IV—Exchanges of M.P.s ecclesiastically similar: (1) English and Welsh boroughs—49, (2) English and Welsh counties—20, (3) Scotland—3." *Nonconformist*, 8 April 1857, p. 252; Minutes of Liberation Society, 13 April 1857, GLRO A/LIB/2, fol. 350; 20 April 1857, fols. 354, 355.

85. Minutes of Dissenting Deputies, 5 May 1857, Guildhall MS. 3083, XIII, 128, 129; 14 May 1857, fol. 131; *Hansard*, CXLV (4 June 1857), 1104; Sir George Grey to Gladstone, 25 May 1857, Gladstone Papers, Add. MS. 44162, fol. 181.

86. Minutes of Dissenting Deputies, 27 May 1857, Guildhall MS. 3083, XIII, 135.

87. Ibid., 2 Dec. 1857, fol. 150; 13 Jan. 1858, fol. 156; 23 Feb. 1858, fol. 163; 14 May 1857, fol. 132; 10 Feb. 1859, fol. 185; Minutes of Liberation Society, 4 April 1856, GLRO A/LIB/2, fol. 257; *Nonconformist*, 8 May 1856, p. 310.

Wilks, who had founded the society in 1811. On 17 November 1857, after protracted discussions, the Protestant Society's unencumbered balance of £800 was legally transferred to the deputies.[88]

The political prospects of church rate defenders waxed as those of the Dissenting Deputies were waning. The evidence contained in several parliamentary papers published in 1857 encouraged Churchmen to step up their defense of the rate. On 17 June 1857 a deputation from the Committee of Laymen met with Palmerston. The marquess of Blandford, the group's spokesman, explained that in its view much of the dissatisfaction with church rates emanated from Churchmen who belonged to district churches and continued to be called on to maintain the parish church as well as their own. Blandford believed that grievance was being defused by legislation that had enabled districts to become independent parishes.[89] Blandford's strongest case was a statistical one, based on the parliamentary church rate return initiated by Robert Cecil. On its authority he was able to assert that 95 percent of the nation's parishes continued to levy and collect church rates. The key question asked in the Cecil survey was whether church rates had been refused in the last fifteen years, and if so whether they had ceased being collected. The overwhelming reply was "no" or "never refused." Some parishes, such as Humbleton in Yorkshire, were more elaborate. A spokesman for it replied, "as far as can be ascertained, such an idea has never entered the heads of any of the parishioners."[90]

Conservative newspapers were jubilant. The *Morning Herald* gloated

88. Minutes of Dissenting Deputies, 3 March 1854, Guildhall MS. 3083, XII, 116, 117; 2 Feb. 1855, XIII, 44, 45; Minutes of Protestant Society, 11 Jan. 1855, 10 April 1855, Dr. Williams's Library, MS. 38.195; Minutes of Dissenting Deputies, 13 April 1855, Guildhall MS. 3083, XIII, 61; 13 July 1855, fol. 69; 26 Dec. 1856, fols. 112, 113; 9 Jan. 1857, fols. 116, 117, 121; 10 March 1857, fol. 127; 20 Nov. 1857, fols. 142–143.

89. *Record*, 19 June 1857. The legislation that enabled districts to become independent parishes was entitled "Formation, etc. of Parishes Bill." The bill had been introduced by the marquess of Blandford (later sixth duke of Marlborough), and it was given a first reading in the Commons on 15 May 1855 and royal assent on 29 July 1856. *Hansard*, CXXXVIII (15 May 1855), 660–662; ibid., CXLIII (29 July 1856), 1491.

90. *Record*, 19 June 1857; Great Britain, *Parliamentary Papers*, "Return of Parishes in Cities or Parliamentary Boroughs in England and Wales in which (during the last fifteen years) Church Rates have been Refused, and since that Refusal have Ceased to be Collected, etc.," 1856, XLVIII. 1, p. 194. The Cecil return has a wealth of information but lacks both a summary and abstract. No contemporary critics questioned whether the *figures* in the report actually indicated a 95 percent compliance rate.

that Parliament should judge "whether it will alter a law with which the majority is satisfied, merely because a small minority chooses to keep up a clamour against it."[91] The *Nonconformist* allowed "that *on the face of the return* there is some room for such exultation." But it went on to argue that in fact the return was extremely "untrustworthy." It showed that a considerable number of parishes no longer requesting rates were listed among those classified as not having refused them. The *Nonconformist* also pointed out that the return was misleading because it gave no indication of the great number of ratepayers opposing the rate in parishes where the majority continued to levy one. Neither did it account for the numbers of illegal rates that were either abandoned or only partially collected.[92] The return's deficiencies did not prevent Churchmen from capitalizing on it. Conservative M.P.s who were wavering on whether to capitulate to the forces of repeal were heartened by the "Cecil Report" to dig in their heels. Church rate defenses received an important fillip.

The cause of church rate defense was given an additional stimulus by the publication of another ambiguous parliamentary return. The body of the "Clay return" catalogued churchwardens' income from Easter 1853 to Easter 1854, distinguishing church rate receipts from other revenues. Initially few people read beyond the summary, which revealed only the undifferentiated total amount of funds received. That sum for England and Wales amounted to the surprisingly large figure of £482,562.[93]

The *Nonconformist* welcomed a third and more accurate return that had been requested by Sir George Grey on 28 May 1857. Grey's return distinguished church rates received from other sources of income for the years 1832, 1839, and 1854. This more refined barometer revealed that in 1854 church rate income for England and Wales was £314,659. Church rate proceeds had decreased by £48,744 since 1839. That was a relatively small drop over a fifteen-year period, however, compared to the dramatic decline of £83,092 recorded from 1832 to 1839. The relatively small decline measured from 1839 to 1854 reflected a lull in

91. *Morning Herald*, 5 Feb. 1857; *Record*, 9 Feb. 1857.
92. *Nonconformist*, 11 Feb. 1857, p. 101; 24 June 1857, p. 482; *Guardian*, 25 Feb. 1857, p. 153; *Liberator*, 1 May 1857, p. 85.
93. Great Britain, *Parliamentary Papers*, "Return of receipt and expenditure by Churchwardens and Chapelwardens in England and Wales, from Easter 1853 to Easter 1854," 1856, XLVIII, 223, p. 2. The return was requested by Sir William Clay in August 1854.

church rate contests during the time covered by the Braintree case. The *Nonconformist* regretted the lack of data reflecting the marked increase in church rate refusals since the Braintree decision. It did not remark on (nor did church papers notice) the remarkable information that in Wales church rate receipts actually increased from £11,332 in 1839 to £13,121 in 1854. The most recent figure was only marginally lower than the £13,918 collected in 1832.[94]

The publication by the Clay return of the amorphous figure of £482,562 as the total income received by churchwardens in 1854 had a riveting effect on the opinions of conservative Churchmen. The Grey return's lower and more exact church rate total came too late to rob the earlier figure of its influence. The conservative *Morning Herald* concluded on the basis of the larger sum: "This shows that it is not a trifling question which we have before us. *Half a million* of money per annum is not to be lightly surrendered."[95] The *Record* declared that the evidence of the Clay and Cecil returns had "utterly destroyed" the liberal conservative view made current by Lord Stanley and *The Times*—that "church-rates are virtually abolished." The *Record*'s position had been confirmed—there was no case "for a mere surrender."[96] The reaction of the staunchly establishmentarian *Record* was not surprising; the response of the Anglo-Catholic *Guardian* was more so. It concluded that "a much larger sum is now received than they have been commonly estimated to produce." The *Guardian* went on to say that Clay's own return "would prevent him from describing the loss of church rates as a mere nominal sacrifice" to be granted without

94. *Nonconformist*, 25 Feb. 1857, p. 141; 24 June 1857, pp. 481, 482; Great Britain, *Parliamentary Papers*, "Amount of Church Rates, etc. received and expended by Churchwardens in 1832, 1839, and 1854," 1857 (Sess. 2), XXXII, 27, pp. 28, 29. Several other points of significance in the church rate debate were also gleaned from this return. One piece of evidence quickly appropriated by the voluntaryists was that in 1854 receipts from "other sources" amounted to £170,195. Voluntaryists claimed that voluntary contributions amounted to more than half of the received church rate figure. They argued that the size of this figure indicated that voluntary contributions could easily replace church rates. They did not comment on the evidence that the amount received from other sources had actually declined from the £215,464 received in 1832. One area in which there had been a definite decline in the church rate burden was the amount of debt secured on church rates. Especially select vestries had tended to borrow money to repair and build churches on the security of church rates to be levied in the future. That practice was declining. In 1830 the debt stood at £535,236; it had fallen to £318,200 in 1854.

95. *Morning Herald*, 6 Feb. 1857.

96. *Record*, 9 Feb. 1857.

compensation.[97] As the *Guardian* leader reflected, some Anglo-Catholics who had long refused to maintain the rate for the sake of the church establishment became ready to defend the rate as an important element of church property.

As Churchmen began to mobilize, they found the Erastian Palmerston (to whom especially the *Record* and the Committee of Laymen had looked) increasingly undependable. The *Record* had learned from Palmerston's meeting with the Committee of Laymen on 17 June that a government bill was unlikely for the present session. The editor continued to believe that Palmerston would probably introduce a bill in 1858 if he remained in office. But John M. Knott, secretary of the Committee of Laymen, had already opened communication with Disraeli, who had recently spoken on church rates. Knott sent material that brought out "important constitutional considerations."[98] Knott had appealed wisely to what would later move Disraeli to lead his own crusade for the preservation of church rates.

VII

In 1858 Trelawny's church rate abolition bill received its largest second-reading majority to date. For the first time, despite an intervening change of government, it passed the third reading and was debated in the House of Lords. The increasing support for repeal reflected both the disunity of church rate defenders and the organizational skill of the Liberation Society. That society's success was not unclouded, however. Militant members—only a vocal minority in 1856—embarrassed an increasingly pragmatic leadership by managing to persuade the society's majority to take parliamentary action linking the hitherto abstract disestablishment question with church rate abolition. That development was eagerly exploited by the Committee of Laymen.

When the new parliamentary session opened in December 1857 the Liberation Society was already working to ensure that the legislative church rate lull of 1857 would not be repeated. The *Liberator* was

97. *Guardian*, 25 Feb. 1857, p. 153.

98. *Record*, 19 June 1857; John M. Knott to Disraeli, 13 June 1857, Hughenden Papers, B/XXI/K/165, LSE microfilm 131; Machin, *Politics and the Churches*, p. 285.

pleased that well-informed minorities in vestry contests increasingly were succeeding in blocking the payment of rates.[99]

On 27 January 1858 a deputation organized by the Liberation Society met with Palmerston. The delegation consisted of at least 140 delegates—fifty-six from the metropolis and eighty-four from the provinces, and included thirteen M.P.s. The invited delegates included several Dissenting Deputies who presented a memorial, although they hardly played the significant role suggested by their own minutes.[100] The deputation wished to accomplish two things: to counteract the credence that had been given to the proposition that 95 percent of the parishes contributed nearly £500,000 annually in church rates, and to determine whether the government would commit itself to introducing a church rate bill that session. If not, it was determined not to repeat last session's barrenness, to break its dependence on the government, and to introduce another private member's bill.[101]

After Palmerston declined to promise a government bill, the deputation retired to the Thatched House, St. James's. There it resolved to bring forward an independent bill for the "'total and uncompensated abolition of church rates.'" Three days later the Liberation Society executive committee agreed to take immediate steps to realize that commitment.[102] Before asking Sir J. S. Trelawny to reintroduce his abolition bill, the executive committee asked the radical T. S. Duncombe and then Milner Gibson whether they would bring in a bill whose abolition provision would not take effect until two or three years after the bill's enactment—an idea they had suggested to Palmerston.

99. *Liberator*, 1 Dec. 1857, pp. 208–209; the question of the right of cottage occupiers to vote on church rates in vestry was decided on 24 April 1858 by the Court of Queen's Bench in the case of Richardson v. Gladwin and others. The court ruled that in cases in which the owner rather than the occupier paid the poor rate, the owner, and not the occupier, had church rate obligations and rights. *Liberator*, 1 June 1858, pp. 112–113.

100. *Daily News*, 28 Jan. 1858; Minutes of Liberation Society, 27 Nov. 1857, GLRO A/LIB/2, minute 765 (the records had ceased using folio numbers); *Liberator*, 1 Feb. 1858, pp. 21–30; Minutes of Dissenting Deputies, 13 Jan. 1858, Guildhall MS. 3083, XIII, 157.

101. *Nonconformist*, 3 Feb. 1858, p. 81; *Liberator*, 1 Feb. 1858, pp. 32–33; *Daily News*, 28 Jan. 1858; "Committee of Laymen, Pamphlet no. 6," in Tait Papers, vol. CVIII, 18 Feb. 1858, fols. 220, 221; Agricola, *Church-Rate Repeal: A Letter to an Abolitionist* (London, 1858).

102. *Daily News*, 26 Jan. 1858; *Nonconformist*, 3 Feb. 1858, p. 81; Minutes of Liberation Society, 30 Jan. 1858, GLRO A/LIB/2, minute 783.

Both men declined, believing Trelawny could better take charge of the bill.[103]

Trelawny's bill, which came up for second reading on 17 February 1858, was simple. The first clause abolished the church rate in England and Wales. Several additional clauses excluded Scotland and Ireland from the bill's provisions and temporarily retained church rate obligations in those parishes that had mortgaged their rates. There was no provision for even a semblance of a substitute.[104]

Lord Robert Cecil, an influential member of the Committee of Laymen, led the opposition. Cecil argued strongly that they should not tamper with church rate law. He introduced his own summary of "his" parliamentary church rate return, which emphasized that no more than 5 percent of parishes refused to pay church rates.[105] Lord Stanley supported Trelawny and criticized the Cecil return, much as the Liberation Society had done. Earlier he had implored Disraeli privately to stop Pakington from attempting to convince Derby and the cabinet to seek a compromise, which Stanley believed to be hopeless.[106]

The home secretary, Sir George Grey, believed that perhaps 10 percent of parishes did not pay church rates, because they either refused or were not asked. He pointed out that these parishes represented approximately 40 percent of the population. Unlike Stanley, he did not back Trelawny's bill. Grey continued to support the principle of partial abolition and exemption, but he admitted that he had erred in 1856 in attempting to introduce that principle in amendments to Clay's bill rather than in a government bill. He would therefore vote against Trelawny's measure and introduce his own bill if Trelawny's were defeated. Grey's intention was not to be realized: Trelawny's bill passed by a vote of 214 to 160.[107] A bill prescribing simple abolition had passed by a majority of fifty-four votes—eleven more than Clay's bill, subject to Grey's amendments, had won in 1856.

The Liberation Society was delighted. The *Nonconformist* warned,

103. Minutes of Liberation Society, 30 Jan. 1858, GLRO A/LIB/2, minute 784; 5 Feb. 1858, minute 786; 19 Feb. 1858, minute 791. The minutes do not record any discussion about the decision to bypass Trelawny in favor of Milner Gibson and T. S. Duncombe.

104. *Hansard*, CXLVIII (17 Feb. 1858), 1165, 1554. The first reading of the bill had been unopposed on 11 February.

105. Ibid., 1560–1564; *Liberator*, 1 May 1858, pp. 92, 93.

106. *Hansard*, CXLVIII (17 Feb. 1858), 1571, 1572; Lord Stanley to Disraeli, 31 Jan. 1858, "Private," Hughenden Papers B/XX/S/631, LSE microfilm 131.

107. *Hansard*, CXLVIII (17 Feb. 1858), 1575–1585.

however, that the constituencies must keep up their pressure as the bill progressed through its remaining stages. It reminded its readers that many Liberals had voted for abolition only because they knew that their seats depended on fulfilling the pledges they had made; they would gladly desert the bill now if they believed they could do so with impunity.[108] The Committee of Laymen was dismayed that the debate had lasted only two hours. But the swiftness and size of the abolitionists' victory goaded the Committee of Laymen to "assume the initiative," as John Knott wrote to London's Erastian Bishop A. C. Tait, in defense of the Church's "rights and revenues . . . despite difficulties in uniting clergy and laity to defend the church."[109]

Cooperation of clergy and laymen was an essential feature of the program of the Committee of Laymen. London banker Henry Hoare had played a prominent role for a decade in advocating such cooperation while working for the revival of convocation.[110] From the beginning, the defense of the church rate was beset with internal conflict. Hoare, who described himself as "severely Protestant," was accused of being "a thoroughgoing Tractarian, if not a Romanizer" by some Evangelicals who mistrusted the Anglo-Catholic support of a revived convocation.[111] Some clergy, led by the Reverend John Sinclair, archbishop of Middlesex, were wary of giving laymen a role in rural deaneries.[112]

Despite its difficulties, the Committee of Laymen was greatly encouraged by the formation on 21 February of a Conservative administration headed by Lord Derby following Palmerston's defeat on the nineteenth. On the day of Palmerston's fall a Committee of Laymen deputation headed by the duke of Marlborough (formerly the marquess of Blandford) met with Derby, attempting to enlist his support to defeat Trelawny's bill. Marlborough relied on the now familiar Cecil return to state that less than 5 percent of parishes had refused to make church rates. Derby pledged to support the rate unless some compromise

108. Minutes of Liberation Society, 19 Feb. 1858, GLRO A/LIB/2, minute 791; *Nonconformist*, 24 Feb. 1858, p. 141.

109. Committee of Laymen (John Knott) to A. C. Tait, 27 Feb. 1858, Tait Papers, vol. VIII, 229.

110. Henry Hoare, *Hints on Lay Cooperation*, 7 vols. (London, 1866). Henry Hoare to A. C. Tait, 14 Jan. 1858, Tait Papers, CVIII, 83, 84; Machin, *Politics and the Churches*, p. 199.

111. Henry Hoare to A. C. Tait, 22 Feb, 1858, Tait Papers, CVIII, 222, 223.

112. John Sinclair, Archdeacon of Middlesex, to A. C. Tait, 25 Feb. 1858, "Private," Tait Papers, CVIII, 225–227.

could be found, although he did indicate that he was cognizant of objections to the accuracy of the Cecil return. Derby suggested the possibility of a voluntary commutation of the rate but expressed pessimism about the probability of agreement being reached on a compromise. He was clearly unhappy that it would fall to the House of Lords to stop Trelawny. The deputation had no such qualms, but the *Record* more insightfully realized that popular support for both the rate and the established church was essential in the long term.[113]

The church rate question "bitterly divided" Derby's cabinet. Sir John Pakington, the liberal Conservative first lord of the admiralty, apparently feared that Spencer Walpole, the traditionalist home secretary, might take too rigid a position. Pakington apologized for interfering in Walpole's department, explaining that he had for two or three years thought much about the topic, "which is, I fear, a rock ahead."[114]

Just how serious an obstruction the church rate had become was glimpsed when the motion was made, on 21 April 1858, to go into committee on the Trelawny bill. An acrimonious three-hour debate on the principle of the bill ensued before agreement could be reached. Sir Arthur Elton, Conservative M.P. for Bath, moved that the bill not take effect for three years. Lord Robert Cecil introduced an amendment that restricted abolition to cities and parliamentary or municipal boroughs. That principle intrigued Gladstone and Sir George Grey, but both amendments were withdrawn because of disapproval from both sides. Disraeli, the chancellor of the exchequer, showed interest in a plan put forth by C. W. Giles Puller, the Liberal M.P. for Hertfordshire, to commute the church rate from a personal tax to a fixed charge on property. Russell agreed, although he opposed Puller's proposal to extend the plan to help build new churches. At the conclusion of that day's sitting, a majority including Disraeli and Russell voted 346 to 104 to have the committee consider the main abolition clause of Trelawny's bill.[115]

Six days later, before the House again considered the Trelawny bill, it debated Puller's Church Rate Commutation Bill, which provided for

113. Committee of Laymen Circular in Tait Papers, Vol. CVIII, March 1858, fols. 235, 236; *Record*, 21 April 1858; 23 April 1858.

114. Angus Hawkins, *Parliament, Party, and the Art of Politics in Britain, 1855–1859* (Stanford, 1987), p. 132. Disraeli lamented (April 1858) that agreement was impossible even if " 'the Angel Gabriel himself were to draw up a Church Rates Bill' "; Sir John Pakington to Derby, 25 March 1858, "Private," Derby Papers 141/10, 25 March 1858.

115. *Hansard*, CXLIX (21 April 1858), 1424–1476.

an annual rent charge to be paid by owners of property. Sir George Cornewall Lewis argued persuasively that members must choose either a compromise or abolition; a new ecclesiastical charge on property was no longer politically possible. Russell, who had been swayed by Puller's proposal on the twenty-first, now agreed (as did Disraeli) that a new rent charge was no longer feasible. He was now ready to assent, with misgivings, to Grey's plan. But he continued to oppose abolition as contrary to the establishment principle.[116]

The most important opinion, however, was that of the home secretary, Spencer Walpole. He asserted that Sir George Cornewall Lewis's objection to a new charge on property was "unanswerable." Walpole then asked that Lewis urge Sir George Grey, who was absent, to bring in such a bill as he had alluded to in 1856. Although Walpole retained some reservations about Grey's plan, he believed Parliament "was now prepared to accept a compromise in this matter." The House apparently agreed. At least it would not introduce new ecclesiastical charges. It defeated Puller's bill by an overwhelming vote of 317 to 54.[117] All but a determined coterie of Conservatives agreed that the clock could not be set back; they had to choose between abolition and compromise. Some members of Derby's cabinet, like Pakington, wondered "whether or not it is *too late for any compromise?*"[118] A substantial number of M.P.s seemed to think it was. On 13 May the Commons sitting in committee passed Trelawny's "clause one," which affirmed abolition, by a vote of 277 to 153.[119]

On 8 June the motion for the third reading was debated. The most dramatic moment came when the Peelite Sir James Graham declared his conversion to abolition. The Erastian Graham remained committed to the establishment, but he hoped abolition might bring ecclesiastical concord. Graham was troubled by growing divisions between High and Low Church factions, which he believed posed a greater threat to the crown than the advance of democracy. His conversion angered High and Low—the *Guardian* and the *Record*. Walpole warned darkly that Graham's concession would not appease Dissenters who sought abolition to achieve the establishment's overthrow. The *Patriot*, on the

116. Ibid., 27 April 1858, 1860, 1861–1863.
117. Ibid., 1864; (27 April 1858), 1867–1869; *Record*, 28 April 1858.
118. Sir John Pakington to Disraeli, 31 March 1858, "Private," Hughenden Papers, B/XX/P/38, LSE microfilm 131.
119. *Hansard*, CL (13 May 1858), 570.

contrary, hailed Graham's turn as a sign "that in the mind of the shrewdest of political statesmen the hour is come."[120]

Trelawny's bill passed by 266 to 203 votes, a majority of sixty-four—nine more than on the second reading, with ninety-five more members present. Both sides had stepped up the pressure on M.P.s. An additional fifty-two votes had gone to the abolitionists and forty-three to the other side.[121]

Liberal and Dissenting newspapers rejoiced because an abolition bill had finally been pushed through a third reading. The *Patriot* praised the bill as the strongest statement yet made by the House of Commons for the voluntaryist principle.[122] The Committee of Laymen agreed with that assessment of the bill and roused Churchmen to action.[123] The Anglo-Catholic *Guardian*, which had long been loath to defend the establishment principle, now took a position similar to that of evangelical establishmentarians. It agreed that church rate abolition was "a stepping-stone to further aggressions." It was particularly upset that even after abolition "improper persons" could still interfere with the parochial affairs of Churchmen. It therefore urged Churchmen to flood the House of Lords with petitions.[124]

Dissenters were delighted that a church rate abolition bill would come before the Lords and sent more than eighteen hundred petitions on short notice.[125] The *Record* was horrified that the bill was unopposed on its first reading in the House of Lords on 10 June 1858, and that the occasion went unnoticed in the parliamentary report of *The Times*.[126] The motion for the second reading in the Lords was made by the Broad Church duke of Somerset. The duke of Marlborough, the Committee of Laymen's noble spokesman, quoted from the *Nonconformist* and the *Liberator* to show that voluntaryists had long tied church rate

120. *Patriot*, 11 June 1858, p. 380; Sir James Graham to Russell, 1 Sept. 1858, "Private," Russell Papers, PRO 30/22 13F, fols. 112, 113; *Record*, 9 June 1858; *Guardian*, 16 June 1858, p. 473; *Hansard*, CL (8 June 1858), 1718–1721.

121. *Hansard*, CL (8 June 1858), 1727–1731.

122. *Nonconformist*, 9 June 1858, p. 445; *Patriot*, 11 June 1858, p. 380; *Daily News*, 9 June 1858.

123. Address from the Committee of Laymen, signed by John M. Knott, in the *Record* (Supplement), 14 May 1858.

124. *Guardian*, 16 June 1858, p. 481.

125. *Nonconformist*, 9 June 1858, p. 467; Minutes of Dissenting Deputies, 16 June 1858, Guildhall MS. 3083, XIII, 172; 7 July 1858, fol. 174; Minutes of Liberation Society, 9 June 1858, GLRO A/LIB/1, minute 824; 6 July 1858, minute 831.

126. The *Record* was cited in the *Liberator*, 1 July 1858, p. 130.

abolition to disestablishment. Derby opposed the bill but suggested, as he had to the laymen's deputation earlier that year, that commutation might still be feasible. The bill was defeated by a vote of 213 to 62, including pairs and proxies.[127]

The *Liberator* was greatly heartened by the progress the abolition cause had made. Its leading opponents in the Lords had favored a compromise. The *Liberator* believed no cabinet could be formed that was committed to "stand by church-rates." It mocked the Committee of Laymen, which at this late date had secured a mere 490 meagerly signed petitions in the rate's defense.[128]

Following the vote in the Lords, the Liberation Society decided to make the rate's defense increasingly expensive for Churchmen by carrying opposition into parishes not yet affected by the church rate conflict. It further appointed two paid agents to increase the Liberation Society's visibility among Dissenters. This step was believed appropriate because the society was rising in public esteem.[129] The Liberation Society's parliamentary success with the church rate question seemed to cement its reputation among Dissenters.

In 1858, however, as in 1856 a militant faction was keen to tie the church rate question to disestablishment. The Liberation Society's church rate subcommittee discovered a novel way to link the two. It recommended that since rate defenders insisted on retaining rates to maintain churches as national edifices, churches should become truly national in the voluntaryist sense. A bill should be introduced to vest "the control of the Parish Churches in the Parish instead of in the Incumbents, with a view to the same being used for other purposes than the worship of the Episcopalian body exclusively. . . ."[130] After hesitation by the society the radical T. S. Duncombe was approached, who actually gave notice of such a bill on 15 August. The proposal elicited considerable disagreement in the Liberation Society. On 17 November, at a special meeting of the council, Miall—who was in a

127. *Hansard*, CLI (2 July 1858), 799–839; *Liberator*, 1 Aug. 1858, p. 139.

128. *Liberator*, 1 Aug. 1858, p. 146.

129. *Nonconformist*, 28 July 1858, p. 590; 13 Oct. 1858, pp. 809, 810; Minutes of Liberation Society, 6 July 1858, GLRO A/LIB/2, minute 833; 1 Feb. 1856–11 April 1856, fols. 235, 243, 247, 248, 254, 258, 259. Apparently parliamentary success, experienced particularly in 1858, was adding to the Liberation Society's respectability; two years before, at the fourth Triennial Conference of 1856, six men (four of them M.P.s) declined to chair the conference.

130. Minutes of Liberation Society, 16 July 1858, GLRO A/LIB/2, minute 836.

minority position in the church rate subcommittee—moved that no further action be taken on Duncombe's bill and that all efforts be devoted to obtaining repeal of church rates. Unlike the situation in 1856, the militants were in the majority and rejected Miall's amendment "after a lengthened discussion."[131] Several days later the canny Dr. C. J. Foster, who realized what damage such an action might have on the practical progress of the church rate cause, apparently convinced the executive to cancel the heads of Duncombe's bill "with a view to deliberation *de novo* and that no publicity be given to them," although the general principles might be discussed in public.[132] The publicity given to this maneuver, together with the Liberation Society's new aggressiveness in rural parishes, only underlined the fear of church defenders that the Liberation Society aimed to overthrow the Church. Not for the last time, the more pragmatic leadership was frustrated by the voluntaryist rhetoric of its followers.

VIII

Shortly after the opening of Parliament in 1859 there were five separate notices of motion to introduce church rate bills or resolutions on the order paper. The only important alternative to Trelawny's abolition measure was Spencer Walpole's government bill, the first official bill since 1837. In it the Conservatives made a momentous concession, relinquishing their insistence on the universality of church rates— something they had been unwilling to concede in 1856.

Within days of the introduction of Walpole's bill on 21 February 1859, there was still disagreement on it in the cabinet. As usual, Sir John Pakington wished to go further than Walpole, and he apparently convinced Derby of the utility of his position. In any event Walpole, who resigned as chancellor of the exchequer shortly after bringing in his bill, feared the political effect the bill might have. A month before he confided to Disraeli, who would soon fill his cabinet post: "Unless we take *some* clear line—what it may be I will not now discuss—I am confident it will do more to [shake] the government, in the estimation

131. Ibid., 26 Nov. 1858, minute 877; Machin, *Politics and the Churches*, p. 292.
132. Minutes of Liberation Society, 26 Nov. 1858, GLRO A/LIB/2, minute 879.

equally of friends and foes, than almost anything, which lies before us."[133]

The aim of Walpole's bill was to free Dissenters from church rate obligations. The plan proposed to establish a permanent substitute for the rate by encouraging landowners to commute the rate into a permanent rent charge on their lands, similar to the commutation of tithes. Tenants could deduct that charge from their rents, ensuring that predominantly Anglican landlords and not Dissenting tenants would pay the church rate equivalent. The permanent fund was to include funds derived from voluntary subscriptions that Walpole now recognized, on the basis of the most recent parliamentary return, to be a growing and dependable source of church income. Walpole defended a perpetual rent charge instead of the rate, "since church rates are a charge which has existed upon property from time immemorial. . . ." Walpole's use of that familiar phrase, dear to defenders of the rate, contradicted his earlier correct definition of the church rate as "a charge on persons in respect of property. . . ."[134] On that difference the legal decision in the Braintree case had turned.

The bill's last proviso ensured that in parishes where rates continued to be necessary Dissenters could exempt themselves by declaring that they conscientiously objected to paying church rates. An exemption did not disqualify them from any rights in their parish church except the right to vote on subsequent church rates.[135] The objections of Dissenters to "ticketing" themselves as such had been taken seriously. Unlike Grey's plan of 1856, this scheme did not require Dissenters to declare themselves Dissenters in order to be exempt. It was necessary only to declare a conscientious objection to paying church rates. Nothing prevented voluntaryist Anglicans or secularists from claiming the same.

There was widespread appreciation in the Commons of Walpole's conciliatory tone. But many, like Sir George Grey, wished to see the bill in print before committing themselves. Trelawny controverted Walpole's basic contention that the rate was a charge on property.

133. Walpole to Disraeli, 21 Jan. 1859, Hughenden Papers, B/XXI/W/42, LSE microfilm 131; Walpole to Derby, 16 Feb. 1859, "Private," Derby Papers 153/2.

134. *Hansard*, CLII (21 Feb. 1859), 610-629; Great Britain, *Parliamentary Papers*, "Return from each Parish within the several Archdeaconries in England and Wales, of amount expended during the last seven years for Church Purposes," 1859 (Sess. 1), XX.1—Supplementary Return, ibid., 469.

135. *Hansard*, CLII (21 Feb. 1859), 625.

Nevertheless, he left open the door to an agreement. He asked the government to cooperate by allowing his bill to be read "a second time, *pro forma*," on 23 February. In the meantime he would consult with his associates to see if Walpole's bill might be adapted to satisfy them, something he thought "quite possible."[136]

The hopes for conciliation were severely clouded by Russell's impassioned attack on Walpole's proposal. Because Walpole's bill did no more than Grey's 1856 amendments to shape a more exclusive church, and because Russell had in the previous session acceded to the principle of exempting Dissenters, it seems surprising that he should have opposed Walpole's bill so passionately. Russell declared that he took deep exception to exempting Dissenters because that necessarily impaired "the principle upon which an Established Church rests."[137] The contradiction may be partly resolved by noting the context within which Russell acted. Consistent with years of defending a comprehensive national church, Russell objected emotionally to Walpole's repeated assertions that those not benefiting from the Church should not be obliged to maintain it. Although Russell had come to accept the exemption of Dissenters as politically expedient, his reply to Walpole that justification of an establishment rested on the "the general benefit to the community at large" suggests that he had kept his Broad Church faith intact. Furthermore, only four months earlier Russell had written to the dean of Bristol that he supposed the church might be disestablished. He added, as one always concerned about the Church's civic importance, that England would then become a republic within ten years. Russell had vowed "to avert, or at all events postpone these results."[138]

Walpole, who was clearly pained by Russell's opposition, acknowledged the debt owed by establishmentarians to Russell's consistent opposition to church rate abolition. But he denied that exempting Dissenters implied a repudiation of the establishment principle. That principle was satisfied, claimed Walpole, when they had, "throughout the country, places of worship and ministers of religion to meet the spiritual wants of the people."[139] Furthermore exemption did not entail destruction of the establishment principle unless that principle meant

---

136. Ibid., 630–638.

137. Ibid., 648; Ellens, "Lord John Russell," p. 252.

138. Russell to dean of Bristol, 4 Oct. 1858, "copy," Russell Papers PRO/30/22 13f, fol. 129; *Hansard*, CLII (21 Feb. 1859), 648; Ellens, "Lord John Russell," pp. 252–253.

139. *Hansard*, CLII (21 Feb. 1859), 658.

"that it was right to enforce on those who did not belong to the Church a compulsory payment of the rate."[140] Sir Robert Inglis, who died four years earlier, might have sat dumbstruck had he been present to hear a Conservative chancellor of the exchequer utter such a statement. For several decades church rate defense had depended on the axiom that universal church rate obligations were but a financial implication of the establishment principle. Walpole's denial indicated the extent of the success that church rate opponents had already achieved; even staunchly conservative church defenders were on the way to voluntaryism.

Conservative and church papers generally supported Walpole's bill as an acceptable compromise. The establishmentarian *Record* welcomed it reservedly. It feared that the bill might attenuate the establishment principle but agreed that because of "the present embarrassed condition of the question, we are not disposed to lay undue stress upon any theoretical difficulty."[141] The *Guardian* was unhappy that exempted Dissenters, although precluded from voting on church rates, might continue "intermeddling in the management of funds" collected from Churchmen. But it did recommend acceptance of "a hard bargain for the Church."[142]

The door left open by Trelawny was slammed shut by "those with whom he acted." The Liberation Society decided that Walpole's bill should be "strenuously opposed." That opinion was shared by the Dissenting Deputies and the liberal and Dissenting press. Miall warned that if the plan were accepted "we surrender *our hold upon the property*, and, in principle, we surrender our local rights of control over the Church, as a State Establishment. . . ."[143]

The debate of 9 March 1859 on the second reading of Walpole's bill was led off by Trelawny, who, having been made quite aware of the feeling of his voluntaryist supporters, stated that he could not accept the measure: only total abolition "would meet the difficulties of the

140. Ibid.
141. *Standard*, 22 Feb. 1859. The editor stated Walpole's bill to be "one of the administrative triumphs of the Ministry"; *Record*, 23 Feb. 1859.
142. *Guardian*, 23 Feb. 1859.
143. *Nonconformist*, 2 March 1859, p. 161; Minutes of Liberation Society, 25 Feb. 1859, GLRO A/LIB/2, minute 910; Minutes of Dissenting Deputies, 4 March 1859, Guildhall MS. 3083, XIII, 188; *Nonconformist*, 2 March 1859, p. 163. The *Nonconformist* gave three pages of excerpts from London and provincial newspapers condemning Walpole's plan.

case."[144] Even more damaging to the bill's prospects was the opposition of Sir George Grey, the former home secretary. He claimed that if this bill succeeded, it would actually revive agitation in those areas where it had "been practically abolished."[145] Perhaps even more serious than the opposition of Whig leaders was the refusal to compromise by Conservative retentionists. The ultra-Protestant Henry Drummond voiced the traditional Tory language of a confessional state, declaring that he "would never consent to have the church rate tampered with or modified. They had now arrived at that point where the question was involved whether as a nation we would worship God or not."[146]

The House divided, defeating Walpole's bill by a vote of 254 to 171, a majority of eighty-three. The compromise attempt failed largely because it had not convinced the body of church rate defenders. Absent from the vote were the Whigs Sir George Cornewall Lewis and Palmerston, and the Conservatives Henry Drummond, Sir William Heathcote, Sidney Herbert, and Lord Robert Cecil. "No" votes were cast by the eminent Whigs Sir George Grey and Russell, and by the Peelite Sir James Graham in keeping with his reluctant conversion to abolition in 1858.[147]

On 16 March 1859 Trelawny brought in his postponed church rate abolition bill for a second reading at the behest of the Liberation Society.[148] The Peelite Sidney Herbert, who had not voted on the Walpole bill, indicated how little separated him from accepting abolition. He did not fear entrusting the Church to voluntary provision, but — true to the concerns that increasingly distinguished Anglo-Catholics from other Churchmen — he would not vote for abolition until voluntarily contributed church funds were protected from outside interference.[149]

The tone of the debate was set by A. J. Beresford Hope and Lord John Manners, both members of the Committee of Laymen. They condemned Trelawny's abolition bill as part of the malevolent design

144. *Hansard*, CLII (9 March 1859), 1567.
145. Ibid., 1577–1581.
146. Ibid., 1589.
147. Ibid., 1598–1601; (10 March 1859), 1653–1662.
148. *Hansard*, CLIII (16 March 1859), 175–197; Minutes of Liberation Society, 4 Feb. 1859, GLRO A/LIB/2, minute 904. The parliamentary subcommittee had recommended that if Trelawny required a summary of the facts of the church rate question for use in the Commons, the cost of printing should be borne by the Liberation Society.
149. *Hansard*, CLIII (16 March 1859), 189–191.

by the Liberation Society to demolish the Church. Their approach prefigured the more virulent tenor that church rate defense was about to take.[150] But for now their warnings had little effect. Trelawny's bill passed by a vote of 242 to 168. Its majority of seventy-four was the largest yet achieved in a full House.[151]

The abolitionists' victory tasted doubly sweet because of Walpole's failure only a week before. Numerous defenders of the rate had despaired of the possibility of a compromise; as yet unwilling to accept abolition, they had abstained from voting. Abstainers included Sir Bulwer Lytton in the cabinet and all the leading Whigs: Palmerston, Russell, Sir George Grey, and Sir George Cornewall Lewis. The *Liberator* concluded: "The Church-rate party is clearly beginning to break up."[152]

Before the abolitionists could press their advantage, they needed to fight a general election. Derby fell on 31 March 1859 over his government's Parliamentary Reform Bill. It was an election in which parliamentary reform and Italian liberation were the weightiest issues, and the ecclesiastical problems, church rates and Maynooth, played a secondary role. In the brief time available before the election, held in late April and early May, the Liberation Society's electoral subcommittee sent the voting records of M.P.s to constituents and found candidates for certain boroughs, although it was unable to place Miall. The voluntaryists made no numerical gain in the election, while the Conservatives won about thirty additional seats. Nevertheless, Derby's administration was defeated by a small majority on a no-confidence vote on 11 June, bringing Palmerston to power once again.[153]

Although the Liberation Society had not repeated its electoral success of 1857, it had continued to place its imprint on the House. Under its tutelage Dissenters had made support of Trelawny's abolition bill an election issue, insisting that "*a pledge* to support that bill should be a

150. Ibid., 175–183, 193, 194; Committee of Laymen, *Church Rates: The Present State of the Church Rate Question, with an Authentic Report of the Lords' Debate, July 8, 1858* (3d ed.; London, 1859); *Standard*, 17 March 1859.

151. *Hansard*, CLIII (16 March 1859), 195–197. A majority of seventy-four votes for abolition had been won in committee, but that was in a House with only 380 members present, on 13 May 1858.

152. *Liberator*, 1 April 1859, p. 58; *Daily News*, 16 March 1859.

153. Machin, *Politics and the Churches*, pp. 295, 296; Minutes of Liberation Society, 14 March 1859, GLRO A/LIB/2, minutes 925–929; 27 April 1859, minute 946; *Nonconformist*, 30 March 1859, p. 241.

sine qua non with every Liberal elector."[154] The most dramatic convert to abolition was one who had not deigned to pledge his vote to Dissenting constituents. Russell declared himself for repeal because he felt that the consistency of his position could no longer be maintained. In a speech on 2 May 1859 he acknowledged that he had long hoped a compromise could be found; both Sir George Grey and Spencer Walpole had tried and failed. Russell now declared, to the archbishop's regret, that it was no longer in the Church's interest to continue reliance on the rate.[155]

With the opening of the second parliamentary session of 1859, the Liberation Society once again made church rate abolition its priority. The *Nonconformist* thought it fitting to add: "If we place Church-rates first in our sessional programme, it is rather from the force of custom, and the present position of the question, than from any sense of its inherent importance."[156] Miall's explanation was a trifle disingenuous. In fact, church rates had been the Liberation Society's key to success. After it had broadened its platform in 1853 to become a more pragmatic extraparliamentary pressure group, the cause of church rate abolition had allowed it to become the spokesman for the mass of moderate as well as the minority of militant voluntaryist Dissenters. In moments of realism Miall acknowledged that repeal of church rates might be not so much a stepping-stone to disestablishment but rather the removal of the last major grievance to pose a threat to the continued establishment of the Church. Following the second reading of Trelawny's abolition bill, Miall reflected with resignation:

> in truth, the most intelligent Churchmen in the House of Commons are beginning to recognise the truth . . . that, in contending for the compulsory system, they have overlooked the real element of their strength. Public opinion is their stronghold. . . . In proportion as they yield to this power, they cut away our ground from under us. If an Established Church be rooted in the sympathies of the people, we shall have hard work to tear it up. But every part of the system which the public have unequivocally condemned, affords us a powerful

154. *Nonconformist*, 13 April 1859, p. 281.
155. Ibid., 4 May 1859, p. 341; J. B. Sumner to Russell, 5 April 1859, Russell Papers, PRO 30/22 13G, fols. 177, 178; *Liberator*, 1 May 1859, p. 77; see also Russell's election speech on 29 April, referred to in the *Daily News*, 30 April 1859.
156. *Nonconformist*, 15 June 1859, p. 473.

leverage for loosening the hold of the rest. Hence, in relation to our ultimate object, we are not anxious to abolish Church-rates. No doubt, we shall thereby gain a victory, but we shall lose a most effective weapon. . . .[157]

The Liberation Society would lose the cooperation of such Anglican Liberals as Trelawny, who sought church rate repeal as a means of strengthening the establishment. But even more important, Miall saw that if church rates were repealed it would be difficult for the Liberation Society to maintain its hold on the moral and financial backing of the Dissenting community. The Liberation Society's adoption of the anti–church rate campaign in 1853 had given it the enthusiastic support of broad sections of Dissent. The sense of unanimity fostered by common opposition to the church rate had fostered the illusion that Dissenters now shared with the Liberation Society a commitment to the militant voluntaryist goal of disestablishment and disendowment. In his darker moments Miall knew this to be a delusion.

In the meantime the Liberation Society prospered. The *Patriot* was satisfied that moderate Dissenters need not fear the society. By way of proof it reminded readers that Edward Baines had agreed to chair the Liberation Society's fifth Triennial Conference, although he had declined the same invitation three years before. The *Patriot* was pleased, too, that when younger militant men at the conference had wished to make the assertion of abstract principles a priority, they had been refuted by men like Miall who themselves had once wished to hear of nothing else.[158]

On 13 July 1859 Trelawny's bill came on for its second reading in the new parliamentary session. One feature of the debate was the degree to which Conservative M.P.s were beginning to broaden the issue to alert the House to the ulterior designs of the Liberation Society against the Church and its property.[159] As the approach of many

157. Ibid., 16 March 1859, p. 201. Jeffrey Cox argues that Nonconformists lost their raison d'être after gaining legal equality; *The English Churches in a Secular Society* (New York, 1982); see also J. F. Glaser, "English Nonconformity and the Decline of Liberalism," *American Historical Review*, 63 (1958), 361–362; Gerald Parsons, "From Dissenters to Free Churchmen: The Transitions of Victorian Nonconformity," in *Religion In Victorian Britain*, vol. I, *Traditions* (Manchester, 1988), pp. 113, 114.

158. *Patriot*, quoted in *Liberator*, 1 July 1859, p. 123.

159. Trelawny's bill had been given an unopposed first reading on 9 June 1859; *Hansard*, CLIV (9 June 1859), 190; 13 July 1859, 1129–1140; *Nonconformist*, 20 July 1859, p. 573.

Conservatives was hardening, the leading Whigs in the government announced that the logic of events had led them to capitulate to the claims of abolition. Apart from the failure of Walpole's compromise bill, the most persuasive factor influencing their decisions was the information contained in the latest parliamentary return that had earlier influenced Walpole to rely in part, at least, on the voluntary contributions of churchgoers.

The return, which the *Liberator* recognized as the most accurate to date, had been requested by Walpole and obtained with the enthusiastic aid of the Committee of Laymen. It revealed the income and expenditures of parish churches from 1851 to 1858. A total of 10,206 parishes had completed their returns. Of these, at least 80 percent continued to levy church rates. But the detailed information in the report offered rate defenders little comfort. Church rates had contributed an average income of £248,838 per year, a much smaller sum than had been claimed recently by the Committee of Laymen. But the truly surprising statistic in the return was that the average annual income from voluntary contributions amounted to £249,542. Even without legal change, parish churches now relied more on the voluntary system than on the rate. A breakdown of the source of income for the 10,206 parishes showed that a bare majority—5,291—still relied solely on church rates for the repair of their fabric and the provision of worship; 2,824 parishes depended on church rates supplemented by combinations of endowments, voluntary rates, or subscriptions; and 1,532 parishes were maintained entirely by some sort of voluntary contribution (559 parishes did not report their sources of income).[160]

The home secretary, Sir George Cornewall Lewis, who brought these figures before the House, underlined the fact that voluntary giving now exceeded church rate income. In light of the defeat of Walpole's bill he believed that a compromise was no longer possible, and he reluctantly declared himself in favor of the abolition bill. Palmerston also declared himself a "convert." He would no longer set his individual preference against the nation's public opinion, which had

160. *Liberator*, 1 March 1859, pp. 43, 44; Great Britain, *Parliamentary Papers*, "Return from each Parish within the several Archdeaconries in England and Wales, of amount expended during the last seven years for Church Purposes," 1859 (Sess. 1), XX.1—Supp. Return, ibid., 469. The supplement provided information on an additional 543 parishes. Both sets of figures were used in public debate. I have used the findings of the original return. Although the amounts were enlarged somewhat by the supplement, the ratios were unchanged.

been expressed "not only out of doors, but in Parliament." Russell, too, announced that he would vote for abolition. He maintained as before that church rates were entirely compatible with religious liberty, but he was convinced that continuing agitation would harm the Church. Consistent with his Broad Churchmanship, he also said that he preferred abolition to exemption of Dissenters. While the Church could remain established under the former, it became a sect with the latter. Russell castigated Disraeli, who decried the apostasy of Russell and Palmerston. Russell caustically inquired why Disraeli had been silent while they steadfastly defended the rate. The House then divided, passing Trelawny's bill by a vote of 263 to 193.[161]

The majority of seventy was treasured by the *Nonconformist*. It was only four less than in the previous vote on Trelawny's bill, despite the loss suffered by the Liberals in the election. The entire Liberal party (including a now predominantly voluntaryist Irish Catholic contingent) led by the cabinet ministers, now sought "abolition without compromise." Only two ministers still stood apart: Sidney Herbert was absent, and his fellow Peelite and now Chancellor of the Exchequer Gladstone voted against abolition.[162]

Following the division on the Trelawny bill Gladstone wrote a gloomy letter to Bishop Samuel Wilberforce: "We have just had a wretched division on Church Rates: 193 to 273—nearly the same majority as in the last Parliament notwithstanding the gain of 25 seats—50 votes to Lord Derby! I hope to see that cloud dispersed which hangs over Hawarden and your labours: but hope is largely

161. *Hansard*, CLIV (13 July 1859), 1161–1164, 1175–1186.
162. *Nonconformist*, 20 July 1859, p. 573; *Hansard*, CLIV (13 July 1859), 1158–1161, 1173. John Pope Hennessy, M.P. for King's County, Ireland, spoke as a Catholic in defense of retaining the church rate. He regretted that Catholic M.P.s seemed to be supporting abolition. In a similar vein, he was sorry that all Irish Catholic M.P.s but himself had voted for the second reading of the Endowed Schools Bill on 6 July. He argued that the diminution of religious distinctiveness, which the bill entailed, was in contravention of Catholic educational teaching. Hennessy urged that, especially in educational and religious subjects, Irish Catholics should not ally themselves with Protestant Dissenters. Hennessy's view was spurned by John Francis Maguire, the Irish Catholic M.P. for Dungarvan. Maguire claimed that all Irish Catholic M.P.s but Hennessy would vote for abolition. Protestant Dissenters had always backed Catholic claims for freedom, said Maguire, and he would now return that favor. Maguire did not share Hennessy's fear that voluntaryism and Catholicism were incompatible. He believed, rather, that the voluntary principle had worked well for the Catholic church in Ireland, and that it would do as much for the Protestant church in England.

mixed with fear."[163] Several days later Gladstone privately circulated another of his plans providing for church vestries free from the interference of nonratepayers in parishes where rates might be discontinued, and exemption for conscientious objectors where they were not. Gladstone feared that defenders would not succeed in saving the rate; yet he was also beginning to fear the results if they should succeed. On the day he had written to Wilberforce about church rates, he also discussed difficulties concerning the Divorce Act Amendment Bill. Two years earlier Gladstone had opposed passage of the bill, which allowed divorce in cases of adultery. Gladstone had acted to enforce the Anglo-Catholic emphasis on the inviolability of marriage. Gladstone now had second thoughts. He asked: "if we insist with all our might on making the church law the Law of the State, do we not justify those who when they get the upper hand insist upon making the State law the law of the Church. . . ."[164] Such concerns for the spiritual independence of the Church were moving Gladstone to accept a less consistent application of his old Tory church and state ideas. The same concerns would prepare him before long to consider relinquishing the church rate altogether if evidence were to suggest that the Church's spiritual mission might be better accomplished by the freedom that repeal could bring.

It was too late in the session to advance the church rate question in the Commons much further that year. T. Alcock withdrew his Voluntary Church Rate Commutation Bill, which seemed pointless in light of the recent majority for abolition. An amendment to Trelawny's bill prescribing commutation, introduced by the Conservative C. N. Newdegate, was defeated roundly in committee. On 28 July 1859 Trelawny withdrew his bill because it had become clear that insufficient time remained to complete its passage that session.[165]

The 1859 parliamentary session had been a momentous one for the church rate question. The Conservative party had relinquished its old

163. Gladstone to S. Wilberforce, 13 July 1859, Bishop Samuel Wilberforce MS. d. 36, fol. 185. Gladstone was mistaken about the number of votes in favor of Trelawny's bill; it was 263, not 273.

164. Ibid., fol. 184; Gladstone to R. J. Phillimore, 26 July 1859, "copy," Gladstone Papers, Add. MS. 44277, fol. 120; Memorandum: "Outline of a plan to alter the law of Church Rate," 26 July 1859, Gladstone Papers, Add. MS. 44748, fols. 116–119.

165. T. Alcock's Church Rates Commutation Bill was given the first reading on 5 July 1859; *Hansard*, CLIV (5 July 1859), 650; CLV (20 July 1850), 134, 135; (26 July 1859), 465–478; (29 July 1859), 671, 729.

insistence that the establishment principle required the enforcement of universal church rate obligations. Walpole's exemption provision was actually more generous to Dissenters than Grey's 1856 amendments had been. But the bill had foundered on the antagonism of the Whigs and disagreements among Churchmen. The victory of Trelawny's bill — and even more, the conversion of the Whigs to abolition — indicated that a new phase in the church rate question was about to ensue.

IX

The success of the Trelawny bill on 13 July 1859, and the desertion of the church rate cause by the Whigs, was a cruel blow to church rate defenders. Anglo-Catholics and Erastian Evangelicals began to defend church and rate in earnest, but their different aims and motives contributed to the movement's lack of cohesion.

Two elements colored the church defense movement in late 1859. First, Churchmen felt at least temporarily estranged from politicians. Anglo-Catholics felt that Derby's government had not done enough; Evangelicals were horrified by the volte-face of Palmerston and Russell. Churchmen of all schools resolved to depend more on their own efforts as the Dissenters had done in the 1840s. Second, the church rate battle was fought as one aspect of Church defense. For Anglo-Catholics this meant guarding the freedom and integrity of a divine institution; for Evangelicals it entailed saving the establishment. They agreed only that the Liberation Society was the enemy.

Conservative papers were bitter about the apostasy of Palmerston and Russell. They found it galling that both men continued to see church rates as just, but that each had capitulated before what he believed to be public opinion. The *Standard*, unkindly alluding to their ages, charged them with "senile ambition." It was also critical of Gladstone, who as chancellor of the exchequer had said nothing in defense of the rate — unlike the case in 1854 when, in the same position, he had defended it vigorously.[166]

The *Guardian*'s criticism of the Trelawny bill illustrated the Anglo-Catholic motivation for joining a church defense movement. The

166. *Standard*, 15 July 1859; *Record*, 15 July 1859.

Guardian had for years supported numerous church rate reforms, such as those proposed by Phillimore and Gladstone, involving the exemption of Dissenters and the concomitant exclusion of nonratepayers from the vestry. It was appalled by the passage of Trelawny's bill not because it repealed church rates, but because it did not compensate the Church by barring Dissenters from intruding in the affairs of "the divine institution."[167] During the preceding decade Anglo-Catholics came to fear increasingly the role in church affairs of a government unfriendly to them. As Evangelicals became ever stauncher establishmentarians under Palmerston's friendly eye, Anglo-Catholics emphasized church self-government—in convocation on the national level and in exclusive church vestries on the local level.

It was the misfortune of church defenders that differences among Churchmen often seemed as intractable as those separating them from the church's enemies. During the election campaign the *Guardian* bemoaned the lack of a coherent church defense policy. The *Guardian* itself, however, failed to allude to a major election address on the church rate question issued by the Committee of Laymen in the pages of its rival, the *Record*.[168]

In spite of serious obstacles, the momentum to organize church defenders was growing. That tendency had become marked after the double shock in March of Walpole's defeat and Trelawny's triumph. On 20 May William Hale, the redoubtable archdeacon of London, declared to his clergy that "the time had come when a decided stand should be made in support of church-rates. . . ."[169] On 22 June the lower house of convocation took up the church rate question. Hale presented a gravamen that charged the House of Commons with acting illegally in proposing to alter the law of church rates without consulting the clergy assembled in convocation. There was considerable difference of opinion about whether to modify church rate law or to keep it just as it was.[170] After agreeing to send an address to the upper house of convocation, both houses agreed on the twenty-fourth to appeal to the queen to safeguard the church rate.[171]

167. *Guardian*, 20 July 1859, p. 625.
168. Ibid., 27 April 1859, p. 373; *Record*, 23 April 1859.
169. *Record*, 23 May 1859; William Hale, *The Abolition of Church Rates: A Measure Preparative to the Overthrow of the Established Church as the National Religion* (London, 1859).
170. *Record*, 24 June 1859.
171. *Nonconformist*, 1 June 1859, p. 429.

As the momentum of church rate defense increased in the early summer of 1859, the people and institutions setting the tone—William Hale, Henry Hoare, the Committee of Laymen, and the evangelical *Record*—insisted that the battle must be fought for the defense of the Church, whose destruction was the ultimate aim of those attacking the rate. The *Record* declared that they must attack the Liberation Society and the gospel of voluntaryism: "The question at issue after all is, not church-rates, but the national acknowledgment of religious obligation, of which they are but one of the forms and expressions. Churchmen will, sooner or later, have to make a stand on this question, and they may as well make it upon church-rates as anything else."[172] The assumption made by the *Record* and shared by numerous establishmentarians was that the origins of church rate opposition lay not in deep disaffection with church rates, but in hostility to the church establishment fomented by the Liberation Society. The *Record* hoped that "some means will be adopted for exposing thoroughly the tactics and proceedings of this Society."[173]

The method adopted to discredit the Liberation Society was the establishment on 7 July 1859 of a House of Lords select committee to investigate the church rate question. The committee was requested by the duke of Marlborough, the leading aristocratic spokesman for the Committee of Laymen. In moving the formation of the select committee, Marlborough argued that the 1851 Commons committee chaired by J. S. Trelawny had been one-sided and had not fairly represented the views of Churchmen. He believed that acknowledged grievances could be removed by careful legislation without destroying the church rate principle. Marlborough argued that the committee should also investigate the work and aims of the Liberation Society. He called the attention of the Lords to a motion at the latest Liberation Society Triennial Conference that called for the question of disestablishment to be brought before the legislature. Miall had replied, said Marlborough, that his friend wished "to take up a faggot bound—we wish to take it up stick by stick." The Liberation Society's official policy, warned Marlborough, was to dislodge piecemeal the individual sticks of church rates, university tests, endowed schools, and churchyards to achieve the ultimate goal of disestablishing the Church.[174] Earl Granville agreed

172. *Record*, 22 June 1859.
173. Ibid., 6 July 1859.
174. *Hansard*, CLIV (4 July 1859), 568–575.

reluctantly to form a committee because Marlborough's motion clearly had wide support, but he felt they already had a surfeit of information and blue books and no shortage of schemes to set the question at rest.[175]

The findings of the select committee would play a key role in helping to mobilize the growing church defense movement, whose impact we will examine in the following chapter. But neither the nature of the findings nor the importance establishmentarians intended to ascribe to them were ever in doubt. The select committee was to be dominated by the duke of Marlborough. As the leading representative of the Committee of Laymen, he would ensure that the committee would reveal that the Liberation Society was seeking church rate abolition as a means of disestablishing the Church. In the middle of the general election campaign, ten weeks before Marlborough was even to request the formation of the select committee, the Committee of Laymen was sufficiently confident that the findings of Marlborough's committee would strengthen its position that it instructed Churchmen to question candidates "whether they will fairly consider and give due weight to the Report about to emanate, in due time, from the Select Committee about to be moved for in the House of Lords, by His Grace the Duke of Marlborough, on the opening of the new Parliament."[176] The issue in the church rate question was about to become the Liberation Society and its ulterior aims.

175. Ibid., 585. The House of Lords select committee was to be chaired by the duke of Marlborough and included the archbishop of Canterbury, Earl Derby, Earl Granville, Lord Eversley, the marquess of Salisbury, Earl Stanhope, Lord Stanley of Alderley, and Lord Monteagle.
176. *Record*, 23 April 1859.

IV

Church Defense

Opportunities Missed, 1859–1865

A new phase in the church rate question began in 1859 with the publication of the House of Lords select committee report on church rates. This report gave the authoritative exposé of the Liberation Society that the Committee of Laymen had sought. It revealed that the society pursued church rate abolition as a means of effecting the separation of church and state. The report put the Liberation Society on the defensive, gave a great impetus to the Church defense movement, and contributed to declining parliamentary votes for church rate abolition.

After 1860 the real conflict concerning the church rate question was no longer between the Church and Dissent,[1] or between the Church and Liberation Society but between Churchman and Churchman. Moderate clergy and Conservative M.P.s wished to utilize a climate that temporarily favored the Church to settle the question by compro-

---

1. By the early 1860s Protestant Nonconformists began to be designated as "Nonconformists" as frequently as "Dissenters." In this chapter both appellations will be used interchangeably, as they were during the period covered here. By 1865 the designation of "Nonconformist" became more common—a practice that is reflected toward the end of this chapter.

mise. Others, who had no sense that there was a tide in the affairs of men and who were encouraged by Disraeli's political opportunism, were intoxicated by the momentum of church defense to believe that they could afford to reject all compromise. By 1861 the success of the church defense movement left the Liberation Society discredited and on the political periphery. Sir J. S. Trelawny, the Anglican parliamentary spokesman for church rate abolitionists, and other moderate Liberals who were no longer awed by the Liberation Society's parliamentary and electoral pressure, negotiated with progressive Conservatives in search of a church rate compromise. The possibility of finding one between 1860 and 1865 no longer depended on the will of Dissent or the Liberation Society. The question had become whether Churchmen and Conservatives could agree among themselves on an alternative to church rate abolition.

II

The publication in August 1859 of the interim report, and the final report issued in February 1860 of the duke of Marlborough's House of Lords select committee on church rates, contained both innovative proposals for church rate reform and "revelations" concerning the "ulterior aims" of the Liberation Society that gave a remarkable impetus to a burgeoning church defense movement.[2] The evidence given to Marlborough's committee by witnesses, who had been as carefully selected to favor the maintenance of the church rate as deponents before Trelawny's Commons committee in 1851 could be counted on to seek its abolition, suggested that the desire for abolition was actually held only by a small segment of political Nonconformists. The report triumphantly declared that the entire abolition of church rates was opposed by most Churchmen and not universally demanded by Dissenters—"and especially not by that large and influential body of Wesleyan Methodists."[3]

2. Great Britain, *Parliamentary Papers*, "House of Commons Report of Select Committee of House of Lords on Church Rates," 1860, XXII. 159; "Report of Select Committee of House of Lords on Church Rates," 1859 (Sess. 2), XVII. 1. 217.

3. *Parliamentary Papers*, 1860, XXII. 159, p. 162; James Murray Dale, *Church Rates: The Present Position of the Question, with Reasons Against Their Abolition* (London, 1860), pp. 3–15.

The key reform proposed by the select committee was an exemption clause that even Miall admitted to be more liberal than expected. The proposal, suggested by T.H.S. Sotheron Estcourt, who had served as home secretary in Derby's cabinet, broke new ground in that an exemption could be claimed by any person desiring it.[4] Establishmentarians protested that exemption abandoned the principle of an established church, but many Anglo-Catholics believed the solution to be in the best spiritual interests of the Church.[5]

The most explosive evidence in the report was given by two prominent members of the Liberation Society executive: Samuel Morley and Dr. C. J. Foster. Under the adroit questioning of the duke of Marlborough and A. C. Tait, the bishop of London, the Committee of Laymen obtained the ammunition they had sought with the formation of the committee. Morley's and Foster's own words openly tied church rate abolition to the further confiscation of church property. Foster frankly answered Marlborough's query about the objects of the Liberation Society. They wished to "separate the Church from the State. We wish to take away all funds and property with which the State has endowed any religious denomination whatever."[6] Both Morley and Foster agreed that Marlborough correctly observed that it was "in furtherance of that object" that the Liberation Society had taken an active part in the church rate question.[7]

Foster's open admission of the Liberation Society's disendowment demand (a policy that Morley personally disliked) catapulted the Liberation Society into the fire of church defense. Miall told a meeting of church defenders in Bristol in February 1860 that his movement had not intended seriously to seek disendowment of the Church in England and Wales until some time in the distant future.[8] It was a topic that Miall and the Liberation Society executive had not publicized for several years for fear of jeopardizing the church rate abolition cause. They had certainly not reissued early anti–state church pamphlets such as Miall's 1848 publication that proposed the secularization of tithes

4. *Parliamentary Papers*, 1859 (Sess. 2) XVII. 1. 217, answer 943; *Nonconformist*, 7 March 1860, p. 181.

5. John M. Knott to Bishop Tait, 17 March 1860, Tait Papers, fols. 350–352; *Guardian*, 14 March 1860, p. 241.

6. *Parliamentary Papers*, 1859 (Sess. 2), XVII. 1. 217, answer 1507.

7. Ibid., answer 773; 1513.

8. Edward Miall, *The "Liberation Society" and Church Property: Two Lectures Delivered . . . in the Broadmead Rooms, Bristol, Feb. 8th and 10th, 1860* (Bristol, 1860).

and all church property except the result of personal bequests and audaciously recommended that parish churches be given to the ratepayers and cathedrals be maintained publicly for nonecclesiastical functions.[9]

The Morley and Foster evidence became a rallying point for establishmentarians, who now had proof that church rate abolitionists threatened the "constitution in Church and State."[10] But Anglo-Catholics, who denied that the Church depended on an establishment, were also alarmed. The *Guardian* affirmed that "the endowments of the Church are a sacred trust; which may not be lightly surrendered. . . ." It was willing to grant church rate concessions to quiet an agitation, but not if these would be taken as merely "a stepping stone to further aggressions."[11] Churchmen of all schools were now prepared to do battle for the Church.

III

Within months of the publication of the first installment of the Lords select committee report, archdeacons, bishops, and (most important) cooperative ventures of clergy and laity were organizing to preserve the church rate, attack the Liberation Society, and defend the Church. On 18 October 1859 the archdeacons of both ecclesiastical provinces met in a London conference chaired by London's inveterate Archdeacon William Hale.[12] They issued a unanimous declaration to Parliament pressing to maintain the rate, which they held to be an integral part of the national church. A petition to that effect was signed by sixty-four of the seventy archdeacons.[13]

The archdeacons appeared to disdain compromise. G. A. Denison,

9. Edward Miall, *What Is the Separation of Church and State?* (London, 1848); J. M. Hare, "The Precise Meaning of the Phrase 'The Separation of the Church from the State,' " in *Proceedings of the First Anti-State-Church Conference*; Edward Miall, *Title Deeds of the Church of England to Her Parochial Endowments* (London, 1862); John Pulman, *The Anti-State-Church Association and the Anti-Church-Rate League, Unmasked* (London, 1864).

10. *Morning Post*, 26 Sept. 1859.

11. *Guardian*, 25 Oct. 1859, p. 909.

12. *Daily News*, 1 Nov. 1859.

13. *Nonconformist*, 2 Nov. 1859, p. 874; "The Visitation Charge of the Ven. G. A. Denison, Archdeacon of Taunton, 1860," in Hoare, *Hints*, IV, 1161, 1162.

the redoubtable establishmentarian archdeacon of Taunton, censured the Lords committee for recommending the exemption of Dissenters, a policy that he scorned as surrendering the principle of an established church.[14] Denison asserted furthermore that they must emulate the tactics used by Dissenters. Petitioning would not suffice. They could not save the rate unless "they made it a hustings' question."[15]

On 23 November the bishops had gathered at the primate's behest. Unlike the archdeacons, the bishops left open the possibility of a future exemption of Dissenters from church rate obligations, having been convinced earlier by Spencer Walpole that only such a concession could ultimately resolve the question.[16] That moderate opinion was rejected by spokesmen for the Committee of Laymen who had been admitted to the bishops' meeting. Sir John Pakington and J. C. Colquhoun declared that the revelation of the Lords committee report had persuaded them to abandon their earlier willingness to grant concessions. They now repudiated compromise.[17] The same hardening of attitude occurred in other Churchmen. At a 9 January 1860 meeting at Newton Abbot, S. T. Kekewich, M.P. for South Devon, said that although he reluctantly had voted for Walpole's bill last session, the question was entirely different now. On 24 February the bishop of Ripon told a meeting of church defenders that he had undergone a similar conversion.[18] "A Churchman" wrote in *Keene's Bath Journal* that "The Puseyites . . . who a short time since advocated the separation of Church and state, are now all alive for the continuance of its union. . . ."[19]

The church defense movement was particularly strong in the west of England, although it was hardly confined to that locality as Miall claimed. Nevertheless, organized church defense was well rooted there. During the 1840s, when Churchmen were fairly somnolent, church defense and lay associations in Bath and Shepton Mallet had often

14. Ibid., pp. 1157–1168; G. A. Denison, *Church Rate: What Ought Parliament to Do?* (London, 1861), pp. 11–13; Denison, *Church Rate: A National Trust* (London, 1861).

15. *Nonconformist*, 22 Nov. 1859, p. 935.

16. "23rd Nov. 1859, record of meeting of bishops, in Tait Papers, CXII, "Private and confidential," fols. 275 a. 12, 275 a. 17; *John Bull*, 28 Nov. 1859, p. 761; Spencer Walpole to Derby, 26 Nov. 1859, "Private," Derby Papers 153/1A, 28 Nov. 1859.

17. *John Bull*, 28 Nov. 1859, p. 761. Other members of the Committee of Laymen present at the bishops' meeting were H. R. Merewether, Lord Robert Montagu, Loftus T. Wigram, and J. M. Knott.

18. *Western Times*, 14 Jan. 1860; *Nonconformist*, 1 Feb. 1860, p. 83.

19. *Keene's Bath Journal*, 28 Jan. 1860.

petitioned alone against church rate abolition.[20] By the spring of 1860 church defense had taken such hold that William Hale was quite optimistic about the Church's prospects. Hale's hopefulness was inspired especially by the new willingness of laymen to work with the clergy. The credit for that he ascribed to the eminent London banker, Henry Hoare.[21] Hoare's theme for decades had been lay cooperation with the clergy. His efforts had been rewarded by the formation of church unions and the revival of convocation. In 1856 he had played a prominent role in organizing the Committee of Laymen.

That committee had endorsed Hoare's scheme of combining clergy and laity in associations based in rural deaneries. On 8 July 1859 the Church Institution grew out of this collaboration. Initially there was friction between the two societies. The *Record* mistrusted the Church Institution for a time, and Miall mocked Churchmen for having High and Low Church institutions even for defense purposes. But Hoare was an ideal bridge builder. He had been raised as an Evangelical and had adopted High Church views after reading the *Tracts for the Times*. Hoare resigned from the Committee of Laymen in March 1862 after failing to unite the societies. But cordial relations were fostered by Hoare, and by the following year John Knott, the laymen's secretary, joined the executive committee of the Church Institution.[22] The institution grew in strength as the Committee of Laymen declined, perhaps

20. *Nonconformist*, 1 Feb. 1860, p. 82; Great Britain, HLRO, *General Index to Public Petitions*, 1833–1852, pp. 135–139. On occasion church defenders could be quite overcome by their own enthusiasm. At a meeting at Kingsbridge, Devon, on 18 January 1860, chaired by Archdeacon John Downall, a clergyman named Cole declared: "Church-rates and tithes are the two pillars that support the Church. Samson is endeavouring to pull them down, he has got his hand to one pillar, and if that falls the other will follow, and down will come the Establishment altogether." The eager advocate of the Church's safety was interrupted by an embarrassed chairman: "I must call you to order, sir; your illustration is a very bad one, for it has *made us out to be the Philistines*." Roars of laughter from the clerical audience followed Downall's remonstration. *Western Times*, 21 Jan. 1860, p. 7; and carried in the *Nonconformist*, 25 Jan. 1860, p. 62.

21. William Hale, *An Address to the Clergy of the Archdeaconry of London, at the Annual Visitation, May 23, 1860, on the Subject of Church Rates* (London, 1860), pp. 3–5.

22. J. B. Sweet, *A Memoir of the Late Henry Hoare* (London, 1869), p. 91; E. A. Gilchrist, *Henry Hoare: The Layman Who Restored England's Synods* (London, 1930), p. 4; *John Bull*, 28 Nov. 1859, pp. 761–762; 3 Dec. 1859, pp. 774, 777; *Nonconformist*, 14 Dec. 1859; Hoare, *Hints*, III, 811–815; 1058, 1059; IV, 1148; V, 1453; M.J.D. Roberts, "Pressure-Group Politics and the Church of England: The Church Defence Institution, 1859–1896," *Journal of Ecclesiastical History*, vol. 35, no. 4 (1984), 560–582.

because the former was more successful in fostering clerical and lay cooperation.

The Church Institution was a national society based on the parochial system. It consisted of laymen who were ultimately responsible to the clergy. Each parochial incumbent was to appoint a "lay consultee." These were to meet annually to choose an executive committee of twenty-nine. By September 1859, 250 consultees had been appointed. Rural deans were to send a lay agent to London through whom they could consult with the executive. Hoare served as treasurer and G. Howels Davies as secretary.[23] Great care was taken to receive episcopal sanction for the society's constitution. Communications from the Church Institution to concerned Churchmen consisted initially of published installments of Hoare's correspondence on church defense matters, which were later bound to become his *Hints on Lay Cooperation*. From 5 March 1862 the *Church Institution Circular* was published to supplement this ad hoc arrangement.[24] On 25 May 1860 Hoare formed the Association of Past and Present Churchwardens as part of his untiring effort to rouse the Church "in its local divisions." As he wrote to the bishop of Rochester, it was his intention "to imitate the Dissenters, whose strength is in the Laity."[25]

IV

Church rate defense during the half-year preceding the opening of the parliamentary session of 1860 had a telling effect. The revelations of the House of Lords select committee came to dominate church rate debate in the Commons, as it had in the country. As a result, the majorities for Trelawny's Church Rates Abolition Bill began to decline.

The Liberation Society again viewed the church rate issue as the leading question in early 1860. Miall noted that church defenders had

23. Ibid., III, 802–806, 814, 815; *Church Institution Circular*, June 1863. The executive committee in 1863 included A. J. Beresford Hope, Lord Robert Cecil, J. M. Clabon, J. M. Dale, the earl of Dartmouth, J. G. Hubbard, G. C. Merewether, Lord Robert Montagu, Earl Nelson, C. W. Packe, T. Salt, and C. J. Selwyn, M.P.

24. G. Howels Davies to Rev. John Haphard, 20 March 1860, Tait Papers, CXVI, 62; Hoare, *Hints*, IV; Machine, *Politics and the Churches*, p. 313.

25. Hoare to bishop of Rochester, 10 March 1862, in Hoare, *Hints*, V, 1590; Gilchrist, *Henry Hoare*, p. 9; Sweet, *A Memoir*, pp. 455–456.

been very active in the country, but he was disdainful of their efforts. The Liberation Society decided not to request petitions in favor of Trelawny's forthcoming abolition bill.[26]

The first bill of the session was a Church Rates Law Amendment Bill brought in on 2 February by J. G. Hubbard and supported by Lord Robert Cecil. Both men were prominent members of the Church Institution. The key provision of the bill, which was modeled after the recommendations of the Lords report, was the granting of wide exemption rights. The bill did not go beyond the first reading and was withdrawn on 4 July, having run out of time.[27]

The bill against which all Church defense efforts had been ranged for months was Trelawny's abolition bill, which came on for its second reading on 8 February. It was opposed in the most important speech of the debate by Lord Robert Montagu, the Conservative member for Huntingdonshire and member of the Church Institution. Montagu stated that all arguments on the question had "long since become trite and worn out." He had "new" evidence, revealed in the report of the House of Lords committee.[28]

Montagu's strongest argument was that the motivation of church rate abolitionists was not conscience, but politics. The church rate question was merely a stalking-horse to attain the severance of the Church from the state. He quoted Samuel Morley's answer to the Lords committee that abolitionists wished to assert " 'a true principle in the theory of government.' "[29] All the differences about church rates were caused by the design of Morley and his collaborators to impose a new theory of government upon the House. Church rate abolitionists repudiated the traditional view that it was the duty of government to lead the nation to follow what was good and consequently to maintain the established religion. According to Morley, said Montagu, "all that is required at the hands of the Government is to insure the security of personal property; he believes that Government is, in fact, nothing but a policeman."[30]

The division list made clear that church defenders were succeeding

26. *Nonconformist*, 1 Feb. 1860, pp. 81–82; 8 Feb. 1860, p. 103; Minutes of Liberation Society, 9 Dec. 1859, GLRO A/LIB/2, minute 1007.

27. *Hansard*, CLVI (2 Feb. 1860), 495–497; CLIX (4 July 1860), 1346–1348.

28. Ibid., CLVI (8 Feb. 1860), 647, 648.

29. Ibid., 652, 651; Great Britain, *Parliamentary Papers*, 1859 (sess. 2), XVII. 1. 217, answer 681.

30. *Hansard*, CLVI (8 Feb. 1860), 652.

in translating aversion to that desacralized liberal view of the state into growing opposition to church rate abolition. Trelawny's bill received 263 votes. That number was unchanged from the second-reading vote of 13 July 1859. But then only 193 had voted "no." Now the opposition had grown to 234, reducing the majority in favor of abolition from seventy to twenty-nine.[31] Absent from the division were Palmerston, Sidney Herbert, and Gladstone, the latter because of illness. The independent Conservative Sir W. Cubitt (Andover) and both M.P.s for South Lincolnshire, T. Mainwaring and G. Hussey Packe, the former a liberal Conservative and the latter a Liberal—all three of whom had voted for abolition in 1859—had now reversed their positions. The weightiest factor to account for the decline of Trelawny's majority, however, was the addition to the opposition of forty-four Conservatives who had previously abstained from voting on the abolition question.[32]

Miall observed ruefully that there remained "more life in the dying system of Church-rates than we had thought. . . ." He recognized that six months of agitation and an "incessant fire of small petitions" without an answer from the abolitionist side had made their mark.[33] A shaken Liberation Society resolved to call for a massive petition campaign, as well as direct pressure on Liberal M.P.s who had abstained, to push the bill through committee. Because the Liberation Society had become so identified with church rate abolition, defeat could be politically devastating. Miall warned, "it is not the fate of the church-rate question alone that is now in the balance, *but the future position of Dissent.*"[34]

In light of its narrow victory at the second reading, the Trelawny bill passed with remarkable ease through the committee stage, with a majority of 222 votes to 49. Miall ecstatically believed that victory had come through an unprecedented rush of petitions, a "majestic inunda-

31. Ibid., 682–686; CLIV (13 July 1859), 1183–1186.
32. *Nonconformist,* 15 Feb. 1860, p. 122; *Guardian,* 15 Feb. 1860, p. 145; *John Bull,* 11 Feb. 1860, p. 89; *Daily News,* 13 Feb. 1860; Sir William Heathcote on the Conservative side was also absent from the division on account of illness, although he might have attended had Gladstone told him that his "no" vote might swing the difference. Sir William Heathcote to Gladstone, 2 Feb. 1860, "Private," Gladstone Papers, Add. MS. 44209, fols. 65, 66; Conacher, *Aberdeen Coalition,* app. B; *Dod's Parliamentary Companion,* 1860.
33. *Nonconformist,* 15 Feb. 1860, p. 121.
34. Ibid., 22 Feb. 1860, p. 141; Minutes of Liberation Society, 10 Feb. 1860, GLRO A/LIB/2, minute 1034.

tion of public opinion" that had swept away every vestige of reaction.[35] The petitions supporting Trelawny had indeed been impressive. In little more than a week, 5,538 petitions bearing 610,877 signatures had been sent to the House of Commons; it had taken months, on the other hand, for defenders of some form of church rate to send 5,575 petitions with only 197,687 signatures.[36]

The passage of Trelawny's bill actually owed more to parliamentary tactics than to abolitionist petitioning, however. Sotheron Estcourt had taken the initiative to invite twenty-seven men—mostly Conservative M.P.s who had taken a prominent role defending the Church, as well as the archbishop of Canterbury and the bishops of London and Oxford—to a private meeting in the tea room the day before the bill was to go into committee to decide on a course of action. Sotheron Estcourt believed that the time was not ripe to originate a measure of their own. They decided to allow the abolition bill to go through committee unamended. The intention, articulated by Lord John Manners in the Commons, was to allow the bill to be defeated in the House of Lords, whereupon with an open field a compromise bill might be introduced. With the abstention of most Conservatives the abolitionists were given the appearance of a landslide victory.[37]

Just how illusory that victory had been became apparent in the vote on the third reading of Trelawny's abolition bill. It passed by a majority of only nine, with 235 votes to 226. The *Nonconformist* expressed shock at the further decline of twenty votes despite the avalanche of proabolition petitions.[38] Church rate abolition was no longer being given the polite reception that it once had. Disraeli, who now was

35. *Nonconformist*, 4 April 1860, p. 261.

36. Great Britain, HLRO, *Reports on Public Petitions*. Session 1860, "54th Report . . . 21–28 Aug. 1860," p. 1817.

37. *Hansard*, CLVII (28 March 1860), 1419–1468; *Record*, 30 March 1860; Sotheron Estcourt to Disraeli, 25 March 1860, Hughenden Papers B/XXI/E/255, LSE microfilm 131. Included among those invited by Sotheron Estcourt to the Tea Room meeting of 27 March were the archbishop of Canterbury; the bishop of London; the bishop of Oxford; the marquess of Salisbury; the peers Derby, Stanhope, Powis, and Portman; and the M.P.s Benjamin Disraeli, Lord John Manners, Sir Stafford Northcote, Lord Robert Montagu, Sir William Heathcote, Spencer Walpole, Lord Henley, C. W. Packe, C. N. Newdegate, and R. A. Cross. Gladstone, who as a member of Palmerston's cabinet had not been invited to Sotheron Estcourt's meeting, nevertheless hoped that it might be possible to introduce an acceptable bill to reform church rates after Trelawny's bill should have been defeated by the Lords. Gladstone to Keble, 24 March 1860, Keble Papers E/90.

38. *Hansard*, CLVIII (27 April 1860), 301; *Nonconformist*, 2 May 1860, p. 341.

beginning to lead the Conservative opposition against Trelawny's bill, delivered a resounding defense of the established church in the third-reading debate.[39]

John Knott's suggestion in June 1857 that Disraeli take up the church rate question as a matter of deep constitutional import had been heard. Sir John Trelawny might remonstrate that he was not a member of the Liberation Society and that church rate repeal should be considered on its own merits. Now that the question had become so much one of the continuation of the church establishment, Trelawny's liberal Anglican argument was losing its appeal.[40] Despite the importance of Disraeli's oratory, the reduced majority given to Trelawny's bill on the third reading owed less to Disraeli than to the careful organizational work initiated by Archdeacon Hale. He had (with Disraeli's endorsement) enlisted the country's archdeacons to "use their local influence" to encourage especially those M.P.s who resided far from Westminster to cast their vote against Trelawny.[41]

Following the division the *Patriot* recognized that reaction had set in. It observed that if the Lords were wise they would use this opportunity to bring in a compromise bill, adding, "[But] the Tories are not wise. . . ."[42] The *Guardian* feared that this was the case, noting that increasingly Churchmen seemed to be hardening their demands. It was apprehensive, too, that the church rate question seemed to have become purely a party question, with the Whigs now almost all on the abolitionist side and with defense of the rate in the Commons dependent on Disraeli's opportunistic leadership.[43]

The reversal suffered by church rate abolitionists influenced the Liberation Society temporarily to reassess its priorities. Since 1853–54, when the goal of attaining church rate abolition had become the society's primary concern, that practical political goal had coexisted uneasily with the Liberation Society's formal aim of disestablishing the Church. At the annual meeting of the Liberation Society's council, chairman William Edwards said that in light of the decreased third-

39. *Hansard*, CLVIII (27 April 1860), 299.
40. Ibid., 300.
41. Hale to Disraeli, 7 April 1860, "Confidential," (printed), Hughenden Papers B/XXI/H/4a and 4b, LSE microfilm 131; circular sent to archdeacons (printed), 2 April 1860, in Hughenden Papers B/XXI/H/5a, LSE microfilm 131; Hale to Disraeli, 11 April 1860, Hughenden Papers B/XXI/H/6, LSE microfilm 131.
42. *Patriot*, 3 May 1860, p. 281.
43. *Guardian*, 2 May 1860, pp. 380, 389.

reading majority for Trelawny's bill, the society should now make "the carrying of the Church-rate Abolition Bill subordinate to outdoor operations on the main question. . . ."[44] Miall reminded those present that they had not taken up the church rate question "on account of its intrinsic importance, but simply as an instrument" to separate church and state. But he admitted that the church rate question "had given them a strong hand with those who could not be brought to take an interest in the abstract question. . . ."[45] The *Patriot* endorsed the position of the Liberation Society executive. It also agreed frankly with Miall: "Dissenters, as a body, have not hitherto sought the abolition of Church-rates with a view to the disestablishment of the Episcopal Church. . . ."[46]

The themes discussed in the House of Lords during the second-reading debate on Trelawny's bill were not dissimilar from those discussed by Miall and the *Patriot*. Lord Lyveden, who moved the second-reading motion, discounted the now popular claim that abolition should be rejected because of the ulterior aims of Dissenters. He held on the contrary that "the country could never be agitated upon a merely theoretical question. Only a real grievance such as church rates . . . could sustain agitation. . . ."[47] The majority was more impressed with the duke of Marlborough's contrary argument. Nevertheless, the measure gained five more votes than it received in 1858. There were now thirty-six pairs, four more than in 1858. But the bill was defeated handily by 128 votes to 31.[48]

V

By the autumn of 1860 the most significant church rate conflict was occurring within the Church. The disagreement was between those (mostly Anglo-Catholics, including many Peelites) who wished to use a climate that seemed to favor the Church to grant timely concessions to Dissent, and those (generally Evangelicals and old High Churchmen) who believed that complete vindication of the church rate princi-

44. *Nonconformist*, 9 May 1860, p. 362.
45. Ibid., p. 364.
46. *Patriot*, 3 May 1860, p. 281.
47. *Hansard*, CLIX (19 June 1860), 624.
48. Ibid., 624–638.

ple and the prerogatives of the national church were within their grasp. The possibility of reconciling these groups became increasingly elusive after Disraeli chose to make the "no compromise" stance the policy of the Conservative party.

On 17 November the *Guardian* carried and endorsed a letter from J. G. Hubbard, the Conservative M.P. for Buckingham, expressing concern that agitation was growing against granting exemptions from church rates to Dissenters and in opposition to his own bill, which he intended to reintroduce that session. The *Guardian* expostulated that if the opportunity gained by the triumph of last session were not seized to bring in an acceptable compromise, it would soon pass away, probably never to return.[49]

Hubbard's letter was answered by G. A. Denison, who strongly opposed exemption from rates as "the one weakness into which defenders of church-rates have been betrayed."[50] A meeting in the Taunton Association rooms on 22 November, attended by seven hundred gentlemen, endorsed resolutions introduced by Denison. These included opposition to pew rents and the proposal that district parishes should be made liable only for their own church. The most controversial resolution was the third—that the exemption of Dissenters from church rate obligations contradicted the principle of an established or national church.[51]

Denison had also sent a copy of his resolutions to Disraeli. He acknowledged that many clergymen and laymen in London seemed scarcely prepared to endorse resolution three; but, said Denison, they were ignorant of the opinion of the laity in country districts. Denison claimed to have found many who leaned "towards Exemption last year wholly against it now."[52] One influential convert to the "no compromise" party was the editor of the *Record*. On 10 December 1860 he announced that he had joined the growing number of those opposed to the self-exemption clause in Hubbard's proposed bill. The editor, who had supported Walpole's bill in 1859, stated: "Churchmen are no longer bound by the conditions which, a year or two ago, they would have accepted. . . . We confess that we are not sorry now that our overtures were rejected."[53]

49. *Guardian*, 14 Nov. 1860, p. 989.
50. Ibid., 21 Nov. 1860, p. 1008.
51. Ibid., 5 Dec. 1860, pp. 1057, 1067, 1068.
52. Denison to Disraeli, 17 Nov. 1860, Hughenden Papers B/XXI/D/109, LSE microfilm 131.
53. *Record*, 10 Dec. 1860.

Anglo-Catholics in particular were horrified that establishmentarians were rejecting compromise. For a decade they had counseled granting concessions—a defensive posture probably accentuated by being a threatened minority among church parties. On 12 December the *Guardian* carried a full page of letters on the exemption controversy. A. J. Beresford Hope warned of the great danger attending the "no-surrender policy." He also wrote to correct the impression that Henry Hoare had spoken as a representative of the Church Institution when he had voiced opposition to exemption at the 22 November Taunton meeting. Beresford Hope, who served with Hoare on the society's executive, indicated that the society could not agree on exemption or "no-compromise."[54]

The disagreement concerning the exemption of Dissenters took an important turn on 4 December 1860, when Disraeli entered the fray. At a meeting of clergy and laity of the rural deanery of Amersham in Prestwood, Buckinghamshire, Disraeli presented himself as the Church's savior. He challenged his hearers "to close this controversy for ever, not by a feeble concession, but by a bold assertion of public right." Disraeli warned that the separation of church and state would precipitate a cataclysmic disintegration of "our parochial constitution."[55] William Hale must have felt gratified with Disraeli's stance. Earlier in the year, two months before Disraeli had (on his own responsibility) led the Conservative opposition against the third reading of Trelawny's bill, Hale had urged Disraeli to consider whether the time had not come for the Commons to consider the church rate question "with just reference to the principles of the English Constitution and the National Jurisprudence."[56]

The *Nonconformist* was certain that by appropriating the "no surrender" cause Disraeli was "forging a weapon, not so much to cut down the claims of Dissent, as to hew himself a way to the Treasury Bench. . . ."[57] Anglo-Catholics feared that Disraeli was set to use the Church to gain a temporary political advantage over the Liberal government. Beresford Hope's *Saturday Review* admonished Churchmen to ponder the fact that the "new champion of Church-rates" had no

54. *Guardian,* 12 Dec. 1860, pp. 1078, 1079.
55. Ibid., supplement, p. 1090; *Nonconformist,* 12 Dec. 1860, pp. 982, 983.
56. Ibid.; Hale to Disraeli, 23 Feb. 1860, Hughenden Papers B/XXI/H/4, LSE microfilm 131.
57. *Nonconformist,* 19 Dec. 1860, p. 1001.

concrete plans to resolve the church rate question, unlike Hubbard, Packe, and the Lords committee.[58]

Derby also had misgivings about Disraeli's activity. He had read about Disraeli's 4 December speech while on holiday and wrote to caution Disraeli against committing himself against exemption. Derby reminded Disraeli that hitherto they had been able to criticize their opponents for being unwilling to consider any compromise; Derby feared that Conservatives might now be open to the same criticism.[59] Disraeli replied six weeks later only after a reminder from Derby. He was quite unrepentant and boasted of how well his campaign was working. The only adversaries he feared were the Anglo-Catholics: "Roundell Palmer, B. Hope, & Co. but they are unceasingly at work. They can do the Ch[urch] no good, for they are utterly incapable of managing England being a . . . fastidious crew, who are more anxious about what they call the Church, than the Church of England."[60]

Disraeli, unlike the Anglo-Catholics, was concerned for the Church primarily as a national institution. He was pleased that defense of the establishment was proving to be a useful lever to attract power to the Conservative party. Increasingly clergy like William Hale looked to the Conservative party as the church party.[61] In October 1861 the *Quarterly Review* published what was in effect a Conservative manifesto, advocating that defense of the church establishment and its prerogatives should become the line of demarcation for political life.[62] That was also the intent of Richard Masheder's *Dissent and Democracy: Their Mutual Relations and Common Object*, published in 1864. Masheder, a fellow of Magdalen College, Cambridge, argued that since 1832, when voluntaryism had developed among Dissenters, Dissent and democracy were two sides of

58. *Guardian*, 12 Dec. 1860, pp. 1073, 1081; *Saturday Review*, 26 Jan. 1861, p. 92; A. J. Beresford Hope, *Church Politics and Church Prospects* (London, 1865), pp. 13–15.

59. Derby to Disraeli, 12 Dec. 1860, Hughenden Papers B/XX/S/277, LSE microfilm 131.

60. Disraeli to Derby, 28 Jan. 1861, "Private," Derby Papers 145/1; Derby to Disraeli, 27 Jan. 1861, "Private," Hughenden Papers B/XX/S/280, LSE microfilm 131.

61. Hale to Disraeli, 26 Jan. 1861, Hughenden Papers B/XXI/H/15, LSE microfilm 131.

62. *Quarterly Review*, Oct. 1861, pp. 544–578. Lord Robert Cecil, later the third marquess of Salisbury, began contributing to the *Quarterly Review* in 1860. In these pages, as elsewhere, he outlined his vision of a conservative society. See M. Pinto-Duschinsky, *The Political Thought of Lord Salisbury* (London, 1967); Paul Smith, ed., *Lord Salisbury on Politics* (Cambridge, 1972); Machin, *Politics and the Churches*, pp. 315, 316.

the same democratic and revolutionary evil that threatened to subvert the country's institutions. Masheder argued that after the Willis's Rooms Compact in 1859 Palmerston and Russell had capitulated to Dissent and radicalism by relinquishing their defense of the church rate and promising the introduction of a parliamentary reform bill. He called on Churchmen to support the Conservative party.[63]

It was that identification of the Conservative party as the church party that the Anglo-Catholic Beresford Hope feared. He warned: "once let the Church be identified with a great political party—and the moral influence of the Church is at an end."[64] Beresford-Hope did continue to support a Christian society guarded by an established church. He attributed "the vulgarization of public morality" in America, Canada, and Australia in great measure to "the absence of the ancestral Established Church." He warned that the Liberation Society was beginning to establish new political battle lines by asking of the electorate, "will you not get rid of this nuisance of an Established Church and receive in exchange the advantages of material prosperity which are now enjoyed in Chicago and Melbourne?"[65]

It was in opposition to the Liberation Society's goal of a desacralized liberal and secular state that Henry Hoare devoted his energies to maintaining the national church as the guardian of the public ethos. Like Beresford Hope he was unwilling to entrust to the Conservative party the interests of the Church. Hoare advocated a realignment of political parties to form a genuinely religious church party.[66] But the possibility of confessional politics on the continental model was not seriously considered. Disraeli won. In making the Conservative party the "church party," the interests and ideals of the Church were subordinated for a time to essentially this-worldly party political objectives. Even as Disraeli was mustering his party in the Commons to defend the rights of the Church, he was contributing to the ongoing desacralization of the country's political life.

VI

The apparent success of the Church defense movement shocked the Liberation Society executive into taking drastic action. The decision

63. Richard Masheder, *Dissent and Democracy: Their Mutual Relations and Common Object* (London, 1864).

64. *Saturday Review*, 26 Jan. 1861, p. 92.

65. A. J. Beresford Hope, *Church Rates and Dissenters* (London, 1861), p. 14.

66. Henry Hoare to Sotheron Estcourt, 23 May 1862, in Hoare, *Hints*.

made only six months earlier to subordinate the church rate question to church disestablishment was overturned in December 1860. The executive committee now was willing to jettison any immediate hope of advancing disestablishment in order to salvage Trelawny's abolition bill.

The Liberation Society decided that because the cause of church rate abolition had been stalled by revelations concerning the society's ultimate objects, a conference should be held early in February that would represent all abolitionists. The intention was to show that the demand for abolition was not restricted to members of the Liberation Society. The Reverend N. T. Langridge, a reform Wesleyan and a member of the Liberation Society, was engaged to organize the conference. Steps were also taken to obtain the signatures of a large number of Methodists in favor of church rate abolition.[67]

The church rate conference was held on 12 February 1861 in the Freemasons' Hall, London. The chair was given to William Scholefield, an Anglican M.P. Setting the tone for the meeting, he asserted, "We are not attacking the Church; we are attacking an abuse. . . ." Scholefield also made it clear that he sought church rate abolition as a means of strenghtening popular attachment to the established church.[68]

The conference resolved to form a Church Rate Abolition Committee (CRAC), to be presided over by Langridge. It was agreed, too, to raise £3,000 (of which £1,000 was immediately subscribed) to secure passage of Trelawny's bill that session. One of the first acts of the CRAC was to reimburse the Liberation Society for money it had already expended in connection with the abolition bill that year.[69] The aim was to carry on the anti–church rate campaign independent of the Liberation Society; it had become too controversial. Just how controversial became apparent in a conference speech by the liberal Anglican church reformer, Lord Henley. The M.P. for Northampton declared that the

67. Minutes of Liberation Society, 21 Dec. 1860, GLRO A/LIB/2, minute 1134; 18 Jan. 1861, minute 1140; *Nonconformist*, 30 Jan. 1861, p. 81. Invited to the church rate conference were prominent Liberals including Edward Baines, M.P., John Bright, M.P., Samuel Courtauld, Samuel Gurney, M.P., George Hadfield, M.P., and Samuel Morley. Representatives were requested from various religious denominations and organizations: the Baptist Union, Congregational Union, London Congregational Board, United Methodist Free Churches, Methodist New Connexion, British and Foreign Unitarian Association, and Dissenting Deputies. *Nonconformist*, 30 Jan. 1861, pp. 81–82.
68. Ibid., 13 Feb. 1861, supplement, p. 141.
69. Ibid., p. 145; Minutes of Liberation Society, 22 Feb. 1861, GLRO A/LIB/2, minute 1146.

question of the separation of church and state had been improperly and unwisely superimposed onto that of church rate repeal. He asked that the conference go on record as seeking simply the repeal of church rates.[70]

Miall attempted to reassure Henley that the Liberation Society had no intention of complicating church rate abolition by using it as a means of achieving its admitted goal of disestablishment. He explained: "We were the victims of a dodge. . . ." Not the Liberation Society but the opponents of abolition in the House of Lords had tied the two issues together. Miall declared: "they never before Parliament, nor before the country, identified the question of Church rates with the wider question. . . ."[71] Miall had conveniently forgotten that only nine months earlier he had declared to the annual meeting of the Liberation Society council that they had not adopted the cause of church rate abolition "on account of its intrinsic importance, but simply as an instrument" to separate church and state.[72] Miall had long held a sometimes conflicting desire to see both immediate political success and the triumph of the disestablishment cause. On this occasion he grabbed for the possibility of a political victory for church rate appeal.

Another indication that church rate abolitionists might be willing to compromise their voluntaryist principles to achieve repeal was the importance they attached to the Methodist petition for church rate abolition, which was presented to the 12 February London conference. Abolitionists rejoiced that fifteen thousand Methodists, of whom seven thousand were ministers and office-bearers, had declared their "emphatic disapproval of this unjust and obnoxious impost." It was clear, however, that this desperately needed Methodist support of the flagging abolition cause had been purchased at a high price. The Methodist petitioners emphatically rejected any link between church rate abolition and separation of church and state. The telling conclusion of their declaration stated that they acted "with a deep conviction that the speedy extinction of Church-rates is essential to the existence of goodwill between the Church of England and the other religious bodies throughout the land."[73] This Methodist view of the issue was identical

70. *Nonconformist*, 13 Feb. 1861, supplement, pp. 144, 145.
71. Ibid., p. 145.
72. Ibid., 9 May 1860, p. 364.
73. Ibid., 6 March 1861, p. 182; *Patriot*, 14 Feb. 1861, p. 101. The petition presented to the Anti-Church-Rate Conference had been signed by Methodists of all schools, including the old-connection Wesleyan Methodists. Opinion on church and

to that of liberal Anglicans like William Scholefield and Lord Henley, who sought church rate repeal as an instrument to save the church establishment. By the spring of 1861 it was becoming clear that church rate abolition could not be achieved without the backing of such moderates. It was an early omen that even if church rate abolition were granted, it would bring the prospect of disestablishment no closer. The abolitionists' inability to advance their cause further without the support of reformist friends of the church establishment presaged the ultimate failure of the Liberation Society to disestablish the Church of England.

VII

By the opening of the parliamentary session of 1861 the initiative in the church rate question had passed from the church rate abolitionists. A chastened Liberation Society had relinquished out-of-doors backing of Trelawny's bill to the less controversial Church Rate Abolition Committee, but the latter now contributed nothing to the deliberations that really mattered. These occurred in Parliament—or more exactly, in the privacy of Westminster's tea and committee rooms. Moderate Liberals who had been influenced by the rush of church defense propaganda to hope that abolition need not be inevitable engaged in behind-the-scenes negotiations with moderate Conservatives in the attempt to arrange a compromise. The church rate question entered its crisis between March and June 1861.

The Liberation Society decided at the beginning of the year that a renewed petitioning campaign would be superfluous in light of the

---

state matters had changed considerably among members of the old connection since the 1830s, when the official view championed church rates and the establishment principle as enthusiastically as any establishmentarian Churchman. See "A Wesleyan," *Watchman*, 22 Feb. 1837, p. 61. In 1860 even the *Watchman and Wesleyan Advertiser* favored exempting Dissenters from church rate obligations (*Watchman and Wesleyan Advertiser*, 14 March 1860, p. 85). Perhaps most Wesleyans by 1861 held the view expressed in the *Watchman and Wesleyan Advertiser* by Henry H. Fowler. He claimed that most Wesleyans had "an intelligent, as well as truly Wesleyan veneration and affection for the Church of England, combined with a decided support of the total abolition of Church-rates" (quoted in *Nonconformist*, 27 March 1861, p. 243). It was a view that might aid the abolitionist cause, but hardly could cheer the hearts of militant voluntaryists.

successful drive of the previous year. It planned instead to rely on what had become a rather refined mode of electoral pressure.[74] Churchmen and conservatives faced the new session buoyed by effective church defense efforts and their recent 4 December endorsement by Disraeli. Denison organized a triple-headed committee composed of representatives of the archdeacons, the Committee of Laymen, and the Church Institution to petition Parliament to maintain the union of church and state. But their enthusiasm could not mask the serious disagreements dividing church defenders. A meeting of the Church Institution on 21 January was marred by bitter exchanges concerning the principle of exemption featured in a forthcoming bill by the Conservative J. G. Hubbard. Lord Robert Montagu contended that the bill entirely denied the establishment principle. Anglo-Catholics such as Roundell Palmer and Beresford Hope argued that the Church would be no less of national establishment if it allowed those with conscientious objections to withhold their church rates.[75]

Hubbard introduced his bill on 12 February 1861. It empowered district churches to rate themselves and placed church rates on a legal footing similar to poor rates. The bill's most controversial feature was its exemption provision.[76] T.H.S. Sotheron Estcourt, Derby's former home secretary, who since 1859 had taken a leading role among the Conservatives in seeking a compromise solution, felt that he could not endorse Hubbard's bill because its exemption provision still discriminated between Churchmen and Nonconformists. Writing to Disraeli about his party's church rate options a month before the introduction of Hubbard's bill, Sotheron Estcourt expressed disquiet about the dilemma facing the Conservative party: "I fear this matter of Church rates will occasion serious difficulties to our party this year. We are not

74. *Nonconformist*, 2 Jan. 1861, p. 2. Miall described methods of discreetly applying pressure on four types of M.P.s: those who were firm supporters of the Liberation Society's objects; members who gave one vote per session for Trelawny's bill but who could not be counted on to vote in further divisions; those never or no longer voting for religious freedom, but who represented constituencies with a considerable number of electors favoring church rate abolition; and last, steady opponents representing a Conservative constituency. Ibid., 16 Jan. 1861, pp. 41, 42.

75. Denison to Disraeli, 27 Nov. 1860, Hughenden Papers B/XXI/D/110, LSE microfilm 131; *Record*, 14 Dec. 1860; *Nonconformist*, 23 Jan. 1861, p. 62; Beresford Hope, *Church Rates*.

76. *Hansard*, CLXI (12 Feb. 1861), 361–365. On 20 February T. Alcock brought in his Church Rates Commutation Bill, which was not seriously considered; *Hansard*, CLXI (20 Feb. 1861), 663.

agreed in opinion, and that Disagreement cannot be suppressed another session, as it was during the last: for Hubbard already will not hold back his Bill, as he was induced unwillingly to do last year."[77] Sotheron Estcourt also feared that Conservatives might simply oppose Trelawny's forthcoming bill without suggesting an alternative. He warned that if they did so, they would lose the support of the Lords. In the Commons, moderates who had abstained from dividing on the Trelawny bill last time in the hopes that Conservatives would bring in a bill based on the report of the Lords committee would feel resigned to vote for abolition. Sothern Estcourt invited Disraeli to meet on 8 February with a group of Conservative M.P.s who had taken a special interest in the question, as well as several peers and the bishop of Exeter, to consider a "common course of action" they might take in the House.[78]

When Trelawny's abolition bill came on for its second reading on 27 February 1861, its rejection was moved by Sir William Heathcote, the leader of the Conservative opposition in the Commons, instead of Lord Robert Montagu, who had taken the lead in 1860. The liveliness of the debate attested to the importance now attached to church rates by the Conservative party.[79]

The weightiest speech against Trelawny's bill was by Gladstone, the chancellor of the exchequer. He had been asked four days earlier by Heathcote to "give us the great benefit" of a speech.[80] His words carried extra weight because he had not spoken publicly on church rates for some time, and because his fellow cabinet members sat silent. In a sophisticated speech he restated in more theoretical fashion his

77. Sotheron Estcourt to Disraeli, 8 Jan. 1861, Hughenden Papers B/XXI/E/259, LSE microfilm 131. Hubbard's bill provided for church rate exemption that could be claimed by any person "not conforming to the Worship of the Church of England."

78. Sotheron Estcourt to Hubbard, 7 Jan. 1861, "copy," in an enclosure to Disraeli, Hughenden Papers B/XXI/E/259a, LSE microfilm 131; Sotheron Estcourt to Disraeli, 8 Jan. 1861, ibid., B/XXI/E/259, LSE microfilm 131; Sotheron Estcourt to Disraeli, 6 Feb. 1861, Hughenden Papers B/XXI/E/2606, LSE microfilm 131. The men invited to the home of Sotheron Estcourt for the purpose of choosing a church rate plan included Disraeli, Sir John Pakington, Sir Stafford Northcote, J. G. Hubbard, C. N. Newdegate, C. W. Packe, the bishop of Exeter, Lord Robert Montagu, Lord Banks Stanhope, Lord Robert Cecil, G. W. Puller, Spencer Walpole, and Sir William Heathcote.

79. Hansard, CLXI (27 Feb. 1861), 1007–1015; Saturday Review, 2 March 1861, pp. 217, 218.

80. Heathcote to Gladstone, 23 Feb. 1861, Gladstone Papers, Add. MS. 44209, fol. 82.

view, first put forward in 1854, that church rates should be allowed to lapse in large urban centers but retained in country parishes. In the latter, he argued, church rate law remained perfectly consonant with its social basis.[81]

The House divided in favor of Trelawny's bill by 281 votes to 266.[82] The previous year's second-reading majority had been cut from twenty-nine to fifteen. The Conservative whip had worked effectively. The abolitionists had also been hurt by the abstentions of eighteen Irish members. Beginning in 1860 Irish M.P.s had not supported abolition in protest against the lack of support for Irish concerns by English and Scottish Liberals and Nonconformists. The Irish M.P. Vincent Scully, with whom Miall corresponded, complained in particular that they consistently supported the Whig government on Irish coercion. Furthermore, Dissenting electors were notorious for refusing to elect Catholic M.P.s.[83]

Despite the reduced majority for abolition, Miall claimed great satisfaction with the result. In spite of all the efforts of church defenders, and the direct intervention of Heathcote, the abolitionists had gained eighteen votes. Miall was pleased, too, that the abolition issue now belonged "to the Liberal party." Only six Liberals had broken ranks to vote against Trelawny; eleven Conservatives had voted for Trelawny. Fourteen Conservatives had been absent unpaired, and twenty-two English Liberals had been absent. Miall exulted in the size of the house: 551 members had voted on the question. The church rate question, crowed Miall, "has forced itself into recognition as the commanding political question of the day. The fate of Governments and of Parliamentary parties has come to turn upon it."[84] Miall's boast about the status of a question that he had often claimed held no intrinsic importance provided a glimmer of his deep yearning for political success.

When Trelawny's bill was considered in committee on 6 March

81. *Hansard*, CLXI (27 Feb. 1861), 1017–1026.

82. Ibid., 1053–1057.

83. *Hansard*, CLXI (27 Feb. 1861), 1053–1057; *Nonconformist*, 27 Feb. 1861, pp. 161, 162; *Guardian*, 13 March 1861, p. 246.

84. *Nonconformist*, 6 March 1861, p. 181; *Guardian*, 13 March 1861, p. 246. The Conservatives who had voted with Trelawny were Edward Bell, C. Bailey, E. Egerton, Sir J. Elphinstone, W. Garnett, Col. William Powell, D. Pugh, Lord Stanley, H. Taylor, Sir H. Willoughby, and E. C. Wynne. The Liberals voting against abolition were W. E. Gladstone, Col. Augustus Andson, F. Cavendish, Sir R. Peel, F. Peel, and C.W.G. Puller.

1861, there were signs that Miall's hopes for the commitment of the Liberals to church rate abolition might be premature. Liberal members, led by G. F. Heneage, the M.P. for Lincoln, showed considerable interest in the amendment proposed by R. A. Cross, the Conservative M.P. for Preston, to the abolition clause of Trelawny's bill. Cross moved that a church rate restricted to maintenance of the fabric of the church and churchyard should be retained; that there should be no rate where none had been made for seven years; and that any person could be exempt who signed a written declaration of a bona fide objection to the payment of church rates.[85] Cross declared himself cheered by unprecedented indications of a desire for a fair settlement. He then withdrew his amendment and promised to introduce a compromise bill, as it had been the predominant feeling that such a concession ought not to be made by amendment. The bill then passed unamended to be considered for the third reading.[86]

Two days later Sotheron Estcourt wrote Derby to say that the committee discussion of Trelawny's bill "took an unprecedented turn. . . ." The Cross resolutions were "received by many Liberals" with the sort of interest that was "clearly indirectly a wish for some compromise. We had been informed that such was the case: but scarcely expected so plain a demonstration. Since that time a communication has passed between these gentlemen represented by Ld Enfield, and Mr. Cross—and in accordance with what was agreed between them."[87]

Two weeks later, on 22 March 1861, Sotheron Estcourt wrote to Derby that they needed "to adopt a distinct mode of action, as a party . . ." on the church rate question. He invited Derby to attend a private meeting on the twenty-seventh with approximately twenty other peers and commoners to decide two questions: whether it was desirable to originate a bill on the basis of the Lords committee report, and what course to take regarding the Trelawny and Hubbard bills. A further meeting with the same participants was scheduled for 3 May.[88]

85. *Hansard*, CLXI (6 March 1861), 1515, 1520–1525.
86. Ibid., 1520–1525.
87. Sotheron Estcourt to Derby, 8 March 1861, Derby Papers 162/2A.
88. Sotheron Estcourt to Derby, 22 March and 1 May 1861, Derby Papers 162/2A. The invited participants in the private church rate conference included the archbishop of Canterbury, the duke of Marlborough, Earl Derby, Earl Stanhope, Earl Romney, Earl Powis, Lord Portman, the marquess of Salisbury, the bishop of London, the bishop of Oxford, Lord John Manners, T.H.S. Sotheron Estcourt, J. G. Hubbard,

The hints of an arrangement between Liberals and Conservatives that had been given by Lord Enfield following the committee stage of Trelawny's bill became firmer near Easter. With evident excitement Sotheron Estcourt informed Disraeli: "unexpectedly Banks Stanhope asked Heathcote and me this afternoon to meet some Liberals in the Tearoom on the subject of Church Rates: Cross being detained in the country."[89] Ten to twelve backbench Liberals, including Trelawny, were present. They offered a deal to Stanhope, Heathcote, and Sotheron Estcourt. The Liberals would come to a further meeting on the twenty-eighth: "they undertake to be there prepared with names of Liberals who will stay away, in sufficient numbers, to throw out Trelawny." In turn the Conservatives should come to their meeting with a draft bill based on the recommendations of the Lords committee, engaging to introduce it when Trelawny's bill had been thrown out on the third reading.[90]

Sothern Estcourt, Stanhope, and Heathcote believed the deal had a reasonable hope of succeeding. They needed Disraeli's counsel and concurrence to continue. Sotheron Estcourt suggested a short meeting with Disraeli on the twenty-seventh to show "how the two proposals depend upon each other. . . ." On 3 June he met with Disraeli, Pakington, Walpole, and Lord John Manners in the room behind the speaker's chair to determine their course on Trelawny's bill.[91]

They apparently decided that they needed additional time, and Sotheron Estcourt asked Trelawny to agree to a fortnight's postponement of the third-reading debate of his bill in order to arrange a compromise. It became apparent that in this stage of the question the views of Dissent counted for nothing. The minutes of the Liberation Society noted that Trelawny had acceded to Sotheron Estcourt's request "without previous consultation with the Church Rate Abolition

---

C.W.G. Puller (a Liberal who had voted against Trelawny), Spencer Walpole, Lord Henley, Lord Robert Montagu, C. W. Packe, C. N. Newdegate, and C. J. Selwyn.

89. Sotheron Estcourt to Disraeli, 28 May 1861 (is the date given in pencil; internal evidence suggests that the date must have been a day or so earlier, perhaps the twenty-sixth), Hughenden Papers B/XXI/E/263, LSE microfilm 131.

90. Ibid. The names of the backbench Liberals who proposed the deal to defeat Trelawny's abolition bill are unfortunately difficult to decipher. Most of them had abstained from the second reading division. They believed that they could convince other Liberals to do the same.

91. Sotheron Estcourt to Disraeli, 28 May 1861 (or several days earlier), Hughenden Papers B/XXI/E/263, LSE microfilm 131; Sotheron Estcourt to Disraeli, 2 June 1861, Hughenden Papers B/XXI/E/265, LSE microfilm 131.

Committee, and after he had received an intimation that postponement was deemed to be undesirable. . . :"[92] Miall was bitter about "Trelawny's Generalship." He feared that the Liberation Society's work since 1853 was about to be wasted.[93]

Sotheron Estcourt now set out to draft a compromise bill that Trelawny might accept as an alternative to his abolition bill. Sotheron Estcourt recommended the formation of two rates. The one should be a compulsory rate, not to exceed one penny, to be paid by all landowners to provide for the essentials: the fabric of the church and churchyard and the necessaries of worship. This rate would not be applied in parishes where no rate had been levied for five years. The other was a voluntary rate for all other expenses to be paid only by those voluntarily joining a church vestry. Sotheron Estcourt explained to Disraeli that he hoped the compulsory landlord rate would placate those Churchmen who demanded that real property should continue to be taxed in recognition of the church and state connection, and that those seeking exemption for Dissenters would be pleased with his voluntary rate.[94]

The proposal did not satisfy Churchmen. Denison adamantly repudiated its support for exemption. The church press, Anglo-Catholic as well as evangelical-establishmentarian, also rejected the draft bill. J. B. Sumner, the evangelical archbishop, wrote: "Unfortunately the friends of the Church can only concur in one point—i.e. in maintaining some rate."[95]

Sotheron Estcourt offered his draft bill to Trelawny in a letter of 7 June 1861. He had to admit that he could give no assurances about the amount of support his own political friends would give the compromise.[96] On 11 June Trelawny informed Sotheron Estcourt that his plan was unacceptable. Trelawny and the Dissenters objected that the

92. Minutes of Liberation Society, 7 June 1861, GLRO A/LIB/2, minute 1182.

93. *Nonconformist,* 5 June 1861, p. 441.

94. The draft of a bill "To abolish the jurisdiction of Ecclesiastical Courts in respect of CHURCH RATES," and an appended letter from Sotheron Estcourt to Sir John Trelawny, 7 June 1861, in Gladstone Papers, Add. MS. 44593, fol. 38; Sotheron Estcourt to Disraeli, 8 Jan. 1861, Hughenden Papers B/XXI/E/259, LSE microfilm 131.

95. Sumner to Sotheron Estcourt, 17 June 1861, Sotheron Estcourt Papers, GRO D 1571-X86; Denison to Sotheron Estcourt, 12 June 1861, ibid.; *Nonconformist,* 19 June 1861, p. 481.

96. Sotheron Estcourt to Trelawny, 7 June 1861, in Gladstone Papers, Add. MS. 44593, fol. 38.

church rate would continue in Sotheron Estcourt's plan—but the deciding factor for Trelawny was apparently that Sotheron Estcourt could not promise the support of the Conservatives. The controversy was now about, said Trelawny, "not so much what is abstractly wise as what is practicable." He would therefore do his duty and proceed with his own bill.[97]

On 19 June the House divided evenly on the motion to give the third reading to Trelawny's bill: both sides mustered 274 votes. The speaker, who now needed to cast the deciding vote, believed that the general opinion in the House favored "some settlement of this question different from that which is contained in this Bill. . . ." With that he cast a "no" vote to defeat Trelawny's abolition bill.[98]

Conservatives were jubilant to have defeated Trelawny for the first time since 1854. Derby had called in Conservative M.P.s two days before the vote to urge them to defeat Trelawny as a preliminary step to further action. Defeating the abolition bill was at least something about which most Conservatives could agree. The Liberal administration, which with the exception of Gladstone continued to vote for abolition, had exerted no pressure on its followers. The defeat of the abolition bill was brought about by the unpaired abstentions of thirty-seven backbench Liberals, compared to twenty-two in the previous vote.[99]

Two days after the crucial division Banks Stanhope explained to Sotheron Estcourt what had induced the Liberals to abstain from voting. Stanhope confessed that a few days before the division he and Cross had met with some Whigs in the tea room, where they had pledged that if Trelawny were beaten Cross would bring in a compromise bill. "The result of that pledge," said Stanhope, "was that it somewhat strengthened your case & . . . that it did make some stay away & consequently enabled us to defeat Trelawny."[100] Stanhope agreed that he and Cross had acted entirely on their "own responsibil-

97. Trelawny to Sotheron Estcourt, 11 June 1861, Sotheron Estcourt Papers, GRO D/1571-X86. When it became apparent that the compromise bill was not likely to win Conservative support, Miall began to speak approvingly of Trelawny once again. *Nonconformist*, 19 June 1861, p. 461.

98. *Hansard*, CLXIII (19 June 1861), 1283–1322.

99. *Nonconformist*, 26 June 1861, p. 501; *Guardian*, 26 June 1861, p. 597; 13 March 1861, p. 246.

100. Banks Stanhope to Sotheron Estcourt, 21 June 1861, Sotheron Estcourt Papers, GRO D 1571-X86.

ity" and on that ground could not complain if the bill proposed by Cross were supported only by Sotheron Estcourt and a few others. But he pointed out that the Conservative party was under considerable pressure to act, since it had committed itself to support a compromise bill. Stanhope believed that the promised Cross bill would receive considerable Whig support. If it were supported by the Conservatives but defeated by their enemies, the position of the Conservatives would be strengthened. But Stanhope warned that if the party should oppose Cross, or not give the bill adequate support, they would face serious danger in 1862 when again they would need to oppose an abolition bill. He asked: "How are we going to fight it? On hopes of a Compromise? Obviously *not* as you will have already destroyed in 1861 that hope." In 1862 the Whigs who had defeated Trelawny would see that "no surrender" was the Conservative motto, and would decide that a vote for Trelawny was the only settlement that remained. Stanhope concluded that he had given his opinion plainly because he was convinced that they had reached "a 'turning point' in the Church Rate fight, a 'turning point' we may not again for many years see."[101]

Sotheron Estcourt wrote to Disraeli in a state of panic. He declared: "We must without delay take our decision, to adopt or decline Cross' Bill. If the latter we must manage to make the rejection come from Miall. . . ." Sotheron Estcourt insisted that they make an offer to the abolitionists — "or *my* offer if you decline complicity," he told Disraeli, who had so far taken no initiative in seeking a compromise, preferring to bask in the adulation following his "no surrender" speeches. Sotheron Estcourt proposed that if abolitionists accepted the laying of rates the Conservatives would concede personal exemptions in any way that would prove acceptable to them.[102]

On 23 June 1861 Sotheron Estcourt wrote to Derby, enclosing the letter from Stanhope stating that whether they proceeded with Cross's bill depended entirely on Derby's nod. Sotheron Estcourt warned that "the danger of postponement to next year is great, and the chance of success at this crisis considerable. . . ." He believed that the moderates on both sides were "so numerous and eager to settle the question, that

101. Ibid.
102. Sotheron Estcourt to Disraeli, 23 June 1861, Hughenden Papers B/XXI/E/264, LSE microfilm 131. Samuel Wilberforce invited Disraeli to speak to a church meeting on 13 April 1864. He promised Disraeli "a great ovation." Wilberforce to Disraeli, 8 April 1864, "private," Hughenden Papers B/XXI/W/365, LSE microfilm 131.

I believe they would carry through almost any Bill." He said also that although the Liberation Society was averse to any accommodation, Bright (with whom he had spoken) wished "for a settlement if it can be had at once."[103]

Derby's reply scuttled hopes for official sanction of the plan. Derby regretted that the arrangement with the Liberals had been made on the personal responsibility of Cross and Stanhope. Derby wrote that he had been hopeful several months ago that they might succeed in bringing in a compromise with the assured support of a group of Liberals. Derby's recounting of his role in the secret negotiations explained why the official arrangements with the Liberals had gone no further. Derby had insisted "as a preliminary, to have the written assurance of the 'thirty or forty Liberals,' who . . . would absent themselves from the division on Sir John Trelawny's motion. . . ."[104] Not surprisingly the Liberals, many of whom had undoubtedly pledged to their electors to vote for abolition, had refused to commit to paper their private willingness to accept a compromise. The official deal had then fallen through, although Stanhope and Cross had carried on their personal arrangements with the Liberals.

Derby counseled that whatever scheme they accepted, it was unlikely that they could obtain for it "anything like the unanimous support of our friends." He believed, therefore, that it was "unwise . . . [to] parade our differences of opinion" unless they could be assured of enough support from the other side of the House to secure its passage. But they could not expect the present government to do anything to guide the deliberations of the House or even to act as moderator between extreme opinions. Derby would not object if Cross and Stanhope wished to proceed on their own, but he believed that the idea of passing such a bill as Cross envisioned, in the hands of private members, was "visionary in the extreme."[105]

R. A. Cross's Church Rates Law Amendment (No. 2) Bill, which received its first reading on 24 June 1861, was based on the Lords recommendations and provided a liberal exemption clause not restricted to Dissenters. It had substantial backing from the peers, including the archbishops of both York and Canterbury. It was brought

103. Sotheron Estcourt to Derby, 23 June 1861, Derby Papers 162/2A.
104. Derby to Sotheron Estcourt, 24 June 1861, Sotheron Estcourt Papers, GRO D 1571-X86.
105. Ibid.

in under the bipartisan authority of Cross and Stanhope with the Liberals G. F. Heneage and W.H.B. Portman. But Sir George Cornewall Lewis, the Whig home secretary, icily refused Cross's request to grant government time to consider the bill.[106]

Time was running out in the parliamentary session of 1861 for the moderates seeking a compromise. In July, first the duke of Marlborough, then J. G. Hubbard, and finally a reluctant R. A. Cross withdrew their church rate bills from the parliamentary order papers. Cross had been advised that it was too late in the session to rely on a sufficiently large House. He asked that during the recess M.P.s should discuss other possible measures with their constituents. If no other compromise were then introduced, he would again bring in a bill next session.[107]

It was an insipid conclusion to a session whose beginning had been so full of hope. The secret offer of backbench Liberals to abstain from voting for Trelawny's abolition bill in exchange for a Conservative pledge to fashion a bill based on the recommendations of the Lords committee had been a golden opportunity to bypass the abolitionists. That opportunity, which Sotheron Estcourt believed to be welcomed by moderates on both sides including even John Bright, had not been grasped. Derby had judged it to be impracticable because of the aimlessness of a rudderless Liberal government, and especially because of the divisions within Conservative ranks. But at least the Cross bill was withdrawn before the Conservatives needed to expose fully their differences. The session of 1862 would reveal whether they would yet seize the chance offered them by Sotheron Estcourt, in cooperation with the moderate Liberals, to forge a compromise solution to the church rate conflict.

VIII

In the autumn of 1861 the Liberation Society executive realized that it should take stock of its position. Its influence and reputation were now

106. Sotheron Estcourt to A. C. Tait, 21 June 1861, Tait Papers, vol. CXXIV; Tait to Sotheron Estcourt, 27 June 1861, Sotheron Estcourt Papers, GRO D 1571-X86; Great Britain, *Parliamentary Papers*, "Church Rates Law Amendment (no. 2) Bill," 1861, I. 443; *Hansard*, CLXIII (24 June 1861), 1749; CLXIV (3 July 1861), 280.

107. *Hansard*, CLXI (22 Feb. 1861), 781–88; CLXIV (1 July 1861), 108; 10 July 1861, 663–73; 24 July 1861, 1420–22.

at a discount. The reaction of *The Times* was fairly representative of popular opinion. As Miall observed bitterly, while Trelawny's bill continued to receive majorities in the Commons *The Times* backed it. It stood firm the day after its third-reading defeat, but within a week it began to favor a compromise bill, and on 1 July it castigated the Liberation Society's folly in having tied abolition to disestablishment.[108]

In September the executive committee of the Liberation Society appointed a subcommittee consisting of Edward Miall, Herbert Skeats, and J. C. Williams to assess the society's situation and to prepare a program for the coming season. The report issued to the executive on 27 September bluntly stated that the society's present position was "critical." Its ability to influence Parliament had been reversed in the church rate question—the issue on which the Liberation Society's reputation had come to rest. The report gloomily asserted: "But the Abolition of Church Rates has, for some years, been our *Cheval de bataille*. We could afford defeat upon other questions so long as we maintained a triumphant position on this."[109]

The subcommittee recommended that for the time being they should cease initiating church rate measures and leave the field clear to opponents of abolition. The subcommittee took courage from the fact that Churchmen were "not agreed amongst themselves" and would probably not be able to agree on a compromise. The report's most controversial proposal was that they should "let it be known that we decline wasting our energies upon the present Parliament, and that we shall concentrate them upon the formation of a Parliament more in unison with our wishes. . . ."[110] The formation of a better Parliament was to be accomplished by influencing public opinion to favor religious liberty. It was suggested that from twelve to twenty lecturers be sent throughout the country. The coming bicentenary of St. Bartholomew's Day was to be used to inculcate Liberation Society principles. Systematic efforts should be made to cultivate the friendship of the proprietors and editors of liberal newspapers. It was hoped that such contacts would make possible the insertion of articles and advertisements about lectures and meetings of the Liberation Society. The parliamentary committee, which would have little to do in the present Parliament

108. *The Times*, 19 June 1861; 20 June 1861; 21 June 1861; 3 July 1861; *Nonconformist*, 10 July 1861, p. 541.
109. Minutes of Liberation Society, 13 Sept. 1861, GLRO A/LIB/2, minute 1203; 27 Sept. 1861, subcommittee report, minute 1206.
110. Ibid.

if the report were accepted, should begin preparing for the next election—especially in Wales, from which few Nonconformists were represented in Parliament.[111]

The recommendations to reemphasize disestablishment reflected the view of Miall, who had written following Trelawny's defeat that he hoped this would advance the cause of disestablishment in the popular mind.[112] Since 1854, when the Liberation Society had made church rate abolition its immediate goal, Miall had cautioned against giving a too-wide exposure to tallk of disestablishment. Now, as in a similar situation in 1860, the banner of disestablishment was unfurled after the practical political campaign had suffered a setback. Disestablishment was becoming a pacifier in time of political defeat.

The voluntaryist message that the subcommittee wished to see proclaimed again in its fullness had undergone a subtle transmutation. The report encouraged speakers to emphasize the social grievances experienced by Nonconformists and to encourage the conviction that "we decline to be dealt with as inferiors." The report went on to say that "the social, political, moral, and spiritual evils produced by the Church Establishment" were all manifestations of the evil of monopoly.[113] The antimonopoly message that had been an effective weapon against the Corn Laws was now turned more fully against

111. Ibid.
112. Ibid.; *Nonconformist*, 26 June 1861, p. 501.
113. Minutes of Liberation Society, 27 Sept. 1861, GLRO A/LIB/2, minute 1206. Even as the Liberation Society was following a more this-worldly course in appealing to the social sensibilities of Nonconformists, rather than their religious convictions, it began to make an almost cynical attempt to gain the support of "religious Dissenters" who had kept aloof from the political activity of the society. In a 4 September 1863 report by Herbert Skeats on the state of the society's church rate publications, Skeats cited the need for new publications—"To excite opp[osition] in parishes where there is no opposition now, and to extend it where it has not been well supported by the body of Dissenters" (Minutes of Liberation Society, 4 Sept. 1863, GLRO A/LIB/3, minute 270, fol. 130). Skeats recommended the publication of "a brief tract, of a high religious tone on the principles of Voluntaryism, as bearing on the question of Church Rates, for the use of what are called "religious Dissenters" (ibid., fol. 131). Several weeks later a report by J. C. Williams and Herbert Skeats recommended that they should prepare new church rate tracts. They suggested that "tracts on the religious aspect of the question . . . may be better written by others." They suggested the pastors Edward White, Charles Short, T. C. Finlayson, E. R. Conder, F. Rugby, and J. J. Waite—men who had the confidence of religious Dissenters. If religious concern no longer was the prime motivator for the Liberation Society, it was an element that could be used; ibid., 30 Oct. 1863, minute 392, fol. 168.

ecclesiastical inequality. The new emphasis was geared to win the support of increasingly prosperous middle-class Nonconfirmists who might be drawn more by the desire for social respectability than by a quest for the spiritual purification of the Church. The only formal barrier that might have slowed this replacement of Christian by temporal ideals had been lost in 1854, when the Liberation Society followed Dr. C. J. Foster's advice to desacralize its constitution. Then a minority, including Miall, had objected; now a proposal backed by Miall to make the society's appeal more this-worldly was not even noticed as such.

The report essentially was accepted by the executive committee. The subcommittee proposed that its costly recommendations could be financed from monies saved by suspending parliamentary work as planned and by increasing the society's income by converting "into regular supporters of the Society the Church Rate correspondents of the last twelve months, and the signers of the Methodist Declaration."[114]

The Liberation Society secured the support of the Reverend N. T. Langridge, the secretary of the Church Rate Abolition Committee, to approach Methodists. Langridge sent to his prospects an expressly drafted letter and a tract "specially adapted to the Wesleyans. . . ." He was to be paid £1 per week for three months, and a 2 percent commission per subscription. The campaign failed. Wesleyans might favor church rate reform or abolition; they did not seek disestablishment.[115]

IX

Late in the parliamentary session of 1861 R. A. Cross had withdrawn his compromise church rate bill, which had the open or tacit support of a number of moderate Liberals. By withdrawing he had temporarily postponed facing the critical question of whether Conservatives could reach an agreement on an alternative to church rate abolition. That question was to be answered in 1862.

114. Ibid., 4 Oct. 1861, minute 1208; 18 Oct. 1861, minute 1213; 27 Sept. 1861, minute 1206.
115. Ibid., 15 Nov. 1861, minute 1228; 1 Aug. 1862, minute 103.

On the eve of the new parliamentary session conservative Church-men continued to be deeply divided about whether they should offer any concessions to church rate opponents.[116] Sotheron Estcourt wrote to Disraeli that "our people are at present divided in opinion, and want the voice of a leader."[117] On 9 January 1862 Cross wrote a fretful letter to Sotheron Estcourt to say that he would need to decide soon whether to bring in the previous year's bill. He feared that their enemies would reintroduce their perennial abolition bill on the first day of the session and chide Conservatives for being no closer than last year to agreeing on an alternative. Cross said too that he was "not in good humour with our Conservative leaders on this point. . . ."[118]

Sotheron Estcourt's reply was not hopeful. He stated that based on his autumn correspondence it appeared that the personal exemption proposal, which was the basis of both the Cross and Hubbard bills, "does not seem . . . to have made any way since the end of last year." He said that Cross's decision to reintroduce his bill must depend on increased support for it. He counseled that those clerical supporters who favored the bill should begin petitioning immediately.[119]

Sotheron Estcourt warned Disraeli that their party would have "a hard time of it" if it met the House unprepared to tell its followers what it meant to do about church rates. He observed that Disraeli had "very cleverly urged" in his Aylesbury speech in late 1861, to a predominantly clerical audience, that the onus be thrown on the government. But what should be their next move, asked Sotheron Estcourt, if the government shirked its responsibility, as he expected it would? He warned that presently no bill from their side could pass because "we are not agreed amongst ourselves." He predicted: "we want at least another Session of hard fighting, to bring us to an Agreement."[120]

116. *Nonconformist*, 4 Dec. 1861, p. 971. Church defense organizations were also experiencing financial difficulties—another sign that church defense was in trouble. At the close of 1861 the Committee of Laymen had a debt of £153 18s. 6d. *Record*, 16 Oct. 1861.

117. Sotheron Estcourt to Disraeli, 23 Nov. 1861, Hughenden Papers B/XXI/E/266, LSE microfilm 131; Banks Stanhope to Sotheron Estcourt, 9 Nov. 1861, Sotheron Estcourt Papers, GRO D 1571-X86.

118. R. A. Cross to Sotheron Estcourt, 9 Jan. 1862, "copy," Hughenden Papers B/XXI/E/267a, LSE microfilm 131.

119. Sotheron Estcourt to Cross, enclosed with letter to Disraeli, 15 Jan. 1862, "copy," Hughenden Papers B/XXI/E/267a, LSE microfilm 131.

120. Sotheron Estcourt to Disraeli, 15 Jan. 1862, Hughenden Papers B/XXI/E/267, LSE microfilm 131.

Until such an agreement could be forged Sotheron Estcourt could think of no policy but to stall. Just days before Trelawny was scheduled to introduce his abolition bill Sotheron Estcourt reminded Disraeli that they should be prepared to inform Parliament of their intended response. Sotheron Estcourt now found the church rate question odious. He had opened his letter by saying, "we must return to that nauseous subject, as a dog to its vomit." Sotheron Estcourt proposed that on the day Trelawny introduced his bill, he or Cross would announce that Cross had "no intention of bringing in his former Bill." He cautioned that with "the field unoccupied, it may fall into awkward hands." He therefore recommended that Disraeli or someone on the front bench should indiate their policy. He enclosed a sketch of a resolution that he believed to be a more positive weapon with which to fight Trelawny than a mere negative vote.[121]

On 11 February, when Trelawny introduced his abolition bill for the first reading, it fell to Sotheron Estcourt to state the opposition's position, since Disraeli had evidently declined to take responsibility. He promised that on the second reading of Trelawny's bill he would move a resolution that would obtain from the House "the recognition of some distinct principle on which legislation on the subject might be founded."[122] The Conservative statement, for which the nation had waited expectantly, was made public shortly after 11 February. It asserted:

> That it is unjust and inexpedient to abolish the ancient customary right, exercised from time immemorial by the ratepayers of every parish in England, to raise by rate amongst themselves the sums required for the repair of their Church, *until some other provision shall have been made by Parliament for the discharge of their obligations,* to which, by custom or statute, the churchwardens, on the part of the parish, are liable.[123]

121. Ibid., 2 Feb. 1862, B/XXI/E/268. The date is entered in pencil and is probably not correct. Sotheron Estcourt talked about Trelawny's bill being brought in on "Tuesday." It was brought in on 11 February. As Sotheron Estcourt appeared to be writing within a week of that date, it would have been several days later than 2 February.

122. *Hansard*, CLXV (11 Feb. 1862), 167.

123. *Hansard*, CLXVI (14 May 1862), 1735; *Nonconformist*, 19 Feb. 1862, p. 162 (emphasis mine).

It was just that "other provision" that the Conservatives had promised to advance. The Conservative elephant had labored and borne a church rate mouse. Miall mocked it, not unfairly, as a "barren resolution."[124]

Sotheron Estcourt's bluff, meant to obscure the lack of an alternative to Trelawny's bill, was called by Trelawny. Following the 20 December recommendation of the Liberation Society executive, Trelawny announced that he would seek postponement of a second reading for his bill to give its opponents ample opportunity to submit their own scheme to settle the question. The Church Rate Abolition Committee applauded Trelawny's move. It recounted that defenders of the rate previously had sought defeat of the abolition bill with the argument that the ground must be cleared before fresh legislation could properly be introduced. It challenged those responsible for defeating Trelawny to accept their duty of introducing their own bill. The *Record* was skeptical of the motives of the Church Rate Abolition Committee but agreed that its challenge was a reasonable one.[125]

On 14 May 1862, after the Conservatives had had almost three months to prepare their position, Trelawny's abolition bill came on for a second reading. Sotheron Estcourt's reply to Trelawny indicated that the Conservatives had made ill use of the time given by Trelawny's postponement. Sotheron Estcourt contended that the government ought to introduce the legislation. If the government failed to do so, he would not add another private member's bill that he believed could not pass. He then moved to counter Trelawny's bill by asking for a vote on his resolution, which had been in the public domain for several months. The House defeated the church rate abolition bill by a vote of 287 to 286. Thereafter the House voted on Sotheron Estcourt's resolution, passing it by the margin of 288 to 271 votes.[126]

The Trelawny bill had been considered by 610 out of 656 members, the largest House yet to have voted on the church rate question. Only six Conservatives and thirty-eight Liberals were absent—nineteen of the latter illegitimately, according to the *Nonconformist*. It was they—mostly Irish, Scottish, and Welsh members—who had defeated the abolition bill. Nevertheless, despite a divided government and only

124. *Nonconformist*, 19 Feb. 1862, p. 162.
125. *Record*, 21 Feb. 1862; Minutes of Liberation Society, 28 Feb. 1862, GLRO A/ LIB/3, minute 31, fol. 26. (In 1862, in vol. III of the Liberation Society Minutes, the Minutes began using folio numbers in addition to minutes numbers.) Minutes of Liberation Society, 20 Dec. 1861, GLRO A/LIB/2, minute 1246; *Record*, 28 Feb. 1862.
126. *Hansard*, CLXVI (14 May 1862), 1674–90; 1727–35.

incidental help from the Liberal whip, the abolition measure had received 286 votes, five more than the previous maximum. The *Nonconformist* claimed that the size of the majority for Sotheron Estcourt's resolution could be explained by the fact that the Conservative party had been well managed by Sotheron Estcourt, while the Liberals had been caught napping. Some members who had voted for Trelawny mistakenly left the House before the vote on the resolution.[127]

The liberal *Daily Telegraph*, which eagerly advocated a compromise, lamented that after twenty-eight years "of ceaseless attack and watchful defence" the church rate question was no closer to a settlement.[128] Sotheron Estcourt apparently concluded too that it was incumbent on the Conservatives to bring in a bill. He decided personally to take the initiative. He informed Disraeli that he was taking the action on his own responsibility and that neither Disraeli nor the party was obliged to support him. He explained that many Conservative members had told him that the party must take positive action on the church rate issue now to ensure their prospects for re-election. If not, they would feel it necessary to vote for abolition.[129]

Sotheron Estcourt's church rate plan dropped the concept of personal exemption that had been the key to most of the important proposals since the publication of the Lords report in 1859. He distinguished between a voluntary rate for services and a compulsory rate to maintain church buildings. His key proposal was that the compulsory rate should be levied on owners of land rather than on occupiers.[130] Derby was taken aback by Sotheron Estcourt's initiative. He wrote saying: "I am rather sorry that you should have thought yourself called upon to give, though in your individual capacity only, a notice of a specific motion; as I fear that it may disclose considerable differences of opinion among our friends. . . ."[131] Derby's apprehensions were well founded. Archdeacon Denison took up his cudgels against Sotheron Estcourt's plan. The Church Institution actually

127. *Guardian*, 21 May 1862, p. 484; *Nonconformist*, 21 May 1862, pp. 441, 442.
128. *Daily Telegraph*, 15 May 1862.
129. Sotheron Estcourt to Disraeli, 17 May ? (1862 in pencil), Hughenden Papers B/XXI/E/269, LSE microfilm 131; *Nonconformist*, 21 May 1862, p. 441.
130. Sotheron Estcourt sketch of a church rate plan, enclosed with letter to Disraeli, 17 May 1862, Hughenden Papers B/XXI/E/269a, LSE microfilm 131; *Nonconformist*, 28 May 1862, p. 469; *Hansard*, CLXVII (24 June 1862), 989–97.
131. Derby to Sotheron Estcourt, 20 May 1862, Sotheron Estcourt Papers, GRO D1571-X86.

decided to petition Parliament against it. It opposed distinguishing between building and service and objected to any form of voluntary rate. The *Guardian* initially opposed the plan, but the editor hinted that he might come around for the sake of peace.[132]

That qualified support did nothing to give Sotheron Estcourt the backing he required. On 24 June 1862, in the course of debate on his plan, he withdrew his resolution. The lack of support on either side of the House was painfully evident.[133] Sotheron Estcourt had failed; the Conservative party had failed. The divisions among Churchmen and within the party had prevented them from agreeing on any alternative to abolition. They agreed only to oppose abolition, but that was no longer enough. The next day Miall exulted: "In truth, last night's debate has given a final death-blow to all compromise schemes, and cleared the way for the simple issue — 'Abolition' or 'no Abolition.' "[134] As was frequently the case in the church rate question, the matter was not so simple. The quest for a form of compromise was not quite exhausted, although Sotheron Estcourt was.[135] As the following session would reveal, compromise initiatives would come from unexpected quarters.

X

In 1863 the wave of conservative reaction to church rate abolition and the specter of disestablishment reached its peak and then collapsed. The Conservative party defeated Trelawny's abolition bill by the largest

132. *Church and State Review*, 1 June 1862, pp. 5–6; *Guardian*, 21 May 1862, p. 485; 18 June 1862, p. 577; *Nonconformist*, 18 June 1862, p. 528.

133. *Hansard*, CLXVII (24 June 1862), 989–1018.

134. *Nonconformist*, 25 June 1862, p. 556. Two bills, besides Trelawny's, were considered briefly in the session of 1862. T. Alcock's Church Rates Voluntary Commutation Bill and C. N. Newdegate's Church Rates Commutation Bill were given a first reading. Neither went to a second reading division. *Hansard*, CLXV (14 Feb. 1862), 266; CLXVII (18 June 1862), 717–19.

135. On 9 June Sotheron Estcourt informed Disraeli that he was becoming most discouraged by the lack of unanimity in his party. He told Disraeli not to feel he was less committed to their cause or his colleagues if he took "some quiet opportunity," probably at the end of the session, to retire to the privacy of the back benches. Sotheron Estcourt to Disraeli, 6 June 1862, Hughenden Papers B/XXI/E/270, LSE microfilm 131.

majority to date; it could agree on nothing to take the bill's place. Yet there were also indications that in the future Churchmen of both parties might agree on a measure that diluted the church rate principle further than any previous proposal, but retained enough of it to frustrate voluntaryists from winning outright abolition as a step toward church disestablishment.

By the beginning of 1863 church defenders, and particularly members of the influential Church Institution, had justifiable pride in their achievement. During its three-and-a-half-year existence the Church Institution had seen the majority in the House of Commons for church rate abolition decrease drastically in 1860 and become a minority in 1861 and 1862. It had distributed approximately 402,650 publications. Despite its successes the organization was plagued by structural weaknesses. The report delivered to the society's annual meeting on 25 February 1863 revealed that of 422 provincial associations in union with it, only two hundred actually sent deputies to London. A large portion of the meeting was preoccupied with the discussion of the Church Institution's finances. Its debt had grown from £300 in 1860 to £700 in 1861 and £1,000 in 1862. A lengthy and unfruitful debate followed a motion that no member of the council be qualified to act until he, or the rural deanery he represented, had contributed £5.[136]

As the 1863 parliamentary session approached, Sotheron Estcourt continued to take a well-deserved rest in Florence. On 9 January he wrote Disraeli to say: "It seems to me rather lucky that I should be out of the way (for a sufficient season) this year, when the annual Infliction of Church Rates comes on. . . ."[137] The Conservative party had moved no closer to agreeing on an alternative to Trelawny's abolition bill. Sotheron Estcourt lamely advised Disraeli that "the safest course this year would be to reaffirm the Resolution of last year. . . ."[138]

The feeble hope that the government might save the Conservatives from the embarrassing bankruptcy of their church rate position was deflated on 16 February. On that day the home secretary, Sir George Grey, indicated that the government had no bill to lay before the House.[139] On 29 April 1863 Trelawny once again brought in his church

136. *Church Institution Circular*, July 1863, pp. 283, 284; *Guardian*, 4 March 1863, p. 202; *Nonconformist*, 4 March 1863, pp. 161, 162.

137. Sotheron Estcourt to Disraeli, 9 Jan. 1863, Hughenden Papers B/XXI/E/273, LSE microfilm 131.

138. Ibid.

139. *Hansard*, CLXIX (16 Feb. 1863), 342.

rate abolition bill for its second reading. He admitted that it had twice been defeated but argued that the defeats could be explained by the hopes of a compromise. Trelawny also revealed that he was one of the Liberals who had "attended the meeting in the tea-room" with the aim of finding a settlement more satisfactory to the opposition. He argued that M.P.s should now vote for abolition because Conservatives had "thrown up the case in despair."[140]

Sir Charles Douglas, the Liberation Society "whip" and Liberal M.P. for Banbury who seconded Trelawny's motion, defended the bill on the voluntaryist principle. But Gathorne Hardy, the Conservative M.P. for Yeominster who moved the rejection of Trelawny's bill in Sotheron Estcourt's absence, alleged that Dissenters had no right to demand abolition based on the voluntary principle. He reminded the House that only days earlier the Dissenters Edward Baines and George Hadfield, Liberal members for Leeds and Sheffield respectively, had voted in favor of the Prison Ministers Bill, which made public provision for non-Anglican chaplains. Gathorne Hardy mocked the voluntaryist claim that the state ought not to interfere in religious matters: "The State not to interfere in matters of religion! Why, the table of the House was groaning with Petitions from Dissenters praying that the House might interfere for the better observance of Sunday."[141] It was a stinging reminder of how far the Liberation Society was from shaping Dissenters into consistent voluntaryists.

Another indication that the Liberation Society might be less than fully successful came in the speech by Lord Alfred S. Churchill. The moderate Conservative M.P. for Woodstock declared that he intended to vote for the second reading of Trelawny's abolition bill. But he added that he wished to see the connection of church and state "maintained in its integrity. . . ." Lord Alfred proposed to introduce a compromise on his own authority. He intended to add in committee a simple clause to the abolition bill "which would completely save the rights of the Church, while at the same time no compulsory payment of the rate could be enforced."[142]

The disarmingly simple device of retaining all facets of the law and the parochial machinery for making and collecting church rates while taking away their compulsory character had been suggested first by

140. Ibid., CLXX (29 April 1863), 927.
141. Ibid., 937, 938, 952, 953.
142. Ibid., 970.

the latitudinarian Baron Ebury in a novel pamphlet published in 1861. The idea was introduced to Parliament by John Bright on 14 May 1862, during the second reading debate on Trelawny's bill. He had said: "I proposed a very simple plan . . . by which you might leave everything as it is, except the power to enforce the rate."[143]

Gathorne Hardy called the plan "perfectly absurd" since Churchmen were to lose all rights of compulsion while abolitionists relinquished nothing. The plan had the merit, however, of intriguing men who had long despaired of the possibility of compromise. Home Secretary Grey, who had voted for Trelawny's abolition bills since 1859, declared that he would again support it but would abstain on its third-reading division if it were not amended as Lord Alfred proposed.[144]

The *Spectator* extolled the Ebury proposal because it gave "a false appearance of victory to both sides. . . ." It said that both sides could so attain what they really cared for, "the representative Church party having long ago disclaimed any wish to insult conscientious scruples, and the representative Dissenter having long ago disclaimed any wish seriously to injure the Church."[145] It was an acute, if cynical, observation. The numerous and increasingly comprehensive exemption schemes proposed since 1859 indicated that most Churchmen had relinquished the claim that the national Church should exact universal rate tribute. The stance of the Church Rate Abolition Committee and the Methodist petition indicated that considerable numbers of Dissenters did not seriously expect to advance the cause of disestablishment by abolishing church rates.

The potential of this compromise was not to be considered seriously until after Palmerston's death. Lord Alfred was unable to move his amendment in committee because Trelawny's bill was defeated by a vote of 285 to 275. The new majority of ten against abolition was a tribute to the effectiveness of the church defense movement allied with the Conservative party whip. It also reflected the decision of the Liberation Society's executive committee to forgo, in this division, the "pressure of moral coercion" on Liberal M.P.s in order to preclude the growth of irritation with the Liberation Society.[146]

The Liberation Society executive was encouraged that the support

143. Robert Grosvenor (Baron Ebury), *The Only Compromise Possible in Regard to Church Rates* (2d ed.; London, 1861); *Hansard*, CLXVI (14 May 1862), 1712.
144. *Hansard*, CLXX (29 April 1863), 942, 963–65.
145. *Spectator*, 17 May 1862, p. 539.
146. *Hansard*, CLXX (29 April 1863), 974–78; *Nonconformist*, 6 May 1863, p. 341.

for repeal had actually held quite steady. It believed that talk of compromise, which had engaged both sides of the House two years ago, was now over. It expressed delight because it had seen the possibility of compromise then as an obstacle to achieving abolition. The unyielding conservative *Morning Herald* likewise was jubilant that compromise had been rejected.[147]

Following the defeat of Trelawny's abolition bill, the Conservative C. N. Newdegate finally pushed his Church Rates Commutation Bill, which he had introduced several times before, to a second reading. His plan envisaged commuting the rate to a permanent charge on land. The burden was to be shifted from occupier to landlord. Parishes that had not paid a rate for seven years were exempt, although the obligation could be revived upon a petition of two-thirds of the parishioners. There was also a provision to convert the permanent charge on land into an endowment controlled by the Queen Anne's Bounty commissioners. Newdegate's plan, which remade the rate to resemble the tithe rent charge, pleased no one. Conservatives opposed it with great reluctance, believing it was too complicated or untimely. Sir Stafford Northcote pleaded with Newdegate not to embarrass his party by pushing his bill to a division. Newdegate could not be swayed, and a small House defeated his measure by a vote of ninety-four to fifty-six.[148] On the same day, T. Alcock, the Liberal M.P. for East Surrey, insisted that his Church Rates Redemption Bill be given a second reading. His measure did no more than to allow parishioners to abolish their church rate obligations by establishing a permanent endowment to maintain the parish church. The plan evoked little enthusiasm and was defeated by eighty-one votes to seventy-two.[149]

Although Conservatives could agree on no alternative to abolition, they had defeated that option decisively for the time being. On 13 August Sir John Trelawny, who had led the abolitionist forces since 1857, announced that he was relinquishing his leadership. He believed it inexpedient to raise the question again in the present Parliament. He intimated, too, that a younger man should take the question in hand following a general election. This led *The Times* to charge that Trelawny had virtually surrendered the principle at issue.[150]

147. *Nonconformist*, 6 May 1863, p. 344; *Morning Herald*, 30 April 1863.

148. *Hansard*, CLXX (6 May 1863), 1264–73.

149. Ibid., 1274–75.

150. *Nonconformist*, 19 Aug. 1863, p. 659; *The Times*, 18 Aug. 1863. The editor said that Trelawny had finally admitted the "impracticability of his measure." He observed too that there was a growing conviction, which he appeared to share, that the church

Near the end of the parliamentary session, agreement on a church rate compromise seemed unlikely. Abolitionists believed that it was only a matter of time until abolition would triumph. However, on 7 July 1863 Lord Alfred S. Churchill introduced a bill whose outlines would not satisfy militant voluntaryists, but which provided the basis for legislation that ultimately would be agreed upon following Palmerston's death. Lord Alfred's bill (which he introduced merely for discussion purposes and which went no further that session), like the amendment he had hoped to affix to Trelawny's bill, provided that the machinery for making the rate should remain intact. Only the penalty for nonpayment should be abolished. Lord Alfred argued that by retaining everything but compulsion "the whole principle of the connection between Church and State and the parochial system of self-government would still be preserved. . . ."[151] The plan offered Churchmen—both Liberals and Conservatives—the option of defusing the church rate dilemma while defeating the Liberation Society's ulterior aim of using church rate abolition to bring on disestablishment of the Church of England.

XI

The defeat suffered by the Liberation Society in the decisive rejection in April 1863 of the Church Rate Abolition Bill, and Trelawny's symbolic capitulation later in the year, contributed to an important reassessment of the society's policy. The immediate response to the second-reading loss of Trelawny's bill followed the pattern set by the reactions to the reverses of 1860, 1861, and 1862. On 5 May the executive committee advised the Liberation Society's members at the annual meeting that they should drop their earlier caution and follow the example of their opponents to "make the Church-rate question

---

rate question was a subject for compromise—not for victory. *Tavistock Gazette*, 21 Aug. 1863.

151. *Hansard*, CLXXII (7 July 1863), 365.

subordinate to the Church Establishment question."[152] In June 1863 Dr. C. J. Foster informed the executive committee that he intended to relinquish his chairmanship of the parliamentary committee to accept a legal position in New Zealand. The departure of the man responsible for so many of the society's earlier successes came as a shock. A subcommittee was formed on 10 July to recommend what should be done in consequence of Foster's resignation.[153]

On 23 October the subcommittee issued its report. It began by surveying the Liberation Society's parliamentary standing. It pointed to the June 1861 tie vote on Trelawny's bill as the point at which the growth of the society's influence in the Commons had ceased. Since then its previously successful attempts to influence M.P.s had aroused impatience and resentment. Furthermore, the society's failure was magnified in that it had failed to bring to the fore in Parliament the fundamental issue of religious equality in the practical measures it had championed. So these reverses could not even be claimed as moral triumphs.[154]

The subcommittee recommended that except for defensive purposes they take no further parliamentary action during the remaining term of the present Parliament. Unlike the case in 1861, when the Liberation Society had considered a similar proposal, it would now be taken seriously. The subcommittee advised in effect that they move from a parliamentary to an electoral strategy; in particular, that friends of the society reverse their habitual tendency of setting their loyalty to the Liberal party above their attachment to religious equality.[155]

The electoral rule that should guide them, said the subcommittee, was that M.P.s "should represent *our* opinions in some proportion to the power *we* put forth to secure their election." In practical terms, in

152. *Nonconformist*, 6 May 1863, p. 344. In September 1862, following the defeat of the church rate abolition bill, a Liberation Society subcommittee had recommended that they should ensure that parliamentary debates on questions promoted by the Liberation Society should advance its "grand design." It was also suggested that they consider introducing bills to disestablish the Church in Scotland, Ireland, and Wales. Minutes of Liberation Society, 19 Sept. 1862, GLRO A/LIB/3, minute 117, fols. 66–68.

153. Minutes of Liberation Society, 26 June 1863, GLRO A/LIB/3, minute 250, fols. 117, 118; 10 July 1863, minute 260, fol. 125.

154. Ibid., 23 Oct. 1863, fols. 142–44.

155. Ibid., fols. 151, 152, 164; D. A. Hamer, *The Politics of Electoral Pressure* (London, 1977), chap. 6.

constituencies with two candidates where Nonconformists contributed at least half of the votes they ought to be entitled to nominate one of the two candidates. Where the number of voluntaryist voters did not warrant such influence the friends of religious equality could make their electoral support depend on a pledge to vote for church rate abolition and open parochial churchyards to Nonconformist ministers. If that measure of justice were denied them, "the *rule*" was that religious equality electors should withhold their vote and influence "*whatever may be the consequences of our abstentions to the Liberal Party.*" In addition, an earlier report to the executive urged that the entire church rate question should be promoted in a way more likely to promote voluntaryism.[156]

Nonconformist reactions to the new electoral policy were initially negative. As D. A. Hamer has pointed out, many Nonconformists had close local ties with the Liberals and feared splitting the Liberal party. The *Leeds Mercury* feared erroneously that the Liberation Society wished "to form an independent political party." It was also anxious lest Dissenting bodies become political rather than religious organizations.[157] By the end of 1863, however, the new policy was widely accepted in Nonconformity. The *Bradford Review* enthusiastically supported the Liberation Society's aim as "the building up of another Liberal party on sounder principles. . . ." This aim captured something of the long-term effects of voluntaryism, which represented much more than Gash's "retreat from politics." Voluntaryism's more lasting legacy was to provide the principles and ethos that Nonconformists brought to the shaping of Gladstonian liberalism.[158] This was also the goal of the young Congregationalist minister R. W. Dale, who had none of the

156. Minutes of Liberation Society, 23 Oct. 1863, GLRO A/LIB/3, fols. 153, 154; 4 Sept. 1863, fol. 132.

157. *Leeds Mercury*, 21 Nov. 1863; *Patriot*, 19 Nov. 1863, p. 757; *Bradford Observer*, 26 Nov. 1863; Minutes of Liberation Society, 11 Dec. 1863, GLRO A/LIB/3, minute 310, fol. 177. The Reverend J. Gordon resigned his seat on the executive committee in protest against the new electoral policy; Hamer, *Electoral Pressure*, 102–12.

158. *Bradford Review*, 28 Nov. 1863; *Nonconformist*, 23 Dec. 1863, p. 1025; *Patriot*, supplement, 26 Nov. 1863, pp. 781, 782; *Manchester Daily Examiner and Times*, 19 Nov. 1863; Minutes of Liberation Society, 29 Jan. 1864, GLRO A/LIB/3, minute 328, fol. 185; John Vincent, *The Formation of the Liberal Party, 1857–1868* (London, 1966), pp. 57–76; Gash, *Reaction and Reconstruction*, p. 76. The best treatment of the religious culture of Protestant Nonconformity and the contribution it made to the development of popular liberalism is in Eugenio F. Biagini, *Retrenchment and Reform: Popular Liberalism in the Age of Gladstone, 1860–1880* (Cambridge, 1992), chap. 4.

old-fashioned apprehension of his fellow Congregationalist Edward Baines, that Nonconformity might become a political rather than a religious body. Before an audience of 1,500 in Birmingham's town hall he challenged Nonconformists on 17 November to sanctify the Liberal party. Dale cautioned his hearers that it would take time to convince the party and country of their church views, and that meanwhile Nonconformists should "stand by the men who, on other great questions of national policy, would vote in harmony with his deepest and most solemn convictions."[159]

Increasingly these "deepest and most solemn convictions" that Dale and his fellow Nonconformists insisted on in the newly forming Liberal party were the sacred tenets of equality and liberty. The defeats suffered by the Liberation Society, in most dramatic fashion on church rate abolition, led to that society's decision to contribute to the refashioning of Palmerston's Liberal party in the image of Nonconformity. In the process Nonconformity itself was being fashioned. By 1877 a Congregationalist could say that " 'Congregationalism is identical with Liberalism. . . .' "[160]

XII

In 1864, following the Liberation Society's decision to adopt a purely defensive posture and with Trelawny out of the field, there was for the first time in over a decade no church rate abolition bill before the Commons. Parliamentary church rate debate this session dealt with the possibility of extending church rate obligations.

The controversy had begun on 20 April 1863 when Solicitor General Sir Roundell Palmer quite innocently introduced his Church Building and New Parishes Act Amendment Bill. Palmer wished to consolidate twenty-six overlapping and often inconsistent church building acts, beginning with the first of 1818 (58 Geo. III, c. 45). He meant to repeal nineteen and to amend another seven, and he attempted to

159. *Patriot*, 26 Nov. 1863, p. 769.
160. *Leicester Chronicle and Leicestershire Mercury*, 13 Oct. 1877, quoted in Johnson, *The Dissolution of Dissent*, p. 57.

reassure the House that all clauses in the church building acts would be left unchanged.[161]

The issue was whether district parishes and new parishes might gain the power to levy church rates for their own churches. The first act, 58 Geo. III, c. 45, had stipulated clearly that new districts were liable for twenty years for the maintenance of the parish's mother church. That stipulation had actually contributed to the beginning of anti–church rate agitation. But the building acts were otherwise silent about church rates. Dissenters had counted on verbal assurances from Peel and others that new district parishes lacked the power to levy their own church rates. The latest such assurance had been given by the marquess of Blandford (later the duke of Marlborough) with respect to his Formation of Parishes Bill, which was given royal assent on 29 July 1856. Its second clause empowered a district containing a church to become a new parish. Blandford stated in the committee stage that these new parishes could not levy church rates. He elaborated that they would resemble those formed by Sir Robert Peel's act of 1843 "under which, as was known, no church rate could be levied."[162]

Dissenters became convinced, however, that the government intended to extend church rates surreptitiously to district and new parishes. Palmer had refused to add a clause stipulating that new districts were ineligible to levy church rates. Dissenting fears stemmed from a comment by Dr. Stephen Lushington in a Court of Arches ruling late in 1862 in the Shrewsbury case (Gough v. Jones). He observed that new parishes could claim " 'the same rights and privileges' " as belonged to " 'a separate parish.' " Dissenters and Churchmen concluded that it was a likely implication that new parishes could therefore also levy church rates.[163] Palmer's consolidation bill had been referred to a select committee in 1863 in which only J. Remington Mills, the Liberal M.P. for Chepping Wycombe and an eminent Congregationalist and member of the Dissenting Deputies, had objected that the bill empowered district churches to levy church

161. *Hansard*, CLXX (20 April 1863), 463; (11 May 1863), 1573; *Record*, 1 May 1863; *Nonconformist*, 20 May 1863, p. 394.

162. *Hansard*, CXLII (22 May 1856), 575; CLXXV (9 June 1864), 1513, 1514; CXLIII (29 July 1856), 1491.

163. Ibid., CLXXV (9 June 1864), 1516; *Patriot*, 21 May 1863, p. 335; *Church Institution Circular*, Dec. 1862, pp. 95, 96; *Liberator*, 1 March 1865, p. 35.

rates. The bill had been withdrawn at the end of the session and was reintroduced on 11 April 1864.[164]

In the spring of 1864 conservative Churchmen called on friends of the Church to ensure that Dissenters should not succeed in altering Palmer's bill, which they believed would enable an estimated 1,600 new parishes to begin laying rates. Such calls roused Dissenters to act. The *Leeds Mercury* said that although they might be patient about some abuses that were "as old as the hills," a new imposition was "absolutely intolerable."[165]

On 15 April the Liberation Society called delegates of the Dissenting Deputies and the Church Rate Abolition Committee together to effect the inclusion of a clause in Palmer's church building bill that would prohibit the levying of church rates by churches built under the acts. The Committee for Preventing the Extension of Church Rates was formed on 26 April, and its 1864 expenses of nearly £52 were shared equally by the three constituent bodies.[166] Even that small share was a burden for the deputies. They now subsisted on dividends paid by their capital investments. Their subscriptions in 1862 had amounted to a mere £36 13s. The secretary, Hull Terrell, had not been reimbursed for his expenses since 1854; the debt owed to him at the end of 1862 was nearly £248.[167]

The Committee for Preventing the Extension of Church Rates sent delegations to both Roundell Palmer and Palmerston. Neither was willing to include in Palmer's consolidation bill the clause desired by church rate opponents. Palmerston said that it was unfair to alter the law; if it were presently ambiguous, the courts should determine the law. But Churchmen were also unhappy with the bill. Evangelicals believed the government was insufficiently bold. Anglo-Catholics ob-

164. *Hansard*, CLXX (11 May 1863), 1573–75; CLXXII (22 July 1863), 1205; (24 July 1863), 1356; CLXXIV (11 April 1864), 853, 854.

165. *Leeds Mercury*, 18 April 1864; the inflammatory letter, which asserted that 1,600 new parishes might be enabled to levy church rates, was submitted by J. M. Knott to the *Morning Herald*, 20 May 1864; *Nonconformist*, 25 May 1864, p. 418.

166. Minutes of Liberation Society, 15 April 1864, GLRO A/LIB/3, minute 373, fol. 198; 29 April 1864, minute 381, fols. 199, 200; Minutes of Dissenting Deputies, 4 May 1864, Guildhall MS. 3083, XIII, 317, 319; 6 July 1864, fol. 322.

167. Minutes of Dissenting Deputies, 29 Jan. 1863, Guildhall MS. 3083, XIII, 272; 16 July 1863, fol. 284; 21 Oct. 1863, fols. 297, 298. Of 110 congregations counted on to return deputies in 1863, only twenty-five had done so by 11 March; ibid., 11 March 1863, fol. 275.

jected that the bill allowed the continuation of pew rents. On 9 June 1864, during the debate on the second reading of the Church Building and New Parishes Acts Amendment Bill, Roundell Palmer asked that the bill be discharged. The government had backed down in the face of the widespread opposition the measure had roused.[168] Although church rate abolitionists could no longer pass an abolition bill through the Commons, they could effectively bar legislation that seemed to entrench the church rate principle.

XIII

The focus of political attention early in 1865 shifted to the expected general parliamentary election, which was held in July. The election signaled the end of the Conservative reaction, brighter prospects for religious liberty, and the emergence of Gladstone, after his defeat in Oxford, as the "unmuzzled" hope of voluntaryists. As the Liberation Society became increasingly determined that church rate abolition should be sought only as an installment of church disestablishment, there were signs in 1865 that this voluntaryist goal would miscarry.

In the spring of 1865 the seventh Triennial Conference of the Liberation Society endorsed the decision of the executive committee to refrain from seeking passage of a church rate abolition bill that session. The executive committee had decided already in the autumn of 1864 to devote its energies to preparing for the approaching general election. By May 1865 a special fund of £13,400 existed to finance electoral expenses. The Liberation Society employed J. M. Hare as an electoral agent, and thirty-three borough constituencies were targeted as ripe for Liberation Society pressure.[169]

The foci of preelection concerns were parliamentary reform and

168. *Nonconformist*, 27 April 1864, pp. 322, 323; 4 May 1864, p. 341; 1 June 1864, p. 439; Minutes of Liberation Society, 20 May 1864, GLRO A/LIB/3, minute 390, fols. 204, 205; 3 June 1864, minute 395, fol. 206; Minutes of Dissenting Deputies, 13 May 1863, Guildhall MS. 3083, XIII, 280; *Guardian*, 1 June 1864, p. 525; *Record*, 3 June 1864; *Hansard*, CLXXV (9 June 1864), 1509–27.

169. *Nonconformist*, 4 May 1865, p. 346; Minutes of Liberation Society, 29 Jan. 1864, GLRO A/LIB/3, fols. 185, 192; 9 Sept. 1864, fol. 218; 21 Oct. 1864, fols. 223, 225; 18 Nov. 1864, fols. 228, 229; 23 Dec. 1864, fols. 232, 233; 20 Jan. 1865, fol. 236; 3 Feb. 1865, fol. 241; 12 May 1865, fol. 265.

church rates. John Bright appealed to Carlisle electors on the basis of his support of an enlarged franchise. Disraeli's election manifesto linked both issues. He charged the Liberals with continually having attacked "the British constitution in Church and state. . . ."[170] Archbishop C. T. Longley expressed relief that the church rate question would be "made a turning-point at the next general election. . . ."[171]

The election was a successful one for the Liberal party. It won a majority of seventy to eighty-four seats, a gain of twenty to twenty-five.[172] An analysis prepared by the Liberation Society's parliamentary and electoral committee expressed satisfaction with the results for the religious equality cause. It claimed that all but eight or ten returned Liberals favored total abolition of church rates. Among the Liberals were seventeen members of the Liberation Society. The report claimed that an additional twenty-two Protestant Nonconformists not belonging to the society had also been returned.[173]

The report claimed that the quality of returned Liberals had improved substantially. It asserted that most defeated Liberals belonged "to the Old Whig party," while most new Liberals belonged to "the advanced liberal party."[174] The report counted as successes the defeats of Liberals who were replaced by conservatives consistent with Liberation Society policy, adopted in November of 1863, to defeat conservative Liberals whatever the cost to the Liberal party. The report acknowledged that the loss of some seats to Conservatives would temporarily yield "hostile votes." But taking the long view, it predicted that ultimately the Liberal party was "likely to be more closely identified than hitherto with the party of Religious Equality. . . ."[175]

170. Disraeli's election manifesto, 20 May 1865, in *Nonconformist*, 24 May 1865, p. 427; 14 June 1865, p. 473.

171. Ibid., 10 May 1865, pp. 369–72. The archbishop expressed his hope regarding the forthcoming election, on 4 May, at a gathering at which J. M. Knott was presented with a piece of plate and purse of £1,000 in acknowledgment of his services as secretary of the Committee of Laymen.

172. Minutes of Liberation Society, 21 July 1865, GLRO A/LIB/3, fol. 281; Machin, *Politics and the Churches*, p. 332; *Nonconformist*, 26 July 1865, p. 602. Machin claims that the Liberal majority was seventy. The Report of the Liberation Society's parliamentary and electoral committee asserts that the final tally was 371 Liberals to 287 Conservatives, or a Liberal majority of eighty-four.

173. Minutes of Liberation Society, 21 July 1865, GLRO A/LIB/3, fol. 282.

174. Ibid.

175. Ibid., fol. 229; Machin, *Politics and the Churches*, p. 332. Machin calls the turnover in seats, from Liberal to Conservative, dubious successes. That they appeared

The defeat of Gladstone by clerical Oxford, and his subsequent election by industrial South Lancashire, stirred the hopes of Nonconformists and Liberals that with time Gladstone would blossom as a consistent proponent of religious equality. The liberal *Daily News* extolled Gladstone as the man destined to lead the Liberal party and to complete the promise of liberalism.[176] Some of Gladstone's Conservative friends were grief stricken that Oxford had rejected Gladstone. One of those, Sir Stafford Northcote, who himself had abstained from voting in the belief that Gladstone could no longer be depended on to defend thoroughly the prerogatives of the established church, explained his position in correspondence with Gladstone.[177] In response, Gladstone confessed to being uneasy about the prospects of religious belief in the country. He believed that there were elements at work in both political parties that tended "to sap its foundations." As a sign that his concern for the Church and the Christian faith had not changed in a quarter-century, he asserted: "To check in some degree the operation of those elements is a chief remaining hope of my political life. . . ."[178]

Gladstone wrote Northcote that he believed they agreed on two propositions: first, "that the highest duty of the Church is to maintain the deposit of faith," and second, that there were "important religious as well as temporal advantages connected with national establishment" that should be retained unless truth were thereby threatened. Northcote, who described himself as inclining "to a somewhat Erastian Conservatism," agreed with Gladstone that their difference was "mainly one of degree."[179] As Gladstone elaborated later, they agreed that "the loss of faith" was more serious "than the loss of Establish-

---

to be, on the face of it. But Machin fails to place the Liberation Society's analysis of the election returns in the context of the society's own electoral policy. When that is done, the claim of success made by the Liberation Society Report is not unwarranted. See Minutes of Liberation Society, 21 July 1865, GLRO A/LIB/3, fol. 286; Hamer, *Electoral Pressure*, pp. 114–16.

176. *Daily News*, 20 July 1865; *Nonconformist*, 19 July 1865, p. 573; 26 July 1865, p. 593.

177. Samuel Wilberforce to Gladstone, 18 July 1865, Gladstone Papers, Add. MS. 44345, fols. 15–17; Northcote to Gladstone, 20 July 1865, ibid., MS. 44217, fols. 90, 91. In a touching letter, Northcote told Gladstone that although he felt unable to vote for him, Northcote had made out a voting paper and entrusted it to Edwin Palmer with instructions to cast it for Gladstone should the election have hinged on a single vote.

178. Gladstone to Northcote, 22 July 1865, "Private," Iddesleigh Papers, Add. MS. 50014, fol. 199.

179. Ibid., 28 July 1865, "Private," fol. 202; also in Gladstone Papers, Add. MS.

ment." But they seemed to part company, said Gladstone, on the question of which of the two evils was more imminent. Gladstone asserted: "I think the change of the loss of Faith has been coming on, for 20 or 25 years, that is ever since the break down of the Tractarian, and the bold development of the rationalizing movement, with a fearful rapidity. . . . But on the other hand the disestablishment of the Church is far off; and the impediments or bulwarks, to be overcome, are many and great."[180]

Gladstone referred to church rates to illustrate his meaning. He pointed out that the attack on church rates was commonly given as "proof of the formidable character of the assault on the Establishment." Gladstone argued that the establishment principle might actually be more secure if church rates were abolished:

> I think it *clear* that in Ireland the Establishment has been . . . made far safer, by the abolition of Church cess. The attack upon Establishment in England is in embryo: it is only as matter of argument that it is respectable: as a political power it is almost contemptible. That some of the Anti-Church-Rate people look upon their measure as a blow to the Establish-ment—, only shows me their feebleness, [and] their Moldigria-fian estimate of Lilliputian proceedings.[181]

Eager voluntaryists were bound to be disappointed in Gladstone. He was committed to redressing the practical grievances, the points of "sore contact" as he saw them, that remained between Anglicans and Nonconformists. But his aim in doing so was to "weaken the invading army" of those seeking disestablishment.[182] Gladstone remained, in 1863, almost as committed to the church establishment as he had been in 1840, although his view of the state had become considerably desacralized.[183]

44217, 28 July 1865, "Private," copy, fol. 98; Northcote to Gladstone, 24 July 1865, Gladstone Papers, Add. MS. 44217, fol. 95; 4 Aug. 1865, fol. 101.

180. Gladstone to Northcote, 9 Aug. 1865, Iddesleigh Papers, Add. MS. 50014, fol. 206.

181. Ibid., fol. 208.

182. Gladstone to Samuel Wilberforce, 21 March 1863, "Private, copy," Gladstone Papers, Add. MS. 44344, fols. 235–39; Machin, *Politics and the Churches*, p. 309.

183. H.C.G. Matthew, ed., introduction to vol. III of *The Gladstone Diaries* (Oxford, 1974); M. D. Stephen, "Liberty, Church, and State: Gladstone's Relations with Manning and Acton, 1832–1870," *Journal of Religious History*, 1 (1960), 222; Perry

Gladstone's dedication to the establishment principle was surpassed only by his Anglo-Catholic devotion to the Church's spiritual vitality. This earned him the bitter enmity of the more rigorous establishmentarians. On 30 July 1865 Archdeacon Denison, who averred that his overriding principle had always been the Church of England as the church national, wrote exultantly to Disraeli about Gladstone's Oxford defeat: "I have been thirteen years endeavouring to turn out Gladstone, and I rejoice to have had a hand at last in doing it."[184] In the same letter Denison informed Disraeli that his *Church and State Review* was to be terminated on 1 August. A deficiency of funds had killed this unbending defender of the "no compromise" establishment school. Denison had fought to extend its life until after the election, lest its demise before or during should "do harm to the Cause, and play into the hands of the Guardian and Gladstone."[185]

The extinction of Denison's journal also signaled the defeat of efforts by Denison, Hale, and Disraeli to align the Church fully with the Conservative party. Instead, the Church was beginning to follow the course advocated by Gladstone and the *Guardian:* of taking its place as a more independent spiritual institution. Contrarily, Nonconformity was becoming ever more closely identified with liberalism and the Liberal party, despite the protestations of older Evangelicals such as Dr. John Campbell and John Angell James.

Late in 1865, in preparation for the approaching parliamentary session, the Liberation Society's parliamentary committee observed that if constitutional reform became an issue, ecclesiasticcal questions would be neglected. It therefore recommended that the society take the initiative only on introducing a church rate abolition bill, to which it was now morally pledged. Ecclesiastical measures introduced by others would be given enthusiastic support, however. The greatest concern of the parliamentary committee was now (as had been Liberation Society policy since 1863) that the questions it adopted should promote the ultimate objects of the society. The issue must be seen by all as a question of church establishments. The report explicated: "We are not

---

Butler, *Gladstone: Church, State, and Tractarianism—A Study of His Religious Ideas and Attitudes, 1809–1859* (Oxford, 1982), pp. 234–35; Boyd Hilton, "Gladstone's Theological Politics," in M. Bentley and J. Stevenson, eds., *High and Low Politics in Modern Britain* (Oxford, 1983), p. 30.

184. G. A. Denison to Disraeli, 30 July 1865, Hughenden Papers B/XXI/D/138, LSE microfilm 131.

185. Ibid., B. XXI/D/136, 9 June 1865.

working for the reward of present success, nor of success in small measures . . . we have to teach abstract truths through the medium of practical measures."[186]

Apart from how best to "teach abstract truths," the Liberation Society also had to face the fact that the cause of church rate abolition was not progressing as smoothly as it tended to claim. On 15 September 1865 J. Carvell Williams had presented a report to the executive committee calling for "no delay in adopting new measures for extending the *parochial* agitation. That, it must be admitted, has, during the last year or two, shown some sign of abatement." He suggested that the decline of anti–church rate agitation must probably "be attributed to the increase of the practice of making what are practically voluntary rates."[187] In effect this growing practice, to which the *Liberator* also referred, involved assenting to rates on the condition that they not be enforced against defaulters. It was the procedure which Baron Ebury had heralded and which Lord Alfred S. Churchill had wished to codify in law on 7 July 1863. On that day he had also claimed—with some justification, it seems—that the system he proposed "was already in operation and fast extending itself in all well regulated parishes."[188] There were other signs that the movement toward church rate abolition was hardly inevitable. The annual summaries of distraints for ecclesiastical taxes suffered by the Society of Friends confirmed that. Distraints for church rates had fallen from approximately £575 in the year before May 1860 to £390 in 1862, and to £355 in 1863. But church rate distraints rose again to £501 in 1864 and £529 in 1865.[189]

Perhaps the weightiest evidence that all signs were not favoring church rate abolitionists can be found in the Home Office's "Local Taxation Returns." These annual returns, which were first published in 1862, tell an interesting story. The first return shows that in the year before June 1861 church rate income in England and Wales amounted to approximately £233,560. The following year's figure indicated a drop, although a small one, to £232,907. That decrease in church rate income followed a pattern seen in each church rate return published since 1832. But the pattern was reversed for the year before June

186. Minutes of Liberation Society, 17 Nov. 1865, GLRO A/LIB/3, fol. 328; *Nonconformist*, 29 Nov. 1865, p. 954.

187. Minutes of Liberation Society, 15 Sept. 1865, GLRO A/LIB/3, fol. 301.

188. *Hansard*, CLXXII (7 July 1863), 365; *Liberator*, 1 Dec. 1865, p. 195.

189. Society of Friends, London Yearly Meeting Minutes, XXVII, 204–8, 493–95, 546, 547, 604–6, 673–75.

1863. Church rate income had climbed to approximately £237,386. The following year it ascended to £241,960, and by June 1865 it had reached £243,523. In three years church rate receipts had increased by £10,616.[190] The rising church rate revenue after 1862 indicated that church defense was being felt on the parish level. Parishes such as Framlingham made a rate after a hiatus of five years.[191] Considerable numbers of parishioners must have consented to a "voluntary rate," although they might have objected to a compulsory one. The church rate figures in the "Local Taxation Returns" helped to demythologize the claim that an inexorably rising tide of parochial anti–church rate agitation made total abolition inevitable. The growth of "voluntary rates" indicated, to the Liberation Society's chagrin, that many Nonconformists could be satisfied with less than the entire abolition of church rates.

Following Gladstone's election in South Lancashire, Miall and other voluntaryists were emboldened to hope that Gladstone might lead them to religious equality. Gladstone was in fact preparing to take an active role in resolving the church rate question. But as his private writings indicate, his motivation was to safeguard the church establishment — not to satisfy voluntaryists. Probably some time in 1865 Gladstone drafted a lengthy memorandum that suggests that a significant factor behind his public resolve in 1866 to settle the church rate question stemmed from his concern about evidence of the declining attachment of Methodists, and particularly of Wesleyans, to the church establishment. Gladstone noted that Wesleyans had fewer objections to paying church rates than did "Methodist secession churches," but that objections were growing among them "owing chiefly to the alarming growth of puseyism & rationalism in the Church. . . ."[192] Gladstone discounted as unrepresentative of Wesleyan opinion the testimony of those — T. P. Bunting and the Reverend George Osborn — who had claimed before

190. Great Britain, *Parliamentary Papers*, "Local Taxation Returns," 1862, III. 127, p. 131; 1863, XXX. 1, p. 4; 1864, XXXIII. 137, pp. 141, 142; 1865, XLVI. 1, p. 5; 1866, LV. 293, p. 297.

191. No church rate had been made in the parish of Framlingham since 1859, but on 21 April 1864 one was carried by a vote of thirty to six. Reported in the *Church Institution Circular*, June 1864, p. 181. Similar reversals occurred in other parishes. Henry Hoare widely publicized his success in carrying and enforcing church rates in his parish of Staplehurst, Kent, where he served as churchwarden. See Hoare, *Hints*, I–III.

192. W. E. Gladstone, "Methodist Statistics, Ch. Rate," circa 1865, Gladstone Papers, Add. MS. 44754, fols. 150, 145–48.

the House of Lords committee in 1859–60 that Wesleyans willingly paid church rates. He also was convinced that the Bunting-Osborn evidence had led to serious dissatisfaction among Wesleyans. Gladstone clearly shared the fear of the Reverend William Arthur that the effect of the agitation among Wesleyans would " 'be to excite a feeling hostile to the established church.' "[193] Gladstone concluded: "from the whole of the above it is clear that the Methodists would be greatly relieved by not being compelled to pay church rates and at the same time one great cause of their growing estrangement from the established Church would be removed."[194] It was telling that after more than thirty years of Dissenting anti–church rate agitation, Gladstone could be so influenced by the relatively new dissatisfaction of Wesleyans. The reason was hardly obscure. He had dismissed the political threat posed by militant voluntaryist Dissenters as "almost contemptible." But the desertion of Wesleyans from at least tacit support of the established church could seriously jeopardize its continuation. To protect the establishment, Gladstone was ready to sacrifice compulsory church rates.

Both the Conservative party and the Liberation Society had suffered serious defeats in their handling of the church rate question. The Conservatives had lost a great opportunity to propose an alternative church rate plan based on the recommendations of the House of Lords select committee. Such a compromise bill, which a considerable number of liberals would have welcomed, would have offered a generous exemption from church rates to all conscientious objectors and allowed the Church to retain a modified church rate principle. It seems likely that had such a scheme been enacted, church rates would have continued in many small and rural parishes. But chronic differences among Churchmen and within the Conservative party torpedoed any possibility of agreement on an alternative to abolition.

The failure of its enemies did not mean full success for the Liberation Society. By 1865 it was again firmly committed to seeking the total abolition of church rates as a step toward the disestablishment of the Church. Yet to save the abolitionist cause from a humiliating rout, the Liberation Society had been compelled to entrust the church rate question to the Church Rate Abolition Committee and to rely on the

193. Ibid., fols. 151–56.
194. Ibid., fol. 156.

anti–church rate petition of Methodists. Both had clearly rejected any link between church rate abolition and disestablishment. Furthermore, there was evidence that by 1865 church rate income was actually increasing, which suggested that the nation (including Nonconformists) might be satisfied with less than total church rate abolition. Finally, the plan suggested by Ebury, Bright, and Lord Alfred, as well as the nature of Gladstone's concerns, suggested that in the future a resolution of the church rate question might yet be found that would stop well short of satisfying the Liberation Society's ideal of using the question to bring on the separation of church and state. The growing bipartisan consensus in favor of preempting that militant goal by settling the church rate issue on a more moderate basis is the subject of the following chapter.

V

Resolution of the Church Rate Conflict, 1865–1868

Early in 1866 Gladstone set out to forge a church rate bill that would be acceptable to moderates in both parties and preclude the necessity of accepting total abolition of the rate. Gladstone introduced a scheme that was essentially Baron Ebury's plan of retaining parochial machinery while repealing the powers of compulsion, with the addition of clauses favored by Anglo-Catholics to exclude noncontributors from interfering in church affairs.

By 1866 tumultuous parochial church rate contests were things of the past. In thousands of parishes church rates were now virtually voluntary, although compulsory church rates continued to be collected in rural parishes throughout the country. It had become clear in 1863 that the conservative church defense reaction had collapsed. Disagreements among conservative Churchmen had prevented moderate Conservatives from taking advantage of the opportunity offered to them by moderate Liberals to pass a compromise church rate bill that would retain the church rate principle in modified form. In the wake of the Conservatives' failure, and because of the changing political climate by the late 1860s, the defeat of the compulsory church rate became inevitable.

In this final stage of the church rate question external pressure counted for little. The shaping of the act to abolish compulsory church rates depended on the balance of church parties within the House of Lords more than on political party strength. The process resulted in an act that pleased the abolitionists but one that paradoxically constituted, on the fact of it, a defeat for the ultimate aims of the Liberation Society.

II

Even before Palmerston's death in October 1865, Nonconformists hoped for unprecedented reforms from a new House of Commons "pledged to ecclesiastical as well as political progress."[1] In the expectation that parliamentary reform would preoccupy the Commons in the 1866 session, the Liberation Society, which now enjoyed the close cooperation of the Dissenting Deputies, had earlier decided to initiate but one ecclesiastical reform—church rate abolition—following a voluntary lapse of two years.[2]

The Liberation Society engaged J. A. Hardcastle to take charge of its church rate abolition bill after being turned down by four other M.P.s. Hardcastle, the Liberal member for Bury St. Edmund's, was, like Trelawny, a Churchman (although of Dissenting parentage) opposed to disestablishment and militant voluntaryism.[3] But it was Glad-

1. *Nonconformist,* 7 Feb. 1866, p. 101; Minutes of Liberation Society, 15 Sept. 1865, GLRO A/LIB/3, fol. 2.

2. Ibid., 17 Nov. 1865, fols. 327, 328; 2 Feb. 1866, fol. 343; Minutes of Dissenting Deputies, 3 Jan. 1866, Guildhall MS. 3083, XIII, 346; 18 Jan. 1866, fol. 347; 14 Feb. 1866, fol. 348. Other ecclesiastical reforms that the Liberation Society would support were the abolition of university tests, reform of parliamentary oaths, and disestablishment and disendowment of the Irish Church. Machin, *Politics and the Churches,* p. 337.

3. Minutes of Liberation Society, 2 Feb. 1866, GLRO A/LIB/3, fol. 346; 16 Feb. 1866, fols. 348, 349. Edward Baines and Thomas Barnes were approached first. Both had "expressed their inability to do so"; ibid., 2 Feb. 1866, fol. 346. Before Hardcastle accepted the task of promoting the Liberation Society's abolition bill, Locke King and Lord Henley also declined to do so. Olive Anderson refers to only two refusals in "Gladstone's Abolition of Compulsory Church Rates: A Minor Political Myth and Its Historiographical Career," *Journal of Ecclesiastical History,* XXV, no. 2 (April 1974), 185. It seems plausible, however, that at least Baines's plea of inability should not be taken at face value. This certainly would not have been the first time that the moderate Baines had excused himself from serving as a spokesman for the sometimes embarrassingly immoderate Liberation Society.

stone's initiative that was to provide the solution to the church rate question. Gladstone recast Hardcastle's bill in 1866 to forge a settlement that was to win the broad support of moderate opinion in both political parties, in the Church, and within Nonconformity.[4]

Hardcastle brought in his church rates abolition bill for the second reading on 7 March 1866.[5] He observed that since 1834 thirty-six different attempts had been made to settle the question, and that on no other issue had both sides of the House been "so resolutely and pertinaciously catechized as on the question of church rates."[6] Hardcastle categorically denied that abolition "would weaken the connection between Church and State."[7] His reassurances to the establishment were a reminder that the Liberation Society could hope for concessions on church rates only by separating that issue from the establishment question.

Spencer Walpole, the Conservative M.P. for Cambridge University, emphasized the ulterior aims of the Liberation Society while moving for a six-month adjournment of the second reading. He also discussed the 1865 church rate returns, which had been published belatedly on 6 March. Church rate income had increased by £4,574 over the previous year. It was now £241,860. Unfortunately it was unclear how much of this increase was derived from compulsory rates and how much had been contributed voluntarily. The *Nonconformist* believed that fully one-third of parishes did not collect compulsory church rates—a figure disputed by Walpole.[8] On 16 March the Liberation Society resolved to institute its own inquiry into the relative numbers of compulsory and voluntary rates. Three months later it claimed that of 1,510 parishes investigated, only 150 exacted compulsory church rates.[9] Although

4. The resolution of the church rate question, achieved between 1866 and 1868, is succinctly and admirably summarized in Anderson's "Gladstone's Abolition of Compulsory Church Rates," 185–91. The second good treatment of this phase of the question, which relies heavily on Anderson, is in Machin, *Politics and the Churches*, pp. 337–43, 349–55.

5. *Hansard*, CLXXXI (7 March 1866), 1632. The first reading was given to the bill on 13 February; ibid., 447.

6. Ibid., 1633.

7. Ibid., 1636.

8. Ibid., 1650, 1652; Great Britain, *Parliamentary Papers*, "Local Taxation Returns," 1865, XLVI. 1, p. 5; *Nonconformist*, 7 March 1866, p. 182.

9. Minutes of Liberation Society, 16 March 1866, GLRO A/LIB/3, fol. 355; 8 June 1866, fols. 377, 378. The Liberation Society return indicated that of 1,510 parishes investigated, 284 parishes levied rates but did not enforce them; 900 parishes

Walpole continued to repudiate church rate abolition, he did indicate that he might be willing to make concessions if Hardcastle demanded less than outright abolition. He noted that Hardcastle had continually referred to the abolition of *compulsory* church rates. Walpole hinted that he might be willing to bargain if such a bill were actually before them.[10]

Gladstone, who was careful to say that he spoke only in his individual capacity, was prepared with a plan he hoped both sides could accept. Gladstone agreed with Walpole that the church rate principle, the policy of taxing the entire community to maintain the edifices of the national religion, was closely related to the establishment principle. But he called on Walpole to recognize two practical points. First, since the Braintree decision every parish was free to "reduce this great theory to nothing in their own case. . . ." Second, since 1859 Walpole himself had been willing to allow individuals to exempt themselves from church rate obligations. Gladstone argued that in practical terms abolishing compulsory rates would remove a point of sore contact between the Church and Dissent and actually strengthen the establishment.[11]

Gladstone stated that he continued to oppose the "simple abolition of church rates." He proposed that they should follow the implications of Walpole's bill of 1859. Its wide exemption provisions entailed, claimed Gladstone, that those remaining to pay the rate would be only those who wished to do so. Gladstone concluded with the core of his proposal: "We should then abolish the compulsory process," restricting "participation in the administration of the church . . . to those who are willing to pay it. . . ."[12]

Beresford Hope, Gladstone's cross-bench friend and fellow Anglo-Catholic, hailed Gladstone's speech as "daylight breaking on this vexed and cloudy question."[13] Bright rightly reminded the House that Gladstone's proposal closely resembled his own plan, which he had placed before the Commons in May 1862. He recommended that they should give Hardcastle's bill its second reading and then amend it in

---

had abolished church rates; 200 parishes had no need of rates, relying on endowments; and 150 parishes relied on a compulsory church rate.

10. *Hansard*, CLXXXI (7 March 1866), 1644.
11. Ibid., 1661–64.
12. Ibid., 1664–66.
13. Ibid., 1668.

committee by extinguishing only all compulsory powers of collecting the rate.[14]

Bright echoed Hardcastle's claim that abolition would not advance the cause of disestablishment. Bright believed that the church establishment, as a political institution, "was destined to many years of life."[15] That opinion was essentially endorsed by Samuel Morley, the wealthy Congregationalist whose testimony before the Lords committee had helped to evoke the conservative reaction beginning in 1860. Although Morley was a voluntaryist and held that in principle church property was national property, he had never been happy with the Liberation Society's disendowment policy. He claimed now that "he did not believe that one Dissenter in [a] thousand desired to touch a shilling of the Church's property."[16] Both Morley and Bright had dissociated their views on the relation of church rates and disestablishment from the official policy of the Liberation Society. It was partly because moderate Churchmen in both political parties were coming to believe that their views were more representative of Dissenting opinion than the positions of Miall and the Liberation Society that agreement on a compromise solution was starting to appear practicable.

Hardcastle, the Liberation Society's moderate spokesman, conceded that although he could not accept alteration of the bill's main principle, he would consider amendments at a later stage. On that note the House divided, passing the abolition bill by a vote of 285 to 252. The majority of thirty-three for Hardcastle's bill was the first majority for abolition since the majority of fifteen for Trelawny's bill on 27 February 1861. Moderate Conservatives like Northcote, Heathcote, and Beresford Hope again cast "no" votes. But Gladstone, for the first time, voted with the abolitionists in the hope of altering Hardcastle's bill so as to win the support of moderates in both parties.[17]

Already on 4 February 1866, nine days before the first reading of Hardcastle's bill, Gladstone had raised the church rate question in the cabinet. He had a three-part proposal to make. First, "All compulsory power for levying Church Rate should cease." Second, persons refusing to pay church rates should "be disabled from acting in the Vestry for Ch[urch] purposes or being Ch[urch] wardens. . . ." Third, a

14. Ibid., 1674, 1675.
15. Ibid., 1678.
16. Ibid., 1689, 1688.
17. Ibid., 1689–95.

vestry might charge additional rates for interments and church seats to poor ratepayers who refused to pay church rates.[18] Gladstone's proposal was in keeping with plans he had been formulating since 1854. Like his most recent sketch of a church rate bill dating to 11 August 1865, Gladstone proposed the formation of a "church vestry" with undiminished powers except over those ceasing to belong to it.[19] Unlike that plan, however, and unlike all the major church rate reforms introduced since Sir William Page Wood's of 1849, the onus was no longer to be on objectors to exempt themselves from church rate obligations, but on Churchmen to assume church rate responsibilities.

Before enunciating his church rate proposals in the Commons on 7 March, Gladstone had shown his plan to the Broad Churchman Sir George Grey, who as home secretary in 1856 had been responsible for the exemption scheme that had been accepted by Dissenters, and to Sir R. J. Phillimore, Gladstone's lifelong Anglo-Catholic friend who was soon to become the dean of the Court of Arches. Both men objected to the third part of Gladstone's plan that proposed additional charges for those refusing to pay church rates. By 17 March, following similar criticisms in the liberal *Daily News* and after discussion with the Anglo-Catholic Attorney General Sir Roundell Palmer, Gladstone was convinced to jettison reliance on extra charges in return for the guarantee that nonratepayers would be barred from interfering in church affairs.[20]

Gladstone's next step was to show the cabinet his proposal. He had decided to introduce his own measure rather than rely on amending Hardcastle's bill in committee. By 12 April he had drafted a bill to abolish compulsory church rates that consisted of amendments to Hardcastle's bill and clauses added jointly by Phillimore and himself.[21]

18. "Mem[orandu]m by WEG on Church Rate Abolition," 4 Feb. 1866, Gladstone Papers, Add. MS. 44755, fol. 9; Matthew, ed., *Gladstone Diaries*, VI, 4 Feb. 1866, p. 416.

19. "Sketch of Church Rate Bill," by Gladstone, 11 Aug. 1865, Gladstone Papers, Add. MS. 44754, fols. 108–14; see also Gladstone's "Plans for Dealing with Church Rate," 25 April 1863, Gladstone Papers, Add. MS. 44752, fols. 292, 293.

20. Gladstone to Phillimore, 4 March 1866, Gladstone Papers, Add. MS. 44277, fol. 287; Phillimore to Gladstone, 6 March 1866, ibid., fols. 289, 290; Sir George Grey to Gladstone, 6 March 1866, Gladstone Papers, Add. MS. 44162, fols. 297, 298; Gladstone to Heathcote, 16 March 1866, "Private," Gladstone Papers, Add. MS. 44209, fol. 174; ibid., 17 March 1866, fol. 175.

21. "Church Rate Abolition. A Bill for the Abolition of Church Rates [Bill 11.]," bill brought in by Hardcastle, Dillwyn, and Baines, in Gladstone Papers, Add. MS. 44605, 13 Feb. 1866, fol. 51. Gladstone added his amendments to this folio, and fols.

The government adopted Gladstone's proposal, contingent on his ability to win bipartisan support for it.[22]

Between 25 April and 3 May Gladstone devoted himself to finding a consensus for his plans. He appealed to abolitionists through Hardcastle and Samuel Morley. Among Conservatives he appealed to friends and fellow Anglo-Catholics on the basis of a shared concern for the Church's spiritual welfare. He wrote first to Heathcote, asking him to communicate with Walpole, Northcote, and Beresford Hope. The initial responses of Heathcote and Northcote were rather negative, but Northcote came to agree (with Heathcote's concurrence) that if Gladstone could promise the approval of Hardcastle and Bright, they would "recommend our friends to accept it. . . ."[23] Beresford Hope reminded Gladstone that there were two materially valuable elements in church rates: "the *power* to enforce them" and "the *prestige* attached to an immemorial institution." He warned that Gladstone's bill, with its language of abolition and talk of a new voluntary rate, surrendered "both power & prestige," and would not satisfy that large body of moderate Churchmen looking to him to settle the question.[24] By 3 May it was clear that Beresford Hope was unlikely to support Gladstone. The same was true for other Conservatives who agreed that Gladstone's bill did not retain sufficient continuity with "the old institution of Church Rates."[25]

53–56 held additional clauses (4–10) added by Gladstone and Phillimore; "Confidential, A Bill for the Abolition of Church Rates," printed at F.O. 12 April 1866, in Gladstone Papers, Add. MS. 44606, fols. 1–3. This was the actual Gladstone bill—a compilation of the amended Hardcastle clauses plus the Gladstone-Phillimore clauses. Oddly, the title did not refer to the abolition of *compulsory* church rates, which was Gladstone's first aim and was achieved by amending clause one of Hardcastle's bill.

22. Gladstone to Heathcote, 25 April 1866, copy in Letter Book, 1866–69, Gladstone Papers, Add. MS. 44536, p. 87.

23. Northcote to Heathcote, 26 April 1866, Gladstone Papers, Add. MS. 44217, fol. 104; Heathcote to Gladstone, 28 April 1866, Gladstone Papers, Add. MS. 44207, fols. 178, 180; Gladstone to Heathcote, 28 April 1866, copy in Letter Book, 1866–69, Gladstone Papers, Add. MS. 44536, p. 89.

24. Beresford Hope to Gladstone, 30 April 1866, Gladstone Papers, Add. MS. 44213, fols. 333, 332; Gladstone to Beresford Hope, 28 April 1866, copy in Letter Book, 1866–69, Gladstone Papers, Add. MS. 44536, p. 90.

25. Beresford Hope to Gladstone, 3 May 1866, Gladstone Papers, Add. MS. 44213, fol. 335. Anderson, in "Gladstone's Abolition of Compulsory Church Rates," p. 188, wrongly gives the impression that Beresford Hope continued to support Gladstone's bill. He did not. On 11 June he supported Sir W. Bovill in bringing in the Church Rates Law Amendment Bill as an alternative to Gladstone's scheme.

The overtures made to Hardcastle and Morley were more warmly received. Both men were sent copies of the draft of Gladstone's bill. Morley quickly replied that he personally could see nothing in it "to which the Dissenters ought not to agree. . . ."[26] On 30 April the Committee of the Dissenting Deputies met to consider the bill. The meeting, which was attended by Hardcastle and Morley, proposed alterations to the bill entailing that the disqualification of nonratepaying parishioners, to which Gladstone attributed such importance, "should be confined to questions involved in the making and Expenditure of the proposed voluntary Rates."[27] The following day, 1 May, at a joint meeting of the executive committee of the Liberation Society and the officers of the Dissenting Deputies, Hardcastle reported that Gladstone was willing to accept the alterations proposed the day before. Those present agreed to accept Gladstone's revised bill, a decision endorsed the following day at the Liberation Society's annual meeting. Miall argued that with compulsion gone there was nothing left of the rate but its name. A minority of more militant voluntaryists objected, however, that by accepting they were de facto relinquishing their rights to the property of parochial churches.[28]

Hardcastle's letter informing Gladstone of the acceptance of his plan by the abolitionists was sent to Beresford Hope and Northcote. Neither man liked the proposal. Northcote said that "the general feeling" among those he had consulted was unfavorable.[29] The prospects of an immediate resolution of the church rate question were dimming rapidly. Conservative Churchmen were not rallying behind Gladstone, and the Liberals were floundering in the Commons on the parliamentary reform issue. Nevertheless, a discouraged Gladstone, backed by Russell and Sir George Grey, believed that it was "due to the Dissenters" to introduce a church rate bill in the Commons.[30]

26. Samuel Morley to Gladstone, 28 April 1866, Gladstone Papers, Add. MS. 44410, fol. 110; Gladstone to Hardcastle, 25 April 1866, copy in Letter Book, 1866–69, Gladstone Papers, Add. MS. 44536, p. 88; 28 April 1866, p. 90.

27. Minutes of Dissenting Deputies, 30 April 1866, Guildhall MS. 3083, XIII, 359.

28. Minutes of Liberation Society, 1 May 1866, GLRO A/LIB/3, fol. 364; *Nonconformist*, 9 May 1866, p. 382; 21 March 1866, pp. 221, 226; *Watchman*, 14 March 1866, p. 85.

29. Northcote to Gladstone, 2 May 1866, Gladstone Papers, Add. MS. 44217, fol. 106; Beresford Hope to Gladstone, 3 May 1866, Gladstone Papers, Add. MS. 44213, fol. 336.

30. Gladstone, "Mem[orandum] on Church Rate Abolition Bill," 4 May 1866, Gladstone Papers, Add. MS. 44755, fols. 70, 71.

On 8 May Gladstone sponsored the first reading of what was now the government bill for the abolition of compulsory church rates. Gladstone briefly outlined the clauses of his bill. The first and preeminent clause provided for the cessation of all legal proceedings "to enforce or compel the payment of any church rate" in the parishes of England and Wales.[31] Clause two allowed compulsory church rates to continue where they were required to pay debts contracted on the security of rates. Clause three provided for the collection of church rates levied before passage of this bill. Clause four enabled parishioners "to assess a voluntary rate upon the owners or occupiers of property" within the parish for the maintenance of church and churchyard and for the provision of church services. Clause five extended the right granted in the previous clause to inhabitants of extraparochial ecclesiastical districts. Clause six provided that in cases in which a vote should be called on a proposed voluntary church rate, voters should sign their names in a poll book that declared their willingness to pay the rate the majority agreed to.[32] The final proviso Gladstone named the "most important clause," because it provided a "compensation" for the loss of compulsion. This was the clause that stopped nonratepayers, and generally non-Anglicans, from interfering in the affairs of the Church. The attainment of this security for the Church's independence from outside interference was the prize in exchange for which Gladstone and other Anglo-Catholic M.P.s were willing to relinquish compulsory church rates. The final clause did ensure that there should be disabilities attached to refusing to contribute to the voluntary rate. First, noncontributors should be " 'ineligible for the office of Churchwarden for ecclesiastical purposes.' " Gladstone explained, showing that the objections of abolitionists had been heard, that noncontributors continued to have the right to function as churchwardens for all but church rate–related duties. The second disability for noncontributors was the loss of the right to vote in vestry for churchwardens for ecclesiastical purposes—that is, for the warden entitled to deal with church rates, and on questions related to the making or distributing of voluntary church rates.[33]

Before the House gave a first reading to the bill, Lord John Manners warned that it would destroy the substance of the rate while retaining a semblance of it. He also alerted members to a recent speech in which Miall had said that although Churchmen might view the bill as a

31. *Hansard*, CLXXXIII (8 May 1866), 619–36.
32. Ibid., 621, 622.
33. Ibid., 622–24.

compromise, it was actually a victory for the Liberation Society.[34] In fact, Gladstone himself had helped to ensure that his bill should be less than a Liberation Society victory. In introducing the government measure he had given fulsome praise to the role of Samuel Morley in arranging this compromise. In a personal letter to Morley a fortnight earlier, Gladstone observed that questions relating to religious liberty required "not only firm but conciliatory treatment." Gladstone believed that Morley amply possessed those qualities as well as a large Dissenting following, and he hoped therefore that progress was possible on vexed religious liberty questions.[35]

Gladstone's praise in the Commons of Morley's moderate and conciliatory manners was a rebuke to the Liberation Society. Although Morley was a member of that society, on 7 March when first supporting Gladstone's proposal he had publicly distanced himself from the liberationists' goal of nationalizing the Church's endowments. In doing so he claimed to voice the views of moderate Dissenters. Morley's stance provided an opportunity for Gladstone to bypass the militant Liberation Society and to deal with Morley as a representative of the moderate majority of Dissenters.

Much credit for bringing Gladstone together with moderate Dissenters belongs to the Reverend Christopher Newman Hall, an eminent and politically moderate London Congregationalist minister. Newman Hall had worked assiduously since the autumn of 1864 to align moderate Dissenters with Gladstone and had introduced Gladstone and Morley at a gathering in his house on 25 January 1866.[36] Shortly after one such important meeting in 1864 Newman Hall wrote a supplementary letter to Gladstone outlining Nonconformist political objectives. Newman Hall asserted that Methodists, who constituted

34. Ibid., 629; for one such statement by Miall, see *Nonconformist*, 21 March 1866, p. 221.

35. Gladstone to Samuel Morley, 21 April 1866, copy in Letter Book, 1866–69, Gladstone Papers, Add. MS. 44536, p. 84; Samuel Morley to Gladstone, 25 April 1866, Gladstone Papers, Add. MS 44410, fols. 99, 100; 11 May 1866, fol. 159; *Hansard*, CLXXXIII (8 May 1866), 621. Morley lost his seat for Nottingham early in 1866. He was unseated on petition, to Gladstone's deep regret, after it was found that several of his 1865 electoral agents had, without his knowledge, bought votes. Edwin Hodder, *The Life of Samuel Morley* (2d ed.; London, 1887), chap. 13.

36. Machin, *Politics and the Churches*, pp. 327–30; Newman Hall to Gladstone, 10 Nov. 1864, Gladstone Papers, Add. MS. 44188, fols. 20, 21; Gladstone to Newman Hall, 11 Nov. 1864, copy in Letter Book, 1863–65, Gladstone Papers, Add. MS. 44534, p. 309; Machin, "Gladstone and Nonconformity in the 1860s: The Formation of an Alliance," *Historical Journal*, XVII (1974), 347–64.

half of Protestant Nonconformity, did not object to the establishment principle. As for the other half, he claimed: "while hoping for the ultimate recognition of the Free Church Theory, they were not expecting it at present, they meditate no political action to bring it about, they make it no question on the hustings, and look for it more as the result of influences within the Church of England than of efforts from without."[37] Thus Newman Hall implicitly denied that the Liberation Society's goals of disestablishment and disendowment reflected anything but a militant fringe of Nonconformist opinion. What Nonconformists did "desire at once," asserted Newman Hall, was free access to the universities, disestablishment of the Church of Ireland, and abolition of church rates.[38] He said in effect that most Dissenters would be content with redress from outstanding "practical grievances." As we have seen, Miall sometimes feared this to be the case.[39] But most important, this was becoming Gladstone's view. He was coming to speak of removing "sore points" between Churchmen and Dissenters to protect the church establishment. Newman Hall probably influenced, or at least reinforced, that strategy.

Conservative church defenders were less successful than Gladstone in defending the establishment. The Church Institution opposed Gladstone's bill ineffectually. Its call for a petitioning campaign yielded no more than 151 petitions against both the Hardcastle and Gladstone bills.[40] The Church Institution had become a dispirited organization devoid of ideas or leadership.[41]

37. Newman Hall to Gladstone, 26 or 28 Nov. 1864, Gladstone Papers, Add. MS. 44188, fols. 30, 31. Machin suggests that the date, which is nearly illegible, should be 16 November; *Politics and the Churches*, p. 327.

38. Newman Hall to Gladstone, 26 or 28 Nov. 1864, Gladstone Papers, Add. MS. 44188, fol. 31.

39. Machin criticizes Newman Hall for minimizing "to an incredible degree the political aims and activity of Dissent" (*Politics and the Churches*, p. 329). If pronouncements of the Liberation Society, and leaders in the *Nonconformist*, are taken as representative of the political aims of Dissent, then Newman Hall's declaration regarding the limited aims of Dissent does seem disingenuous. However, even Miall recognized that Nonconformist support for a political campaign to disestablish the Church of England was shallow and likely to crumble if practical grievances such as church rates were redressed.

40. Great Britain, HLRO, *Reports on Public Petitions*, Session 1866, "34th Report . . . 31 July–10 Aug. 1866," pp. 887, 888; *Nonconformist*, 7 March 1866, p. 182; 30 May 1866, p. 430.

41. The Church Institution's founder, Henry Hoare, died on 16 April 1866 from wounds suffered in a freak railway accident a year earlier. On 30 March 1865, en route from London to Cambridge, Hoare's head hit a telegraph post while he was "looking out of his carriage window on entering a tunnel." Sweet, *A Memoir*, p. 518.

III

The second reading of Gladstone's Compulsory Church Rates Abolition Bill was delayed by the defeat of Russell's ministry on 18 June
1866 over Gladstone's parliamentary reform bill. When Derby formed
a minority government on 25 June Gladstone was left to advance his
church rate scheme as a private member. But the franchise question
had left Liberals deeply divided, and all moderate Churchmen were
not yet convinced that Gladstone's scheme was the best solution to the
church rate question. Among Conservatives strong opposition remained to Gladstone's plans — but neither was there general enthusiasm
for alternatives to it. Disraeli, as leader in the Commons of a minority
government, now relied on his parliamentary skills to stall in the hope
of finding a compromise in the following session that would not alienate
his die-hard backbench supporters.

On 18 July 1866 Gladstone moved (with the blessing of the Liberation Society) that his bill be given a second reading. Initially it
appeared that bipartisan agreement on the question was finally in sight.
Gladstone opened his speech by informing the House that it had been
intimated to him through the normal channels that the government was
"willing to accede to the principle of the Bill by voting for the second
reading" on the understanding that the bill go no further that session
and that the Conservatives remained free to move amendments in
committee.[42] But Disraeli, now chancellor of the exchequer, rose
dramatically to say that Gladstone had misconceived the arrangements
that had been made. Because of the lateness of the session "and other
circumstances," the government had thought it best to allow the bill to
be read the second time. But, declared Disraeli to a dismayed Gladstone, the government "do not accept the principle of the Bill, nor do
they mean to vote for the second reading, but will not vote against it."[43]

Most of the speakers in the debate opposed Gladstone's measure. A
common concern, reflecting particularly antiritualist feelings, was that
it would allow certain ecclesiastical parties to usurp power in particular
parishes. Another frequently voiced refrain was that the bill was not a
real compromise.[44] Perhaps Gladstone's greatest disappointment was

42. Minutes of Liberation Society, 6 July 1866, GLRO A/LIB/3, fol. 383; *Hansard*,
CLXXXIV (18 July 1866), 1029–52.
43. *Hansard*, CLXXXIV (18 July 1866), 1032.
44. Ibid., 1033–39.

that Beresford Hope came out publicly against his bill on the grounds that it failed to retain the identity of the old rate. Five weeks earlier he had joined with Sir William Bovill, now the solicitor general, to bring in a church rates amendment bill that offered all conscientious objectors the possibility of "contracting out" of church rate obligations. That bill joined C. N. Newdegate's familiar but unpopular commutation bill.[45]

Because of the lateness of the hour, Gladstone's bill was then adjourned to 24 July and again to 1 August. Gladstone reflected ruefully that in light of the agreement with the government he had not expected elaborate speeches from government ministers in opposition to the bill. On 1 August 1866 the House gave the bill its second reading without dividing. On the same day, Hardcastle's abolition bill, Newdegate's commutation bill, and Bovill's exemption bill were withdrawn to clear the deck for the end of the session.[46]

Gladstone had gained a second reading for his bill, but he had been outmaneuvered by Disraeli. The Conservative House leader had managed to avoid a hostile division; by flouting accepted parliamentary procedure, he had not committed himself to the principle of the bill, thus leaving himself room to move in the next session. The *Nonconformist* was outraged, but other liberal papers understood that Disraeli's position had been a difficult one. Disraeli saw that he could not count on a majority in a division, but neither could he afford to allow Gladstone's bill to pass in silence and thus affront a phalanx of supporters who, according to the *Daily Telegraph*, "would almost sooner go back into opposition, and pass a Reform Bill, than accept such a measure."[47] Die-hard Conservative church defenders took hope from the tone of the debate, Beresford Hope's repudiation of a scheme he had once praised, and from the volte-face of *The Times*, which now rejected Gladstone's plan as unacceptable after having backed it in March.[48] The time was not yet ripe for a consensus solution to the church rate question.

45. Ibid., 1041–46; (11 June 1866), 114; CLXXXI (13 Feb. 1866), 460; (20 Feb. 1866), 810.

46. *Hansard*, CLXXXIV (18 July 1866), 1444–53; (1 Aug. 1866), 1847–85. Lengthy speeches against Gladstone's bill were made by Lord John Manners, the commissioner of works; G. W. Hunt, the secretary to the treasury; and Sir William Bovill, the solicitor general.

47. *Nonconformist*, 25 July 1866, p. 589; *Daily Telegraph*, 19 July 1866; *Morning Star*, 19 July 1866.

48. *Record*, 20 July 1866.

IV

In the 1867 session the politics of parliamentary reform overshadowed all other political questions. Gladstone did not reintroduce his church rate measure that session. In its absence Hardcastle again brought in his bill for total abolition. It served the useful function of reminding moderate Conservatives in both Houses that perhaps Gladstone's bill ought to be considered seriously.

Before the opening of the new session, the Liberation Society's parliamentary committee recommended that in light of the unfavorable reaction to Gladstone's bill "by those whom it was intended to conciliate," and because Gladstone was no longer a member of the government, they should support Hardcastle's bill for total abolition.[49] On 20 March 1867 Hardcastle brought in his bill for a second reading. Gladstone greatly regretted his action; and Hardcastle himself was reluctant, apparently wishing that Gladstone might undertake the bill in his stead.[50] The most striking feature of the debate was that it was concerned less with Hardcastle's measure than with Gladstone's bill of the previous session. It was a portent that movement toward a solution of the church rate question was imminent.

Beresford Hope moved an amendment for a six-month adjournment. Edward Baines, who seconded Hardcastle's motion for a second reading, expressed regret—not that Beresford Hope opposed Hardcastle, but that he opposed Gladstone's bill. Baines reminded him that Dissenters were willing to make the concessions to the Church sought in Gladstone's bill.[51] Sir George Grey stated that at the close of the last session there had been a general feeling that Gladstone's measure "contained the germ at least of a settlement. . . ." Although he preferred Gladstone's measure to Hardcastle's, he would vote for the latter with the aim of amending it in committee to make it "more generally acceptable."[52]

49. Minutes of Liberation Society, 25 Jan. 1867, GLRO A/LIB/3, fols. 420, 421. Other proposed legislation that the parliamentary committee recommended support for included the Oxford Tests Abolition Bill, Irish Church disestablishment, and removal of bishops from the House of Lords. The committee was considering the expediency of bringing in a bill to enable non-Anglican ministers to officiate in parochial churchyards.

50. Gladstone to Roundell Palmer, 25 Jan. 1867, Selborne Papers, MS. 1862, fol. 250; *Hansard*, CLXXXVI (20 March 1867), 215–50.

51. *Hansard*, CLXXXVI (20 March 1867), 215–50.

52. Ibid., 227, 228.

Sir William Heathcote declared himself pleased with the tone in which the church rate question was now being discussed in the House. He was happy with Baines's statement, which indicated the readiness of Dissenters to meet the susceptibilities of Churchmen. But, he said, now showing more interest in Gladstone's plan to abolish compulsory rates than he had a year ago, it made no sense to vote for the principle of absolute abolition now before considering some compromise. The same conciliatory note was struck by Lord John Manners, the chief commissioner of works and not long before a foremost proponent of the "no surrender" wing of church rate defense, who now favored the exemption of Dissenters.[53]

Gladstone pointed out that those Conservatives who argued that church rates were an inherited charge on property became inconsistent when, like Manners, they agreed to exempt Dissenters. Gladstone said that he had not reintroduced his bill on the grounds that amendments that George Waldegrave-Leslie, the Liberal M.P. for Hastings, intended to move in committee would accomplish what he had hoped to effect with his bill. Gladstone therefore agreed to vote for a second reading. With that the House divided, voting by 263 votes to 187 for Hardcastle's bill.[54]

Immediately thereafter, C. N. Newdegate's perpetual church rates commutation bill came on for the second reading. It was roundly defeated by 177 votes to 45. J. G. Hubbard, who with Beresford Hope had brought in a church rates regulation bill that allowed an exemption to any person objecting to church rates, wisely asked that a second reading be postponed for a week.[55] Under the guise of allowing M.P.s time to become better acquainted with their bill, they were spared the embarrassment of having their bill dispatched by a House that had proved receptive to Hardcastle and Gladstone.

Hardcastle's bill won an impressive majority of seventy-six votes. But the *Nonconformist* admitted that this increase was not due to a gain in the strength or zeal of abolitionists, but to "the unprecedented disorganization of the Conservative party."[56] Hardcastle's bill had come on after Disraeli had introduced his parliamentary reform bill, which offered household suffrage. As a result, the Commons and his

53. Ibid., 228–33.
54. Ibid., 245–50.
55. Ibid., 266.
56. *Nonconformist*, 27 March 1867, p. 245.

own party had been thrown into disarray. The conservative *Morning Post* mourned: "All around us there is nothing but doubt and anxiety."[57]

The liberal *Daily Telegraph*, which supported Gladstone's proposal, warned that Hardcastle's majority should not be interpreted as a victory for the Liberation Society. Rather, it argued, Churchmen had decided to satisfy the conscientious scruples of Dissenters without injuring the Church. The *Daily Telegraph* called on Nonconformists to support the abolition of compulsory rates and to relinquish all ideas of getting rid of the church establishment.[58]

The hopes entertained by Gladstone and Grey that Waldegrave-Leslie's amendments might transpose Hardcastle's abolition bill into the likeness of Gladstone's measure did not materialize in the 1867 session. Preoccupation with the parliamentary reform bill precluded any serious attention to Hardcastle's bill in the Commons. It passed through committee almost unnoticed. On 24 July it passed a third reading unamended, by the meager vote of 129 to 99. On the same day, Hubbard's exemption bill was withdrawn without having been debated.[59]

The reform bill crisis also contributed to the dearth of attention paid to several "church rate martyrs" during the 1867 parliamentary session. Contemporaries were astounded that it still was possible to jail church rate defaulters. But it was difficult to canonize them, as men like John Childs and William Baines once had been, because their nonpayment did not arise from a principled opposition to the church rate.

James B. Grant, a Unitarian brewer from Kettleburgh in Suffolk, was imprisoned in London's Whitecross Street prison in March 1867. Grant had refused to pay an 1863–64 church rate of £1 13*s*. 5³⁄₄*d*. on the grounds that the assessment of £50 made against his house was unequal and unjust. The Court of Arches had ruled against him, and after paying expensive legal costs amounting to £257, which were said to have ruined him, Grant was jailed.[60]

57. *Morning Post*, 21 March 1867.
58. *Daily Telegraph*, 21 March 1867.
59. *Hansard*, CLXXXVII (8 May 1867), 207, 208. When Hardcastle's bill first was considered in committee it might conceivably have been amended. But Waldegrave-Leslie was not in attendance due to illness. Hardcastle suggested that they allow the bill to pass that stage and consider amendments when the report was brought up. That was agreed, but the pressure of parliamentary reform gave no further opportunity to amend the bill. Ibid., CLXXXVIII (25 June 1867), 507; CLXXXIX (24 July 1867), 34, 35.
60. *Suffolk Mercury*, 23 March 1867; 30 March 1867. An investigation by the *Suffolk Mercury* suggested that Grant may have had cause to complain of his assessment. The paper examined the Kettleburgh assessment rolls after Grant's house had been

The *Nonconformist* was aghast at what it considered an anachronistic proceeding. But it gave little further publicity to Grant's case, believing the point of the dispute could "hardly be elevated to the dignity of a principle. . . ."[61] Once in prison Grant wrote a friend that he wanted Dissenters "to make use of him" to get rid of a law that, although condemned on all sides, could still land men in prison. He complained that "Some of those who led the anti-movement are not over sympathetic with me now they find I am a heretic, and Unitarians seem to care very little about it." He claimed that his "best friends and supporters" were the Wesleyans, and he fantasized that Unitarian views might one day spread through the working classes thanks to his martyrdom.[62]

On 8 August 1867 Hardcastle's abolition bill came on for the second reading in the House of Lords. The most striking feature of the debate was not the steady opposition to outright church rate abolition, but the readiness—almost eagerness—to go on record in favor of a compromise. Earl Morley, who moved that the bill be given a second reading, set the tone by asserting that he believed the bill's promoters would be happy to accept any compromise in committee that did not violate their demand for the abolition of compulsory church rates. Morley urged too that this was a most propitious time to settle the church rate question. He thought it certain that when the new reform bill came into effect "a large number of Dissenters would get into Parliament," and therefore it would be wise, before that occurred, to remove this "source of contention between Nonconformists and the Church Establishment. . . ."[63] Even the duke of Marlborough, who reminded his colleagues of his select committee report of 1860 and of the ultimate aims of the Liberation Society, urged that each party should "surrender something of their extreme claims." The Lords then defeated Hardcastle's measure by the vote of eighty-two to twenty-four.[64]

For the third time the Lords had thrown out a church rate abolition

sold to another owner. It found that the assessment for Grant's former house had been decreased from £50 to £18. The paper wondered whether Grant had been discriminated against because of his religious convictions. *Nonconformist*, 10 April 1867, p. 285.

61. Ibid.

62. *Unitarian Herald*, 31 May 1867, pp. 173, 174. Another man, Phocion Foster of North Curry, Somerset, was jailed in late July 1867 in the Taunton country gaol. Foster had originally refused to pay a church rate of 15*s*. 7³/₄*d*. He had been unable to pay subsequent court and defense costs. *Somerset County Gazette*, 3 Aug. 1867; *Nonconformist*, 7 Aug. 1867, p. 638; 31 July 1867, p. 620.

63. *Hansard*, CLXXXIX (8 Aug. 1867), 1081.

64. Ibid., 1089–94.

bill. But the debate indicated that the time merely to defeat abolition had passed. The message given by both sides of the House was clear—a compromise measure that came before the Lords would now be seriously considered. The failure of the Church and the Conservative party to push through Parliament an acceptable alternative to abolition had prepared the Lords to accept a more radical measure; the passage of the parliamentary reform bill readied them to welcome one quickly.

Some Churchmen felt that they had been betrayed by the Conservatives. On the day of the Lords debate, Bishop Tait wrote an anxious note to Samuel Wilberforce:

> . . . I take it for granted that you will smash Mr. Hardcastle's Bill. You will not fail to urge that the Bishops a[nd] the Church generally have been in favor of a fair compromise. The real reason why such compromise was not made a[nd] accepted was that Dizzy humbugged our Hale a[nd] some others into the belief that he was the Church's all-powerful friend, a[nd] w[oul]d maintain Church rates with no surrender. Surely the government who have led us into this mess by playing o[n] the folly of the clergy will not be so dastardly as to abandon us.[65]

No vestige remained of the Conservative reaction that had seemed so formidable in 1860 and 1861. Disraeli had used the Church then for political advantage. He and his party were now being asked, for the Church's sake, to accept the least damaging compromise available to settle the church rate question. Disraeli was ready to accede to that request now that it was politically expedient to do so.

V

In the parliamentary session of 1867–68 the government reluctantly agreed that compulsory church rates should be repealed. Once that principle had been adopted—the basic and minimum demands of Nonconformists—Nonconformists counted for little in the actual shaping of the legislation. What really mattered was the agreement reached among Churchmen, and between the government and the Liberals.

65. A. C. Tait to S. Wilberforce, 8 Aug. 1867, Bishop Samuel Wilberforce Papers, d. 47, fols. 102–4.

The obvious interest in his bill shown by the Lords while rejecting Hardcastle's measure in August emboldened Gladstone, together with Sir George Grey and Sir Roundell Palmer, to reintroduce on 28 November his Compulsory Church Rates Abolition Bill.[66] Gladstone reassured Russell several weeks earlier, in light of the dissension that continued to plague the Liberal party because of the parliamentary reform controversy, that his bill was "hardly political as it now stands; at least it is hardly a party question."[67] But despite signs of a growing consensus three other bills were given a first reading. Hardcastle reintroduced his unconditional abolition bill. Hubbard and Beresford Hope brought in their bill, which, like all the major Conservative attempts since 1859 to achieve a compromise, offered a generous exemption from church rate obligations. And once again Newdegate offered his commutation bill, in spite of its overwhelming defeat in the previous session.[68]

Before Gladstone's measure came on for its second reading abolitionists expressed deep concern about a section of what was now clause six of Gladstone's slightly revised bill. Roundell Palmer had added the stipulation that nothing in the act should prevent any agreement to make a voluntary rate "on the faith of which any Expenditure shall have been made, or any Liability incurred, from being enforced in the same Manner as other Contracts of a like Nature might be enforced in any Court of Law or Equity."[69] Roundell Palmer insisted that the added words were necessary, in light of the bill's references to "voluntary" rates, to enable churchwardens to enter contracts in confidence that funds promised by voluntary contributors would be forthcoming.[70]

Abolitionists were now more reluctant than in the previous session to support Gladstone's bill because they believed that Roundell Palmer's sixth clause, conjoined with clause five, which provided that voluntary contributors should sign their names when being polled as a promise to abide by the will of the majority, reintroduced compulsion

66. *Hansard*, CXC (28 Nov. 1867), 417.

67. Gladstone to Russell, in G. P. Gooch, ed., *The Later Correspondence of Lord John Russell, 1840-1878*, vol. II (London, 1925), p. 363.

68. Church Rates Abolition Bill [21] and Church Rates Regulation Bill [22], first reading—*Hansard*, CXC (3 Dec. 1867), 573; Church Rates Commutation Bill [10], first reading—ibid. (27 Nov. 1867), 314.

69. Great Britain, *Parliamentary Papers*, House of Commons Bills, "A Bill for the Abolition of Compulsory Church Rates," 1867–68, i. 13, pp. 314, 315.

70. Roundell Palmer to Gladstone, 21 Dec. 1867, Gladstone Papers, Add. MS. 44296, fols. 101, 102; *Hansard*, CLXXXVI (20 March 1867), 221.

to voluntary church rates. A difference of opinion existed between the Liberation Society's parliamentary committee and the more moderate executive committee. The former initially recommended, on 24 January 1868, that Gladstone's bill not be supported without the withdrawal of the offending proviso in clause six. Both sides were placated by Gladstone's willingness to meet with a delegation headed by Hardcastle.[71] The planned meeting, which included members of the Liberation Society and Dissenting Deputies, took place on 17 February. Gladstone answered the delegation that he had been advised legally that the sixth clause did not alter the voluntary character of the rate. He did say that he was willing to consider alteration to remove all doubts. But he went no further than to extend verbal reassurances to the abolitionists. That was probably as far as he could conciliate voluntaryists without alienating Roundell Palmer.[72]

By 19 February 1868, when Gladstone moved that his bill be given a second reading, the Commons found the consensus that had so long eluded it. The government and the moderate majority of the Conservative party capitulated. Conservatives followed the lead of that most eminent church defender Viscount Cranborne (formerly Lord Robert Cecil) and accepted the principle of repeal of compulsory church rates.

Gladstone opened the debate by saying that all indications now were that both sides would accept his compromise. But he warned that this would be his last attempt. If the House rejected this solution, he would leave the field to Hardcastle's bill for total abolition. Gladstone argued that his bill offered a fair settlement to both Churchmen and Nonconformists. He told Dissenters that they were offered the "absolute abolition of the principle of compulsion." With respect to clauses five and six, Gladstone was firm; he stated that they were needed to provide legal protection to churchwardens identical to that enjoyed by officers of any voluntary organization.[73] Gladstone reminded Churchmen that the retention of parochial machinery was valuable especially in rural parishes, "where things go on from generation to generation

71. *Nonconformist*, 18 Jan. 1868, p. 49; Minutes of Liberation Society, 24 Jan. 1868, GLRO A/LIB/4, fols. 13, 14; 7 Feb. 1868, fols. 19, 20.

72. Minutes of Liberation Society, 21 Feb. 1868, GLRO A/LIB/4, fol. 23; Minutes of Dissenting Deputies, 13 Feb. 1868, Guildhall MS. 3083, XIII, 398; Roundell Palmer to Gladstone, 21 Jan. 1868, Gladstone Papers, Add. MS. 44296, fol. 111.

73. *Hansard*, CXC (19 Feb. 1868), 959, 960.

with little change. . . ."[74] Gladstone reminded the followers of Hubbard and Beresford Hope that the church rate principle held that since all in the community received benefits from the parish church, all were obliged to contribute to its maintenance. But, declared Gladstone, the vast majority on both sides of the House had for some time been unprepared to entertain that principle. Driving home that uncomfortable fact, he pointed out that the church rate principle was no more an issue in Hubbard's exemption bill than in his own. Finally, he denied that a surrender of the church rate principle would harm the established church. Oddly, in light of the motion he would himself make within a month that the Church of Ireland be disestablished, he used the illustration he had apparently become fond of in the past three years: that the Irish church might no longer exist if church cess had not been abolished in 1833.[75]

Only a scattered remnant of Conservatives remained adamantly opposed to Gladstone's plan. Oxfordshire's J. W. Henley believed the bill was equivalent to total abolition. C. N. Newdegate agreed. He preferred Hardcastle's bill because it at least left the vestries unimpaired. He warned that the Church needed to fear not only disestablishment from without but also "the narrow spirit of ecclesiasticism and sacerdotalism within her own pale. . . ."[76] Newdegate and other antiritualists increasingly became suspicious that Gladstone's exclusive church vestry was designed to allow wealthy Anglo-Catholics to dominate churches that they would finance with voluntary rates.

Although that warning against ritualism would be heeded in the House of Lords, the Conservatives in the Commons were swayed more by Cranborne's argument. As he wrote later to Lord Carnarvon, he did his best "to adapt himself to the altered condition of affairs. . . ."[77] Cranborne admitted that he had always preferred the exemption principle of Hubbard's bill. But Gladstone's bill did allow the Church to retain its parochial machinery, and it allowed subscribers of funds to determine how they should be spent. With an eye on what he considered the disastrous course Disraeli had taken on parliamentary reform, he warned against years of obstruction to be followed by

74. Ibid., 961.
75. Ibid., 963, 964.
76. Ibid., 971, 966.
77. Cranborne to Carnarvon, 27 Feb. 1868, typescript, Salisbury Papers D/31/14, fol. 17.

"giving way to an unreasonable panic. . . . We may go further and fare worse."[78]

Hardcastle was delighted with Cranborne's speech and expressed general satisfaction with Gladstone's bill. Charles Gilpin, a Quaker and member for Northampton whose name was on the back of Hardcastle's bill, declared that he would support Gladstone's measure and attempt to alter clause six in committee. Hubbard, whose exemption bill remained the only alternative with any real following among Conservatives, rose to say that he would not vote against the second reading. It now seemed to him that their two bills were very similar.[79]

Gathorne Hardy, the home secretary, rose at the end of the debate to state the government's position. He disagreed that Hubbard's bill and Gladstone's were similar. Hardy accurately pointed out that in Hubbard's bill, as in Walpole's in 1859, exemption from church rates needed to be claimed by those who wished it. In Gladstone's bill the onus was on Churchmen to come forward. Hardy was also skeptical about the likelihood of Gladstone's provisions being carried out in many parishes. But although the government was clearly unenthusiastic, Hardy indicated that it was now prepared to submit to the bill's principle. There were two conditions: when being considered in committee the bill's clauses should be open to amendment, and the date for going into committee should be set subsequent to debate on the other church rate bills now before the Commons so that the committee could fully consider the question. Gladstone agreed, and his bill to abolish compulsory church rates was given the second reading without a division.[80]

With the acquiesence of the government, the remaining fire left the conservative movement for church rate defense. The Anglo-Catholic *Guardian* was satisfied that the bill allowed church people to direct the spending of their own money. It concluded, and praised Cranborne and Hubbard for recognizing, that Gladstone's offer included nearly all that it had insisted on "as essential, since it became apparent that the opportunity of setting the old system of Church-rates upon an improved and permanent basis had passed away."[81] Staunchly establishmentarian papers railed at the bill as a "mockery of a compromise."

78. *Hansard*, CXC (19 Feb. 1868), 970.
79. Ibid., 967, 974.
80. Ibid., 977.
81. *Guardian*, 26 Feb. 1868, p. 225.

But spokesmen occupying the vast middle ground, including Miall in the *Nonconformist,* acknowledged that they could do no better than to resign themselves to Gladstone's solution. The liberal *Daily Telegraph* said it was "the only plan which the country would sanction."[82]

On 11 March, before Gladstone's bill could be considered in committee, the House needed to deal with Hubbard's bill. Hubbard requested that it be given a second reading so that it could be studied in committee with Gladstone's bill. He believed that parts of his bill might beneficially be engrafted on Gladstone's bill. But Hardcastle objected that whereas he might support Gladstone, he must oppose Hubbard. Gladstone balked too at the suggestion that their bills rested on a similar principle and could be considered together. The government backed down, because it was now clear that agreement on Gladstone's bill might be reached in committee. The former Home Secretary Spencer Walpole asked that Hubbard agree to defer a second reading to 8 April alongside the other church rate bills.[83]

During the committee's consideration of Gladstone's bill there was a division only on clause one. The House in committee divided at the insistence of J. W. Henley, affirming the principle of the repeal of compulsion by a vote of 167 to 30. Northcote, who abstained, spoke for most Conservatives when he said that "he thought it was their duty to pass the Bill in the best shape possible."[84]

The lengthiest discussion was on clauses five and six. Clause five stipulated that those voting on a requested rate pledge abide by the will of the majority. Clause six enabled churchwardens who had incurred liabilities on the basis of promised rates to enforce their payment in courts of law. Prior to consideration of the bill in committee, another Liberation Society deputation met with Gladstone. Backed by legal advice, they urged that clauses five and six be deleted. Baron Ebury separately had made a similar request.[85] But in committee Gladstone agreed only to make a technical alteration to clause five. There was wide-ranging opinion against clause five. But the most

82. *Daily Telegraph,* 12 March 1868; *John Bull,* 22 Feb. 1868, p. 133; *Churchman,* 27 Feb. 1868, p. 140; *Nonconformist,* 22 Feb. 1868, p. 169.

83. *Hansard,* CXC (11 March 1868), 1399–1415.

84. Ibid., 1416, 1415.

85. Ibid., 1422–25; Minutes of Liberation Society, 6 March 1868, GLRO A/LIB/4, fol. 26; "Compulsory Church Rate Abolition. Copy Opinion of Mr. B. Braithwaite," 6 March 1868, Gladstone Papers, Add. MS. 44608, fols. 95, 96; Ebury to Gladstone, 3 March 1868, "Private," Gladstone Papers, Add. MS. 44395, fol. 202.

important was that of Northcote, who feared that because of it parishioners would be reluctant to sign a poll book lest they commit themselves to a liability of which they were ignorant. Northcote argued that clause eight would effect what Gladstone sought in clause five. Clause five was negatived after Gladstone said he would not press it in light of Northcote's opinion. It was a reminder of the limits to pressure group influence that Northcote's comment had accomplished more with Gladstone than two Liberation Society deputations—although that did not prevent the Liberation Society's parliamentary committee from taking credit for the withdrawal of the fifth clause.[86]

Gladstone refused to budge at all on clause six, which abolitionists had found most objectionable. Gladstone asserted that "if he were to abandon this clause he should be breaking . . . [the] understanding on which he had brought forward the measure."[87] The only amendment offered and accepted was by Sir Charles James Selwyn, the Conservative solicitor general, providing that the nominal plaintiff in any legal action against subscribing parishioners should be the churchwardens, chapelwardens, or treasurer instead of all the subscribing parishioners, who would need to act as plaintiff as the bill now stood.[88]

Clauses seven and eight, to which Gladstone and the Anglo-Catholics attached such importance, were accepted without controversy. The latter disqualified persons from voting on a requested voluntary rate (and disqualified churchwardens from disposing of such rates) who had not paid their voluntary rate, or an equivalent, in the preceding year. Clause seven provided for the election of a treasurer where churchwardens were ineligible for the foregoing reasons.[89]

Although abolitionists were satisfied that the bill did away with legal compulsion (social pressure in rural parishes might remain), they found it hard to swallow. They had to bow to the political necessity of bipartisan agreement, but the *Nonconformist* admitted that it acquiesced only "with sincere and unconcealed reluctance."[90]

On 24 March 1868 at one o'clock in the morning the Compulsory Church Rates Abolition Bill came on for the third reading in a House with few Conservatives present. Charles Schreiber, the Conservative

86. *Hansard*, CXC (11 March 1868), 1422–25; Minutes of Liberation Society, 20 March 1868, GLRO A/LIB/4, fol. 31.
87. *Hansard*, CXC (11 March 1868), 1425.
88. Ibid., 1425, 1426.
89. Ibid., 1426, 1427.
90. *Nonconformist*, 14 March 1868, p. 241.

member for Cheltenham, attempted to adjourn the debate but was defeated by a vote of 131 to 28. It was the last division in the Commons on the vexed question. Newdegate, who had fought for years to commute the rate to a charge on property payable by landlords, had the last word. He gave up his fight, concluding: "He would only say that the Bill would destroy the parochial system of the Church of England." With that the bill was given its third reading without a division.[91]

VI

The Compulsory Church Rates Abolition Bill that passed through the Commons was a fragile compromise. Voluntaryists had acceded to it as the least they could accept. Gladstone had convinced conservative Churchmen that in exchange for the loss of compulsion the Church would retain its ancient parochial machinery to make voluntary rates. Many Anglo-Catholics were reconciled to the bill because its compensatory clauses facilitated the development of their ideal—a church cleansed of external interference. On practical grounds, too, the bill facilitated the election of sympathetic churchwardens, less likely to be used (as wardens under the comprehensive system were) to put down ritualism. Only a remnant in the Commons, of die-hard establishmentarians, was left in impotent gloom.

But the ecclesiastical balance was different in the House of Lords. Anglo-Catholics were in a minority there. Well-placed establishmentarians were able to strip the bill of the clauses that alone had made Anglo-Catholics in the Commons willing to pass it. As a result of antiritualist feeling, Gladstone's bill was transformed into one more nearly satisfying Nonconformists, something they had been unable to achieve by their own influence in the House of Commons.

On 23 April 1868 Russell moved in the House of Lords that a second reading be given to Gladstone's bill. He gave a surprisingly brief introduction, basing his request for support from the Lords primarily on the fact that the bill had been received in the Commons "with almost unanimous support."[92] Because the government had capitulated

---

91. *Hansard*, CXCI (24 March 1868), 207.
92. Ibid. (23 April 1868), 1113; first reading in the House of Lords was given on 26 March 1868, ibid., 255.

and decided that the second reading should not be opposed, the Lords fell unwillingly into line. Derby, who no longer was burdened with the leadership of the government, had actually attended with the intention of voting against the bill, although he had promised Disraeli that he would not originate a division. He was bitter that the bill, however amended, could not be rid of its basic vice—that, as he saw it, it surrendered the establishment principle. He voiced regret that the Commons should "apparently from sheer weariness, upon this subject, have acquiesced in this Bill. . . ."[93] Longley, the archbishop of Canterbury, had actually come prepared to move a six-month adjournment. But he also submitted to the government's wishes.[94]

Although there was a general recognition among the Lords that they would need to give a second reading to the bill, there was an equally strong resolve to reshape the bill in committee. Bishop Tait pointed out that the second clause, which had passed unnoticed through the Commons, repealed the right of parishes governed by local acts of Parliament to levy statutory compulsory rates. Tait had a petition from the rector of St. Botolph's, Bishopsgate, which functioned under a local act. Under its provisions church rates had been abolished, and the church and service were to be maintained instead out of the tithe. Tait had a similar petition from St. Paul's Covent Garden. He warned that clause two must be recast to protect the property rights of parishes governed by such acts.[95]

The strongest and most consistent criticism of the form of the bill focused on clauses seven and eight, which embodied the raison d'être behind the support given the bill by Gladstone and Conservative Anglo-Catholics in the Commons. These clauses, which excluded those not contributing voluntary rates from voting on a new rate or serving as churchwardens for the purpose of maintaining the church and its services, were opposed by Evangelicals and Broad Churchmen—by all who championed a comprehensive national church establishment. The duke of Buckingham and Earl Grey expressed the typical concern that the clauses would lead to the affairs of parishes becoming vested in the hands of a few wealthy parishioners. Grey feared with a latitudinarian evenhandedness that in a few years parishes would fall under the

93. Ibid. (23 April 1868), 1124; Derby to Disraeli, 20 April 1868, "Private," Hughenden Papers B/XX/S/491, LSE microfilm 131.
94. *Hansard*, CXCI (23 April 1868), 1123, 1124.
95. Ibid., 1122.

RESOLUTION OF THE CONFLICT, 1865–1868   249

domination of one or another of the extreme factions within the Church. But probably the greater animus against the clauses was rooted in a particular aversion to the aspirations of Anglo-Catholics and the spread of ritualism. Tait, the Erastian bishop of London who was to be translated to Canterbury before year's end, warned against a clique of "visionary theorists" in the Church "who were in favor rather of a so-called free than of an Established Church."[96] Tait's views were shared by others in influential positions, including the new lord chancellor, Hugh Cairns. It was agreed to give the bill a second reading without dividing on the understanding that it would be rewritten in a select committee. Almost alone, Samuel Wilberforce, the bishop of Oxford, praised the bill's fairness in demanding that only those paying their fair share should share in the Church's management.[97] But his was a lone High Church voice crying in an Erastian wilderness.

On 29 April, the day before Gladstone's bill was to be considered in committee, Newdegate's commutation bill was debated in the Commons. Not one government member attended. On the grounds of the paucity of the House and the determination of the majority to disestablish the Irish church, he asked that the second-reading order be postponed until the following day. With fitting irony, he could get no time then, as the House continued debate on the Irish church. So was extinguished a scheme that had long since ceased to be practicable.[98]

On 30 April Gladstone's bill came before the Lords in committee. Russell, who was in charge of the bill, accepted the amendment by Malmesbury, the lord privy seal, calling for the bill to be considered by a select committee. So a committee of nineteen considered and radically rewrote the bill.[99] The select committee was headed by Lord Chancellor Cairns, who had replaced the aging Lord Chelmsford when Derby resigned in late February. Cairns, the only major new figure in Disraeli's cabinet, was a zealous evangelical Orangeman, perfectly positioned to redraft the bill in order (in his view) to save the parishes

96. Ibid., 1116–23, 1130–33.
97. Ibid., 1134–46.
98. Ibid. (29 April 1868), 1535.
99. Ibid. (30 April 1868), 1570–74. The members of the select committee were: Lord Chancellor, Hugh Cairns; archbishop of York; Lord Privy Seal, Malmesbury; duke of Somerset; duke of Richmond; duke of Buckingham and Chandos; Earl Shaftesbury; Earl Carnarvon; Earl Romney; Earl Beauchamp; Earl Russell; Earl Kimberley, Viscount Halifax; bishop of London; bishop of Oxford; bishop of Carlisle; Lord Delamere; Lord Stanley of Alderley; and Lord Westbury.

from ritualism.[100] The most influential men in the committee shared Cairns's antipathy to Gladstone's compensatory clauses. The Evangelical Halifax, the Erastian Tait, and the antiritualist archbishop of York were keen in their support of Cairns's designs. The Broad Church Russell gave his silent blessing to his colleagues' determination to redraft the bill.[101]

In the select committee the principle that compulsory rates be repealed was retained. But the efforts at reconstruction by Gladstone and Phillimore were nullified. Clauses seven and eight—the former providing for a treasurer to replace a noncontributing churchwarden, the latter prohibiting those not paying voluntary church rates from voting on a rate for the following year, or from interfering with the distribution of voluntary rates—were boldly struck out.[102]

Even before the select committee was established Gladstone had expressed his concern to Russell that his bill might be destroyed if it were allowed to go before such a committee. Gladstone had warned that especially clause eight should not be altered. It was, he said, "an essential, perhaps the main part, of the tacit compact—under which I obtained the votes of a multitude of Conservatives. If therefore, it is omitted or materially altered I should have no choice but to drop the Bill."[103]

Respecting clause seven, Russell declared to Gladstone that it was necessary to delete the power of appointing a treasurer to prevent "a clique in the parish" from getting "the Church into their own hands."[104] A grieved Gladstone observed in a memorandum that while the law and the theory of church and state remained that there was one lawful

100. Ibid.; Robert Blake, *Disraeli* (New York, 1967), pp. 487, 488.

101. *Hansard*, CXCI (30 April 1868), 1574; Anderson, "Gladstone's Abolition of Compulsory Church Rates," p. 190; Great Britain, *Parliamentary Papers*, House of Lords Sessional Papers, "Report from the Select Committee of the House of Lords on the Compulsory Church Rates Abolition Bill, with the Proceedings of the Committee," 1867–68, XXX (143).

102. Great Britain, *Parliamentary Papers*, House of Commons Bills, "A Bill Instituting an Act for the Abolition of Compulsory Church Rates as Amended by the Lords, 1867–1868," i 232, pp. 329–30.

103. Gladstone to Russell, 28 March 1868, Russell Papers, PRO 30/22 16E, fol. 165. The date on the letter should perhaps be April rather than March. The second reading of the Gladstone bill in the Lords was held on 23 April. It was then that it was suggested, publicly at least, that the bill should be considered by select committee.

104. Russell to Gladstone, circa 14 June 1868, Gladstone Papers, Add. MS. 44608, fol. 177.

church to which all were compelled to contribute, it was consistent that Dissenters should be allowed to serve as churchwardens. But his bill had destroyed the old theory and had legally established that Dissenters need not maintain the Church. Therefore it appeared "utterly indefensible" that the select committee should reinforce that part of the old law that allowed Dissenting churchwardens to manage the voluntarily subscribed funds of Churchmen.[105]

An early sign that the select committee aimed to transform Gladstone's bill had been given by its handling of clause five. The clause had simply provided that parishioners in vestries could make a voluntary church rate. The effect, when joined with clauses seven and eight, was to create two vestries, one consisting of voluntary contributors to deal with church matters and the other open to all for the regulation of all other parish concerns. But the majority on the select committee wished to maintain the traditional vestry open to all on all questions, as much it wished to preserve a comprehensive church. Therefore clause five was crossed out and an amendment by Halifax agreed to. The new clause began: "This Act shall not affect Vestries, or the making, assessing, receiving, or otherwise dealing with any Church Rate, save in so far as it relates to the Recovery thereof. . . ."[106] The emphasis now was, as Cairns told the Lords in full committee on 3 July, to retain in its entirety the traditional parochial machinery with the exception of compulsion.[107] The Lords bill was to approximate, more nearly than the Commons bill had, the scheme originally proposed by Ebury and Bright.

Carnarvon fought valiantly in the select committee to reintroduce the old clause five, but his amendment was beaten by more than two to one. Thereafter, he wrote to Gladstone, he had considered with the Bishop of Oxford "how far it was possible or expedient to raise other points on the subsequent clauses and we were both of opinion that nothing further could be done."[108] Both High Churchmen concluded that the principle of excluding non-Anglicans from interfering in

105. Gladstone, "Memorandum," circa June–July 1868, Gladstone Papers, Add. MS. 44608, fols. 188, 187.

106. Great Britain, *Parliamentary Papers*, House of Commons Bills, 1867–68, i 232, pp. 331, 329; Russell to Gladstone, circa 14 June 1868, Gladstone Papers, Add. MS. 44608, fol. 177.

107. *Hansard*, CXCIII (3 July 1868), 598.

108. Carnarvon to Gladstone, 12 June 1868, "Private," Gladstone Papers, Add. MS. 44608, fol. 173.

church affairs, upon which Anglo-Catholic support for the bill had been predicated, had been defeated even before clauses seven and eight were extinguished. Carnarvon added that Russell, "who had charge of the bill," and who should have "endeavoured to maintain its general character was a consenting party to this great change—that is to say so far as his vote was concerned, for he never opened his lips on the subject."[109]

Two other changes, which Gladstone and supporters of the bill considered particularly important, were made to the bill in the House of Lords. Clause six, which allowed the legal enforcement of rates pledged by voluntary contributors, was crossed out. What the concerted pressure of Nonconformity had failed to accomplish with Gladstone had been effected effortlessly in a House of Lords select committee, which was swayed by Cairns's argument that compulsion would frighten people and inhibit contributions.[110] The other major amendment was of clause two. Following Tait's lead, the select committee exempted parishes governed by private or local acts of Parliament from the jurisdiction of the abolition bill. This was the only amendment for which Phillimore and Roundell Palmer felt sympathy.[111] It ensured that the church rate conflict was not to be concluded entirely neatly, for antagonism to the rate would continue in parishes where rates could continue to be compelled by statutory power after common law rates were made voluntary in 1868.

The *Nonconformist* was very pleasantly surprised that the select committee had actually "improved" the bill. The Liberation Society gave the amended bill its support with only minor reservations. But Phillimore wrote glumly to Gladstone, "I see Ld. Cairns' hand. . . ."[112] When the revised bill came before the full committee of the House of Lords on 3 July, grieving High Churchmen vented their anger and disappointment. Salisbury and Derby mourned the loss of clauses

109. Ibid.
110. *Hansard*, CXCIII (3 July 1868), 599, 600.
111. Great Britain, *Parliamentary Papers*, House of Commons Bills, 1867–68, i 232, pp. 328, 331; *Hansard*, CXCI (23 April 1868), 1120–22; Phillimore to Gladstone, 21 June 1868, Gladstone Papers, Add. MS. 44608, fols. 181, 182.
112. Phillimore to Gladstone, ibid., fols. 183, 184; *Nonconformist*, 17 June 1868, pp. 593, 594; Minutes of Liberation Society, 26 June 1868, GLRO A/LIB/4, fols. 64, 65. The parliamentary committee's sole objection to the amended bill was to clause D, added by the select committee, which enabled corporate bodies in possession of "Lands, Houses, or Tenements" to pay voluntary church rates. Great Britain, *Parliamentary Papers*, House of Commons Bills, 1867–68, i 232, p. 332.

seven and eight. Thomson, the archbishop of York who was delighted that the Anglo-Catholics had been thwarted, relied on moderate practical arguments to defend the altered bill. He reminded the Lords that the system proposed by their bill already existed in thousands of parishes, in which rates were levied without resorting to compulsion. Thomson argued that excluding noncontributors from vestries would have bred ill feeling. He advocated generosity. He also predicted that Dissenters would not attend vestries "to discuss rates and expenditures which did not affect their pockets, and that Churchmen would be elected as Churchwardens."[113]

Thomson's view was psychologically astute. Anglo-Catholics had often faulted establishmentarians for refusing rigidly to grant church rate exemptions for fear of violating their church-state principles. Now Anglo-Catholics were guilty of the same sin. They fought tenaciously to exclude Dissenters from parish vestries in the attempt to realize their ideal of a confessionally and liturgically more exclusive church. They did not yet see, as Thomson shrewdly realized, that once Nonconformists were freed from personal financial obligations to the Church, few would be sufficiently motivated by voluntaryism to continue insisting on exercising their parochial rights in the established church.

Bishop Wilberforce made one last attempt, when the bill reached the report stage on 9 July, to restore the clauses deleted by the select committee. He failed in each instance. On 13 July the bill received its third reading without a division.[114] Late at night on 24 July the Lords sent the bill down to the House of Commons. Gladstone was now in an awkward situation. This bill was considerably different from the one he had proposed. Phillimore had urged him to reject it. Gladstone himself had warned Russell only several months earlier that he would feel compelled to drop the bill if clause eight were deleted or destroyed. But he could hardly forgo a solution to the church rate question that was at long last in sight. Gladstone could not assume renewed support from the Conservative government for another bill, or that the House of Lords would again agree to pass a church rate bill. Gladstone needed this success to rally Liberals still smarting from the divisions occasioned in 1866 and 1867 by parliamentary reform. He wished to consolidate the support of Nonconformists, whom he had courted since 1864. With deep reluctance Gladstone indicated that he would agree

113. *Hansard*, CXCIII (3 July 1868), 596–602.
114. Ibid. (9 July 1868), 896–903; (13 July 1868), 1098–1101.

to the Lords amendments.[115] The *Nonconformist* described the passage of the bill on Saturday, 25 July at 3:15 A.M.: "The House was tired, thin, and quiet. A few stayed to see the Bill through, but the process did not take more than five minutes. Just as the dawn was coming, almost silently, without any excitement, without any controversy, the Bill was allowed quietly to pass, and the Church-rate system was finally extinguished."[116] On 31 July royal assent was given to "an Act for the Abolition of Compulsory Church Rates" (31 & 32 Vict. C. 109).[117] So ended the often tumultuous church rate conflict — "not with a bang, but a whimper."

VII

The *Nonconformist* hailed 31 July as the day on which "an agitation of more than thirty years' continuance, which had caused more strife and bitterness than any agitation which has ever taken place in England, was brought to a quiet and peaceful end."[118] The writers' hyperbolic forgetfulness of the seventeenth-century Civil War may be forgiven. In the nineteenth century, no other political issue could claim to have so long and so consistently engaged the political passions of the nation on both the local and national levels.

Carvell Williams, the secretary of the Liberation Society, sent special acknowledgment to the men who had played a key role in resolving the church rate conflict. Gladstone was thanked, as were J. A. Hardcastle, Sir William Clay, and Sir John Trelawny, all of whom had proposed solutions in Parliament. Sir Charles Douglas was recognized for his important role as the Liberation Society's parliamentary "whip."

115. Ibid. (24 July 1868), 1773, 1774; Anderson, "Gladstone's Abolition of Compulsory Church Rates," p. 191; Machin, *Politics and the Churches*, p. 350; Phillimore to Gladstone, 12 July 1868, Gladstone Papers, Add. MS. 44278, fol. 19; Foot and Matthew, eds., *Gladstone Diaries*, VI, 24 July 1868, 613. For Gladstone's own report, see the *Guardian*, 29 July 1868.

116. *Nonconformist*, 29 July 1868, p. 738.

117. *Hansard*, CXCIII (31 July 1868). On 21 July Hardcastle's Church Rate Abolition Bill was withdrawn. On 29 July both Hubbard's Church Rates Regulation Bill and Newdegate's commutation bill were withdrawn. Ibid. (21 July 1868), 1553; (29 July 1868), 1921.

118. *Nonconformist*, 5 Aug. 1868, p. 773; neither the *Guardian* nor the *Record* mentioned the enactment of the abolition bill.

Finally, Samuel Courtauld and William Baines were honored, the former for his role in the Braintree case and the latter as the foremost "church rate martyr." The Liberation Society recognized, as Carvell Williams wrote in the *Nonconformist*, the invaluable role played by those who had conducted the agitation in the parishes, without whom "the long struggle . . . could never have been maintained."[119]

The *Liberator* rejoiced that passage of the bill indicated the acceptance by the legislature of the voluntary principle that "no one shall be forced to contribute towards the support of religion, whether it be his own or any one else's. . . ." It was the loss of compulsion, even against Churchmen, which all conservative exemption bills had sought to retain in modified form, that constituted the essential victory of the voluntaryists. The *Liberator* crowed that in fact the Church was now "disestablished in regard to one part of its administration. . . ."[120]

The deepest cause of voluntaryist excitement was the belief that the church rate struggle had opened the doors for public debate on the larger question of religious establishments. The church rate issue was hailed as the "local irritant" that had kept alive that deeper issue and had goaded Dissenters into supporting the disestablishmentarian Liberation Society. Miall admitted that had Churchmen gracefully relinquished compulsory church rates ten years earlier, the Liberation Society would have had a difficult time convincing languorous Dissenters to make disestablishment a parliamentary question. Yet now that fundamental question was being debated at Westminster in the form of the debate on the Irish church.[121]

The majority support in the Commons for disestablishment of the Irish church gave Miall hope that the Liberation Society no longer moved toward its goal alone, but "in company with the whole Liberal body of the country. . . ."[122] The eighth Triennial Conference of the Liberation Society on 5 and 6 May 1868, attended by eight hundred delegates, inspired the same euphoric hopes. Yet in a reflective moment Miall noted the absence at the conference of "most of the foremost political and ecclesiastical men of the day." He admitted that the society continued to be "a veritable hobgoblin to the apprehension of thousands. . . ."[123]

119. Ibid., 12 Aug. 1868, p. 790; Minutes of Liberation Society, 11 Sept. 1868, GLRO A/LIB/4, fol. 84.
120. *Liberator*, 1 Sept. 1868, p. 157.
121. *Nonconformist*, 8 July 1868, p. 665.
122. Ibid., 15 April 1868, p. 361.
123. Ibid., 7 May 1868, pp. 432, 457–63.

Miall's hope that the Liberation Society and the Liberal party together would work to disestablish the Church of England might have been tempered had he properly appreciated how the agreement between Gladstone and the abolitionists had been arranged. Gladstone had worked with Hardcastle, an Anglican, and Samuel Morley, an Evangelical Congregationalist, precisely because both men refused to tie church rate abolition to the Liberation Society's wider goal. It was fitting that on 3 December 1868 Samuel Morley resigned from the executive committee of the Liberation Society. Earlier, while standing for election in Bristol, he had come out against the society's policy of secularizing church property. It was a policy that he had never been comfortable with; nor did he and other moderate Nonconformists believe that it was desired by the mass of moderate Nonconformists. Gladstone could count on moderates like Morley, and those whom he continued to meet through Newman Hall, to support the Liberal party.[124] They would be satisfied that their grievances had been addressed without the disestablishment or disendowment of the English church. The settlement of the church rate question probably did much to sublimate Nonconformist antipathy to the church establishment.

VIII

A new era in the funding of parochial churches began on 1 August 1868. After centuries of reliance on compulsory church rates, the Church needed to learn to trust in voluntary support. It was unclear how practically useful voluntary rates might prove to be. There were anomalies, too. The greatest was that in an era in which voluntary provision for churches was becoming the rule, compulsory church rates continued as before in parishes governed by local and private acts of Parliament.

After decrying the passage of the new church rate law, Churchmen began to follow the advice of a number of archdeacons to give it a fair trial. They recommended relying on two of its provisions. One was to appoint three trustees to form a corporation empowered to receive

124. Minutes of Liberation Society, 4 Dec. 1868, GLRO A/LIB/4, fol. 111; Newman Hall to Gladstone, 1 Jan. 1868, Gladstone Papers, Add. MS. 44188, fols. 76, 77; 10 Feb. 1868, fols. 80, 81.

bequests and donations, an organizational model that resembled that of Nonconformist chapels. It was hoped that landowners would feel conscience-bound to make over to their parish church the equivalent in land or money of the increase in the value of their property accruing from raised rents that could be demanded once church rates were repealed. The second was to hold vestry meetings as before to make voluntary rates. If occupiers declined to pay they should apply to the landlords, who could, according to the act, pay the rate and temporarily replace the occupier in vestry. The archdeacons had recommended that "only when that method has failed should recourse be had to any other."[125]

It soon became clear, as cynics had predicted, that the voluntary rate could not be relied on to replace the compulsory rate, although the former continued for years in a number of rural parishes, especially in the south of England.[126] With considerable reluctance Churchmen began turning to offertories, subscriptions, and special collections. By 1878 Churchmen were pleasantly surprised to find that compulsory church rate abolition might not be the financial calamity they had feared. At the 1878 church congress, Bernard Wake of Sheffield praised the reliability of offertories and voluntary contributions. He referred to the testimony of a clergyman that in his parish a legal rate had formerly raised £30 or £40, leaving the church " 'always in debt. . . .' " An offertory, on the other hand, provided " 'a balance of cash in the bank. . . . I ask and have.' " Wake challenged the congress, asserting: "Facts are stubborn things! How many of these facts are now to be found; and do they not prove that a voluntary offering is better than a legal rate?"[127] At the church congress of 1888 a paper on "proportionate giving" was presented. It emphasized that increasingly the Church needed to rely on voluntary gifts. The church rate was mentioned in neither the paper nor the discussion that followed.[128]

At the church congress of 1894 Robert Long, archdeacon of Auckland, presented a paper on offertories and subscriptions. Long observed how greatly thinking had changed on the topic of voluntary giving in a

125. Richard Brindley Hone, *Churchwardens' Duties: The New Church Rates Act* (London, 1869), p. 11.

126. *Churchman*, 27 Feb. 1868, p. 140; *Nonconformist*, 9 May 1866, pp. 370, 371; Charles James Burton, *Considerations on the Abolition of Compulsory Church Rates* (London, 1869), pp. 4, 10, 11; Chadwick, *The Victorian Church*, II, 195.

127. *Church Congress Report* (London, 1878), pp. 240, 241.

128. Ibid., 1888, pp. 537–66.

few decades. He had noticed in surprise in looking at reports of earlier congresses that the subject of offertories had been debated with "bated breath." Speakers had apologized for advocating offertories "as the only way in which, after Church rates had been done away with, the needs of the Church were to be met. . . ." He had been told that many country churches did not yet use offertories, but so far as the north of England was concerned, he did "not think there is a single church in which the offertory is not a regular institution."[129] By the 1890s different modes of maintaining parish churches remained. Southern rural parishes seemed to rely less on offertories and probably more on endowments and subscriptions; but everywhere voluntary rates were anachronisms.[130] The 1921 edition of Cripps's *Practical Treatise on the Law Relating to the Church and Clergy* stated: "The power to levy a voluntary church rate has in practice been found to be of little use."[131]

The same could not be said of compulsory church rates that could continue to be levied on parishes governed by statute under a wide variety of local parliamentary acts. Russell had observed during the debate on Gladstone's bill that there were at least seven hundred parliamentary acts allowing the making of church rates. Of the £232,903 collected in church rates according to the "Local Taxation Return" of 1863, £32,694, or approximately 14 percent, represented rates that could continue to be collected compulsorily after 1868.[132]

Initially some people living in parishes not under common law were surprised to find that their church rate obligations continued unchanged after 1868. That was frequently the case in London, where there were many parishes with statutory church rates. The 1872 Yearly Meeting minutes of the Society of Friends reported seven cases of restraints for church rates, for an amount of almost £56. The Committee for Sufferings noted that in some London parishes the recent

129. C. Dunkley, ed., *The Official Report of the Church Congress* (October, 1894), p. 612.

130. After 1890 the *Official Year Book of the Church of England* never mentions voluntary church rates. For this information I am indebted to K. W. Orr of Nuffield College, Oxford, who in the spring of 1980 was researching the finances of the Church of England, 1870–1920, for an Oxford D.Phil. thesis.

131. Henry William Cripps, *A Practical Treatise on the Law Relating to the Church and Clergy* (7th ed.; London, 1921), p. 438.

132. *Hansard*, CXCIII (3 July 1868), 594; Great Britain, *Parliamentary Papers*, "Local Taxation Returns," 1863, XXX. 1, p. 6.

Compulsory Church Rates Abolition Act had "offered no relief whatever."[133]

There was popular opposition at times to these compulsory church rates. These were often called ministers' rates or rectors' rates because they typically involved cases in which church rates had been commuted before 1868 in return for the obligation to compensate the clergy, who were charged with maintaining the church and services. An early case of opposition to the continuation of such a compulsory rate occurred in the parish of St. Saviour's, Southwark. Legal action was sought there to prevent the justice of the peace from enforcing payment of a church rate made under a local parliamentary act. In 1870 the Court of Queen's Bench upheld the right to enforce the rate under the fifth clause of the Compulsory Church Rates Abolition Act. Prideaux, in his *Practical Guide to the Duties of Churchwardens*, observed in his 1880 edition that there were in London and in other urban areas of the country many parishes with the same rights. As a staunch defender of the church establishment, he believed there was "every reason to hope that the 5th section of the Act will prove of great practical utility."[134]

Prideaux was proved right in the short run. The remaining compulsory church rates were legal and enforceable, and they were generally paid. But in the long run their financial value was outweighed by the cost of collecting them, and although the right to collect them was never abolished by Parliament, the Church was happy to have them commuted by local authorities.

By 1911 the London County Council had become concerned about the cost of collecting compulsory church rates in the boroughs in and around London. The Local Government Records and Museums Committee was commissioned to investigate. It reported on 14 July 1911 that "both the cost of collection and the amount of leakage in connection with these rates are very high in proportion to the amounts which are required to be raised."[135] A rectory rate in St. Olave's,

133. Society of Friends, London Yearly Meeting Minutes, 22–31 May 1872, XXVIII, 343–45.

134. Charles Greville Prideaux, *A Practical Guide to the Duties of Churchwardens* (14th ed.; London, 1880), p. 103; Manning, *Dissenting Deputies*, pp. 194–97.

135. London County Council, "Report of the Local Government, Records and Museums Committee, 14 July 1911," in Church Rates, General File, Commutation of Church Rates in the Metropolitan Area, Ecclesiastical Commissioners for England, MS. 85385.

Southwark, levied under 57 Geo. III, c. 7, was to raise £600 payable annually to the rector in lieu of tithes. But the cost of collection and clerical work was £60. In Christchurch, Southwark, a minister's rate was levied under 11 Geo. II, c. 21 to raise £60 annually to pay the minister of the parish. Collection expenses there for 1906–7 amounted to approximately £53, or 89 percent of the sum payable to the minister. The amount of leakage—the difference between the amount collected and levied—was also great. The amount for Christchurch in 1909 was 24 percent. In Shadwell, Stepney, it was as high as 31 percent; in others it was 8 or 11 percent. The committee explained that the high costs of leakage were caused partly by the small amounts of the rates in question, which were always more expensive than larger ones. It added that these rates probably were not enforced "with as much stringency as the general rate. . . ." That trend undoubtedly reflected the now general feeling that ecclesiastical contributions ought to be voluntary. The committee observed that it would be more efficient to collect the church rate with the general rate as was done in metropolitan boroughs, but borough councils lacked the power to follow that course of action.[136]

The report pointed out that in a number of parishes the compulsory church rate had been commuted. In 1898 a rate for St. Matthew, Bethnal Green, was commuted by a payment of £20,000 by the vestry to the ecclesiastical commissioners. A new rate was added to the general rate to repay the debt incurred to make that payment and was scheduled to be paid by 1959. A church rate for All Saints, Poplar, was commuted in 1903 by a payment of £19,000, to be repaid by general rate by 1963. In its report of 14 July 1911 the committee recommended "that all compulsory church rates in London shall be commuted." That recommendation was communicated to the ecclesiastical commissioners and to the appropriate metropolitan and borough councils.[137]

The ecclesiastical commissioners agreed on 2 November 1911 to cooperate with London boroughs to commute remaining compulsory church rates; they recorded no commutations in other parts of the country. But it took time before particular cases were resolved. The ecclesiastical commissioners communicated with the borough of Southwark in July 1912, for example, offering to accept redemption

136. Ibid.
137. Ibid.

for an annual £60 ministers' rate in the parish of Christchurch. The borough inexplicably took no action, and nothing further was done in that parish until 1939. By then the issue there, as in other places, was in no sense a church rate controversy but had become merely a bookkeeping question.[138]

The parishes of the Church of England today rely on voluntary financial support. Only occasionally do they still attempt to make use of their statutory right to levy voluntary church rates. Between 1972 and 1975 the High Church London parish of All Saints', Margaret Street, to whose foundation Gladstone and Phillimore contributed generously, levied voluntary church rates. A minimum of £275 and a maximum of £350 were collected during those years from the predominantly Jewish merchants in the heart of London's garment district. The practice was discontinued, however, because the amount of money collected was less than the value of the time and work required to raise it.[139] The Church of England has retained its established status, but the voluntary church rate is a legal anachronism of no financial importance.

The time was ripe between 1866 and 1868 to settle the church rate question. The movement to defend the church rate was broken. Conservatives had been unable since the height of their power in 1860-62 to agree on an alternative to abolition. The passage of a liberalized franchise and the prospect of a more radical Commons convinced prudent conservative Churchmen that there was no advantage in postponing agreement on a solution. Finally, there was a growing realization among Conservatives that they themselves had long since relinquished the core of that church rate principle which they had defended so tenaciously. Every major Conservative church rate proposal since 1858 had offered conscientious objectors a wide exemption from church rate obligations. In abandoning universality

138. "Church rates, General File, Commutation of Church Rates in the Metropolitan Area," 1 Aug. 1911, Ecclesiastical Commissioners for England and Wales, MS. 85385; P. H. Gray, town clerk, borough of Southwark, to Ecclesiastical Commissioners, 11 June 1912, ibid.: "Report of the Estates Committee," 27 June 1912, adopted at general meeting on 4 July 1912; letter sent to clerk of borough of Southwark, 8 July 1912, ibid.; comptroller of London to secretary of Ecclesiastical Commissioners, 2 Feb. 1939, ibid.; Ecclesiastical Commissioners to comptroller, 3 March 1939, ibid.

139. Based on an interview in June 1980 with Mr. John Hanvey, treasurer at All Saints', Margaret Street, London.

Conservatives had emasculated the principle that all in the parish ought to maintain the parish church.

By 1866 the question for Conservatives had become how to accept the inevitable loss of compulsory church rates with minimal damage to the established church. In the Commons Gladstone cooperated with influential Anglo-Catholics in both parties to frame a bill that pleased voluntaryists by abolishing compulsory church rates while frustrating their ultimate designs by effectively excluding Nonconformists from interfering in parochial church affairs. In the House of Lords, however, establishmentarian Evangelicals, Broad Churchmen, and old High Churchmen had the power to truncate the bill. Their desire for a national comprehensive church and their fear of ritualism transformed the bill into one that was paradoxically more radical and pleasing to abolitionists than the Commons bill had been.

It is noteworthy, however, that the bill's final transformation owed nothing to pressure exerted by voluntaryists. Indeed, it was striking how negligible was the influence of the Liberation Society once Gladstone took the church rate question in hand. Also in its moment of greatest triumph the Liberation Society followed the pattern of the Anti-Corn-Law League. Hardcastle, the Liberation Society's church rate spokesman, and Morley and Bright, with whom Gladstone cooperated, all dissociated themselves from the liberationists' linking of abolition to disestablishment. Their stance enabled Gladstone to win agreement for a compromise bill from moderate Nonconformists and Churchmen in both parties. His ability to do so paradoxically augured the Liberation Society's ultimate political failure, even as that society hailed its victory in defeating the compulsory church rate.

Conclusion

An Established Church and Voluntary Rates in a Liberal State, 1868

The abolition in 1868 of compulsory church rates ended a sustained political and ecclesiastical conflict that for thirty-six years had caused greater rancor and strife than any other in the nineteenth century. The social concord of countless parishes had been seriously disrupted by acrimonious and festering disputes over church rates. The bitter contests set Nonconformists against Churchmen and furthermore created fissures within the Church and Nonconformity as well. The abolition of compulsory church rates meant that for the first time in a millennium the established church was deprived of legally prescribed financial support from parishioners. The Church retained its established status, but on the parish level it now needed to depend on endowments and voluntary contributions, as did congregations of every other denomination.

Forty-nine bills or motions of bills were introduced in Parliament during the course of the church rate conflict in the attempt to settle the question. Most of them foundered on the fact that the church rate could not be considered apart from the question of the church establishment. The issue at stake was the church rate principle — the right of the parish churches of the established church to rely for maintenance on all the ratepayers of the parish.

Perhaps the most remarkable feature of the almost four-decade-long conflict was that few at the end, including Conservative church rate defenders, remembered what the church rate principle had entailed in 1832. At the beginning of the church rate struggle Tories still professed the traditional Christian European belief in a confessional state of which compulsory church rates were a manifestation. The legitimacy of church rates had been understood in light of two assumptions: the state was a moral agent with a divine mandate; and the state, in order to be consecrated, required the established church to exercise civil privileges in alliance with the state. The exalted status of neither state nor church was an end in itself; both had the object of maintaining a social order based on a religious footing and directed by an Anglican confession.

During the course of the church rate conflict less and less was said about the traditional view of the state as a divinely instituted moral agent. Few of the Conservatives who championed church rates to the end did so explicitly as a means of maintaining a Christian state and society; the establishment had become almost an end in itself. The apparent loss of memory regarding the original purpose for church rates and a religious establishment occurred because of a fundamental, but often imperceptible, shift in beliefs about the nature of state and society. Conservatives and Churchmen, no less than Liberals and Nonconformists, had come to accept the liberal state. They had come to assume that the objects of state and society were essentially this-worldly; the state's concerns were property and either order or liberty, not morality or spirituality. Therefore, it had become difficult to continue to defend the church rate as a symbol of confessionally defined purpose. The rate had become an archaic ecclesiastical privilege, cherished somewhat sentimentally by a shrinking coterie of Conservatives and relinquished as a too costly privilege by the rest.

The final debate in the House of Lords on Gladstone's church rate bill illustrates how far removed from the disputed church and state principles of the 1830s were the concerns of 1868. No one spoke about the state or about traditional claims concerning its moral or spiritual obligations. Differences now centered on the nature of the Church. Peers, no less than M.P.s, now assumed the validity of the claims of a pluralistic society and a liberal state. The members of the House of Lords spoke less as statesmen than as High, Broad, or Low Churchmen as they disputed those parts of the church rate legislation that had a bearing on shaping the Anglican church toward or away from their brand of churchmanship. The final debate about the rate was, unlike the debates of a generation earlier, not about political philosophy but about ecclesiology. The old political debates about "the Constitution in Church and State" had been reduced to an internal denominational squabble.

The defeat of the church rate principle and the triumph of the principle of voluntary financial support for all religious denominations are tied closely to the political pressure exerted by Nonconformists between 1832 and 1868. Parochial vestry contests and church rate refusals endangered social peace and threatened the well-being of parish churches and therefore commanded the attention of Parliament. National leadership of the anti–church rate agitation was provided first by the Dissenting Deputies and after 1853 by the Liberation Society. The latter especially was able to use the church rate question to become an effective political pressure group. The Liberation Society developed the machinery, finances, and support that enabled it to create a climate of opinion that forced both political parties to attempt to redress the church rate grievance. By the late 1850s the society had grown in influence to such an extent that it was able to exact and enforce pledges from large numbers of Liberal M.P.s committing them to vote for church rate abolition.

The influence Nonconformists were able to exercise in the church rate agitation was considerable but limited. Nonconformists had the power to convince both the Church and Parliament of the necessity for legislation to free Nonconformists from church rate obligations; but in this period they did not have the political power to force the Church to accept the principle of voluntary financial support, any more than the Anti-Corn-Law League had been able to shape the legislation abolishing the Corn Laws a generation earlier. Voluntary funding of parish churches came about by default because Churchmen could not agree on a modified compulsory church rate that would have given some form of exemption either to Nonconformists or to all conscientious objectors.

At several crucial points during the thirty-six-year church rate struggle the issue might have been settled in a way that would have allowed the Church to retain compulsory support at least from Churchmen. In 1856 Palmerston's government offered to exempt self-declared Nonconformists from church obligations. The Liberation Society accepted the offer because it depended on the support of moderate Dissenters and liberal Churchmen who did not then insist on total abolition. The plan was stillborn because of opposition from the Conservative party, divisions in the Liberal party, and Palmerston's lack of interest in the scheme. In 1861, after the Liberation Society had been discredited by a successful church defense movement, moderate Liberals including Trelawny, the parliamentary spokesman of the church rate abolitionists, were willing to break their pledges to the Liberation Society and to cooperate with progressive Conservatives in search of a church rate compromise. They failed not because of a resurgence of pressure from the Liberation Society, but because of serious disagreement within the Church and within the Conservative party. In the end the repeal of compulsory church rates owed less to the strength of Nonconformists than to the impotence of the Church, which lacked the nerve and vision to adapt the church rate principle to fit the demands of an increasingly pluralistic society.

When the Conservatives were unable to agree on a compromise church rate bill, there was no realistic alternative but to adopt a form of church rate abolition. Neither political party could afford to continue to alienate Nonconformists after the extension of the franchise in 1867. The very inevitability of church rate legislation may be seen as a triumph for the Liberation Society. Nevertheless, it was a limited victory because Gladstone was able to work with moderate Nonconformists such as Samuel Morley to bypass militant voluntaryists in the Liberation Society. In so doing, and by abolishing only compulsion but not the church rate or the machinery to levy it, Gladstone's bill gave notice that abolition of compulsory church rates should not be seen as a step toward disestablishment of the Church. The termination of the church rate conflict, therefore, while a victory for Nonconformist anti–church rate agitation, also constituted a failure of militant voluntaryists. The ultimate objective of the Liberation Society was not realized.

In light of Gladstone's continuing allegiance to the established church, it might seem paradoxical that by 1868 Gladstone was becoming the spokesman for the political aspirations of Nonconformists. But that relationship was possible because Gladstone's continued commitment to the church establishment decreased in practical importance to moderate Nonconformists, after the repeal of compulsory church rates and the opening of the ancient universities and parish churchyards to Nonconformists. In public affairs Gladstone and the Nonconformists could find common ground in political liberalism.

Religion was the route by which both Gladstone and the Nonconformists became liberals. Ecclesiastically Gladstone and the Nonconformists shared only a deep piety and a common savior. Gladstone's sacramental piety and highly liturgical Anglo-Catholicism differed greatly from the biblicistic faith and spare meeting-hall worship of many Nonconformists. It was in the evolution of their public faiths that Gladstone and the Nonconformists found each other.

The beginning of Gladstone's pilgrimage from an Anglican politics to merely being an Anglican in politics has been sketched in a variety of ways. Perry Butler has shown that as early as 1845 Gladstone realized, in light of Peel's Maynooth decision, that the state could no longer claim to have an undivided conscience. Gladstone's letter to John Henry Newman in April 1845 outlined the approach Gladstone was to take in politics in the decades to follow. He proposed that when government continued to act as if it had a conscience, much good might result. Gladstone would attempt to maintain the Church's public position where that was feasible. In cases in which that was no longer possible he would promote social justice under natural criteria.[1]

Gladstone's overriding concern now became, as he wrote to Newman: "to extricate the Church from the more constricting trammels of its attachment to the State in order that it might proclaim more effectively the Catholic truths to which it witnessed."[2] His stance toward the Church was governed consistently by the Anglo-Catholic principle that the Church's religious integrity ought to be valued above its privileges as an establishment. Because of his fear of Erastianism and " 'legislative Christianity' "[3] Gladstone came increasingly to treasure religious liberty as essential to provide justice, social peace, and "the maintenance of Divine Truth itself."[4] As Perry Butler and Peter Stansky have shown, the motivation for Gladstone's adoption of liberalism came from a deep conviction that religious liberty and full toleration were essential for the spiritual integrity of the Christian faith. His Anglo-Catholicism led him to embrace liberalism.[5]

    1. Perry Butler, *Gladstone: Church, State, and Tractarianism—A Study of His Religious Ideas and Attitudes, 1809–1859* (Oxford, 1982), p. 127.
    2. D. C. Lathbury, ed., *Correspondence on Church and Religion of William Ewart Gladstone*, vol. 1 (London, 1910), p. 73.
    3. Butler, *Gladstone*, p. 137.
    4. Ibid., p. 147.
    5. Ibid., p. 150; Peter Stansky, *Gladstone: A Progress in Politics* (New York and London, 1979).

It would be erroneous, however, to assume that because Gladstone discovered liberalism along the Anglo-Catholic road, there was an organic affinity between these two faiths.[6] Gladstone's view of the Church was never altered by this-worldly liberalism. However, his view of politics and the state became quite thoroughly desacralized and not fundamentally distinguishable from that of unbelieving liberals.

H.C.G. Matthew argued that after Gladstone saw his earlier Anglican Tory church and state principles collapse in 1845, he "came to invest the general concept of free trade with the moral role in the nation's ethical progress earlier attributed to the Established Church."[7] It can be argued not only that there was considerable discontinuity between Gladstone's earlier Tory statecraft and his later liberalism, but that as a mature Liberal there was a break between his ecclesiastical and political lives.[8] In politics, Gladstone paid increasingly less attention to the transcendent. Whereas he had once assumed that in both church and state truth came to man through revelation, in politics, according to Boyd Hilton, he turned "from a faith based on revelation to one based on nature."[9] God's omnipotence was revealed, therefore, not in divine revelation but within human experience, in the "moral improvement of society."[10]

It was on the road of Victorian fascination with the forces of development, with improvement in society traced in moral progress no less than in political, economic, and intellectual melioration, that Gladstone and the Nonconformists found each other. The incongruity of their similar ecclesiastical pilgrimages was bridged because, as Hilton has argued, Gladstone and the Nonconformists shared the same redemptive view of the world.[11] Hilton maintains that this sympathy "was based on their common acceptance of a fundamentalist theology. . . ."[12] It may be, however, that an even deeper common ground than theology was the growing attachment to liberty that came to motivate and inspire both Gladstone and the Nonconformists.

6. Butler, *Gladstone*, p. 150.

7. H.C.G. Matthew, *Gladstone, 1809–1874* (New York, 1988), p. 76.

8. M. D. Stephen, "Liberty, Church, and State: Gladstone's Relations with Manning and Acton, 1832–1870," *Journal of Religious History*, 1 (1960), 222; Butler, *Gladstone*, pp. 234–35.

9. Boyd Hilton, *The Age of Atonement: The Influence of Evangelicalism on Social and Economic Thought, 1785–1865* (Oxford, 1988), p. 350.

10. Ibid., p. 343.

11. Ibid., p. 358.

12. Ibid.

Among Nonconformists, that commitment to human freedom came to be expressed in voluntaryism. After 1832 Nonconformists came in growing numbers to translate their ecclesiological commitment to independent chapels into an ideology in whose name they aimed fundamentally to restructure society. Voluntaryism was a subtle mixture of traditional Dissenting ideals and political liberalism. The voluntary principle was, according to Richard J. Helmstadter, "a version of *laissez faire* with religion and education at its heart, couched in the language of political liberty."[13] Voluntaryist Nonconformists became determined to break down what remained of the Constantinian legacy in the nineteenth century. That entailed disestablishing the Anglican church and removing the remaining elements of a confessional state and society. Anglican privileges concerning education and ecclesiastical taxation became the points of conflict between voluntaryists and establishmentarians. Because even the most moderate voluntaryists objected to the validity of the church rate, opposition to that tax became a powerful engine to draw together moderate and militant Nonconformists into an apparently unified political movement.

In principle all voluntaryists opposed the legitimacy of the church establishment. But it was militant voluntaryists who insisted on seeking immediate disestablishment as a practical political goal. So long as militant disestablishmentarians appeared to represent the political goals of Nonconformity, Gladstone and the Nonconformists were politically incompatible. By 1865, however, it had become clear—in light of the humbling of the Liberation Society at the hands of the church defense movement, and following fruitful meetings between Gladstone and moderate Nonconformists such as Newman Hall[14]—that many Nonconformists could be satisfied with less than disestablishment.

It was then that Nonconformists began to see Gladstone as their champion. He introduced the church rate bill that freed them from what had long appeared to them to be a vexatious tax. When Gladstone agreed to disestablish the Irish church his reputation as a rising proponent of religious liberty was further secured. Increasingly Gladstone and the Nonconformists were drawn together to build a moral

13. Richard J. Helmstadter, "The Nonconformist Conscience," in P. March, ed., *The Conscience of the Victorian State* (London, 1979), p. 149; Ian Sellers, *Nineteenth-Century Nonconformity* (London, 1977), p. 72.
14. Machin, "Gladstone and Nonconformity," *Historical Journal*, XVII (1974), 347–64.

society on the basis of religious liberty, free trade, fiscal probity, and balanced budgets.

It was in Gladstonian liberalism that Gladstone and the Nonconformists joined forces to remove religious privilege and impediments to liberty. For both, it was their Christian faith that provided the moral fervor for reform. For this reason recent studies of Gladstone, including Richard Shannon's biography,[15] acknowledging the centrality of religion in Gladstone's political life are much-needed correctives to John Morley's classic study, which neglects the influence of religion on his politics. In one respect, however, the agnostic Morley may inadvertently have been more accurate than recent, and otherwise excellent, studies in assessing the actual role of religion in Gladstone's statesmanship. There is reason to argue that although much of the enthusiasm and moral energy of Gladstonian liberalism is inexplicable apart from the ferment of religion, the substance of Gladstone's politics belonged to classical liberalism and had little to do with the historic Christian faith.

For this reason one could speak, as M. D. Stephen and Perry Butler have done, of a "divorce" or "a gulf" between Gladstone's religious and political selves. Hilton, however, has argued that this gulf was bridged by Gladstone's insistence, when acting in politics as "a Lockeian," in tracing "the operational workings of divine providence" in a liberal state.[16] If we grant Hilton's contention that the liberal Gladstone was guided by profoundly religious motives, however, we must observe that Gladstone's once-coherent Christian view of church and state now rested on a contradiction. His churchmanship was based on dogma and authority; his liberal polity was subject primarily to human freedom and will. As a Churchman, Gladstone's view of truth remained based on the objective pillars of divine revelation and Christian tradition; as statesman, Gladstone had become a historicist. The purposes of God were revealed now in the subjective process of history, in the progressive unfolding of human freedom, dignity, and power. However much Gladstone might seek signs of divine providence in human affairs, his lack of a normative religious framework to anchor his politics would make it increasingly difficult to distinguish the voice of

15. R. Shannon, *Gladstone, 1809–1865* (London, 1982).
16. M. D. Stephen, "Liberty, Church, and State," p. 222; Butler, *Gladstone*, pp. 234–35; Boyd Hilton, "Gladstone's Theological Politics," in M. Bentley and J. Stevenson, eds., *High and Low Politics in Modern Britain* (Oxford, 1983), p. 30.

the people from the voice of God. By the time that voluntaryist Nonconformists ranged themselves under the banner of Gladstonian liberalism in the 1860s the pilgrimages of Gladstone and the Nonconformists had become one. Both Gladstone and Nonconformity had embraced liberty for similar reasons. Gladstone had fought against Erastianism, and Nonconformists against the establishment principle itself, out of a desire to achieve authentic religion free of political control. They enjoyed considerable success in freeing church and chapel from political bondage. In the process, however, neither had reflected about the conscience of the state, or about how traditional Christian teaching about politics and the state might be applied in a pluralistic society. Both assumed that liberal ideology and morality, and the interests of the middle classes, were indistinguishable from Christian political teaching. Both consequently identified Christianity with the impermanent social forces of the Victorian era.[17] The long struggle to repeal compulsory church rates in the name of voluntary religion had contributed to a paradox. Religion by 1868 had become freer of state control, as both Gladstone and the Nonconformists desired; but the state, in becoming more liberal, had also become denuded of religious influence. This conclusion represented the defeat of Gladstone's primary goal, stated in 1838 in his *The State in Its Relations with the Church*, to maintain an Anglican Christian conscience in the state. Equally, it marked a substantial departure from the common Nonconformist aim as late as 1834, when only the vanguard of Dissenters were becoming voluntaryists, to rely on state sanctions to enforce nondenominational Christian religion in public life.[18] The desacralized liberal state emerged in England and Wales not from the malevolent design of godless revolutionaries but from the absentmindedness of men whose zeal for voluntary religion and ecclesiastical independence led them to neglect the conscience of the state.

17. A. D. Gilbert, *Religion and Society in Industrial England, 1740–1914* (London, 1976), pp. 148, 149.
18. *Congregational Magazine* (1834), new series, II, 358.

Appendix

Bills, or motions to introduce bills, to repeal or amend the law of church rates, introduced in both houses of Parliament, 1834–68. (Based on Great Britain, Parliamentary Papers, 1861, XLVIII.83; 1867, LIV.647; Hansard's Parliamentary Debates, vols. XXII–CXCIII. All bills were introduced in the House of Commons unless otherwise indicated.)

1834   Bill to Abolish Church Rates, and to Make Provision for the Repair of Churches (Lord Althorp)

1837   Resolution to abolish church rates and to maintain church fabrics from income derived from better-managed church lands (Thomas Spring Rice)

1839   Motion to introduce bill to exempt Dissenters from church rate obligations (T. S. Duncombe)

1840   Motion to introduce bill to exempt Dissenters from church rate obligations (T. S. Duncombe)

1841   Motion to introduce bill to abolish church rates and make other provisions for churches and chapels in England and Wales (Sir John Easthope)

1842   Motion to introduce bill to abolish church rates and make other provisions for churches and chapels in England and Wales (Sir John Easthope)

1853   Motion to introduce bill to exempt Dissenters from church rate obligations (R. J. Phillimore)

1854   Dissenters Church Rates Relief Bill (C. W. Packe)
Church Rates Abolition Bill (Sir William Clay)

1855   Church Rates Abolition Bill (Sir William Clay)
(HL) Church Rate Reform Bill (J. B. Sumner, Cantuar)

1856   Church Rates Amendment Bill (C. W. Packe)
Bill to Abolish Church Rates and to Make Other Provision in Lieu Thereof (Sir William Clay)

1857   Church Rates Abolition Bill (Sir William Clay)

1858   Church Rates Abolition Bill (J. S. Trelawny)
Voluntary Church Rates Commutation Bill (T. Alcock)
Church Rates Commutation Bill (C. W. Giles Puller)

1859   Church Rates Abolition Bill (J. S. Trelawny)
Voluntary Church Rates Commutation Bill (T. Alcock)
Church Rates Bill (Spencer Walpole)
(HL) Church Rate Relief Bill (Duke of Marlborough)
(HL) Bill to Abolish Church Rates and to Make Provision for Church Fabrics (Baron Portman)

1860   Church Rates Abolition Bill (J. S. Trelawny)
Church Rates Law Amendment Bill (J. G. Hubbard)

1861   Church Rates Abolition Bill (J. S. Trelawny)
Church Rates Law Amendment Bill (J. G. Hubbard)
Church Rates Commutation Bill (T. Alcock)
Church Rates Law Amendment (no. 2) Bill (R. A. Cross)
(HL) Church Rates Assessment Bill (Duke of Marlborough)

1862   Church Rates Abolition Bill (J. S. Trelawny)
Church Rates Commutation Bill (C. N. Newdegate)
Church Rates Voluntary Commutation Bill (T. Alcock)

1863   Church Rates Abolition (no. 2) Bill (J. S. Trelawny)
Church Rates Redemption Bill (T. Alcock)
Church Rates Commutation Bill (C. N. Newdegate)
Church Rates Recovery Bill (Lord Alfred Churchill)

1864   Church Rates Commutation Bill (C. N. Newdegate)

1865   Church Rates Commutation Bill (C. N. Newdegate)

1866   Church Rates Abolition Bill (J. A. Hardcastle)
       Church Rates Commutation Bill (C. N. Newdegate)
       Church Rates Amendment Bill (Sir William Bovill)
       Compulsory Church Rates Abolition Bill (W. E. Gladstone)

1867   Church Rates Abolition Bill (J. A. Hardcastle)
       Church Rates Commutation Bill (C. N. Newdegate)
       Church Rates Regulation Bill (J. G. Hubbard)

1868   Church Rates Abolition Bill (J. A. Hardcastle)
       Church Rates Commutation Bill (C. N. Newdegate)
       Church Rates Regulation Bill (J. G. Hubbard)
       Compulsory Church Rates Abolition Bill (W. E. Gladstone)

—

Bibliography

I. Manuscripts

Bishop Samuel Wilberforce Papers. Bodleian Library, d. 35–47; c. 13–16.
Braintree Assessment Book. Essex Record Office, D/P 264/4/4.
Braintree Church Rate Case. Bocking Church Rate. Typescript copy of letters exchanged between S. Courtauld and Sir H. Oakeley. Essex Record Office, T/P 116/43.
Braintree Church Rate Case. Church Rate Meeting at Braintree, Friday, 2 June 1837 (typescript copy). Essex Record Office, T/P 116/43.
Braintree Vestry Book, 1811–1814. Essex Record Office, D/P 264/8/16.
Broadlands Papers. Royal Commission on Historical Manuscripts, London.
Chelmsford Vestry Book, 1835–1843. Essex Record Office, D/P 94/8/16.
Church Rates. General File. Commutation of Church Rates in the Metropolitan Area. Ecclesiastical Commissioners for England, MS. 85385.
Consistory Court Cause Papers (incomplete). London Diocese. Guildhall Library, MS. 12, 185/7.
Court of Arches. H-Series (record of cases before the court). H. 253–end, 1818–1849. H. 745–996, 1849–1880. Lambeth Palace Library, London.

Derby Papers. In the care of Lord Blake. The Queen's College, Oxford.
Gladstone Papers. British Library Add. MSS. 44095–44790.
Holland House Papers. British Library Add. MSS. 51558–51871.
Howley Papers. Lambeth Palace Library MS. 1812.
Hughenden Papers. British Library of Economic and Political Science Microfilm. Film 131.
Iddesleigh Papers. British Library Add. MSS. 50014, 50015.
Keble Papers. Keble College, Oxford.
Lambeth Churchwardens Accounts. Minet Library, London.
Lambeth Vestry Minutes. Minet Library, London.
Minutes of the British Anti-State-Church Association. Vol. II. Greater London Record Office, County Hall, London.
Minutes of the Liberation Society (executive committee). Vols. II–V. Greater London Record Office, County Hall, London.
Minutes of the Protestant Dissenting Deputies. Vols. V–XIII. Guildhall MS. 3083.
Minutes of the Protestant Society for the Protection of Religious Liberty. Dr. Williams's Library, London.
Minutes of the United Committee to consider the grievances under which Dissenters now labour with a view to their redress. Vols. I and II. Guildhall MS. 3086.
"Nomad." A Miscellany (typescript). Essex Record Office, T/P 116/18.
Notes of Minutes of the Church Rate Abolition Society, 1836–1839. Greater London Record Office, County Hall, London.
Notes on Nineteenth-Century Braintree (typescript). Essex Record Office, T/P 116/25.
Peel Papers. British Library Add. MSS. 40333–40423.
Persons Summoned for Arrears of Old and New Church Rates commencing 18 July 1823. Parish of Lambeth. Greater London Record Office MS. P85/MR41/112.
Pusey Papers. H. P. Liddon Bound Volumes. Pusey House, Oxford.
Russell Papers. Public Record Office, 30/22.
Salisbury Papers. Hatfield House, Hertfordshire.
Selborne Papers. Lambeth Palace Library, London.
Society of Friends. London Yearly Meeting. Great Book of Sufferings. Vols. XL–XLIV. Friends' House, London.
Society of Friends. London Yearly Meeting. Meeting for Sufferings Minutes. Vols. XLIV–XLVII. Friends' House, London.
Society of Friends. London Yearly Meeting Minutes. Vols. XXIII–XXVIII. Friends' House, London.
St. Martin's, Leicester Vestry Book. Book no. XXII, 1826–1851. Leicestershire Record Office.
Tait Papers. Lambeth Palace Library, London.
Thomas Barrett Lennard Papers. Essex Record Office, MS. DL c. 61.
Thomas Henry Sutton Sotheron Estcourt Papers. Gloucestershire Record Office.
Warner Papers. Bodleian Library MS. Top. Essex C/8. On microfilm in Essex Record Office, T/A 242.
Woodbridge Local Taxation Returns. St. Mary's Woodbridge, Suffolk.

Woodbridge Vestry Minute Book. Vols. 1856–1865; 1865–1879. St. Mary's Woodbridge, Suffolk.

II. Parliamentary Documents (organized chronologically within categories)

Great Britain. *Hansard's Parliamentary Debates* (3d series). Vols. XXII–CXCIII.

Great Britain. *General Index to the Reports on Public Petitions, 1833–1852.* House of Lords Record Office.

Great Britain. *Public Petitions and Appendix, 1833.* Vols. I and II. House of Lords Record Office.

Great Britain. *Reports of the Select Committee of the House of Commons on Public Petitions with Appendix.* Sessions 1834–1868. House of Lords Record Office.

Great Britain. *Parliamentary Papers.* Poor Rates, County Rates, Highway Rates, and Church Rates. 1830–1831 (52.), XI. 205.

Great Britain. ———. *Report of Commissioners Appointed to Inquire into the Practice and Jurisdiction of Ecclesiastical Courts in England and Wales.* 1831–1832 (199.), XXIV. 1.

Great Britain. ———. *First Report of Commissioners on the State of the Established Church, with Reference to Duties and Revenues.* 1835 (54.), XXII. 1.

Great Britain. ———. *Suits for Recovery of Church Rates in Ecclesiastical Courts since 53 Geo. III, c. 127.* 1835 (487.), XLVI. 91.

Great Britain. ———. *Second Report of Commissioners on the State of the Established Church, with Reference to Duties and Revenues.* 1836 (86.), XXXVI. 1.

Great Britain. ———. *Memorandum of the Visiting Justice and Governor of the Gaol of Chelmsford, Transmitted to the Secretary of State for the Home Department, with Reference to the Treatment of John Thorogood, a Prisoner in That Gaol.* 1839 (444.), XXXVIII. 397.

Great Britain. ———. *Amount of Church Rates in the Year Ending Easter 1827; of Church Rates and Other Monies Received and Expended by the Churchwardens in the Year Ending Easter 1832; and of Church Rates and Other Monies Received and Expended in the Year Ending Easter 1839* (in 562.), XLIV. 47.

Great Britain. ———. *Abstract of Returns Relating to Church Rates.* 1845 (428.), XLI. 51.

Great Britain. ———. *Report of Select Committee of House of Commons on Church Rates.* 1851 (541.), IX. 1.

Great Britain. ———. *House of Lords Sessional Papers. Reports from the Select Committee of the House of Commons on Church Rates.* 1851, XXXII. 1.

Great Britain. ———. *Abstract of Return from Each Parliamentary Borough in England and Wales, 1833–1851.* 1852 (346.), XXXVIII. 19.

Great Britain. ———. *Return of Church Rates Made or Refused in Parishes of the Thirty-six Registration Districts of London during 1851, 1852, and 1853, etc.* 1854, L. 117.

Great Britain. ———. *Return of Parishes in Cities or Parliamentary Boroughs in England and Wales in which (during the last fifteen years) Church Rates Have Been Refused, and since That Refusal Have Ceased to Be Collected, etc.* 1856, XLVIII. 1.

Great Britain. ———. *Return of Receipt and Expenditure by Churchwardens and Chapelwardens in England and Wales from Easter 1853 to Easter 1854.* 1856, XLVIII. 223.

Great Britain. ———. *Amount of Church Rates, etc., Received and Expended by Churchwardens in 1832, 1839, and 1854.* 1857 (Sess. 2), XXXII. 27.

Great Britain. ———. *Return from Each Parish within the Several Archdeaconries in England and Wales, of Amount Expended during the Last Seven Years for Church Purposes.* 1859 (Sess. 1), XX. 1. Supplementary return, ibid., 469.

Great Britain. ———. *Report of Select Committee of House of Lords on Church Rates.* 1859 (Sess. 2), XVII. 1. 217.

Great Britain. ———. *Return of Rateable Value of Property Assessed to Poor Rate in Parishes in which, According to Above Returns, No Church Rates Were Made.* 1859 (Sess. 2), XIX. 115.

Great Britain. ———. *House of Commons. Report of Select Committee of House of Lords on Church Rates.* 1860, XXII. 159.

Great Britain. ———. *Return of Bills Introduced into Both Houses, with Names of Persons Introducing Same, 1841 to 1861.* 1861, XLVIII. 83.

Great Britain. ———. *Local Taxation Returns: 1862, XXX. 127; 1863, XXX. 1; 1864, XXIII. 137; 1865, XLVI. 1; 1866, LV. 293.*

Great Britain. ———. *Return of Bills and Clauses Proposed as Amendments to Bills Introduced into the House of Commons, with Names of Persons Introducing or Proposing Such Clauses, 1861 to 1867.* 1867, LIV. 647.

Great Britain. ———. *House of Commons Bills. A Bill for the Abolition of Compulsory Church Rates.* 1867–1868 (13.), 1.

Great Britain. ———. *House of Commons Bills. A Bill Instituted an Act for the Abolition of Compulsory Church Rates as Amended by the Lords.* 1867–1868 (232.), 1.

Great Britain. ———. *House of Lords Sessional Papers. Report from the Select Committee of the House of Lords on the Compulsory Church Rates Abolition Bill, with the Proceedings of the Committee.* 1867–1868 (143.), XXX. 9.

Journals of the House of Commons.

III. Newspapers and Victorian Periodicals

Albion
Aris's Birmingham Gazette
Birmingham Advertiser
Birmingham Journal
Bradford Observer
Bradford Review
Bury and Norwich Post
Chelmsford Chronicle
Cheltenham Examiner
Church and State Review
Church Institution Circular
Churchman
Colchester and Chelmsford Gazette
Congregational Magazine

Daily News
Daily Telegraph
Essex Herald
Essex Standard
Examiner
Globe/Globe and Traveller
Guardian
Ipswich Journal
John Bull
Keene's Bath Journal
Leeds Mercury
Leeds Times
Leicester Journal
Leicestershire Chronicle
Leicestershire Mercury
Liberator
Manchester Courier
Manchester Daily Examiner and Times
Manchester Guardian
Manchester Times and Gazette
Morning Advertiser
Morning Chronicle
Morning Herald
Morning Post
Morning Star
Nonconformist
Patriot
Plymouth and Devonport Weekly Journal
Quarterly Review
Record
Saturday Review
Somerset County Gazette
Spectator
Standard
Suffolk Mercury
The Times
True Sun
Unitarian Herald
Watchman/Watchman and Wesleyan Advertiser
Welshman
Wesleyan Times
Western Times

IV. Victorian Books and Pamphlets

Abbott, Edwin A., ed. *The Anglican Career of Cardinal Newman.* Vol. II. London and New York, 1892.

Account of Distraints Made on Members of the Religious Society of Friends for Tithes and Other Ecclesiastical Imposts. London, n.d.

Agricola. *Church-Rate Repeal: A Letter to an Abolitionist.* London, 1858.

Aitken, R. *Hints, Suggestions, and Reasons for the Provisional Adjustment of the Church-Rate, for the Reformation of the Church's External Administration, and for the Union of Church and Dissent.* London, 1859.

Allin, Henry. *Some Brief and Serious Reasons Why the People Called Quakers Do Not Pay Tithes, and Other Ecclesiastical Demands.* London, 1840.

An Archdeacon in the Province of Canberbury. *Church Rates, "the Question of the Day," Considered in a Letter to Loftus T. Wigram, Esq., M.P. for the University of Cambridge.* London, 1856.

Arnold, Thomas. *Principles of Church Reform.* London, 1962. First published in 1833.

Attree, W. Wakeford. *The Braintree Church Rate Case.* Report of the case of Gosling v. Veley, in the House of Lords. London, 1853.

Ayliffe, John. *Parergon Juris Canonici Anglicani; or, A Commentary, by Way of Supplement to the Canons and Constitutions of the Church of England.* 2d ed. London, 1734.

Barnes, Ralph. *A Letter on Church Rates.* London, 1837.

Bennett, William J. E. *Why Church Rates Should Be Abolished.* 2d ed. London, 1861.

Bentham, Jeremy. *Church of Englandism and Its Catechism Examined.* London, 1818.

Beresford Hope, A. J. *Church Politics and Church Prospects.* London, 1865.

————. *Church Rates and Dissenters: A Speech Delivered at the Council of the Church Institution, January 21, 1861.* Revised. London, 1861.

Beverley, R. M. *A Letter to His Grace the Archbishop of York, on the Present Corrupt State of the Church of England.* London, 1831.

Bligh, E. V. *Church Rates: Concession Advocated, by a Clergyman.* London, 1861.

Blomfield, Alfred. *A Memoir of Charles James Blomfield.* 2d ed. London, 1864.

Bristol Church Defence Association. *Report Read at the Meeting Held in the Victoria Rooms, April 9, 1866.* London, 1866.

British Anti-State-Church Association. *Proceedings of the First Anti-State-Church Conference, Held in London, April 30, May 1 and 2, 1844.* London, n.d.

————. *Tracts for the Million.* London, 1847.

————. *The Ultimate Principle of Religious Liberty.* London, 1860.

Burke, Edmund. *Reflections on the Revolution in France.* Edited with an introduction by Thomas H. D. Mahoney. Indianapolis and New York, 1955.

Burn, Richard. *The Ecclesiastical Law.* Vol. I. 8th ed. Edited by Robert Philip Tyrwhitt. London, 1824.

————. *The Justice of the Peace and Parish Officer.* 6 vols. 28th ed. rev. by J. Chitty and Thomas Chitty. London, 1837.

Burnet, John. *The Church of England and the Church of Christ.* London, n.d.

Burton, Charles James. *Considerations on the Abolition of Compulsory Church Rates.* London, 1869.

Campbell, Sir John. *Letter to the Right Hon. Lord Stanley, M.P. for North Lancashire, on the Law of Church Rates.* 3d ed. London, 1837.

The Case of the Dissenters, in a Letter Addressed to the Lord Chancellor. London, 1833.

Chalmers, Thomas. *The Works of.* Vol. XVII. *On Church and College Establishments.* Glasgow and London, n.d.

The Chronicle of Convocation. London, 1860.

The Chronicle of Convocation. Lower House of Convocation of Canterbury. Report of Committee on Deficiencies of Spiritual Ministration. London, 1876.

Church Congress Report. London, 1878, 1888.

Church Defence Institution. *List of Associations in Union Throughout the Country.* Westminster, 1872.

Churton, Edward. *The Assembled Commons.* London, 1837.

A Clergyman of the Diocese of London. *Church-Rates: What a Vestry Can, and What It Can Not Do.* London, 1856.

Coleridge, Samuel Taylor. *On the Constitution of the Church and State According to the Idea of Each.* Edited with an introduction by John Barrell. London, 1972.

Committee of Laymen. *Church Rates.* The Present State of the Church Rate Question: "No. 5. Suggestions for Maintaining the Church Rate." London, 1859.

———. *Church Rates.* The Present State of the Church Rate Question, with an Authentic Report of the Lords' Debate, July 8, 1858. 3d ed. London, 1858.

Conder, Eustace R. *Josiah Conder: A Memoir.* London, 1857.

Correspondence of John Henry Newman with John Keble and Others, 1839–1845. New York, 1917.

Coventry, George. *On the Revenues of the Church of England: Exhibiting the Rise and Progress of Ecclesiastical Taxation.* London, 1830.

Cripps, Henry William. *A Practical Treatise on the Law Relating to the Church and Clergy.* 6th ed. London, 1886. 7th ed. Edited by Aubrey Trevor Lawrence. London, 1921.

Curteis, W. C. *Report of Cases Argued and Determined in the Ecclesiastical Courts at Doctors' Commons.* Vol. I and III. London, n.d.

Dale, James Murray. *Church Rates: The Present Position of the Question, with Reasons Against Their Abolition.* London, 1860.

———. *The Clergyman's Legal Handbook.* 2d ed. London, 1859.

Deacon, Edward A. *Another Letter to the Right Hon. Lord Stanley, M.P. on the Law of Church Rates; Being in Answer to the Letter of the Attorney General.* London, 1837.

Degge, Simon. *The Parson's Counsellor; with the Law of Tithes or Tithing.* 7th ed. With additions by Charles Ellis. London, 1820.

Denison, George Anthony. *An Appeal to the Clergy and Laity of the Church of England, to Combine for the Defence of the Church, and for the Recovery of Her Rights and Liberties.* London, 1850.

———. *The Charge of the Archdeacon of Taunton, April 1860.* London, 1860.

———. *Church Rate: A National Trust.* London, 1861.

———. *Church Rate: What Ought Parliament to Do?* London, 1861.

Denison, Louisa Evelyn. *Fifty Years at East Brent—The Letters of George Anthony Denison, 1845–1896.* London, 1902.

Dodsworth, William. *A House Divided Against Itself.* London, 1850.

A Dorsetshire Incumbent. *Three Articles on Mr. Gladstone's Compulsory Church-Rate Abolition Bill.* Dorchester, 1866.

D'Oyly, George. *A Letter to the Right Honourable Earl Grey, on the Subject of Church Rates.* London, 1834.

Dunkley, C., ed. *The Official Report of the Church Congress.* London, 1894.

Elliot, Gilbert. *A Letter to a Yeoman in Favour of Abolition of Church Rates.* London, 1837.

Epistles from the Yearly Meeting of Friends Held in London. Vol. I, 1681–1769; vol. II, 1770–1857. London, 1858.

Evans, James Cook. *A Letter to the Inhabitants of St. Luke, Chelsea, on the Subject of Church Rates.* Chelsea, 1836.

———. *Report of the Judgments Pronounced by the Judges of the Court of Exchequer Chamber, in the Braintree Church-Rate Case, Gosling v. Veley, in Error from the Queen's Bench, in Hilary Term, 1850.* London, 1850.

Extracts from the Minutes and Proceedings of the Yearly Meeting of Friends Held in London, 1857–1866. London, n.d.

Fendall, James. *Exemption from the Payment of Church Rates on Personal Grounds, Considered in a Letter to J. G. Hubbard, Esq., M.P.* London, 1860.

Forster, William. *The Duties of Sunday School Teachers in Relation to State Churches.* London, 1846.

Fox, W. J. *The Church-Rate Imposition.* London, 1837.

Galton, Theodore H. *Church Courts and Church Rates: A Letter to the Rt. Hon. W. E. Gladstone, M.P.* London, 1854.

Girdlestone, Charles. *Church Rates Lawful, but Not Always Expedient.* London, 1833.

Gladstone, W. E. *Church Principles Considered in Their Results.* London, 1840.

———. *Gleanings of Past Years, 1843–1878.* 7 vols. London, 1879.

———. *The State in Its Relations with the Church.* London, 1838. 4th ed., enlarged into 2 vols., 1841.

Gooch, G. P., ed. *The Later Correspondence of Lord John Russell, 1840–1878.* Vol. II. London, 1925.

Goode, William. *A Brief History of Church Rates.* 2d ed. London, 1838.

Gordon, Arthur H., ed. *Selections from the Correspondence of the Earl of Aberdeen.* Vol. X, 1852–1854; vol. XI: 1854–1855. London, 1885.

Grosvenor, Robert (Baron Ebury). *The Only Compromise Possible in Regard to Church Rates.* 2d ed. London, 1861.

Guedalla, Philip, ed. *The Palmerston Papers. Gladstone and Palmerston: Being the Correspondence of Lord Palmerston with Mr. Gladstone, 1851–1865.* London, 1928.

Hale, William Hale. *The Abolition of Church Rates: A Measure Preparative to the Overthrow of the Established Church as the National Religion.* London, 1859.

———. *An Address to the Clergy of the Archdeaconry of London, at the Annual Visitation, May 23, 1860, on the Subject of Church Rates.* London, 1860.

———. *The Designs and Constitution of the Society for the Liberation of Religion from State Patronage and Control.* London, 1861.

———. *An Essay on the Supposed Existence of a Quadripartite and Tripartite Division of Tithes in England, for Maintaining the Clergy, the Poor, and the Fabric of the Church.* London, 1832.

———. *Few Words on the Church Rate Question.* London, 1861.

Hall, C. Newman. *Newman Hall: An Autobiography.* London, 1898.

Harvey, Frederick Burn. *Church Rate Opposition: Its Fallacies Exposed and Refuted.* London, 1866.

Heaton, George. *A Letter to R. M. Beverley, Esq., on the Subject of His Late Address to His Grace the Archbishop of York, on the "Present Corrupt State of the Church of England."* 2d ed. Doncaster, 1831.

Henley, Lord. *A Plan of Church Reform.* London, 1832.

Hills, Walter. *The Law of Church Rates.* London, 1837.

Hinton, J. H. *Address to the Wesleyan Methodists of Great Britain and Ireland.* London, 1851.

———. *Church Property and Revenues in England and Wales.* London, 1851.

———. *Church Property — Whose Is It?* London, 1851.

———. *It's the Law; or, The Churchman's Defence of Church-Rates Examined.* London, 1851.

Hoare, Henry. *Hints on Lay Cooperation.* 7 vols. London, 1866.

Hodder, Edwin. *The Life of Samuel Morley.* 2d ed. London, 1887.

Hone, Richard Brindley. *Churchwardens' Duties: The New Church Rates Act.* London, 1869.

Hubbard, J. G. *The Church and Church Rates: A Letter to the Electors of the Borough of Buckingham.* 2d ed. London, 1861.

Irons, William J. *The Present Crisis in the Church of England, Illustrated by a Brief Inquiry as to the Royal Supremacy.* London, 1850.

James, John Angell. *A Pastor's Address to His People, on the Principles of Dissent, and the Duties of Dissenters.* London, 1834.

Johnson, Cuthbert W. *The Judgments of the Consistory Court of London, Court of Queen's Bench, Court of Exchequer Chamber, and the Arches Court of Canterbury, in the Braintree Church-Rate Case.* London, 1843.

———. *Report of the Braintree Church-Rate Case, Veley and Joslin v. Burder, and Veley and Joslin v. Gosling, to which Is Appended Gaudern v. Silby.* 3d ed. London, 1843.

[Keble, John.] "Review of 'The State in Its Relations with the Church,' 3d ed., London: John Murray, 1839." *British Critic*, LII (Oct. 1839), 355–97.

Keble, John. *"Sermon on National Apostasy," in the Christian Year — Lyra Innocentium — and Other Poems.* London, 1914.

A Kent Incumbent. *An Easy Solution and Amicable Settlement of the Church-Rate Question.* London, 1861.

Kenworthy, James Wright. *A Brief History of St. Michael's Church, Braintree.* Braintree, 1899.

Lathbury, D. C., ed. *Correspondence on Church and Religion of W. E. Gladstone.* 2 vols. London, 1910.

Liberation Society. *The "Liberation Society": A Jubilee Retrospect.* London, 1894.

The "Liberation Society" and Its Triennial Conferences: An Historical Review. London, 1880.

Locke, John. *Epistola de Tolerantia* (A Letter on Toleration). Edited with a preface to the Latin text by Raymond Klibansky. English translation and introduction by J. W. Gough. Oxford, 1968.

———. *Two Treatises on Government.* Edited with an introduction by Peter Laslett. New York and Toronto, 1965.

[Macaulay, T. B.] "Review of 'The State in Its Relations with the Church,' by W. E. Gladstone, Esq." *Edinburgh Review*, LXIX (April 1839), 231–80.

Mackarness, Frederick Coleridge. *Prideaux's Practical Guide to the Duties of Church-wardens.* 16th ed. London, 1895.

Manning, James. *Letter to Earl Fitzwilliam, upon the Power of Compelling the Assessment of a Church Rate, by Proceedings in Courts of Law.* London, 1837.

Martin, George. *A Brief Statement of the Effect of the Judgments Given in the Braintree Case on the Law of Church Rates.* Exeter, 1854.

———. *Observations on a Bill on Church Rates, Presented to the House of Lords, by the Archbishop of Canterbury.* Exeter, 1855.

Masheder, Richard. *Dissent and Democracy: Their Mutual Relations and Common Object.* London, 1864.

"Mathetes." *Religious Reform Impracticable, Without Separation from the State: An Earnest Appeal to Pious Members of the Established Church.* London, 1834.

Meck, Robert. *Methodism, the Church, and the Dissenters.* London, 1834.

Merewether, Francis. *A Letter to the Right Honourable Lord John Manners, M.P., on Church Rates.* London, 1855.

———. *A Reply to Lord Stanley's Pamphlet on Church Rates.* London, 1853.

———. *A Respectful Address to the Ratepayers of the County of Leicester, on Church Rates.* Leicester, 1855.

Metcalfe, William. *The Opinion of Sir John Campbell on the Law of Church-Rates, as Stated in His Letter to the Right Hon. Lord Stanley, Examined, and Contrasted with the Highest Authorities and Judicial Decisions on the Subject.* London, 1837.

Miall, Arthur. *Life of Edward Miall.* London, 1884.

Miall, Edward. *The British Churches in Relation to the British People.* 2d ed. London, 1850.

———. *The Fixed and the Voluntary Principles: Eight Letters to the Right Hon. the Earl of Shaftesbury.* London, 1859.

———. *The "Liberation Society" and Church Property: Two Lectures Delivered . . . in the Broadmead Rooms, Bristol, Feb. 8 and 10, 1860.* Bristol, 1860.

———. *Religious Establishments Incompatible with Rights of Citizenship.* 2d ed. London, 1846.

———. *Title-Deeds of the Church of England to Her Parochial Endowments.* London, 1862.

———. *What Is the Separation of Church and State?* London, 1848.

Molesworth, I.E.N. *Resistance to Church-Rates: A Letter to the People of England.* 3d ed. London, 1836.

Morgan, Thomas. *A Lecture on the Views and Designs of the Birmingham Voluntary Church Society.* Birmingham and London, 1836.

Morris, A. J. *An Address to Dissenters on the Religious Bearings of the State-Church Question.* 3d ed. London, 1846.

———. *The Anti-State-Church Catechism Adapted for Popular Use.* London, 1845.

Mursell, Arthur. *James Phillippo Mursell: His Life and Work.* London, 1886.

Nicholl, John. *Observations on the Attorney General's Letter to Lord Stanley.* London, 1837.

A Nonconformist of the Old School. *Primitive Nonconformity Opposed to Modern Dissent.* London, 1837.

The Official Report of the Church Congress, Held at Manchester, October 1888. London, 1888.

The Official Report of the Eighteenth Annual Meeting of the Church Congress, Held at Sheffield, 1878. Sheffield and London, 1879.

Paley, William. *The Principles of Moral and Political Philosophy.* 2d ed. London, 1786.

Palmer, William. *A Treatise on the Church of Christ.* 2 vols. 3d ed. London, 1842.

Parliament and the Church-Rate Question: An Historical Sketch. London, 1861.

Percevel, A. P. *The Origins of Church Rates, with Remarks on the Proposal of His Majesty's Government.* London, 1837.

Phillpotts, Henry. *Correspondence between the Bishop of Exeter and His Archdeacons, on Church Rates.* 1861.

A Political Volunteer. *Sixpennyworth of Rifle-Shot.* London, 1860.

Pott, Joseph Holden. *A Letter to the Clergy of the Archdeaconry of London.* London, 1837.

The Present Law as to Church Rates. London, n.d.

Prideaux, Charles Grevile. *A Practical Guide to the Duties of Churchwardens.* 7th ed. London, 1855. 14th ed. London, 1880.

Prideaux, Humphrey. *Directions to Church-wardens for the Faithful Discharge of Their Office.* Norwich, 1701. 7th ed. London, 1805.

Protestant Dissenters' Almanac, 1875: "Mr. J. Carvell Williams and the Liberation Society." London, n.d.

Pulman, John. *The Anti-State-Church Association and the Anti-Church-Rate League Unmasked.* London, 1864.

The Real Character of the Provisions of the Bill for Abolishing Church Rates, Viewed Chiefly with Reference to the Coronation Oath. Durham, 1837.

Report of the Proceedings on the Occasion of the Presentation of a Testimonial to Samuel Courtauld, Esq., at Braintree, on 25 September 1855. London, 1857.

Robertson, Max A. *The English Reports.* Vols. X, CXV, and CXVI. London, 1911.

Rogers, J. Guinnes. *The Story of the Struggle for Religious Equality.* London, 1882.

Stanley, Lord. *The Church-Rate Question Considered.* London, 1853.

Stovel, C. *A Letter to the Right Honourable Lord Henley, Containing Remarks on His Plan of Church Reform, etc.* 2d ed. London, 1832.

Strachey, L., and R. Fulford, eds. *The Greville Memoirs, 1814–1860.* 8 vols. London, 1838.

Swan, Robert. *Church Repairs and the Remedies for Enforcing Them.* London, 1841.

———. *The Principle of Church Rates; from the Earliest Evidences of Their Existence to the Present Time, Comprising a Period of Nearly Twelve Hundred Years.* London, 1837.

Sweet, J. B. *A Memoir of the Late Henry Hoare.* London, 1869.

Tottenham, E. *A Speech on the Subject of the Established Church and Church Rates.* London, 14 Feb. 1837.

Vaughan, Robert. *Thoughts on the Past and Present State of Religious Liberty in England.* London, 1838.

Veley, A. C. *An Argument on the Braintree Church-Rate Question, with an Appendix of Authorities.* Pamphlet in Essex Record Office, n.d.

Walling, R.A.J. *The Diaries of John Bright.* London, 1930.

Wardlaw, Ralph. *National Church Establishments Examined.* London, 1839.

Wardlaw, William. *The Alliance Between Church and State.* 3d ed. London, 1748.

White, H. Master. *Church Rates: A Paper Read at the York Church Congress, on Thursday, October 11, 1866.* London, 1867.

Wilkins, George. *A Letter to the Right Honourable Lord John Russell, on the Subject of the Church Rates.* London, 1837.
Will You Have Your Church Repaired? London, 1837.
Williams, J. Carvell. *The Progress of Toleration Toward Religious Equality from 1688 to 1888.* London, 1888.
Wills, Alfred. *The Powers and Duties of Parish Vestries in Ecclesiastical Matters.* London, 1855.
Young, David. *The Law of Christ for Maintaining and Extending His Church.* 2d ed. London, 1846.

V. Recent Books and Journal Articles

Addison, William George. *Religious Equality in Modern England, 1714–1914.* London, 1944.
Anderson, Olive. "Gladstone's Abolition of Compulsory Church Rates: A Minor Political Myth and Its Historiographical Career." *Journal of Ecclesiastical History,* XXV, no. 2 (April 1974), 185–98.
Arnstein, Walter L. *Protestant versus Catholic in Mid-Victorian England: Mr. Newdegate and the Nuns.* Columbia, Mo., 1982.
Bebbington, D. W. *Evangelicalism in Modern Britain: A History from the 1730s to the 1980s.* London, 1989.
———. *The Nonconformist Conscience: Chapel and Politics, 1870–1914.* London, 1982.
Bellamy, Richard, ed. *Victorian Liberalism: Nineteenth-Century Political Thought and Practice.* London, 1990.
Bentley, Michael, and John Stevenson, eds. *High and Low Politics in Modern Britain: Ten Studies.* New York, 1983.
Best, G.F.A. "The Constitutional Revolution, 1828–1832, and Its Consequences for the Established Church." *Theology,* LXII, no. 468 (June 1959), 226–34.
———. *Temporal Pillars: Queen Anne's Bounty, the Ecclesiastical Commissioners, and the Church of England.* Cambridge, 1964.
Biagini, E. F. *Liberty, Retrenchment, and Reform: Popular Liberalism in the Age of Gladstone, 1860–1880.* Cambridge, 1992.
Binfield, C. *So Down to Prayers: Studies in English Nonconformity, 1780–1920.* London, 1977.
Blake, Robert. *Disraeli.* New York, 1967.
Bowen, Desmond. *The Idea of the Victorian Church.* Montreal, 1968.
Brent, Richard. *Liberal Anglican Politics: Whiggery, Religion, and Reform.* Oxford, 1987.
———. "The Whigs and Protestant Dissent in the Decade of Reform: The Case of Church Rates, 1833–1841." *English Historical Review,* 102, no. 405 (Oct. 1987), 887–910.
Brose, Olive. *Church and Parliament: The Reshaping of the Church of England, 1828–1860.* Stanford, 1959.
Brown, Kenneth D. *A Social History of the Nonconformist Ministry in England and Wales, 1800–1930.* Oxford, 1988.
Brown, Richard. *Church and State in Modern Britain, 1700–1850.* London, 1991.

Butler, Perry. *Gladstone: Church, State, and Tractarianism—A Study of His Religious Ideas and Attitudes, 1809–1859.* Oxford, 1982.

Chadwick, Owen. *The Victorian Church.* Parts I and II. 3d ed. London, 1966–70.

Champ, Judith F. "Priesthood and Politics in the Nineteenth Century: The Turbulent Career of Thomas McDonnell." *Recusant History,* 18 (May 1987), 289–303.

Clark, G. Kitson. *The Making of Victorian England.* New York, 1969.

Clark, J.C.D. *English Society, 1688–1832: Ideology, Social Structure, and Political Practice during the Ancien Regime.* Cambridge, 1985.

Coleman, D. C. *Courtauld's: An Economic and Social History.* Vol. I. Oxford, 1969.

Conacher, J. B. *The Aberdeen Coalition, 1852–1855.* Cambridge, 1968.

———. *The Peelites and the Party System, 1846–1852.* Newton Abbot, 1972.

Cornick, David. "William Baines in Leicester Gaol—A Note." *Journal of United Reformed Church History Society,* 3 (Oct. 1986), 388–91.

Courtauld, S. A., ed. *Courtauld Family Letters, 1782–1900.* 8 vols. Cambridge, 1916.

Courtauld, S. L. *The Huguenot Family of Courtauld.* Vols. I. and III. London, 1957, 1967.

Cowherd, Raymond G. *The Politics of English Dissent.* New York, 1956.

Cowling, M. *1867: Disraeli, Gladstone, and Revolution: The Passing of the Second Reform Bill.* Cambridge, 1967.

———. *Religion and Public Doctrine in Modern England.* Cambridge, 1985.

Cox, Jeffrey. *The English Churches in a Secular Society: Lambeth, 1870–1930.* New York, 1982.

Crowther, Margaret A. *Church Embattled: Religious Controversy in Mid-Victorian England.* Newton Abbot, 1970.

Curry, R., A. Gilbert, and L. Horsley. *Churches and Churchgoers: Patterns of Church Growth in the British Isles since 1700.* Oxford, 1977.

Davies, G.C.B. *Henry Phillpotts, Bishop of Exeter, 1778–1869.* London, 1954.

Davis, R. W. *Dissent in Politics, 1780–1830: The Political Life of William Smith, M.P.* London, 1971.

Davis, R. W., and R. J. Helmstadter. *Religion and Irreligion in Victorian Society.* London, 1992.

Dictionary of National Biography.

Dod's Parliamentary Companion.

Ellens, J. P. "Lord John Russell and the Church Rate Conflict: The Struggle for a Broad Church, 1834–1868." *Journal of British Studies,* 26 (April 1987), 232–57.

———. "Protestant Dissent in Mid-Nineteenth-Century England: A House Divided." *Fides et Historia,* XVIII, no. 1 (Jan. 1986), 15–24.

Evans, Eric J. "The Church in Danger? Anticlericalism in Nineteenth-Century England." *European Studies Review,* 13, no. 2 (1983), 201–23.

———. *The Contentious Tithe: The Tithe Problem and English Agriculture, 1750–1850.* London, 1976.

Everitt, Alan. *The Pattern of Rural Dissent: The Nineteenth Century.* Leicester, 1972.

Foot, M.R.D., and H.C.G. Matthew, eds. *The Gladstone Diaries.* Vols. I–IV. Oxford, 1968–74.

Gash, Norman. *Pillars of Government, and Other Essays on State and Society, c. 1770–1880.* London, 1986.

————. *Reaction and Reconstruction in English Politics, 1832–1852.* Oxford, 1965.

Gilbert, A. D. *Religion and Society in Industrial England, 1740–1914.* London, 1976.

Gilchrist, E. A. *Henry Hoare: The Layman Who Restored England's Synods.* London, 1930.

Glaser, J. F. "English Nonconformity and the Decline of Liberalism." *American Historical Review,* 63 (1958), 352–63.

Gloyn, Cyril K. *The Church in the Social Order: A Study of Anglican Social Theory from Coleridge to Maurice.* Forest Grove, Oreg., 1942.

Haig, Alan. *The Victorian Clergy.* London, 1984.

Hamburger, Joseph. *Macaulay and the Whig Tradition.* Chicago and London, 1976.

Hamer, D. A. "Gladstone: The Making of a Political Myth." *Victorian Studies,* XXII (1978–79), 29–50.

————. *The Politics of Electoral Pressure.* London, 1977.

Hammond, J. L., and Barbara Hammond. *The Village Labourer, 1760–1832.* New York, 1967.

Hanham, H. J. *Elections and Party Management: Politics in the Time of Disraeli and Gladstone.* London, 1978.

Harrison, J.F.C. *The Early Victorians, 1832–1851.* London, 1971.

Hawkins, Angus. " 'Parliamentary Government' and Victorian Political Parties, c.1839–c.1880." *English Historical Review,* 104 (July 1989), 638–69.

————. *Parliament, Party, and the Art of Politics in Britain, 1855–1859.* Stanford, 1987.

Hempton, David. *Methodism and Politics in British Society, 1750–1850.* Stanford, 1984.

Hennock, E. P. *Fit and Proper Persons: Ideal and Reality in Nineteenth-Century Urban Government.* London, 1973.

Hilton, Boyd. *The Age of Atonement: The Influence of Evangelicalism on Social and Economic Thought, 1785–1865.* Oxford, 1988.

Hobsbawm, Eric, and George Rudé. *Captain Swing: A Social History of the Great English Agricultural Uprising of 1830.* New York, 1975.

Hole, Robert. *Pulpits, Politics, and Public Order in England, 1760–1832.* Cambridge, 1989.

Hollis, Patricia, ed. *Pressure from Without in Early Victorian England.* London, 1974.

Hooker, Richard. *Hooker's Ecclesiastical Polity.* Book VIII. Introduction by Raymond Aaron Houk. New York, 1931.

Inglis, K. S. *Churches and the Working Classes in Victorian England.* London, 1964.

Isichei, Elizabeth. *Victorian Quakers.* London, 1970.

Jenkins, T. A. "Gladstone, the Whigs, and the Leadership of the Liberal Party, 1879–1880." *Historical Journal,* XXVII (1984), 337–60.

————. *Gladstone, Whiggery, and the Liberal Party, 1874–1886.* Oxford, 1988.

Johnson, Mark D. *The Dissolution of Dissent, 1850–1918.* New York and London, 1987.

Kain, Roger J. P., and Hugh C. Prince. *The Tithe Surveys of England and Wales.* Cambridge, 1985.

Keith-Lucas, Bryan. *The Unreformed Local Government System.* London, 1980.

Kenyon, J. "R. W. Dale and Christian Worldliness." In *The View from the Pulpit: Victorian Ministers and Society,* edited by P. T. Phillips. Toronto, 1978.

Kinzer, Bruce L., ed. *The Gladstonian Turn of Mind: Essays Presented to J. B. Conacher.* Toronto, 1986.

Koss, S. *Nonconformity in Modern British Politics.* London, 1979.

Lovegrove, Deryck W. *Established Church, Sectarian People: Itinerancy and the Transformation of English Dissent, 1780–1830.* Cambridge, 1988.

Lyon, David. *The Steeple's Shadow: On the Myths and Realities of Secularization.* Grand Rapids, Mich., 1987.

Machin, G.I.T. "Gladstone and Nonconformity in the 1860s: The Formation of an Alliance." *Historical Journal,* XVII (1974), 347–64.

———. *Politics and the Churches in Great Britain, 1832–1868.* Oxford, 1977.

MacKintosh, William H. *Disestablishment and Liberation.* London, 1972.

Manning, B. L. *The Protestant Dissenting Deputies.* Cambridge, 1952.

Marsh, Peter, ed. *The Conscience of the Victorian State.* Syracuse, N.Y., 1979.

Martin, Roger H. "The Place of the London Missionary Society in the Ecumenical Movement." *Journal of Ecclesiastical History,* XXXI, no. 3 (July 1980), 283–300.

Marty, Martin E. *The Modern Schism: Three Paths to the Secular.* New York, 1969.

Matthew, H.C.G. "Disraeli, Gladstone, and the Politics of Mid-Victorian Budgets." *Historical Journal,* 22 (1979), 626–30.

———. *Gladstone, 1809–1874.* Oxford and New York, 1988.

———. "Gladstone, Vaticanism, and the Question of the East." In D. Baker, ed., *Studies in Church History,* vol. XV. Oxford, 1978.

Meacham, S. *Lord Bishop: The Life of Samuel Wilberforce.* Cambridge, Mass., 1970.

Morley, John. *The Life of William Ewart Gladstone.* 2 vols. London, 1905.

Newbould, Ian D. C. "The Whigs, the Church, and Education, 1839." *Journal of British Studies,* 26, no. 3 (July 1987), 332–46.

Nicholls, David. *Deity and Domination: Images of God and the State in the Nineteenth and Twentieth Centuries.* London, 1989.

Norman, E. R. *Christianity and the World Order.* Oxford, 1979.

———. *Church and Society in England, 1770–1970.* Oxford, 1976.

Obelkevich, James. *Religion and Rural Society: South Lindsey, 1825–1875.* Oxford, 1976.

Obelkevich, James, Lyndal Roper, and Raphael Samuel, eds. *Disciplines of Faith: Studies in Religion, Politics, and Patriarchy.* London, 1987.

O'Gorman, Frank. *Voters, Patrons, and Parties: The Unreformed Electoral System of Hanoverian England, 1734–1832.* New York, 1989.

Parry, J. P. *Democracy and Religion: Gladstone and the Liberal Party, 1867–1875.* Cambridge, 1986.

Parsons, Gerald, ed. *Religion in Victorian Britain.* Vols. 1–4. Manchester, 1988.

Patterson, A. T. *Radical Leicester, 1780–1850.* Leicester, 1954.

Peel, Albert. *These Hundred Years: A History of the Congregational Union of England and Wales, 1831–1931.* London, 1931.

Perkin, H. J. "The Development of Modern Glossop." In *Small Town Politics: A Study of Political Life in Glossop,* edited by A. H. Birch. Oxford, 1959.

Phillips, Paul T. *The Sectarian Spirit: Sectarianism, Society, and Politics in Victorian Cotton Towns.* Toronto, 1982.

Ramm, A. "Gladstone as Politician." In *Gladstone, Politics, and Religion: A Collection*

of Founder's Day Lectures Delivered at St. Deiniol's Library, Hawarden, 1967–1983,
edited by P. J. Jaggar. London, 1985.

————. "Gladstone's Religion." *Historical Journal,* 28 (1985), 327–40.

Rashid, Selim. "Anglican Clergymen and the Tithe Question in the Early Nineteenth Century." *Journal of Religious History,* 11, no. 1 (1980), 64–76.

Read, Donald. *Peel and the Victorians.* London, 1987.

Robbins, K. *John Bright.* London, 1979.

Roberts, M.J.D. "Pressure-Group Politics and the Church of England: The Church Defense Institution, 1859–1896." *Journal of Ecclesiastical History,* 35, no. 4 (1984), 560–82.

Robson, Robert, ed. *Ideas and Institutions of Victorian Britain.* New York, 1967.

Sangster, Paul. *A History of the Free Churches.* London, 1983.

Sellers, Ian. *Nineteenth-Century Nonconformity.* London, 1977.

Semmel, Bernard. *The Methodist Revolution.* London, 1974.

Shannon, R. *Gladstone.* Vol. 1, *1809–1865.* London, 1982.

Stanley, Brian. "Nineteenth-Century Liberation Theology: Nonconformist Missionaries and Imperialism." *Baptist Quarterly,* 32 (Jan. 1987), 5–18.

Stansky, Peter. *Gladstone: A Progress in Politics.* Boston, 1979.

Steele, E. D. *Palmerston and Liberalism, 1855–1865.* Cambridge, 1991.

Stephen, M. D. "Liberty, Church, and State: Gladstone's Relations with Manning and Acton, 1832–1870." *Journal of Religious History,* 1 (1960), 217–32.

Stewart, Robert. *Henry Brougham, 1778–1868: His Public Career.* London, 1985.

Tate, W. E. *The Parish Chest.* Cambridge, 1946.

Taylor, E. R. *Methodism and Politics, 1791–1851.* Cambridge, 1935.

Thompson, David M., ed. *Nonconformity in the Nineteenth Century.* London, 1972.

Thompson, F.M.L. *English Landed Society in the Nineteenth Century.* London, 1963.

Trevelyan, G. M. *The Life of John Bright.* London, 1913.

Vidler, Alec R. *The Orb and the Cross.* London, 1945.

Vincent, John. *The Formation of the Liberal Party, 1857–1868.* London, 1966.

Virgin, Peter. *The Church in an Age of Negligence: Ecclesiastical Structure and Problems of Church Reform, 1700–1840.* Cambridge, 1989.

Waddams, S. M. *Law, Politics, and the Church of England: The Career of Stephen Lushington, 1782–1873.* Cambridge, 1992.

Ward, W. R. *Religion and Society in England, 1790–1850.* London, 1972.

————. "The Tithe Question in England in the Early Nineteenth Century." *Journal of Ecclesiastical History,* XVI (1965), 67–81.

Ward-Jackson, C. H. *A History of Courtaulds.* London, 1941.

Wasson, Ellis Archer. *Whig Renaissance: Lord Althorp and the Whig Party, 1782–1845.* New York, 1987.

Webb, R. K. *Modern England: From the Eighteenth Century to the Present.* New York, 1970.

Wickham, E. R. *Church and People in an Industrial City.* London, 1957.

Wolffe, J. "The Evangelical Alliance in the 1840s: An Attempt to Institutionalise Christian Unity." In *Voluntary Religion,* edited by W. J. Sheils and D. Wood. Oxford, 1986.

VI. Ph.D. Dissertations

Fong, William Jesse. "The Ritualist Crisis: Anglo-Catholics and Authority, with Special Reference to the English Church Union, 1859–1882." University of Toronto, 1977.

Kenyon, J.P.B. "High Churchmen and Politics, 1845–1865." University of Toronto, 1967.

Martin, H. R. "The Politics of the Congregationalists, 1830–1856." University of Durham, 1971.

Newton, J. S. "The Political Career of Edward Miall." University of Durham, 1975.

Welch, A. H. "John Carvell Williams, the Nonconformist Watchdog (1821–1907)." University of Kansas, 1968.

Index